Internetworking SNA with Cisco Solutions

George Sackett
Nancy Sackett

CISCO SYSTEMS

CISCO PRESS

Cisco Press
201 West 103rd Street
Indianapolis, Indiana 46290 USA

Internetworking SNA with Cisco Solutions
George Sackett
Nancy Sackett

Copyright © 1999 Cisco Press

Cisco Press logo is a trademark of Cisco Systems, Inc.

Published by:
Cisco Press
201 West 103rd Street
Indianapolis, IN 46290 USA

Printed in the United States of America 1 2 3 4 5 6 7 8 9 0

Library of Congress Cataloging-in-Publication Number 98-86496
ISBN: 1-57870-083-3

Warning and Disclaimer

This book is designed to provide information about internetworking SNA with Cisco routers. Every effort has been made to make this book as complete and as accurate as possible, but no warranty or fitness is implied.

The information is provided on an "as is" basis. The author, Cisco Press, and Cisco Systems, Inc., shall have neither liability nor responsibility to any person or entity with respect to any loss or damages arising from the information contained in this book or from the use of the discs or programs that may accompany it.

The opinions expressed in this book belong to the author and are not necessarily those of Cisco Systems, Inc.

Feedback Information

At Cisco Press, our goal is to create in-depth technical books of the highest quality and value. Each book is crafted with care and precision, undergoing rigorous development that involves the unique expertise of members from the professional technical community.

Readers' feedback is a natural continuation of this process. If you have any comments regarding how we could improve the quality of this book, or otherwise alter it to better suit your needs, you can contact us through email at `ciscopress@mcp.com`. Please make sure to include the book title and ISBN in your message.

We greatly appreciate your assistance.

Associate Publisher	Jim LeValley
Executive Editors	Alicia Buckley
	Julie Fairweather
Cisco Systems Program Manager	H. Kim Lew
Managing Editor	Caroline Roop
Acquisitions Editor	Brett Bartow
Development Editor	Lisa M. Thibault
Project Editor	Brad Herriman
Technical Editors	Craig Brown
	David Merrell
Acquisitions Coordinator	Amy Lewis
Cover Designer	Karen Ruggles
Production Team	Argosy
Indexer	Kevin Fulcher

Trademark
Acknowledgments

About the Author

George C. Sackett is Managing Director at NetworX Corporation, a Cisco Professional Services Partner consulting to the financial, telecommunications, consumer, entertainment, medical, pharmaceutical, transportation, and hospitality industries. NetworX specializes in merging legacy systems and networks to all-service networks. Mr. Sackett has 17 years experience in the networking arena and has previously authored and co-authored publications with McGraw-Hill on networking. He has an M.S. in Management of Technology from Polytechnic University. More information on NetworX Corporation can be found at http://www.networxcorp.com.

Nancy E. Sackett is Director of Operations at NetworX Corporation. She has 14 years of experience in the field of telecommunications, concentrating in large-scale global enterprise networks. Ms. Sackett has been responsible for international telecommunications operations along with strategic and tactical network planning. Ms. Sackett has a B.B.A. in MIS from Iona College.

About the
Technical Reviewers

Craig Brown is technically responsible for the Cisco Data Center products. His responsibilities include assisting product managers, sales and engineering, specifically sales specialists and SE Virtual Teams in developing technical information and solutions. Craig also produces white papers and design guides on many topics based upon research performed in his lab. He also performs competitors' analysis including features, performance and positioning. The products that Craig supports are TN3270 Server, CSNA, IP Datagram, TCP/IP for MVS, Cisco IOS for S/390, TCP Offload, APPN, DLSw, Network Management (from the mainframe perspective), and Web Enablement products in relation to n-tier solutions.

David Merrell is a member of Cisco's Interworks Business Unit (IBU) in Research Triangle Park, North Carolina, and focuses on solutions for Mainframe and Data Center migration and integration. David has worked for Cisco for more than 4 years and has been part of the computer and communications industry for more than 13 years. During this time he been involved in the design and implementation of many large and complex multiprotocol networks both in Australia and overseas. He holds a bachelor's degree in Engineering (Electronics and Communications Engineering).

Dedications

The first influence any person has on their life and character is his parents. I dedicate this book to my mother, June, and my father, Ray, for providing me with a wonderful childhood, for being there when I needed them and for their constant encouragement and positive outlook on life.

George

As I grow through life I realize that much of what I am and what I will grow to be is based on where I come from. So, as such, I dedicate this book to my late mother, Margaret Susan Russo, and my dad Joseph Russo.

Mom, you may not be here to tell me what you think, but somehow I know.

Dad, I know you are proud of all your children. I may not say it enough, but I am thankful of all that you have given and proud to be part of you.

Nancy

Acknowledgments

I believe that encouragement from those you respect and hold in high regard is the foundation for accomplishment. My wife and partner, Nancy, provides this to me on a daily basis. Her complete understanding of the time and effort needed to produce a book of this nature and her constant support lead me to believe that I could not have found a better partner in life and for this book. Thank you Nancy for all your love, help and guidance.

Thanks to our children for understanding that Pop was not around a lot over the past year.

Finally, I would like to express my appreciation to Jim LeValley, Julie Fairweather, Brett Bartow, Lisa Thibault of Macmillian Technical Publishing and Cisco Press for their patience and dedication to making this book the best it can be. All your time, effort and concern is greatly appreciated. I would also like to extend our thanks to Craig Brown and Dave Merrill of Cisco Systems, Interworks Business Unit, for their many hours spent reviewing the manuscript for readability, accuracy and timeliness. Though we may have had some inroads, I believe the outcome of the finished product is one of excellence thanks to you. Much thanks goes to Gary Stewart of Cisco Systems, Technical Illustrations, for working with me on identifying and then providing the Cisco Systems icons used for the line art in this book.

George

There are many people that were a part of this book. First and foremost my partner in this collaboration and more importantly in life, George. There is a spiritual poem called "Footsteps" that describes a person who sees two sets of footprints during the journey of his life. When the tough times came, he questioned why he was deserted and saw only one set of footprints. The answer was, "That's when I was carrying you." I thank you George for when, during this process, there was only one set of footprints. Though I never said this, I know they were yours.

To all the children we have been blessed with: Pamela, James, Meredith, Chelsea and our little one on the way. There is no greater accomplishment than the pride I feel when I see your happy and healthy faces each morning.

Nancy

Contents at a Glance

Introduction

Contents

Introduction

The IBM mainframe and SNA form the foundation of 90% of the Fortune 1000's information delivery to corporate end users and customers. At one time, IBM's mainframe and its Systems Network Architecture (SNA) owned the corporate networking arena. However, corporate America's embrace of TCP/IP and routers have dethroned IBM and SNA from its once dominant perch. However, this did not diminish the importance of delivering the information from mainframe computers with applications written in support of IBM's SNA.

One company, early on in the rapid corporate growth of TCP/IP realized the importance of delivering SNA data over TCP/IP routers. That company is Cisco Systems. Cisco Systems is now the premier provider of solutions for internetworking SNA. As such, this book *Internetworking SNA with Cisco Solutions* provides all the real-world information you will need to know to internetwork SNA on a Cisco router based network.

It is the intent of this text to provide the reader with an understanding of internetworking terms, networking architectures, protocols and implementations for internetworking SNA with Cisco routers. The text uses many illustrations to educate the reader on terms, protocols, transport techniques and configurations.

The text is divided into two sections. The first section will provide the reader with an overview of the various architectures and protocols that are used in corporate networks. The second section discusses Cisco Systems specific issues, architectures, and implementation of internetworking SNA. The appendixes included with this book provide detailed router and SNA parameter mappings in addition to tips on implementing SNA with Cisco Systems routers and technology.

Internetworking SNA over router networks is a paradigm shift. The majority of SNA network professionals are not TCP/IP and router savvy. Likewise, TCP/IP router network professionals are foreign to the world of SNA networks. This text provides information that is applicable to both professionals. The information found in this text provides the knowledge necessary for any SNA or TCP/IP professional to become a well-versed SNA internetworking professional using Cisco Systems solutions.

We sincerely hope you find this book educational and useful for internetworking SNA with Cisco Systems solutions. Since we have used real-world scenarios the book is ideal as a reference for your own SNA integration challenges.

If you would like to reach us you can do so by contacting George Sackett at email address gsackett@ networxcorp.com or Nancy Sackett at email address nsackett@networxcorp.com with your questions and/or comments.

George Sackett

Nancy Sackett

PART I

Overview

CHAPTER 1

Overview of Corporate Networks

Corporate networks have become the foundation for businesses. The idea of conducting business today without a corporate network leaves a company at a competitive disadvantage. The use of the Internet shows that networks have not only become the foundation for business but are quickly becoming a means of generating business.

The network is now a vital part of conducting business; managing and growing this new corporate asset has evolved two schools of networking beliefs:

- Centralized control and management
- Decentralized control and management

Two different approaches to networking are hierarchical and peer.

1.1 HIERARCHICAL NETWORKS

The concept of a *hierarchical network* is that of a master and slave. The master dictates and controls while the slave listens and obeys. This top-down architecture centralizes processing and maintains a manageable structure. Hierarchical networks were first chosen for computer networks due to their predictive and deterministic qualities. The slaves—the computer terminals—cannot access data without the master—the centralized processor—recognizing their connection or establishing their connection to the network.

As business became dependent on a network to connect workers in remote offices, a standard for hierarchical networking became a necessity. The standard that emerged from this requirement became the *IBM Systems Network Architecture (SNA)*, a networking protocol.

The majority of all large corporations rely in some manner on IBM mainframe computers to access their vital corporate data. Corporations use interactive applications executing on these mainframes to process the data into information that's useful to the business processes. Interactive applications deliver the information to office workers using computer terminals through network connections. As shown in Figure 1-1, the mainframe (master) sends information to the front-end processor (slave), which then distributes it to the controllers, terminals, and printers.

Figure 1-1
The hierarchical network model applied to SNA.

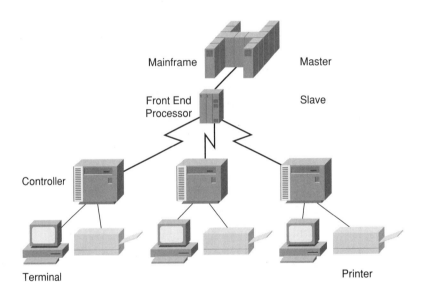

The traditional terminal type used for accessing information from IBM mainframe interactive applications is the IBM 3270 terminal. Applications using the IBM 3270 terminal for displaying and requesting information from the mainframe are collectively known as *3270 applications*. 3270 applications grew in popularity because of their inherent predictive and deterministic behavior as predicated by SNA. This growth required a means to increase the size of the network while maintaining reliable delivery of information. SNA bases its architecture on static network knowledge and includes a networking scheme for large networks using the concept of subareas and static routes.

1.1.1 SNA Subarea Networking

SNA *subarea routing* uses the simple question: How do I get there from here? SNA defines the answer to this question in every SNA device responsible for delivering information to the 3270 terminal.

SNA subarea networks are composed of three types of devices:

- Mainframe
- Front-end processor (FEP)
- Controller cluster

The mainframe in an SNA subarea network is the master, which controls all other resources in the network. The FEP is an extension of the master. The FEP handles redundant duties of the master, in particular, the network communications functions.

However, the FEP cannot perform these duties without a directive from the mainframe. The FEP also assists in the delivery of the information.

Cluster controllers connect the printers and 3270 terminals to the SNA network. The controllers themselves connect to the FEP (as shown in Figure 1-2). Again, we find that the controllers cannot deliver information to the 3270 terminals until they receive permission from the mainframe.

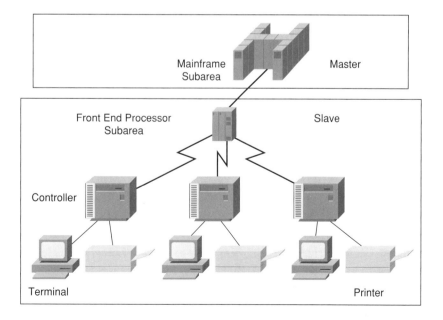

Figure 1-2
SNA subarea network components.

Static, or predefined, routes in the mainframe, and FEPs identify the path taken by information messages from the mainframe to the terminals. The assignment of subarea numbers to the mainframe and FEPs is the foundation of SNA subarea networking. When a mainframe or FEP has a subarea number assigned, it becomes an SNA subarea. Both forward and reverse routes in each subarea provide the mapping information to deliver messages.

Multiple routes through multiple subareas provide alternate paths for the delivery of messages. However, after a route is selected, the messages between the two subareas must traverse the same forward and reverse routes. Figure 1-3 illustrates the subarea and SNA route concepts. If a link or subarea fails during the delivery of messages, all connections through the disabled path will fail and need re-establishment in order to use a predefined alternate route.

The larger the subarea network is, the more possible routes there are to define. This leads to a complex static route definition with the potential for errors without dynamic rerouting of messages.

Figure 1-3
SNA subareas and routing.

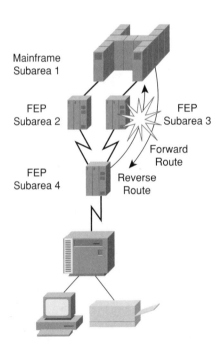

Implementation in a hierarchical network requires you, at some point in time, reinitializing the master, or FEPs, to keep changes permanently. This disruption causes valuable downtime on the network. In the end, SNA's inherent need to know caused it to lose its place as the dominant networking architecture, which gave rise to reliable, yet dynamic, peer-to-peer networks.

1.2 PEER NETWORKS

Peer networking involves the ability to establish connections between two stations independent of any other resource. In a peer network, there is no one resource that controls the entire network. This independence has given rise to the delivery of messages in the form of *dynamic routing*.

Dynamic routing in peer networks, as compared to static routing in hierarchical networks, is a learned process versus a defined process. The network devices in a peer network communicate with each other to learn the topology of the network, as you can see in Figure 1-4. Network resources added or removed dynamically are learned almost instantaneously, allowing for uninterrupted network topology changes.

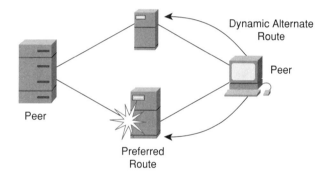

Figure 1-4
Peer network topology and routing.

There are three dominant peer network architectures in the majority of large corporations:

- Transmission Control Protocol/Internet Protocol (TCP/IP)
- Novell/Internet Packet eXchange (Novell/IPX)
- Advanced Peer-to-Peer Network (APPN)

Both TCP/IP and Novell/IPX deliver SNA messages in encapsulation techniques. APPN delivers SNA messages in native SNA format. The two architectures discussed throughout this book are APPN and TCP/IP.

1.2.1 APPN Networking

Peer networking APPN removes the hierarchical controls while maintaining predictive yet dynamic networks. APPN owes its roots, beginning in the early 1980s, to connecting small business networks based on IBM System/36 (S/36) computers. The S/36 is the precursor platform to IBM's Advanced Series/400 (AS/400) computing platform.

Small companies with disparate physical offices required a network for connecting their S/36 or AS/400 computers; however, they lacked the technical staff to manage the infrastructure. APPN's ability to dynamically manage the changes in the small business network became an advantage and was adapted to handling large corporate SNA networks (see Figure 1-5).

Figure 1-5
APPN network
topology.

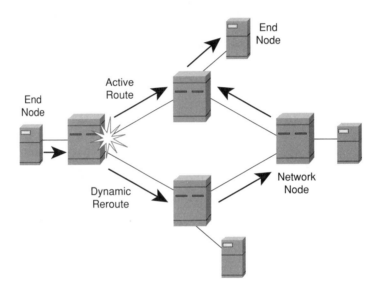

APPN networks revolve around applications communicating with other applications. The basis of this communication is the *network node (NN)* and the *end node (EN)*. For the most part, applications reside on APPN ENs. APPN NNs provide the core of the networking services under APPN architecture. NNs maintain directories, network resources (for example, applications), and the topology of the network. NNs communicate with each other, keeping themselves informed of network topology changes. Topology maps kept by the APPN NNs using High-Performance Routing (HPR) allow the rerouting of application-to-application messages without disrupting the connection as found in hierarchical networks.

1.2.2 TCP/IP Networking

TCP/IP has its origins not in the business world but in the government and educational sectors. In the mid-1970s the now infamous ARPAnet, based on TCP/IP networking, fostered communication between military and educational research facilities. Initially,

TCP/IP networks were used for remote file access, file transfer, and electronic mail. Today, TCP/IP networking and its dynamic abilities have proven to be an asset to corporate networks, allowing a structured yet dynamic rapid growth.

Typically, a TCP/IP network consists of four networking resources (as shown in Figure 1-6):

- IP network
- Host
- Bridge
- Router

An IP network is akin to the SNA subarea because network resources assigned to the same IP network are addressed by using the IP network number. An IP network maps to a physical networking media. Therefore, IP network numbers associate a logical network to a physical network.

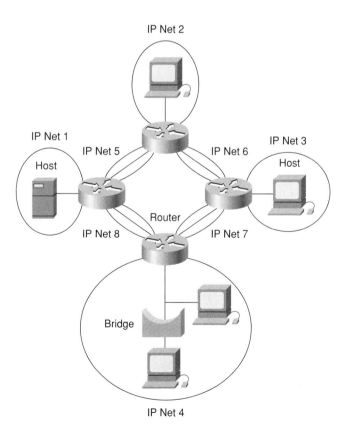

Figure 1-6
TCP/IP network topology.

TCP/IP networks were first based on local area networks (LANs). Limitations to LAN wiring restricted the number of network resources on the LAN. Increasing the size of LANs and, therefore, the IP network became a concern for early network engineers. The answer to this concern is bridging. *Bridges* extend the physical LAN limitations and thereby, theoretically, increase the number of resources assigned to an IP network.

Multiple IP networks require a router to provide connectivity between them. *Routers* have the ability to connect multiple IP networks simultaneously, which transports messages between IP networks transparently. Routers contain network topology maps detailing the number of known IP networks and the best route between each network. The routers share information between them, keeping an up-to-date database dynamically.

1.3 LOCAL AREA NETWORK

LANs allow computers (that is, hosts) to share LAN resources. These resources may be printers, CD-ROM servers, file servers, fax servers, and shared access to the corporate wide area network (WAN) as well as the Internet. An LAN is described as being a "broadcast medium," and the most widely used LAN architecture is Ethernet.

1.3.1 Ethernet

The development of Ethernet paralleled the development of TCP/IP. Like TCP/IP, Ethernet LANs are dynamic. Every host on an Ethernet LAN may send messages at any time without formal requests. The host "listens" on the LAN for the opportunity to send a message. When the host believes the LAN is available, it sends a message. However, other hosts may also be listening, and if they sense that the LAN is available, they send their message. The result is message collision on the LAN. Ethernet uses this collision technique to maintain host independence.

Ethernet LANs use a bus topology (see Figure 1-7). A *bus topology* connects all hosts to the same wire. Each host copies the message from the wire. The host looks at the message to determine if the message is for that particular host. If the message is not for the host, the host discards the message. Meanwhile, the original message on the wire has been traveling to all the other hosts on the LAN. Each host on the Ethernet receives a copy of the original message whether or not the message was destined for the host.

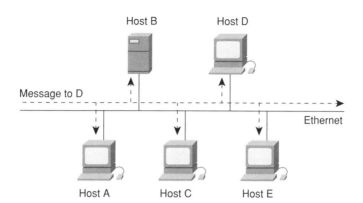

Figure 1-7
Ethernet bus topology.

1.3.2 Token Ring

Another LAN that is an alternative to Ethernet was developed by IBM in the mid-1980s. It is known as *Token Ring*. IBM maintains its approach to predictive and deterministic networking by implementing an orderly approach to LANs. Token-Ring LANs use either a ring or star-wired ring topology to ensure that only one host on the LAN sends messages at any one time.

Like Ethernet LANs, Token-Ring LANs are dynamic. They can grow and change with ease just like Ethernet LANs. However, Token-Ring LANs have the controls in place to ensure that only one host may send a message at any time. Token-Ring LANs accomplish this using a *token message,* or *frame.* Any host wanting to send a message must first claim the token frame prior to sending the message. Claiming the token frame is dynamic; the process ensures that only one host may send a message at any given time.

Figure 1-8 shows the Token-Ring topology. Token-Ring hosts receive messages from the LAN and remove the message from the wire. The host removes the message from the wire and inspects the message to determine if it is for this host. If the destination of the message is indeed this host, the host copies and processes the message. The host sends the message back to the originating host with an indicator stating that the message has reached the destination and the host successfully copied the message. If the message is not for this host, it places the message back on the wire and sends it to the next host on the ring. The originating host releases the token frame after receiving successful or unsuccessful confirmation of message delivery.

Figure 1-8
*Token-Ring
topology.*

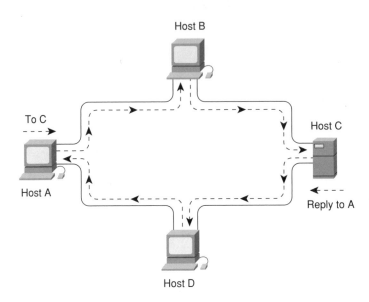

Due to the serial approach of sending messages on a Token Ring, not all hosts receive the message. This reduces network overhead by maintaining a deterministic approach to networking while allowing for dynamic network change. Reducing network overhead allows a Token Ring to sustain a higher rate of productivity.

1.4 WIDE AREA NETWORK

Connecting LANs over geographically dispersed locations requires a WAN infrastructure. WANs expand networks by allowing them to grow and connect not only corporate offices but customers and suppliers. The WAN is the network backbone because it is the common connectivity point for the transmission of messages between offices.

SNA and TCP/IP networks use WAN backbones as the conduit for delivering messages. There are typically three variations of WAN backbone infrastructures, which are described in detail in the following sections:

- Serial line backbone

- Multiplexed network backbone

- Switched network backbone

1.4.1 Serial Line Backbone

The simplest of the WAN backbone configurations is the *serial line backbone* (see Figure 1-9). Serial lines are the basis of the other backbone infrastructures. Serial lines connect two endpoints at full bandwidth speeds.

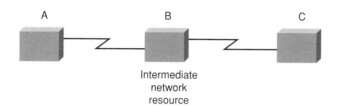

A   B   C

Intermediate
network
resource

Figure 1-9
*Serial line
WAN
backbone
topology.*

Connection between two locations may require messages to traverse an *intermediate network resource (INR)*. Although this type of communication works, it does not bode well for resources off the INR when large amounts of data are passing through the INR to a far endpoint. This concern leads to the idea of logical lines multiplexed over a physical line.

1.4.2 Multiplexed Network Backbone

Multiplexed backbone infrastructures allow network engineers to build complex logical networks over a single physical network. The bandwidth typically used for engineering a multiplexed backbone is a minimum of 1.544 Megabits per second (Mbps) or *T1*. Network devices called *multiplexers* connect the T1 lines. Unlike a point-to-point serial link, where the endpoints are reserved for the exclusive use of a single network, the multiplexed link allows multiple networks to each believe that they have its exclusive access and use.

The topology of a multiplexed backbone is similar to that of a serial line backbone configuration. However, by using multiple logical lines, the network becomes more useful (see Figure 1-10).

Figure 1-10
*Multiplexed
WAN
backbone
topology.*

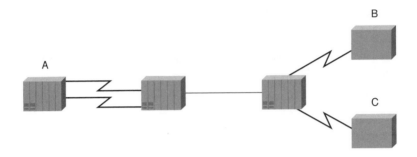

As an example, the serial line configuration shown in Figure 1-9 is now logically placed on a multiplexed network as shown in Figure 1-10. Note that the far endpoints connect directly through the multiplexer backbone rather than traversing through the INR. This provides efficient utilization and a cost-effective means for adding network resources to the multiplexed backbone versus a direct connection between locations. However, not all multiplexed networks support the ability to reroute messages dynamically and, therefore, still have the problem of interrupted services due to network resource outages.

1.4.3 Switched Network Backbone

Switched backbone networks combine the benefits of both serial line and multiplexed backbone configurations. Typically, a switched backbone network consists of either a frame relay network or an Asynchronous Transfer Mode (ATM) backbone network (see Figure 1-11). In some cases, you may see a combination of the two making up the backbone. These networks bring the concept of multiplexing down to the location level without using a multiplexer.

As an example, a location is configured over a frame relay or ATM network to have virtual point-to-point connections between itself and the other office locations. These virtual circuits share the same physical medium; however, they are assigned different quality attributes based on the type of service required between the locations.

As the name implies, frames are switched dynamically through a switched backbone. This ability to reroute messages dynamically through the network gives switched backbones a greater advantage to delivering dynamic, large-scale network infrastructures supporting both SNA and TCP/IP.

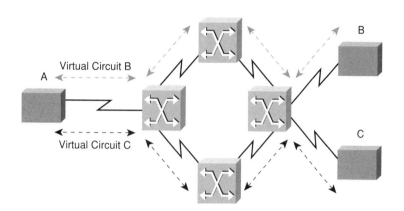

Figure 1-11
Switched WAN backbone topology.

1.5 SNA NETWORK CONFIGURATIONS

SNA is still the dominant networking architecture for vital corporate data accessed using IBM mainframe applications. Through the years, the typical IBM SNA network has evolved into various configurations supporting small to worldwide networks.

SNA uses the word *domain* as a means of describing the scope of resource control by the master or mainframe. In actuality, there is a software program executing on the mainframe called *Virtual Telecommunications Access Method (VTAM),* which acts as the SNA master. VTAM's control over other SNA resources defines a domain.

1.5.1 Single Domain

In SNA, a *single domain* consists of a single VTAM that controls, or owns, all of the SNA resources attached to the network. These include the terminals, printers, controllers, lines, and FEPs.

A single domain (as depicted in Figure 1-12) may comprise a single mainframe with one or more FEPs directly or remotely attached through subarea connections and all of the controllers attached to each FEP. Each terminal or printer attached to a controller is owned by VTAM. Every communications line, controller, terminal, and printer is defined to the FEP through the use of the Network Control Program (NCP). During VTAM's activation sequence of network resources, it becomes aware of the resources attached to each FEP and, hence, determines the bounds of its domain.

Figure 1-12
*SNA single
domain
network.*

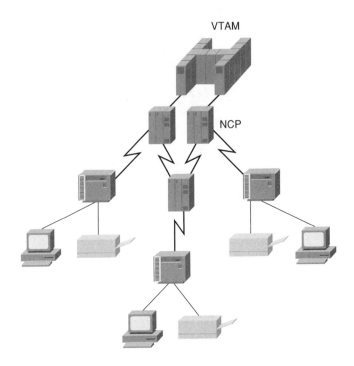

1.5.2 Multidomain

In an SNA multidomain network, there is more than one VTAM controlling network resources. Each VTAM is in communication with the others; however, they do not share network topology information. Each VTAM may share control of the FEPs (as shown in Figure 1-13) in an SNA network if the physical and logical connections are defined appropriately.

Shared FEPs may have their lines and associated controllers, terminals, and printers owned by different VTAMs as long as the FEP itself is co-owned by VTAM. Shared ownership enables one VTAM to take control of the failing VTAM's resources, thus providing continued network service.

1.5.3 Multinetwork

At one point, though, the size of some SNA networks reached practical limits. Many corporations created multiple independent networks only to find out later that these independent networks needed communication between them. This requirement led to *SNA Network Interconnection (SNI)*.

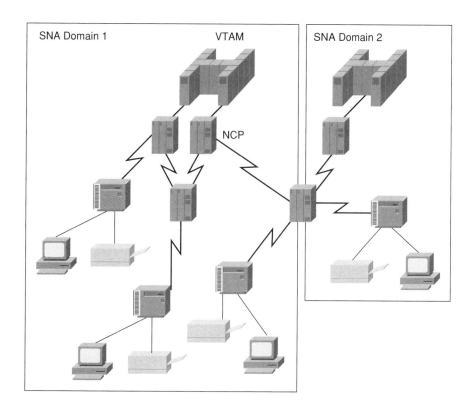

Figure 1-13
SNA multidomain network.

SNI connects two disparate, independent networks (depicted in Figure 1-14) for allowing communication between the VTAM network resources. Communication between the networks happens through an NCP SNI gateway. An *SNI gateway* is an FEP that shares its existence between two SNA networks. The distinction between SNA network resources is found in the addition of a network identifier (NETID) to the SNA resource name.

1.5.4 Point-to-Point

The simplest of SNA network configurations is the point-to-point connection. *Point-to-point connections* (as illustrated in Figure 1-15) provide remote locations with dedicated bandwidth to an FEP. Point-to-point connections between FEPs are similar to the serial line backbone scenario discussed earlier. However, use of a multiplexer allows for enhanced connectivity solutions while still preserving bandwidth for the SNA resources.

Figure 1-14
*SNA SNI
network
example.*

SNA NETID: UseNet

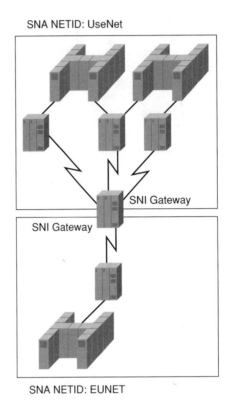

SNA NETID: EUNET

Figure 1-15
*SNA
point-to-point
and multipoint
network
example.*

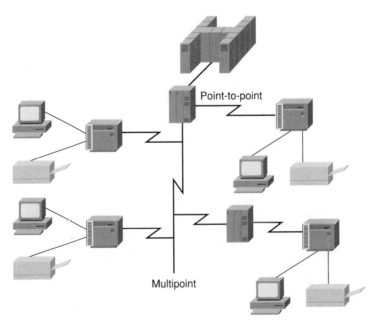

1.5.5 Multipoint

The evolution of SNA communications includes the requirement of having multiple locations connected to an FEP over a single line. Each location connected to the line is considered a *point* or *drop* on that line. Figure 1-15 shows a multipoint or multidrop line configuration.

The first incarnation of multipoint lines required that the same type of controllers attach to the line. The increasing cost efficiencies of corporations, however, fostered a mixed multipoint line. *Mixed multipoint lines* allow different types of network resources to connect to, and share, the communications line. On a mixed multipoint line, both controllers and FEPs attach to the same communication line.

1.5.6 SNA LANs

SNA controllers and FEPs, as well as the mainframe, attach to LANs. The most popular method, depicted in Figure 1-16, has been controller connectivity over the LAN to an FEP. The FEP attaches to the mainframe using channel communication links. LAN connectivity is typically Token Ring. However, Ethernet and Fiber Distributed Data Interchange (FDDI) are also used.

FEP connectivity to a Token-Ring LAN uses a *Token-Ring interface coupler (TIC)*. Controllers attached to the Token Ring use the network address of the TIC to connect to the FEP.

SNA, being deterministic, is a nonroutable protocol and requires a LAN bridging technique for use on Token-Ring LANs called *source route bridging (SRB)*. SRB embeds the description of physical paths, to and from the TIC, in the message. If any network resource described on the SRB path fails, the controller must re-establish connectivity to the FEP TIC to discover a new path through the network.

1.5.7 Frame Relay

A standard technique for sending SNA over frame relay is the *Internet Engineering Task Force (IETF) Request for Comment (RFC) 1490*. The RFC 1490 describes an encapsulation technique for placing SNA messages in frame relay messages and sending them through the network. IBM's FEP (IBM 3745) platform, using NCP version 7 or higher, enables the front end to participate directly in a frame relay network.

There are two types of frame relay devices:

- Frame relay terminal equipment (FRTE)
- Frame relay switch equipment (FRSE)

Figure 1-16
*SNA
connectivity
over
Token-Ring
LANs.*

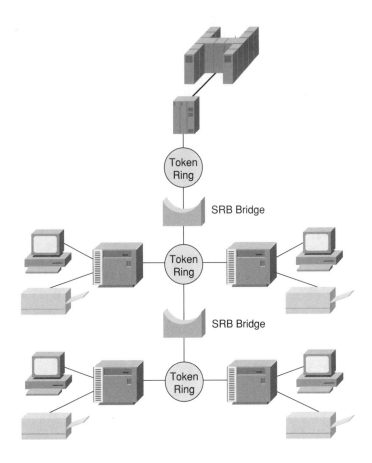

An FRTE is an end device on a frame relay network. It is the access device for remote network resources to send messages over the frame relay network to another FRTE. Both the IBM 3745 and the IBM controller, IBM 3174, participate in a frame relay network as FRTE devices. The IBM 3745 is also capable of acting as an FRSE device in a frame relay network. As a switching device, FRTE devices attach to the IBM 3745, which in turn switches the messages from the FRTE to the appropriate far-end FRTE.

As shown in Figure 1-17, an IBM 3174 FRTE connects to an IBM 3745 FRSE, which in turn, has two virtual connections to the mainframe. Each virtual connection terminates in different IBM 3745s that are channel-attached to the mainframe. This configuration provides alternative paths for the remote FTE device with the ability to switch within the network should an intermediate FRSE experience an outage.

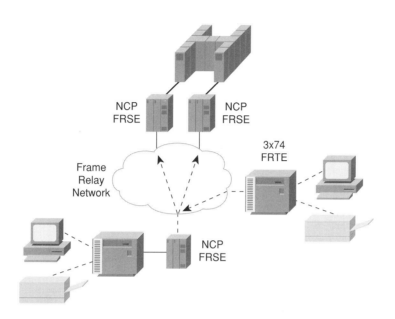

Figure 1-17
*SNA over
frame relay
network
example.*

1.5.8 SNA Subarea Network

The traditional SNA subarea network uses static routes called *explicit routes (ERs)*. Each subarea in an SNA subarea network uses ERs to map the path between origin and destination subareas. ERs map to the physical communications line connecting the subareas. These subarea lines, or links, are defined as *transmission groups*. Multiple subarea links may be grouped together to form a single transmission group. Multiple ERs may be mapped to a transmission group.

SNA subarea nodes perform *intermediate network node (INN), boundary network node (BNN)*, or both functions (as shown in Figure 1-18). INN subareas participate in the forwarding of messages to subarea destinations attached directly to the INN subarea or to subareas beyond the directly attached subareas. BNN subareas deliver messages to the directly attached controllers. BNN subareas also perform polling and activation/deactivation procedures with the directly attached controllers.

1.5.9 APPN Network

APPN provides SNA with the dynamics of peer networks and the predictive deterministic qualities of traditional SNA subarea hierarchical networks. APPN networks have the ability to nondisruptively reroute SNA messages using a feature called *high-performance routing (HPR)*. HPR allows APPN networks to maintain SNA sessions even when a network resource used for forwarding SNA messages fails. The APPN NNs sense this failure and reroute messages around the failing NN (see Figure 1-19).

Figure 1-18
*SNA network
subarea node
functions
example.*

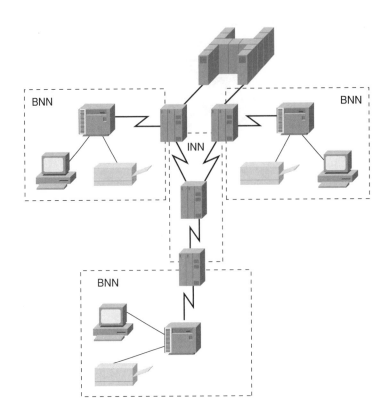

Each NN uses a type of service qualifier for each SNA message. ENs contain the applications used in an APPN network, and register the application name and the type of service the application expects with the NN attached to the EN. In APPN, applications establish a conversation between applications using an application name. The EN requests the NN to discover the EN location of the requested application. The ENs assist in setting up the application session. The use of application names makes APPN very flexible in allowing the movement of applications to different ENs dynamically.

APPN networks, like SNA networks, have NETIDs, or network names. Unique APPN networks are connected using an APPN *border node (BN)*. An APPN BN is similar to an SNA SNI gateway. The BN connects to both APPN networks and assumes an EN type of function registering applications found in one APPN network with the attached NN in the other APPN network. Different types of Border Node exist, providing different levels of routing and topology support. They are *Peripheral Border Node (PBN)* and *Extended Border Node (EBN)*.

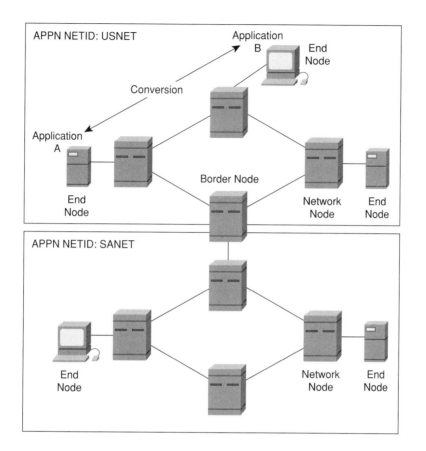

Figure 1-19
*APPN
internetwork
example.*

CHAPTER 2

IBM Systems Network Architecture (SNA)

As IBM grew its computing power and reach into the business arena, it also had to grow the reach of its data processing. The answer to IBM's need to provide flexible communications from the main computing system out to the remote offices was *Systems Network Architecture,* or *SNA.* SNA was born in September of 1974. The objective of SNA was to further the batch processing into interactive terminal and print applications. This was accomplished by using a hierarchical structure that was composed of seven layers.

2.1 FOUNDATION SNA CONCEPTS

Some fundamental concepts to understanding SNA are as follows:

- SNA is a hierarchical network (master-slave).

- SNA uses predefined routes for transporting data between source and destination.

- ACF/VTAM is the master of an SNA network.

- SNA is the network architecture enabling communication between network-addressable units.

2.1.1 Network Components

An SNA network is made up of basic hardware and software components. In a classic SNA network, key hardware components would include the following:

- Mainframe CPU

- Communications controller and front-end processor—37X5 (3725, 3745)

- Cluster controller—3X74 (3174, 3274)

- End-user workstation/printer

The master/slave relationship was the mode in which this network operated. The master portion executes on the mainframe CPU, termed the *access method,* and the slaves were the rest of the network components. Early on, to allow for the increase of network functionality, a new hardware/software component was created to front-end the mainframe processing and control the network; thus, the birth of the network control program occurred.

To support the aforementioned network hardware list, the following software was developed:

- Advanced Communications Function/Communications Access Method (VTAM)

- Advanced Communications Function/Network Control Program (NCP)

Another vital piece of the IBM SNA strategy is the applications software that communicates with the access method. The relationship created between these two software programs allows for each software product to specialize on core competencies. The access method takes care of the transport of the data, and the application manages data integrity. An excellent example of this genre of software is IBM's Customer Information Control System, CICS. Figure 2-1 portrays the quintessential SNA network.

2.1.2 Nodes

The hardware and software categories define the physical and logical components of an SNA network. This section will discuss the functions of each of the areas. There are three types of nodes:

- Host subarea nodes

- Communications controller subarea nodes

- Peripheral nodes

Notice that Figure 2-2 uses the same diagram as Figure 2-1; the only difference is that it uses SNA nodal terminology instead of representing each component as its physical/logical function.

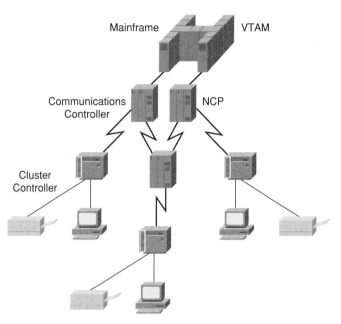

End user workstation/printer

Figure 2-1
The SNA network.

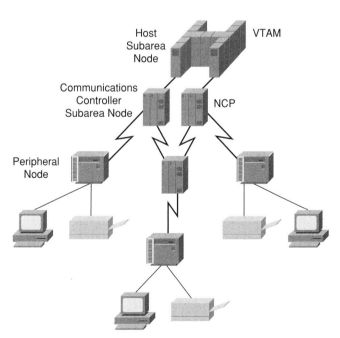

End user workstation/printer

Figure 2-2
SNA nodes.

Let's discuss the role of each node:

- A *host subarea node* is the main engine for network functionality. Its hardware platform is the mainframe CPU, and the software component is VTAM.

- The *Communications Controller subarea node* is the outboard engine that runs and dispatches network packets throughout the network. Its hardware platform is the communications front-end processor, and the software component is the network control program.

The remainder of the network components comprise the peripheral nodes. This list includes cluster controllers, distributed processors, end-user workstations, and printers.

2.1.3 Subareas

In SNA, sections of the total network are broken down into smaller segments. The rule in creating a smaller section, or *subarea,* is that there must be a VTAM or NCP to manage the area. When defining and working with SNA networks, subarea numbers are present in many definitions ranging from VTAM to the AS/400 emulating as a peripheral node. Figure 2-3 shows a representation of subareas composed of VTAMs and NCPs.

2.1.4 Links

Simply stated, an *SNA link* is any connection used to join two subareas. The physical connection could be a fiber channel, the classic telecommunications circuit, or even satellite communications. There can be—and good networking sense would employ—more than one link between subarea nodes. Even if there is only one physical connection, a good design includes multiple links to better segregated logical sessions for better data control and flow and to provide redundant routes in the event of a link failure.

At the end of each side of the logical link is the link station. The *link station* transmits data over the link using data link control protocols. Figure 2-3 has the same network diagram, only this time with the links and link stations highlighted.

SNA supports the following data link control protocols:

- System/390 data channel
- SDLC
- BSC
- S/S
- X.25

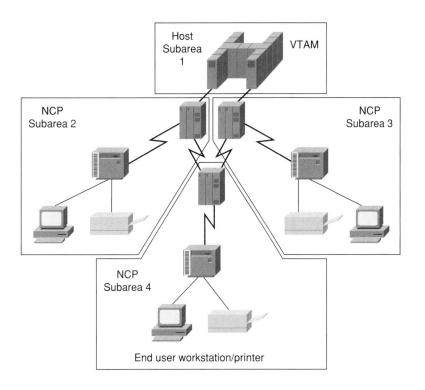

Figure 2-3
*Subarea
networking.*

Figure 2-4 shows a diagram of a network with attached lines.

2.1.5 Network-Addressable Units

The magic of computer networking is the cohesive manner in which disparate components communicate. The communication of these individual functions is accomplished under the designation of *Network Addressable Units*, or *NAUs*. NAUs are elements within an SNA network that are the endpoints for sessions. As their name suggests, NAUs must be addressable by the network using addresses that are unique within that network.

In SNA, there are three types of NAUs:

- The logical unit (LU)
- The physical unit (PU)
- The Systems Services Control Point (SSCP)

Figure 2-4
*Networking
with attached
lines.*

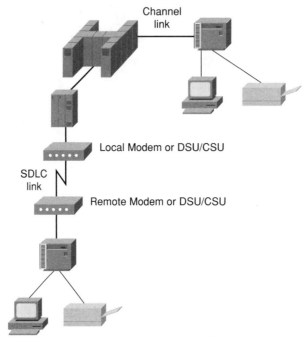

Figure 2-4
*Networking
with attached
lines.*

Channel link

Local Modem or DSU/CSU

SDLC link

Remote Modem or DSU/CSU

End user workstation/printer

2.1.5.1 Logical Units

The *logical unit (LU)* is the outermost access point into the network. We commonly think of only a terminal or printer as an LU, but an application program is also an LU in the SNA network. There is a one-to-one relationship between a "port" in the network and the presence of the logical LU. The ultimate goal of the network is to establish a working relationship between the workstation and the application, thus creating an LU-LU session.

All LUs are not created equal. Some application programs can have multiple sessions simultaneously; we would call this *parallel LU-LU sessions*. In a further classification of LUs, different capabilities are possible for each subtype:

- LU type 1: SNA Character String printer (SCS)

- LU type 2: 3270 Interactive Terminals

- LU type 3: Data Stream Compatible printer (DSC)

- LU type 6.2: Application programs

2.1.5.2 Physical Units

These LU sessions are managed by a *physical unit (PU)*. A mainframe processor, communications controller, or cluster controller represents a PU. The job of a PU is to present the LU data to the link for transport. There is a one-to-many relationship between a PU and LUs.

Again, as with LUs, there are different classifications of PUs:

- PU type 1: Legacy distributed systems controller—S/3X

- PU type 2: Cluster controllers

- PU type 2.1: Advanced peer-to-peer networking nodes

- PU type 4: Communications controllers

- PU type 5: VTAMs

2.1.5.3 Systems Services Control Points

The final NAU type is the *Systems Services Control Point (SSCP)*. The SSCP functionality lies within the access method up at the mainframe, thus VTAM. The host subarea node is the only network component that can "activate," control, or "inactivate" network resources. In SNA jargon, under a VTAM's control is called "in its domain." Small networks that have only one VTAM image are called *single domain,* and those that have more than one VTAM are called *multidomain.*

2.1.6 Network Addressing

Network addresses uniquely identify NAUs, links, and link stations in a subarea network. These addresses allow for the routing of messages between subareas. An SNA network address comprises two components:

- A subarea address

- An element address

The *subarea address* is a unique number defined and allocated for each subarea node in the network. VTAM and NCP define the element addresses during system generation and network activation. Consequently, these addresses have no significance to human operators or users. Instead, SNA allows the definition and allocation of a name to a given NAU, which VTAM associates with the SNA network address. In this way, VTAM performs a function similar to that of a domain name service (DNS).

In recent times, the terminology has changed whereby the term *subarea addresses* is used to describe what was previously referred to as network addresses. This change has been brought about by the advent of different network addressing requirements needed in Advanced Peer-to-Peer Networking (APPN).

Much akin to the TCP/IP addressing schema, underneath the shell of an LU name is a "network/host" numerical representation. SNA uses a subarea/element number to identify each and every device in the network. SNA uses names to allow for an easier nomenclature that enables users to operate more comfortably—again, another analogy to DNS under TCP/IP structure.

Building upon the concept of a subarea, a VTAM or NCP in a network, we can begin to describe the addressing in an SNA network. The subarea number for VTAM is defined by the HOSTSA parameter, and the subarea number for NCP is determined by an NCP definition parameter, SUBAREA. The element addresses are then assigned from a pool of addresses that both VTAM and NCP maintain for their attached resources.

SNA networks are generated and defined in an offline process. Unlike the network routers of today, programs are created and syntax checked prior to the load. The terminology that SNA systems programmers use is to *perform gen*. During the generation process, the Network Definition Facility (NDF) of NCP manages the process of handing out a unique address for every "element" defined in that subarea. There are many more elements inside an SNA network than just LUs. For example, we need to address each SDLC line; PU; and Token Ring–attached LINE, PU, and LU. After the generation of devices is completed, network changes are usually still required. As the NCP cannot be reloaded without creating a disruptive environment, dynamic configuration is also available for many devices.

When resources are locally attached to the mainframe, VTAM handles all of the addressing assignments for those physical devices as well as all of the applications.

SNA networks hand out these addresses at the time they "load" the network. This occurs when VTAM is started at the host and when a new copy of NCP is loaded into the front-end processors (FEPs).

SNA networks have a 31-bit address field. The first portion of the address, 16 bits, is used for subarea number and the next 15 bits are used for element. As a result, we can have 65,535 subareas and 32,768 elements within a given subarea. The introduction of VTAM Version 4 Release 1 (V4R1) enabled the use of 16 bits for the element address. This allows VTAM to address 65,535 elements within a given subarea. Most recently an enhancement to VTAM V4 has expanded the element addresses from 65,353 to 1.6 million elements per subarea.

2.1.7 Routes

Another aspect of SNA networking is the concept of routes. Routes are logical notions of physical connections in a network. These logical roadways are defined and used in such a manner as to provide quick response time and alternate pathways through the network. With the building blocks of priority and performance in place, SNA routes will enable terminal sessions to have quicker response time than printers.

When connecting NCPs to each other, more than one connection is possible. If multiple links are used—and of course this makes tremendous sense—they are called *parallel links*. The parallel links are coupled together and are called a *Transmission Group (TG)*. A TG can be viewed as a single, logical, or composite link for the purposes of routing. Within sub-area networks, only PU4 nodes define multilink TGs, whereas all other nodes define only single-link TGs.

To define these links to the systems, we create PATH statements. PATH statements are the definitions that tell the VTAMs and NCPs how to get to the next hop in the network. A PATH statement consist of routes, both physical and logical.

2.1.7.1 Explicit Routes

An explicit route (*ER*; also known as a *physical route*) is the definition of a physical connection between two subareas. This can be a communications line or a channel. This ER is mapped to a TG. You can have more than one ER in a specific TG. It would make a lot of sense to have two separate physical circuits compose one TG for nondisruptive backup in the event of a circuit failure (see Figure 2-5).

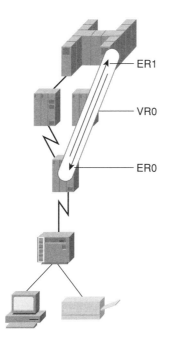

ER1

VR0

ER0

Figure 2-5
*Explicit and
virtual routes.*

The following rules are involved when defining ERs:

- They must have a forward and reverse path.
- They must traverse the same set of subarea nodes and TGs.

2.1.7.2 Virtual Routes

Virtual routes (*VR*; also known as *logical routes*) are the logical connections between two subareas. A VR is mapped to an ER. One or more VRs can be mapped to an ER. This many-to-one relationship allows for greater flexibility in data flow control. The primary usage of a VR is to separate out one type of traffic over another. A good example is the prioritization of terminal over printer traffic.

2.1.7.3 Class of Service Table

So we have all of the highways to provide multiple logical circuits over physical media, and the ability to prioritize one type of data over another. The remaining question is: How do we tag the type of data? The answer is the *Class of Service Table (COS)*. The COStab is assembled up at VTAM and has three classes that can be attached to the data. The three classes are up to the user to define, but are typically high, medium, and low. Each session that is created has characteristics attached to it: one of them is the *COS name*.

In traditional subarea SNA, routes do not get dynamically distributed throughout the network. You can think of them as static routes that are predefined and contain only the adjacent neighbor's information. Although there is no mechanism for the network itself to know a change in the path and propagate it automatically, we can make a change and issue a VTAM operator command to update all the participant's tables.

2.1.8 Layers

SNA is built on a layered architecture. Each layer is designed to be autonomous from the other yet still be able to communicate freely. The seven layers to the SNA protocol set are defined as follows (note that I will discuss them from the bottom up):

- Physical Control Layer
- Data Link Control Layer
- Path Control Layer

- Transmission Control Layer
- Data Flow Control Layer
- Presentation Services Layer
- Transaction Services Layer

Figure 2-6 shows the classic representation of the seven-layer SNA model.

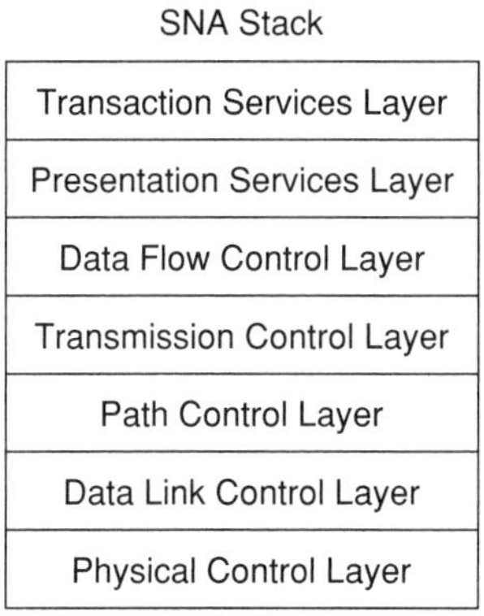

SNA Stack

| Transaction Services Layer |
| Presentation Services Layer |
| Data Flow Control Layer |
| Transmission Control Layer |
| Path Control Layer |
| Data Link Control Layer |
| Physical Control Layer |

Figure 2-6
*The Systems
Network
Architecture
model.*

2.1.8.1 Physical Control Layer

This portion of the model describes the physical interface for the transmission medium. Here we define the electrical signaling characteristics.

2.1.8.2 Data Link Control Layer

In the second layer of SNA, you see the workings of software/firmware that handles the logical components of data communications. At the Data Link Control Layer, the scheduling and error recovery take place in the SDLC and mainframe OS/390 channel protocols.

2.1.8.3 Path Control Layer

All of the routing information and data movement is controlled under the notion of paths located in the Path Control Layer. All of the different types of SNA sessions use these fundamental principles for getting data from "here" to "there." Here we start to implement the aforementioned concepts of routes, whether virtual or explicit, and the idea of TGs. The Path Control Layer has three subgroups:

- Transmission Groups—Provide connections between subarea nodes.

- Explicit Routes—Determine which TG will be chosen between subarea nodes.

- Virtual Routes—Provide the physical path the logical session will take as it works its way through the network.

2.1.8.4 Transmission Control Layer

The function of this layer is to provide for the delivery of usable data. We accomplish this by the use of *sequence number checking*.

2.1.8.5 Data Flow Control Layer

All of the session flow between the LUs is handled at this point. The packet of information that is sent out by the application is handed to VTAM for delivery. At this point, VTAM must organize related requests and responses into request/response units (RUs). VTAM creates chains to link single packets of information together that are too big for one buffer size of data. VTAM uses brackets to maintain the application-to-LU session until all of the data has been received. The final product of the data product is called a *Path Information Unit (PIU)*. Figure 2-7 shows the SNA PIU.

Figure 2-7
SNA Path Information Unit.

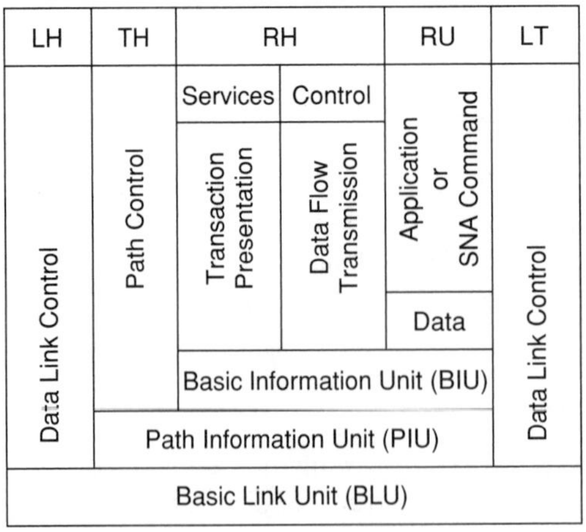

2.1.8.6 Presentation Services Layer

This layer of the SNA model is where application programs define verbs for transaction programs. The verbs determine the appearance of the output of the data to a terminal, printer, or application.

2.1.8.7 Transaction Services Layer

The Transaction Services Layer contains all of the rules for the end user to access the network and send requests to the Presentation Layer. The functions of control and operation are also housed here. SSCP-to-PU sessions are controlled here and are vital for the operation of the network. The SSCP-to-PU session is used to activate and deactivate links, load the same domain software, and assign dynamically created addresses.

In this layer, you also see the function of session establishment between two LUs. The SSCP-to-SSCP session and the SSCP-to-LU sessions are controlled out of this layer. User password validation, access authority, and session parameters are selected.

Management services are performed in this layer. These services perform the monitoring, testing, tracing, and statistical recording for all of the myriad session partners.

2.1.9 Sessions

Using the SNA terminology, four permutations of SNA sessions can exist:

- SSCP to SSCP
- SSCP to PU
- SSCP to LU
- LU to LU

Figure 2-8 shows a representation of these session types.

2.1.9.1 SSCP to SSCP

SSCP to SSCP is the Session Services Control Point (SSCP) of VTAM that communicates with another VTAM. This is used to pass information from one VTAM to another, usually to set up LU-to-LU sessions in a cross-domain environment. This SSCP-to-SSCP session will house either same-network or a different network (for example, SNI) session.

Figure 2-8
Session types.

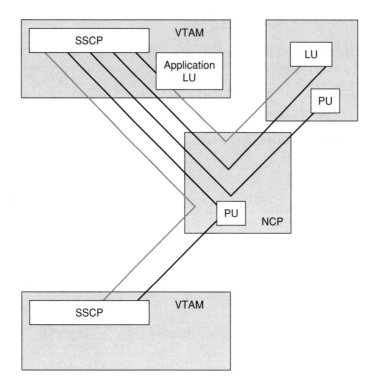

2.1.9.2 SSCP to PU

SSCP to PU is the conversation between a VTAM and a subordinate controller. This can be a large and smart communications controller (FEP—37X5) or a smaller cluster controller (3X74). This session is established during the activation process of loading or starting the network. The main aim for this session is to act as a conduit for subordinate resources.

In the case of a FEP, the subordinate resources are large in number, consisting of an entire subarea's portion of network devices. For a small cluster controller, it is probably just the LUs. Requests can be either the activation/deactivation of LUs or the passing of network management information.

2.1.9.3 SSCP to LU

The SSCP-to-LU session occurs during network activation/loading when the endpoint LU acknowledges the request. In the case of a terminal or printer, LU activation occurs when the remote device responds positively to the ACTLU request.

As for the scenario for an application, this session is established when the Access Control Block, ACB, has been activated. It is this all-important contact that allows for the ultimate activation to occur—the joining of the end user to its desired application. Acknowledgment of this session occurs when the end user reaches the company logon screen. In VTAM jargon, the company logon screen is known as the *USSMSG10 screen.*

2.1.9.4 LU to LU

The LU-to-LU connection is most familiar and probably the most relevant to the MIS community at large. After a request is received from an LU to VTAM to start a session, VTAM will go through its routine to fulfill the request. VTAM will search for the device/application (session establishment), present to each other the possible characteristics for the session (BIND), and ultimately perform the transport of data from "here" to "there."

Application LUs can have more than one session at a time, called *parallel sessions.* In many situations, you can think of the application as the *primary LU (PLU)* and the terminal/printer or the end user as the *secondary LU (SLU).*

2.1.10 Open Systems Interconnect and SNA

We have focused our discussions on IBM's Systems Network Architecture, a proprietary model that has been designed for and used by IBM product sets. Standards committees have created an open model for all other market participants to share. One such model was developed by the International Standards Organization (ISO), called *Open Systems Interconnection (OSI).*

OSI was designed to allow for disparate and autonomous systems to communicate by using standard communications protocols and architectures. As SNA, it was designed to allow for the communication of IBM products. Although no direct correlation can be drawn between the layers, the functions provided by each are quite similar. Figure 2-9 outlines two architectures and their close technical relationship.

Note that the SNA Path Control Layer functions are found in the OSI Network and Transport Layers. Likewise, the SNA Physical Control Layer and OSI Physical Layer both describe the physical medium for transmission.

2.1.11 Downstream Physical Units

As SNA grew and spread its wings, it adapted to LAN protocols, namely, Token Ring. The method of attaching 3X74 controllers to an SNA NCP is by means of a *leased line* (discussed in the next section). Let's look at its newer, faster Token Ring–attached offering: gateways and downstream PUs.

Figure 2-9
*The SNA and
OSI models.*

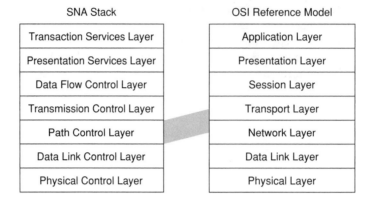

SNA Stack	OSI Reference Model
Transaction Services Layer	Application Layer
Presentation Services Layer	Presentation Layer
Data Flow Control Layer	Session Layer
Transmission Control Layer	Transport Layer
Path Control Layer	Network Layer
Data Link Control Layer	Data Link Layer
Physical Control Layer	Physical Layer

When users began to wire LANs on their premises, they also began to use this connection for connectivity to the mainframe (see Figure 2-10). One way to attach these systems to the mainframe was by using a "gateway" 3174.

Figure 2-10
*Downstream
PUs.*

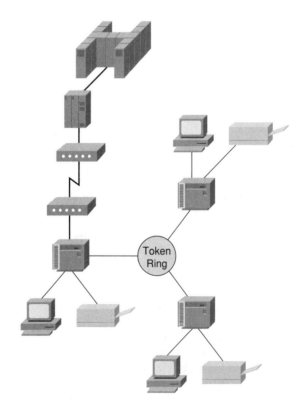

The 3174 gateway Token Ring Media Access Control (MAC) Layer address is the destination MAC address for the non-gateway 3174 Token Ring–attached controllers. The 3174 gateway is therefore providing an FEP function to the non-gateway 3174s (downstream PUs) and a single PU that represents all the downstream PUs to the FEP and the mainframe.

2.2 SNA/SDLC FRAME FORMATS

Let's look in a little closer detail at the format of the data as it passes over an SNA line. We are on the second layer of the SNA seven-layer model—Data Link Control Layer. *Synchronous Data Link Control (SDLC)* is a very orderly and controlled method for sending information, checking that it got there correctly, and retransmitting it if an error occurred.

There are three types of frames that make up an SDLC approach:

- The Information frame
- The Supervisory frame
- The Unnumbered frame

Here's how they break down:

1. The Information frame (I-frame) passes SNA requests and responses.

2. The Supervisory frame acknowledges I-frames and reflects the status of the NAU as either ready to receive more data—a.k.a. *receiver ready (RR)*—or not ready to receive more data—a.k.a. *receiver not ready (RNR)*.

3. The Unnumbered frame passes SDLC commands used for data link management.

2.2.1 Message Unit Formats

In SNA, there are three types of message units, and depending upon where your data is along the path, their destination will dictate what that message unit is composed of:

1. Network-Addressable Units (NAUs) use the *Basic Information Unit (BIU)* to pass information between other NAUs. The BIU is created by the LU and the LU attaches a Request Header (RH) to the Request Unit (RU). Only NAUs use Request Headers. When this has been assembled, the LU passes this on to the Path Control Layer for the additional routing information.

2. The Path Control Layer affixes a Transmission Header (TH) to the BIU. With the transmission header attached, the BIU is then promoted to the stage of a Path Information Unit (PIU).

3. The Path Control Layer then passes this packet to the Data Link control mechanism for preparation to transmit the PIU.

4. The Data Link Layer adds a Link Header (LH) and Link Trailer (LT) to the PIU.

5. Now, completely compiled, the packet of data has been formally assembled into an SDLC frame, also known as a *Basic Link Unit.*

The following sections discuss the details of each of these concepts.

2.2.2 Link Header

The Link Header (LH) contains three fields (see Figure 2-11):

- The flag
- The SDLC station address
- The Link Header control field

Figure 2-11
Link header.

The flag is always a hexadecimal value of 7E. This value notifies the Data Link Layer that this is the start of a new SDLC frame.

The SDLC station address can be the address of a single station or a group of stations. In the case of a multipoint configuration, it denotes the destination of the frame. In a traditional NCP, it's the PU ADDR= parameter. It is always a hexadecimal address.

We can also use a broadcast function, a value of FF to alert all stations. Similarly, we can define a "no stations" address, which is reserved as 00.

The Link Header Control field is quite important as it describes the contents of the field. The field can be unnumbered, supervisory, or information. The unnumbered frame says that the SDLC link-level command is being issued. The supervisory frame will convey the status of the state of the receiver, RR or RNR, or of the prior frame was rejected. The I-frame keeps tally of the frames being sent and received.

2.2.3 Transmission Header

SNA supports a plethora of devices. In order to discern each device type from the next, SDLC has employed the use of five formats. The format identifiers (FID) are as follows:

Non-SNA FID	Type 0	Used for non-SNA traffic between adjacent nodes
PU4 and PU5 FID	Type 1	SNA traffic between subarea nodes
PU4, PU5, PU2 FID	Type 2	SNA traffic between subarea nodes and PU2.1 adjacent peripheral nodes
PU4 and PU1 FID	Type 3	SNA traffic between an NCP and a peripheral PU1 node
PU4 and PU4 FID	Type 4	SNA traffic between subarea nodes that support virtual route protocols
PU4 and PU5	FID Type F	Specific SNA commands between subarea nodes that support virtual and explicit router protocols

The most commonly used FIDs are 2 and 4. The Transmission Header houses the detail as to which FID type we are discussing. Figure 2-12 shows the format of the Transmission Header (TH).

The TH's purpose is to aid the path control level of the SNA seven-layer model. Remember that the Path Control Layer gets data from "here" to "there." It is in this TH that "here" and "there" are denoted in the Origin Address Field (OAF) and the Destination Address Field (DAF). Also found in the TH is the sequence number of this PIU, the length of the Request Unit (RU), and whether it is first, last, middle, or only in this transmission.

For FID type 4s, we also see additional information regarding explicit and virtual route (ER and VR) information, origin/destination subarea, and element addresses.

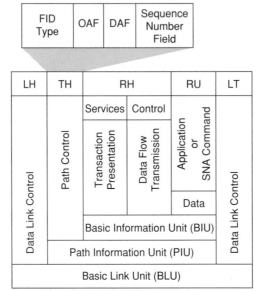

2.2.4 Request/Response Header

Figure 2-13 shows the format of the request/response header.

Directly following the TH is a 3-byte header that informs us of the type of information being transmitted. The header type is indicated by the first bit, Bit 0. If Bit 0 is equal to 0, it is a request header. If Bit 0 is equal to 1, it is a response header.

The request header provides information to the PIU as to how to control the session. Certain information that's provided includes whether or not you're running this session with definite response, pacing, bracketing, or its position in a chained packet.

The response header is used to provide appropriate information back to the SDLC protocol. If there are negative responses due to an error in the transmission, the Response Header will contain related information concerning the reason for the error. A negative response to a request sets the sense indicator bit equal to 1, which indicates that SNA sense data will follow.

2.2.5 Request/Response Units

Request units (RUs) follow request headers. This unit can vary in length and may contain some end-user data or an SNA command. The RUs can, in theory, be infinite in size. In practice, you would want to limit the size of the RU to the size of the buffer at the end device. In traditional SNA networks that were composed of 9.6Kbps analog lines and 3x74 controllers, a value of 256 bytes was a good rule of thumb. In today's expanding high-bandwidth networks, values of 256 bytes are not optimum.

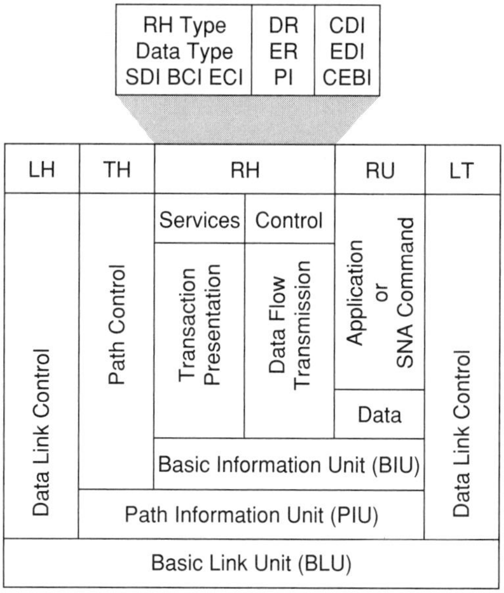

Figure 2-13
*Request/re-
sponse header.*

BCI = Beginning Chain Indicator
CDI = Change Direction Indicator
CEBI = Conditional End Bracket Indicator
DR = Definite Response
ECI = End Chain Indicator
EDI = Enciphered Data Indicator
ER = Exception Request/Response Indicator
PI = Pacing Indicator
SDI = Sense Data Indicator

2.2.6 Link Trailer

The final field in the SDLC format frame is the *link trailer (LT)*. It houses two fields (see Figure 2-14):

- The Frame Check Sequence
- The Link Trailer Flag

The *Frame Check Sequence (FCS)* is used to keep cadence of the packets going in and out on the network. The transmitting link station executes an algorithm based on *Cyclic Redundancy Checking (CRC)*. The data for the computation is the link header address field through the RU. The receiving link station performs a similar computation and checks its results against the FCS. If the results are incorrect, a transmission error is sent back to the originating link station and a retransmission will be scheduled.

Figure 2-14
Link trailer.

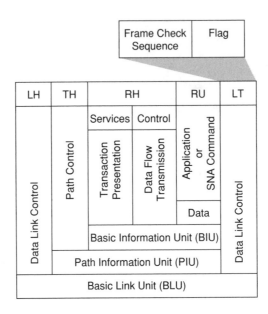

The *Link Trailer flag* indicates that the frame has ended and new frame is expected. This too is depicted by a hexadecimal 7E.

2.3 SNA MAINFRAME SOFTWARE

Certain software that runs on the mainframe is necessary to support and operate a traditional SNA network. The backbone of the SNA network is IBM's Advanced Communications Function/Virtual Communications Method, called VTAM.

2.3.1 IBM's Advanced Communications Function/Virtual Communications Access Method (VTAM)

Virtual Communications Access Method (VTAM) is a software package developed and supported by IBM that runs on a mainframe platform and is the cornerstone of an SNA network. It directly controls the transmission of data to and from the network at large. It has many complex abilities to manage, operate, and control the flow of data from application to end user.

Let's talk about the role VTAM plays in the network. Let's say we have an SSCP-to-LU session established with a remote terminal, and the user comes in and wants to log on to an application.

VTAM will receive that request and try to establish an LU-to-LU session for that terminal (see Figure 2-15). Remember, the terminal is an LU and the application is an LU.

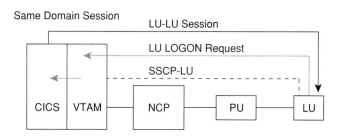

Figure 2-15
*Same-domain
session
LOGON
example.*

The first thing VTAM will do is to check to see if the application is available within its own control (in other words, has an SSCP-LU session active). We would then term this a *same-domain session*. Let's say VTAM does have an active SSCP-LU session with the requested application. VTAM passes the request over to the application, and after session startup procedures, a session is established. At this point VTAM is out of the flow of data. The data will flow between the application and the terminal until VTAM is in some way required to terminate the session.

Now let's go back to the first example. Suppose that the application was not residing on the same mainframe image as VTAM (see Figure 2-16).

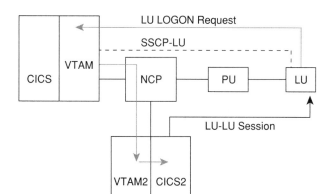

Figure 2-16
*Cross-domain
session
establishment.*

VTAM will check a table built to reference a list of LUs it knows about that are not within the scope of control or domain. These entries are entitled *Cross-Domain Resources (CDRSC)*. They can be created by hard-coded entries, or are dynamically created when VTAM searches and discovers a resource. VTAM checks the CDRSC tables to see if the requested LU is known. If the resource is found, the LU (representing the user who is trying to log on) is presented to the other owning VTAM for session establishment, and the process will begin. If the LU resource is not found, VTAM will check with other VTAMs over SSCP-SSCP sessions for the LU resource. If no other VTAM has knowledge of the requested LU, the LU-LU session request is denied.

This is another function in VTAM that has a separate name, *Cross-Domain Resource Manager (CDRM)*. CDRMs are the function in VTAM that handle the interaction between two VTAMs. If the other CDRM has knowledge, VTAM will:

- Pass along the resource for session establishment

- Update its own CDRSC table so as to save a repetitious search act for the next resource that wants that particular application

Let's change this same example for the last time. Let's say VTAM has exhausted all of the VTAMs within its network. Look at Figure 2-17 to see what happens next.

Figure 2-17
VTAM cross-network session establishment.

Cross Network Session

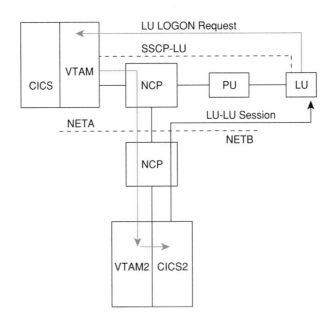

VTAM will now go outside its network and check with its cross-network connections. Much akin to firewalling, autonomous SNA networks can communicate without the interdependence of being in the same network by using Systems Network Architecture Interconnect (SNI). VTAM will contact its SNI-connected CDRMs in hopes of finding the destination resource. If it's found, the same procedure happens with:

- Session establishment commencing
- Updates to CDRSC tables for future reference

Now, let's say there was no such active resource in the network. VTAM would send a response back to the terminal indicating that the session could not be bound. That response is not so cryptic as it may first appear. In SNA networking after the two partner resources have been located, the next step is to establish the session. To do that, VTAM must, in our example, present the terminal (SLU) to the application (PLU) for connection. VTAM must know the details about the capabilities of the resource; VTAM gets its information through the definitions. There is a specific reference in the LU definition to a VTAM LOGMODTAB (LOGon MODe TABle) and entry. This table/entry has a list of characteristics and features that comprise each and every resource in VTAM's network.

The next step is as follows: VTAM gathers the session information (that is buffer sizes, screen sizes, types of data streams, definite/exception response mode, and so on) to the destination resource.

This presentation of the request of a session between the device and the application is called a *bind*. In legacy SNA, binds are either accepted or refused. In current Advanced Peer-to-Peer Networking (APPN) networks and with the advent of intelligent devices out in the field (that is, LU 6.2-capable), some binds can be negotiated.

2.3.2 Network Control Program (NCP)

IBM's *Network Control Program (NCP)* runs outbound of the mainframe in the communications controller. Typically today, we see a traditional IBM 3745 as the hardware platform for this software. NCP is designed to handle the end station traffic and management of the device and act as a conduit up to VTAM. Defined in NCP are all of the SDLC lines, Token-Ring connections, adjacent subarea link stations, PUs, and LUs.

An *NCP gen* is created up at the mainframe host and is loaded into the box during activation. Another, less highlighted piece of IBM software actually performs any loading and/or dumping of the NCP; it is called *Systems Support Program (SSP)*.

NCP can be likened to the IOS router configuration as it pertains to form and function, but not in process. An NCP gen is assembled beforehand and has software checks before loading into the device.

Figure 2-18 shows how NCP fits in the SNA network.

Figure 2-18
NCP in an SNA network.

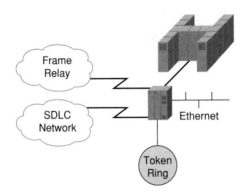

CHAPTER 3

Advanced Peer-to-Peer Networking (APPN)

Advanced Peer-to-Peer Networking (APPN) is an outgrowth of SNA. In APPN's original incarnation, it was designed for networking IBM small business computers—namely the IBM System/36 and System/38 computing systems, which are the predecessors to IBM's most successful line of computers, the IBM AS/400. With the introduction of the AS/400, IBM made its investment in peer networking with APPN as the cornerstone. It was not until quite recently that VTAM, which has remained very much hierarchical in nature, adopted a peer networking approach.

A fundamental use of APPN is to provide a flexible network that will allow peers to communicate with each other without having to work with the restriction of SNA, which is that all sessions must pass through the SSCP. Using the methods discussed in the rest of the chapter, APPN provides the flexibility for peer-to-peer relationships using LU T2.1 and LU T6.2 nodes.

3.1 APPN CONCEPTS

The strength behind the APPN architecture is the ability to dynamically learn the entire network topology and to allow individual network nodes to update the network with its topology changes. Any change in the network topology will result in all nodes learning of this and altering their network database accordingly. Another key feature of APPN is the ability to store the location of applications after they have been learned. The advantage to having the ability to locate applications within the network is being able to move them without impacting connectivity from a user's perspective.

APPN peer networking has become a dominant means of communicating with applications on IBM mainframes, due in large part to its roots in deterministic SNA. Guarantees of delivery and predictive response time are paramount to corporations with delivering information. At the same time, companies need to remain flexible with their networks to answer the fast-paced environment of today's competitive marketplace. The outcome of these needs is a peer networking environment that provides:

- Ease of use, but that can change, be manageable and grow

- Decentralized network control with centralized network management

- Support for any type of network topology

- Flexible support for physical connectivity

- Continuous operation using High-Performance Routing (HPR)

To meet these requirements, APPN specifies unique services:

- *Configuration Services* define the means for simple physical attachment to the peer network.

- *Directory Services* function to locate any resource in the network dynamically.

- *Topology and Routing Services* selection of the most efficient route and the ability to provide an alternate route between peer network resources.

- *Data Transport Services* reliable transport of variable length messages using flow control to prevent deadlocks.

- *Management Services* offer control and management of the peer network.

3.2 APPN Architecture

The architecture of APPN is an extension of the early PU Type 2.1 node. The APPN Type 2.1 node (T2.1) added support for directory functions, dynamic update of network topology, routers, and directories. APPN defines four types of nodes as shown in Figure 3-1.

The Low Entry Networking (LEN) T2.1 node was the first APPN node to be supported. Being the foundation of all T2.1 nodes, the LEN lacked the majority of dynamic functions afforded by the subsequent EN implementation. However, it did establish the ability for an LU to establish a session without the need or intervention of a Session Services Control point (SSCP), in the form of VTAM. LEN did, however, limit connectivity to adjacent and predefined partner applications—*transaction programs (TPs)*.

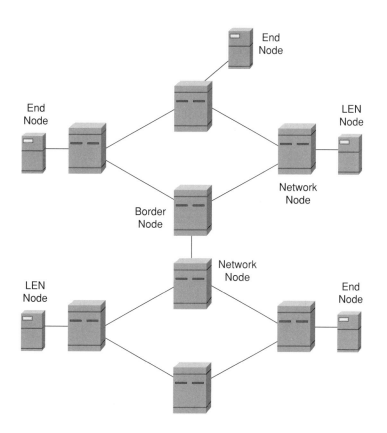

Figure 3-1
APPN node network topology.

The APPN End Node (EN) T2.1 supports many of the APPN T2.1 node service enhancements. As its name implies, it must be the end of a route in APPN.

The APPN Network Node (NN) T2.1 is the keeper of all APPN network topology. Additionally, the NN assists ENs and LENs in locating APPN resources throughout the network.

Finally, interconnecting unique APPN networks is accomplished using an APPN Border Node (BN). A BN acts as an NN to its native network and an EN to the non-native network. This allows each APPN network to isolate its topology while integrating its directory services for locating APPN resources in either network.

All APPN nodes have a function called a *control point (CP)*. Figure 3-2 diagrams the functions of the CP. NNs establish CP-CP sessions with directly attached NNs or ENs. The CP-CP session is established using APPC LU 6.2 communications. A CP is then, by definition, an LU 6.2 application, that the CP uses to establish a conversation with other

CPs. Because the CP is actually an application, it is given a fully qualified unique resource name made up of the network identifier and a unique individual identifier. Using the CP-CP conversations, an NN can perform additional services on behalf of the ENs with which it communicates. When performing these services, the NN node is called a *Network Node Server (NNS)*. As a single EN can connect to multiple NNs, the EN will be configured to adopt one of the NNs as its NNS. Each NNS and the ENs it communicates with define the NNS domain.

Figure 3-2
APPN CP functions.

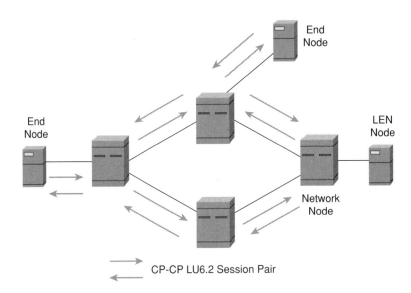

APPN nodes communicate over physical links called *transmission groups (TGs)*. In the early releases of APPN, a TG could only be a single link. Today, however, multiple links are possible within a TG, and these links may be mixed media. Multilink TGs are supported only when using HPR. ISR supports parallel TGs. As seen in Figure 3-3, NN1 has multiple TGs, one to each adjacent NN, and NN2 has a multilink TG to NN3. Each TG is uniquely identified by a TG number and the name of the partner CP. This allows the TG to be unique between the adjacent partners while reusing the TG numbers.

NOTES

By default all APPN TGs begin at number 21 unless specific parameters are set. So, in most networks, all single links between CPs will start sequentially as TG21, TG22, and so on.

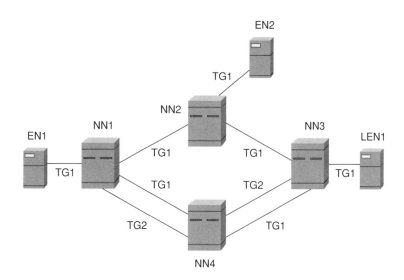

Figure 3-3
*TG
configuration
between APPN
nodes.*

3.2.1 Low Entry Network Node

Although LEN T2.1 nodes utilize a CP function, they do not establish CP-CP communications. The LEN CP supports the five services of APPN but with reduced functionality for Directory Services, Topology, and Routing Services. The LEN CP functions are described in Figure 3-4.

LEN nodes may attach to an APPN network through an adjacently attached NN. The LEN does not provide network services to other nodes because it lacks the ability of a CP-CP session. The Directory Services on an LEN node are manually defined for supporting local resources and communicating to remote resources. Without a CP-CP session capability, the LEN knows only what is defined to it. LEN nodes may only use a single TG link to another node and do not propagate or populate a topology database dynamically.

An LEN believes there to be only two adjacent devices in a network connection—itself and its session partner. In summary, an LEN lacks the dynamic abilities of its successor, the end node.

3.2.2 APPN End Node

The T2.1 APPN EN is the device that contains the logical units (LUs) used in an APPN network. The ENs may connect to adjacent ENs directly or to remote ENs through the assistance of an NNS. Figure 3-5 illustrates direct EN-EN connectivity supporting LU-LU sessions.

Figure 3-4
*CP functions
used by LENs.*

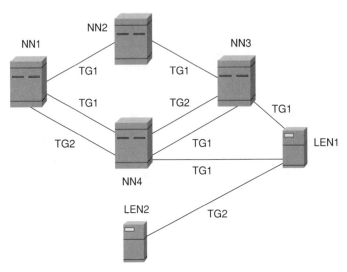

LEN Functions: Manual Configuration Services
Manual Directory Services
Limited Topology and Routing Services
Session Services for local resources only
Data Transport Services
No CP-CP session support
Only functions as a session end point
No intermediate routing through LEN nodes

ENs discover the location of partner LUs for their own LUs either by manually entered local definition or through the APPN LOCATE request command issued to the EN's NNS. LU-LU sessions between directly connected ENs require local definition of the partner resource. The EN participates in CP-CP communications with its NNS using a single pair of LU 6.2 sessions. One LU 6.2 session is used for sending the other for receiving.

The CP-CP communications are established when the EN starts its links to the NNS. Initially, the CP-CP communications are used for exchanging topology information and the registration of the EN LUs with the NNS. It is the registration process of the EN LUs that enables APPN to locate network resources anywhere in the network. ENs may have more than one NN connection, but only one NN serves as the NNS at any given time.

3.2.3 APPN Network Node

The APPN network node implements the APPN services completely. All NNs are characterized as having a domain as shown in Figure 3-6.

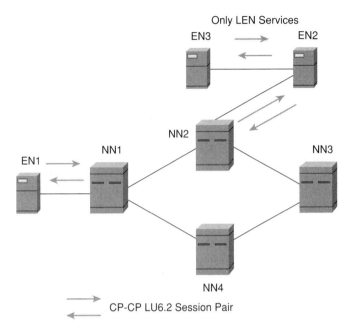

Figure 3-5
EN-EN direct connectivity without the use of an NNS.

Only LEN Services

EN3   EN2

NN2

NN1   NN3

EN1

NN4

CP-CP LU6.2 Session Pair

EN Functions: Configuration Services
Local and LOCATE Request Directory Services
Local Topology and Routing Services
Local Session Services
Data Transport Services
CP-CP session support to one NN at a time
Only functions as a session end point
No intermediate routing through EN

An NN domain spans its own resources and the EN resources with which the NN maintains CP-CP communications. LENs are not considered part of the NN domain because they do not support CP-CP communications. However, an NN will perform directory services for the LEN and represent the partner resource as if it were on the NN; hence the LEN is in the NNs domain.

Network nodes are the portal to the APPN network for ENs and LENs. The APPN NN provides:

- LU-LU session services for its own LUs

- Session routing functions

- Network directory searches and route selection

- Management services as a focal point or relay point for network problem management

Figure 3-6
*Network node
domain
configuration.*

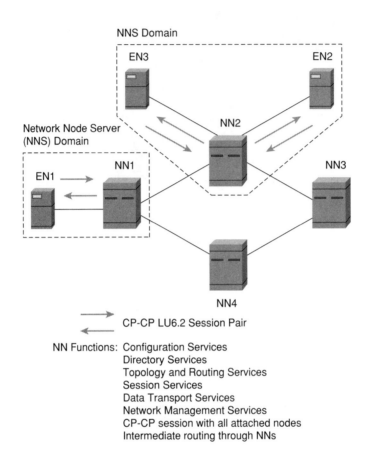

Figure 3-6
Network node domain configuration.

NNSes maintain the APPN directory entries for resources residing on the NN, LEN-defined LU resources, and registered LUs from attached ENs.

3.2.4 APPN Border Node

Each APPN network in an enterprise may be unique unto itself. Some are engineered this way to isolate outages or to maintain a more manageable network. Connecting these two unique APPN networks is accomplished by using an APPN Border Node (BN). This is because the APPN architecture does not allow for the establishment of CP-CP sessions across a connection between two APPN networks with different NETIDs. As illustrated in Figure 3-7, the BN will act as an EN to one network and be an NN to the other network. As an EN, the BN maintains a local directory of all the applications that exist in the native network that can be reached by the non-native LUs. As an NN, the BN can participate in all NN functions for locating, routing, and maintaining network topology databases.

The BN is used in environments where networks need to be isolated due to network constraints. An example of such a network is when the network topology is so large that changes in the network can impact network performance. The performance impact would be realized due to Topology Database Updates (TDUs).

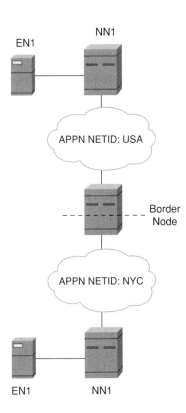

Figure 3-7
*APPN BN
network
topology.*

3.2.5 Link and Transmission Groups

The *APPN link* is defined as the physical transmission media between two adjacent endpoints. Each endpoint connects to the link using link stations. The link, as diagrammed in Figure 3-8, may be point-to-point or over a shared transmission media such as a LAN.

LANs, however, are truly a multipoint connection. APPN architecture handles this through implementing *Shared Access Transport Facility (SATF)*. SATF enables APPN over LANs through the definition of a virtual routing node (VRN) as shown in Figure 3-9.

Figure 3-8
*APPN link
station
connectivity
configuration.*

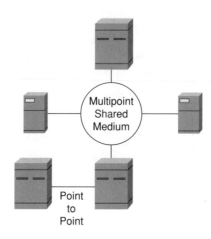

Figure 3-9
*SATF feature of
APPN over
LANs.*

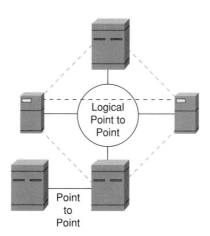

ENs participate in an SATF configuration by defining a VRN link. The purpose of providing a VRN is to eliminate unnecessary routes via an NN when both ENs have the same NNS. As illustrated in Figure 3-10, EN1 defines a connection over a TG to a VRN and one TG link to a true NN attached to the LAN. EN2 is configured similarly. The route vectors generated by the ENs identify two routes for connecting to each other. One route is through the VRN, and the second route is through the NN. LU-LU session establishment between EN1 and EN2 are directed by NN1 to use the VRN route. This allows the ENs to communicate directly without the overhead of going through a real NN. This SATF configuration is also called a *connection network*.

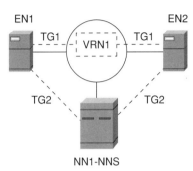

EN1   EN2

TG1   VRN1   TG1

TG2   TG2

NN1-NNS

Potential Routes for both ENs:
EN1 - TG2 - NN1 - TG2 - EN2
EN1 - TG1 - VRN1 - TG1 - EN2

Figure 3-10
*VRN and NN
connectivity
for an EN
attached to a
SATF LAN.*

3.2.6 Comparing APPN to SNA Layers

Because APPN is an outgrowth of SNA, comparing its services to the SNA layers is prudent. Figure 3-11 diagrams this comparison. The heart of APPN resides in the Path and Transmission Control Layers of SNA. APPN supports any Layer 1 and Layer 2 connectivity. Session services functions are provided through the use of LU 6.2 at the SNA Data Flow Control and Presentation Services Layers. APPN resources are located through APPN Directory Services as a function of the CP, which resides at SNA Transaction Services Layer.

3.3 APPN SERVICES

The sophisticated APPN architecture lends itself to a dynamic network topology. These dynamics significantly reduce the coordination of resource definitions between nodes. Resource location, adaptation to network changes, topology updates, route optimization, class of service, and transmission priorities are provided by APPN services.

SNA Architecture	APPN Architecture
Transaction Services Layer	SNADS, DDM, DIA, CNOS, CP
Presentation Services Layer	LU6.2
Data Flow Control Layer	Session
Transmission Control Layer	APPN
Path Control Layer	
Data Link Control Layer	Data Link Control Type 2.1 XID3
Physical Control Layer	Physical Layer

3.3.1 Configuration Services

Each APPN node control point incorporates a configuration services component. Configuration services maintain the APPN node's resource definitions. The definitions are manually entered through the use of the Configuration Services Network Operator Facility (NOF). Using NOF, a network administrator defines start, stop, and query configuration services components. Following are the node definitions and characteristics defined using NOF:

- Data link control

- Ports

- Links and link stations

- Attached connection network (VRN)

3.3.1.1 Data Link Control

Data link control (DLC) ensures reliable delivery of information between a pair of nodes through the use of a protocol that provides frame sequencing, acknowledgment, error recovery, and the establishment and synchronization of the information between the node partners over a common communication medium. Using configuration services, the CP creates a DLC manager and a DLC element for each type of DLC in use.

Figure 3-12 identifies the list of DLC protocols supported by APPN. The configuration services offered by the DLC Manager are as follows:

- Activation and deactivation of DLC elements and links
- Coordination between the DLC element and the CP
- CP notification when a station or port becomes operative or inoperative
- Exchanging with adjacent DLC elements
- Transfer of data to the physical communications medium

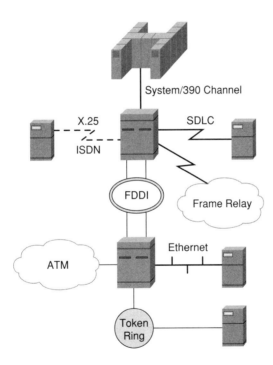

Figure 3-12
*DLC protocol
support with
APPN.*

Configuration Services maintain information regarding an APPN node's DLC characteristics. These characteristics can be thought of as a hierarchy that, in descending order, are the DLC, PORT, and Link Station.

3.3.1.2 Ports

The DLC Manager can associate with many ports. Each port is associated with a DLC process acting as the physical connection to the link hardware. Ports are associated to a specific DLC manager, which in turn learns of the following port characteristics:

- Link station activation limits and timeout values
- Transmission group characteristics
- Buffer sizes
- Connected networks

3.3.1.3 Links and Link Stations

Link stations manage the connection between two nodes. Configuration Services through NOF define a name for each link station. Each link station performs a role on the connection. The role is determined at link activation time. The role is learned either through predefinition, or negotiation with the adjacent link station. If a predefined role is used, one link station must take on the primary role and the other the secondary role.

If a link activation and both link stations are predefined as either primary or secondary, the activation will fail. This is avoided when using negotiated activation. Using negotiable activation on just one of the link stations allows the predefined link station to maintain its specified role, either primary or secondary. In this case, the link station defined as negotiable will take on the opposite role.

A link having both link stations defined as negotiable is resolved through the exchange identification fields at link activation time. APPN nodes use the exchange identification format 3 (XID-3) when activating links. There are three phases of link activation and subsequent XID exchange:

- Connect
- Prenegotiation
- Contact

The Contact phase, consisting of `Negotiation proceeding` XID-3, exchanges the following capabilities information between adjacent nodes:

- Adjacent link station name

- CP capabilities:

  Network node provided services on this link
  Network node does not provide service on this link
  End node supports CP-CP sessions on this link
  End node does not support CP-CP sessions on this link
  End node supports and requests CP-CP sessions over this link

- CP name

- Link characteristics

- TG number

- A subarea PU name is applicable

- The Product Set ID (PSID)

- Node capabilities:

  Parallel TG support
  Multilink TG support
  Type of DLC support
  BTU size

NOTES

Multilink TG support was not included in the architecture of APPN. Its use is restricted to HPR.

3.3.1.4 Attached Connection Network

Configuration services through NOF allow the network administrator to define a connection network and a VRN. Recall that the connection network is composed of an SATF and its representation through the use of a VRN. The connection network is defined with a fully qualified network name, which also matches the CP name associated with the VRN. Any nodes on a LAN that want to communicate with each other must use the same connection network name specification.

Any-to-any communication on the LAN, as shown in Figure 3-13, using APPN requires
that each end node have at least one CP-CP session with a common NNS or a CP-CP
session with an NNS that has a CP-CP session with another NNS connecting to the
partner end node. The use of VRN and connection networks reduces the amount of
TDUs flowing over the SATF, thereby reducing the overhead on the LAN and the
NNSes.

Figure 3-13
*Connection
network
configuration.*

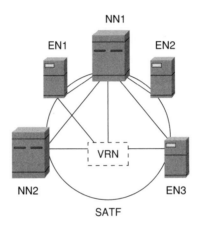

3.3.2 Topology and Route Selection Services

Each APPN node maintains a database that reflects the node's knowledge of the network topology and the various class of services available for the resources found in the
topology data base. LENs and ENs maintain the data bases only for their own local
resources. The full network topology and router selection data bases for the entire
APPN network are found only in the NNs. The topology and route selection data base
specify the information for end-to-end routes between nodes in an APPN network.

Figure 3-14 illustrates the three components that comprise the Topology and Route
Selection Services (TRSS):

- Topology Database Manager (TDM)

- Class-of-Service Manager (COSM)

- Route Selection Services (RSS)

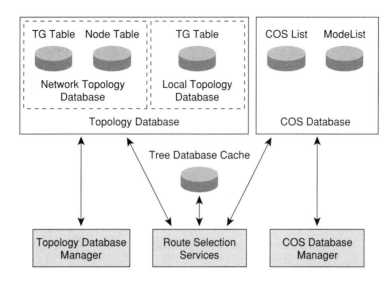

Figure 3-14
The three components of TRSS.

TRSS is aware of the local resources through network administrators' entries using the NOF for initialization parameters pertinent to TRSS. Following are the parameters:

- Type of node (NN, EN, or LEN)

- CP name of this node

- Network ID associated with this node

- Class of service/transmission priority field (COS/TPF) support

- COS database file name

- Topology database file name

The primary function of TRSS is the provision of optimal routes between two APPN nodes in the network. The optimal route is based on information from several sources.

First among these sources is the *topology database,* which is composed of information that allows each NN to build a map of the entire APPN network. Recall that APPN nodes are connected over links that are assigned to a TG. Intermediate routing TGs connect NNs to NNs, or VRNs to NNs, and form the network topology database. Endpoint TGs connect ENs to NNs, or ENs to ENs, or VRNs to ENs, and populate the local network topology database. ENs may only have the local network topology database. NNs maintain a local network topology database and a network topology database.

The network topology database contains a *node table*. Characteristics of each known node and the node's associated definitions are specified in the node table. Within both the local network and network topology databases is a *TG table*. Each TG entry contains a TG vector and a TG record. The entries exist for both forward and reverse TG direction. The topology data collected by each NN is transmitted to each adjacent NN through the use of TDUs.

Each TDU also contains information on the class of service (COS) possible for each TG. The COS database information is obtained from Configuration Service definitions from the TGs and COS definitions. The COS database includes a list of mode names, COS names, and a weight index.

Figure 3-15 lists the TG and node characteristics used in the default COS database. The COS name associates one of three user-assigned transmission priorities (high, medium, and low) which are associated to rows of TG and node characteristics. The mode names are kept in a table and each entry specifies session characteristics and points to a COS name for use by LU session requests.

NOTES

This is similar in the functionality used by IBM VTAM and VTAM's mode table. The LU passes the mode name to use to the CP, and the CP requests the COSM to select the COS entry from the table.

The weight index structure of the COS database is a mechanism for computing the cost of using a TG. This information along with data provided by the topology database allows RSS to decide on the optimal route between two endpoints.

RSS calculates the optimal route for each LU-LU session supported by the NNS. In the first incarnation of APPN, the optimal route selected by RSS was a deterministic route. This means that after the route was selected, all information flowing on the LU-LU session traversed the same physical connection. If any piece of this connection were to fail during the LU-LU session, the LUs would have to re-establish the session to determine a new optimal route. The ability to reroute an active LU-LU session to overcome a network resource outage is a function of a new APPN routing feature called *High-Performance Routing (HPR)*. HPR is discussed in the section "HPR" later in this chapter.

Mode Name	Corresponding COS Name
Default	#CONNECT
#BATCH	#BATCH
#INTER	#INTER
#BATCHSC	#BATCHSC
#INTERSEC	#INTERSEC
CPSVCMG	CPSVCMG
SNASVCMG	SNASVCMG

TG Characteristics	Node Characteristics
Cost per Byte	Route Addition Resistance
Cost per Connect Time	Congestion
Effective Capacity	Weight Field
Propagation	
Security Level	
User Defined-1	
User Defined-2	
User Defined-3	
Weight Field	

Figure 3-15
TG and node characteristics in the COS database.

An ordered sequence of nodes and TGs between two end nodes comprises an APPN route. The selection of an optimal route is determined by RSS on a session-by-session basis. RSS calculates all possible routes based on the COS and TG requirements identified by the LU requesting a session with a remote LU using the mode name. RSS selects the optimal routes by first excluding all unacceptable routes at the time of session request. Next, RSS excludes potential routes by examining:

- Current TG characteristics and network topology congestion on intermediate nodes between the two end nodes

- Depletion of resources on the intermediate nodes or the endpoint itself

- Nodes along the route that are quiescing

- An infinite weight assigned to a route by TRS, and user-definable values for increasing route resistance

The information just listed, regarding intermediate node characteristics, is stored in the node's topology database and is learned from TDU exchanges.

However, RSS does not always go through a calculation for every session request. RSS uses a routing tree cache for quick lookup of available routes between two end nodes. The routing tree entry is computed from the origin NNS and a given COS. Each NN calculates and maintains its own routing tree cache.

The tree is a representation of the optimal routes between the original NNS and any other NN in the network. The routes in the routing tree cache are unidirectional. The routing tree is specific to a COS, and thus each COS requires its own routing tree. RSS calculates and caches the routing tree only once, or when there is a network resource change. If multiple routes exist and some have the same weight, only one route is chosen at random, and an aging algorithm is used to cause the routing tree to be deleted and then recalculated for this entry.

After the routing tree calculations are complete and the tree is cached, RSS selects the route with the least weight.

3.3.3 Directory Services

Logical units request sessions with other LUs by sending session requests to their CP. The CP determines which node in the network the session request is directed to by using the Directory Services function. Each CP maintains a directory of LUs for its own node. These available LUs are entered manually through the NOF of Configuration Services. These LUs may be the CP LU and application LUs.

LEN nodes do not participate in a distributed directory search across the network, because they do not support CP-CP sessions. All LUs remote to a LEN node must be defined in the LEN local directory database.

Figure 3-16 illustrates a LU-LU session request for LEN nodes. As seen in Figure 3-16, LENb has predefined LUa and LU1 as being reachable using NN1 and TG2. The reverse is applicable to the APPN node adjacent to the LEN node. The APPN NN eases the definitions by using a wildcard character to define all the resources on the adjacent node.

APPN ENs can also have their resources manually entered on the NNS. However, true APPN ENs have a feature that allows them to dynamically register all their locally defined resources to the NNS. In Figure 3-17, ENa registers its resource named LUa with NN1 after CP-CP session establishment. The registration process is used only if the EN is defined as an authorized EN. An authorized EN allows the NNS to query it for LU resources that may have not been registered with the NNS.

Requests for a *destination LU (DLU)* are handled by the EN CP by querying its own local directory database first. If the DLU is found in the local directory database, the session establishment process begins. If the DLU is not found in the local directory database, the EN CP on behalf of the requesting LU issues a LOCATE request to its NNS for assistance on locating the DLU somewhere in the APPN network. The LOCATE request is forwarded to the NNS on the CP-CP session that exists between the EN and the NNS.

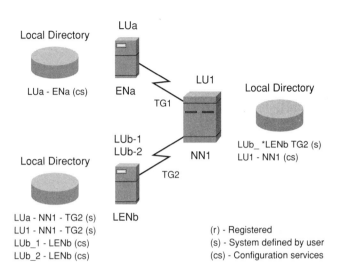

Figure 3-16
LEN LU-LU session request.

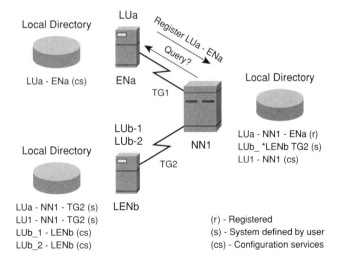

Figure 3-17
EN resource registration.

Three types of searches are used by Directory Services. Figure 3-18 diagrams the one-hop, broadcast, and directed search techniques. In locating a DLU, the EN issues the LOCATE request to its NNS. If the NNS knows of a route to the DLU, the search is accomplished in one hop.

However, suppose the NNS does not have directory information for the DLU in the NNS local directory database. At this point, the NNS can send a LOCATE(Broadcast) search command. The LOCATE(Broadcast) search request flows to all NNs and ENs adjacent to the issuing NNS via the node's CP-CP sessions.

The broadcast is categorized into either a *domain search* or a *network search*. The broadcast is a domain search when the LOCATE(Broadcast) are only sent to adjacent ENs if the ENs adjacent to the NNS had indicated that they will participate in a LOCATE(Broadcast) request during CP-CP establishment. A network search is performed when the NNs adjacently attached to the issuing NNS propagate the LOCATE(Broadcast) request to their adjacent NNs, thereby passing the request on to every NN in the network.

After an NN receives the LOCATE(Broadcast) request for the DLU and determines that the DLU is found in the NN local directory database, it forwards a LOCATE(Find) request to the EN that registered the DLU entry. The LOCATE(Find) request is issued to verify that the DLU still exists on the registered EN. The EN, after verifying that the DLU is indeed in its local directory database, returns a LOCATE(Found) response to the originating EN through the same path used to discover the DLU location. At this juncture, TRSS begins optimal route selection.

Predefined network paths to known resources may be used instead of broadcasted paths. These directed search requests (as shown in Figure 3-18) reduce network overhead and establish connectivity faster. In Figure 3-18, LUc in NN1 is still in the RSS cache. The LUa on ENa requests a second session with LUc on ENc. NN1 sends a LOCATE(Directed) request over the path found in the RSS cache. The NNS for ENc verifies that LUC is still on ENc with a LOCATE(Find) request. ENc returns a LOCATE(Found) response to ENa. Using directed searches uses only two LOCATE requests through the network versus a LOCATE(Broadcast) request, which can potentially flood a network, affecting performance and throughput.

For LEN nodes, if the DLU is not found in the local directory database, the session is not established. However, LENs understand their partner resource (the DLU) to be adjacent. Consequently, when the DLU is remote, the LEN will send a BIND to its adjacent node (in this case the NN). The NN will use one or more of the search methods described earlier to locate the DLU.

A *Central Directory Server (CDS)* is also supported by Directory Services. As the name implies, the CDS is a centralized server acting as the repository for all NN local directory databases. IBM's VTAM on the mainframe computer is an example of a CDS.

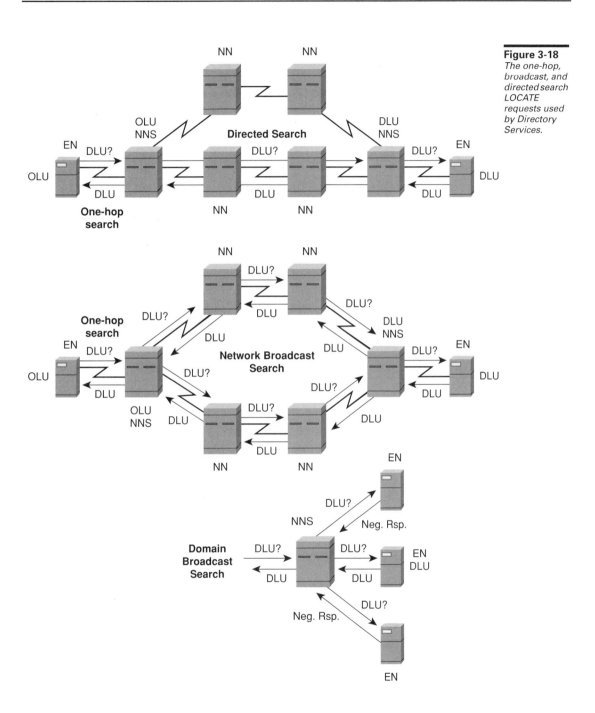

Figure 3-18
The one-hop, broadcast, and directed search LOCATE requests used by Directory Services.

3.3.4 Session Services

The establishment of sessions between EN resources and CP-CP sessions between ENs and NNs is performed by Session Services. The information required for Session Services is supplied through the NOF. Session Services perform the following functions:

- Generating a unique session identifier

- Activating and deactivating of CP-CP sessions

- Assisting in LU-LU session initiation

- Invoking directory services to locate DLU partners

- Invoking TRSS to determine optimal route

- Notifying management services of the CP-CP session status

- Requesting Configuration Services to activate TGs

All sessions are assigned a unique network called a *fully qualified procedure correlation identifier (FQPCID)*. This identifier is used to correlate requests and replies between APPN nodes, recovery procedures, problem determination, accounting, auditing, and performance monitoring. The originating node creates the FQPCID. The FQPCID is a fixed-length (8-byte) field. The contents of this field are a 4-byte value derived from the CP's qualified network name, and a 4-byte sequence number.

3.4 VTAM/NCP SUPPORT FOR APPN

VTAM and NCP are the cornerstone of communications to IBM mainframe computers. As such, VTAM and NCP must provide enhanced SNA support to include APPN. The initial APPN support for IBM mainframes was very similar to LEN nodes. This allowed IBM CICS or IBM APPC/MVS applications to establish LU 6.2 sessions with APPN EN resources that were not on the mainframe. Today, IBM VTAM and NCP support pure APPN nodal functionality with simultaneous support of subarea-based SNA networking.

3.4.1 VTAM/NCP as a Composite Network Node

LEN support on VTAM and NCP is diagrammed in Figure 3-19. VTAM and NCP combine functions of an APPN node and form a unique mainframe APPN node called a *Composite Network Node (CNN)*. A CNN is created when a VTAM is started with both a HOSTSA definition and the NODETYPE=NN start parameter coded and then by activating an NCP from that VTAM. A CNN appears to an APPN network as a single

APPN NN. LU 6.2 sessions traverse between pure APPN networks; and SNA-based VTAM uses APPN routing decisions through the APPN network and static SNA sub-area routing within the SNA network. CNN support on VTAM and NCP requires coordination of LU and routing definitions on all partner nodes.

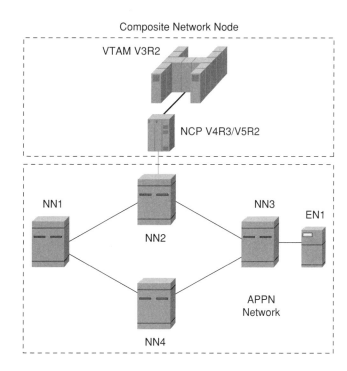

Composite Network Node

Figure 3-19
LEN support on VTAM and NCP define the CNN.

3.4.2 VTAM/NCP Support for APPN

It was not until VTAM V4R1 and NCP V6R2 that VTAM/NCP received full APPN support for NNs and ENs. Along with NN and EN support, VTAM became the first APPN node to act as a CDS. Figure 3-20 illustrates the VTAM/NCP APPN support.

In order for VTAM/NCP to participate as fully functional APPN nodes, extensions to the APPN architecture for providing a migration path from subarea networking to APPN were mandated. The extensions allow VTAM to isolate subarea-specific traffic from APPN nodes while supporting APPN and subarea LU 6.2 session flow through, and/or into, APPN and subarea networks.

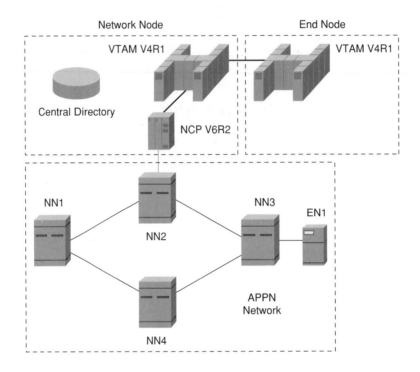

Figure 3-20
*APPN node
support
configuration
on VTAM and
NCP.*

CP-CP sessions from VTAM to adjacent APPN nodes are either established through the boundary function of NCP or through connection networks. The VTAM CP-CP sessions with other nodes integrate the APPN and subarea directories enhancing resource search functions to allow searches to take place through the SNA subarea network. The traditional role of VTAM as the center of SNA communications makes it a valid choice as the CDS. VTAM can handle thousands of CP-CP sessions. Acting as an NN, VTAM can take on the functions of a CDS, which reduces the number of APPN broadcast searches.

NOTES

CP-CP sessions are not supported through a VRN. The CP-CP sessions on a CNN must have predefined link stations.

VTAM's support of parallel and multitail TG connections greatly enhances options for APPN-to-subarea connectivity. Using parallel TGs, two APPN nodes can connect through multiple physical paths. Multitail supports independent LUs to establish sessions to, or through, a subarea network with multiple physical connections.

VTAM has a function that allows another VTAM to take over ownership of SNA resources should the owning VTAM fail. This functionality of VTAM has been extended to support APPN nodes participating in a CP-CP session with the VTAM CP. The connectivity is nondisruptive to SNA and APPN sessions flowing through the NCP. The takeover is performed by issuing a nonactivation XID request that provides the new CP name of the VTAM and assuming the NN function for the CP-CP sessions.

3.4.3 VTAM Node Types to Support APPN

In order for VTAM to function as an APPN node while supporting SNA subareas, it must be defined as one of five different node types. Table 3.1 lists the various VTAM start options and the combinations of NODETYPE and HOSTSA parameters needed to define the functionality. The five different node types that VTAM is capable of supporting include the following:

- A pure subarea network

- An interchange node

- A migration data host

- A pure EN

- A pure NN

Table 3-1   *Node type functional summary.*

Node	Node Type	HOSTSA	CP-CP Sessions	SSCP-SSCP Sessions	NCP Ownership	Inter-Change Function
Subarea	Not coded	Coded	No	Yes	Yes	No
Interchange	NN	Coded	Yes[1]	Yes	Yes	Yes
Migration Data Host	EN	Coded	Yes[1]	Yes	No[2]	No
Pure Network Node	NN	Not coded	Yes[1]	No	No[2]	No
Pure End Node	EN	Not coded	Yes[1]	No	No[2]	No

1. Node level default for CP-CP start option is Yes.
2. Activation of an NCP is not allowed.

3.4.3.1 Pure Subarea Networks

Traditional SNA PU Type 5 functionality is determined in the VTAM start options list by not coding the NODETYPE parameter and defining the HOSTSA parameter. Using this definition enables VTAM to participate in an APPN network as shown in Figure 3-21.

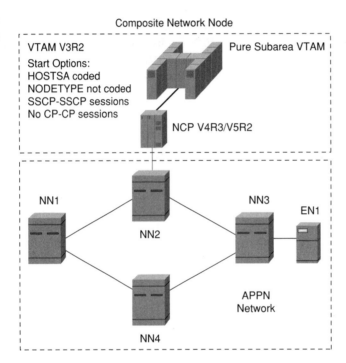

Figure 3-21
VTAM and NCP as a CNN.

Composite Network Node

VTAM V3R2
Start Options:
HOSTSA coded
NODETYPE not coded
SSCP-SSCP sessions
No CP-CP sessions

Pure Subarea VTAM

NCP V4R3/V5R2

NN1

NN2

NN3

EN1

NN4

APPN
Network

3.4.3.2 Interchange Nodes

VTAM acts as an *interchange node (ICN)* when the NODETYPE VTAM start options parameter is defined as NN and the HOSTSA parameter contains a valid SNA subarea number. Acting as an ICN, VTAM may own one or more NCPs and support subarea networks with SSCP-SSCP sessions and APPN networks with CP-CP sessions. Looking at Figure 3-22, you can see that an ICN VTAM node facilitates the routing of sessions from APPN nodes into, and through, an SNA subarea network.

The routing of the data is supported using APPN T2.1 connectivity over the APPN NNs to the ICN subarea domain where the data is delivered using SNA ERs and VRs. As its name implies, an ICN transforms a type of interchange between two different platforms. ICN performs forward and reverse translation of APPN LOCATE requests to SNA subarea Direct Search List (DSRLST) or Cross-Domain Initiate (CDINIT) requests. Two possible ICN configurations are shown in Figure 3-23.

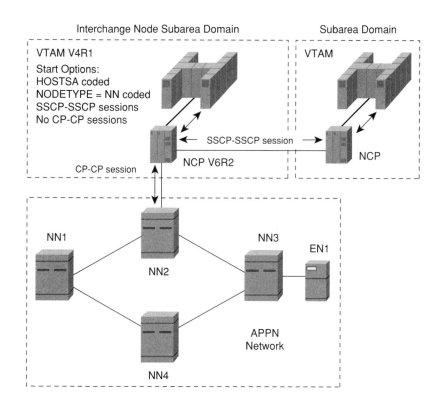

Due to the ability of an NCP to have its ownership shared between VTAMs, multiple ICNs may communicate with an NCP. In support of this, ICNs can be interconnected either by using an APPN TG connection between the NCPs of the ICN or by using sub-area networking between the ICN-owned NCPs.

3.4.3.3 Migration Data Hosts

VTAM supports a unique configuration (illustrated in Figure 3-24) called *Communication Management Configuration (CMC)*. In such a configuration, there are multiple VTAMs; however, only one VTAM owns all the resources attached to NCPs and their downstream devices. The other VTAMs in the network are called *data hosts*. In a CMC configuration the data hosts support communications to and from the applications that execute on that host. CMC functionality is maintained in an APPN VTAM network through the migration of the CMC to an ICN. This is a prerequisite step to migrating the data hosts to MDHs.

Figure 3-23
*Support of two
ICN VTAMs in
one APPN
network.*

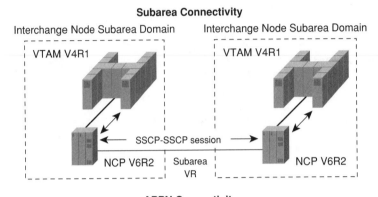

Support of this type of configuration became a requirement for migration to APPN. During an APPN migration, the data hosts are defined as *migration data hosts (MDH)*. The MDH function is defined in the VTAM start options parameter list by specifying a valid SNA subarea number and defining the NODETYPE parameter with the EN value. Specifying NODETYPE=EN denotes that this VTAM will participate in an APPN network as an EN. Acting as an EN, the MDH can perform resource registration to an NN after the NN TG is activated and a CP-CP session is established.

The adjacent NN for an MDH is the ICN. Connection to the ICN is either over a channel to an NCP, or a LAN. The MDH supports both CP-CP and SSCP-SSCP sessions; however, these sessions may not traverse the same physical links. This requires two diverse links: one link supporting the SNA network traffic between the MDH and the SNA nodes and the second link supporting the APPN traffic.

VTAM 4.2 introduced the *virtual route transmission group (VRTG)* to allow FID2 flows across FID4 links and APPN Host-to-Host Channel (AHHC) support to allow CP-CP sessions between VTAMs without the need for an intermediate NCP. AHHC connections are made by means of multipath channel (MPC) links.

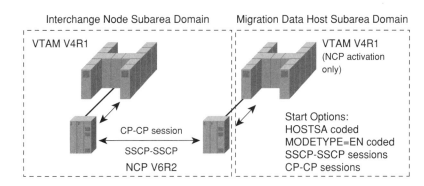

Figure 3-24
VTAM CMC configuration and functional configuration in an APPN network.

3.4.3.4 Pure End Nodes

Pure EN functionality for VTAM is defined by the absence of the HOSTSA VTAM start options parameter and specifying EN on the VTAM start options parameter NODETYPE. As a pure EN, VTAM does not support SNA subarea networking, and therefore it does not support SSCP-SSCP sessions. However, as an EN, it does support CP-CP sessions. Because VTAM is performing the functions of an EN, it can register its resources with an NNS or CDS. VTAM EN does support dependent LUs.

3.4.3.5 Pure Network Nodes

VTAM can also perform the functions of an NN. Figure 3-25 depicts VTAM as an EN and an NN. As an NN, VTAM performs all the functions of APPN NNs. One enhancement to a VTAM NN is its ability to function as an APPN CDS. NN functionality is specified by defining NODETYPE=NN in the VTAM start options list. CDS functionality allows VTAM to act as the global APPN repository of all APPN network resources. Hence, with this type of service, VTAM still continues its role as the focal point within the network. Like VTAM ENs, VTAM NNs can own dependent LUs and support their communication over an APPN network.

3.4.4 Central Directory Service

A benefit of APPN is reduced definition requirements for locating network resources. VTAM acting as an NN can further enhance this benefit by providing Central Directory Server (CDS) functions for all the nodes in the network. The CDS function reduces network search broadcasts by allowing APPN nodes to issue directed broadcasts, which in turn leads to better network performance.

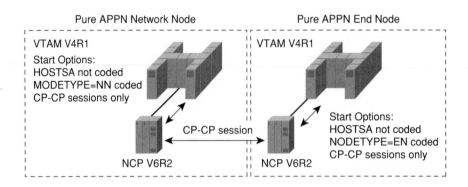

Figure 3-25
VTAM acting as an EN and an NN.

As diagrammed in Figure 3-26, multiple CDS nodes are allowed in APPN. Multiple CDS nodes provide backup for each other and, again, increase performance by distributing the directed searches.

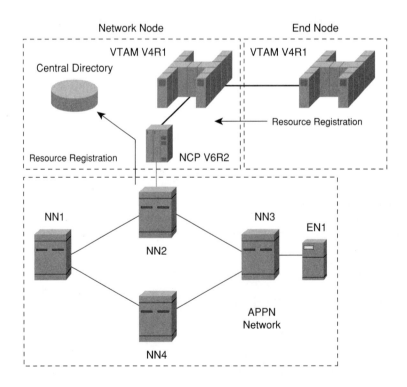

Figure 3-26
CDS configuration using VTAM.

3.4.5 Connection Network Support

The TRS function in VTAM supports connection networks and VRNs. Figure 3-27 diagrams a connection network with VTAM and a Cisco channel-attached router. ENa and ENb both define a VRN and the TG connection to VTAM by specifying the MAC address and SAP address of the Cisco channel-attached router with a *Channel Interface Processor (CIP) card*.

The EN definitions define VTAM as the preferred NNS. VTAM defines dynamically after the EN line and port definitions of the Cisco CIP router have been defined to VTAM. The CP-CP sessions between ENa and ENb and VTAM are established, and the TG tail vectors are exchanged identifying to VTAM that the direct route through the VRN should be used. If the two ENs were other VTAMs, LU-LU sessions between them would route either through the NN VTAM or through a direct connection (channel) between the VTAMs.

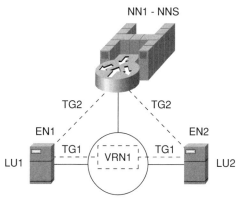

NN1 - NNS

TG2   TG2

EN1   EN2

TG1   VRN1   TG1

LU1   LU2

Potential Routes for both ENs:
EN1 - TG2 - NN1 - TG2 - EN2
EN1 - TG1 - VRN1 - TG1 - EN2

Figure 3-27
VTAM and connection network connectivity.

3.5 APPN ROUTING

IBM's Advanced Peer-to-Peer Network (APPN) is the network architecture most enterprise networks will use when their traffic characteristics are predominantly SNA and when there is a need for providing a deterministic network performance model to the end-user community.

The first generation of APPN used a routing mechanism akin to SNA subarea networking called *Intermediate Session Routing (ISR)*. ISR includes the route within the message header and requires that the session flow be bound to the same physical path for the entire session. Should any link in the connection break, the session fails and must be re-established.

APPN overcomes this deficiency with a second generation routing mechanism called *High-Performance Routing (HPR)*. HPR takes the best of both traditional SNA deterministic characteristics and merges this with the dynamics of IP routing. Using HPR, a session can maintain its required performance level while still having the ability to be re-routed dynamically, without session failure, should any link in the session connection fail.

3.5.1 Intermediate Session Routing

ISR uses a connection-oriented DLC for sessions. The connection is made on a hop-by-hop basis with error correction and retransmission. Sessions between LUs that are not found on adjacent nodes are facilitated by the intermediate routing functions of APPN NNs. After the NNs have determined the optimum route, the originating LU can issue a BIND request to the DLU to establish a connection. This BIND is similar to the SNA BIND but has been extended to support APPN and LU 6.2. The BIND now contains such information as a Route Selection Control Vector (RSCV), the FQPCID, the COS/TPF value, and Basic Information Unit (BIU) indicator to determine whether the RUs sent on the session can be segmented.

Each session traversing a TG is assigned a unique identifier by the Address Space Manager function of Session Services. The identifier is called a *Local Form Session Identifier (LFSID)*. The LFSID is used in an extended FID Type 2 transmission header (TH). This extended FID Type 2 is used for communications between APPN nodes. The LFSID value changes between each intermediate NN found in the selected path.

Figure 3-28 illustrates the format of the LFSID in the extended FID Type 2 TH. In SNA Type 2.0 nodes, the address field is 8 bits in length. This address field is used to identify the PU of the sending and receiving LUs. Due to this 8-bit limit, the maximum number of sessions on a PU allowed is 255.

In an APPN Type 2.1 node, both the origin and destination fields are combined to create a local form address identifier (LFAI) providing for up to 65,024 (64K) unique sessions that can travel over the TG. Bit 6 of the TH is also used to identify the session and is called the Origin Address Field (OAF)-Destination Address Field (DAF) Assignor Indicator (ODAI). This bit partitions the address field. Because each Address Space Manager on each endpoint APPN node can define 65,024 addresses, the total number is the aggregate of 130,048 addresses that can be used to identify unique sessions over a TG.

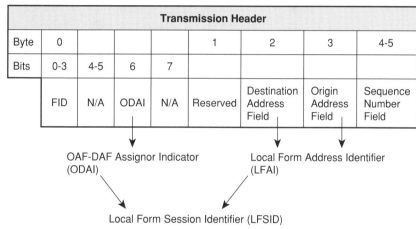

Figure 3-28
LFSID format.

Intermediate NNs found on the route between the two endpoints create *session connector blocks (SCBs)*. The SCB is used to map the incoming LFSID to an outgoing LFSID. The BIND used in session establishment is forwarded to the next adjacent node determined from the route found in the RSCV. The SCB also stores pacing values, transmission priorities, and whether the RU can be segmented. Figure 3-29 illustrates a session between two end nodes using intermediate session routing.

A session using ISR is broken up into sections. Each section uses the unique LFSID created. In the example (see Figure 3-29) ENa establishes a session with ENb through NN1 and NN2. Each hop of the connection uses a different LFSID associated with the session. Session services use the information from the SCB to effectively swap the LFSID label of the incoming messages with the matching outgoing label. This label swapping reduces overhead for decision making, as compared to traditional SNA subarea networking that decides on which outbound port the message should be sent.

Figure 3-29
*Intermediate
session routing
for connecting
two ENs.*

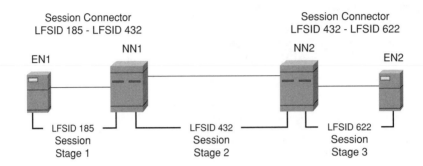

Although the decision-making process on delivering the message is an improvement over legacy SNA subarea networking, its impact is reduced by each node having to buffer the entire message to perform error detection, error correction, flow control, and resegmentation. This induced latency defeats APPN's purpose of providing high-speed networking for SNA-type applications. Also, as in SNA, sessions using ISR routing must use the same physical path after the session is established.

This requirement, again, does not address the need for dynamic routing of disrupted connections. Sessions disrupted over ISR routes must be re-established to discover new routes through the network.

3.5.2 High-Performance Routing

The shortcomings of ISR have been addressed in the development of High-Performance Routing (HPR). Improved performance through the NNs is achieved by putting the responsibility of error processing, flow control, and segmentation on the edge nodes of a session. An enhancement to the flow control mechanism is also realized through the use of *Adaptive Rate-Based (ARB)* flow control, which optimizes flow in high-speed networks. Finally, with HPR, sessions between LUs can reroute around failed connections without session disruption.

HPR consists of two networking layers. The first is *Automatic Network Routing (ANR)*, which provides a connectionless layer for dynamic rerouting of messages that are similar in functionality to IP. The second layer is *Rapid Transport Protocol (RTP)*, which provides a connection-oriented layer for end-to-end guaranteed delivery of messages with similar functionality to TCP. Although HPR is a much-needed improvement over ISR, it was architected to coincide with an APPN/ISR network.

3.5.2.1 Automatic Network Routing

ANR is more of a switching mechanism than a routing mechanism. ANR reduces memory and processing requirements on the NN, because it no longer employs the error correction and retransmission of messages for each NN in the route. There are three functions specific to ANR.

ANR fast packet switching/forwarding is enabled by the network layer structure and its use of "sourcing" the path within the header of the packet. The ANR transport frame contains a network layer header as shown in Figure 3-30.

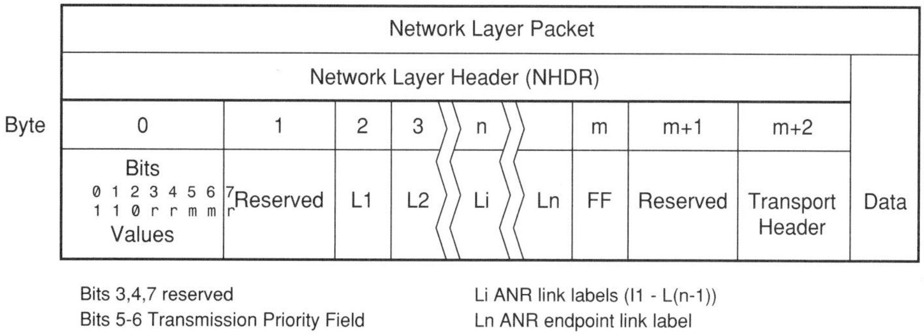

Figure 3-30
HPR/ANR transport frame network layer header format.

Bits 3,4,7 reserved
Bits 5-6 Transmission Priority Field

Li ANR link labels (l1 - L(n-1))
Ln ANR endpoint link label

The first byte of the transport frame identifies the frame as either an ANR network layer header or an SNA FID 2 PIU. As a network layer header, the first 3 bits are represented as binary 110 followed by two reserved bits. Bit 5 and 6 specify the transmission priority associated with the data in the frame and bit 7 is reserved. Byte 1 on the network layer header is reserved. Byte 2 begins the ANR routing field. The ANR routing field is made up of a string of link labels that describe the path of a frame through the APPN/HPR network. The ANR routing field is populated during route setup by the endpoint of an RTP connection.

In processing the HPR ANR routing field, the HPR node interprets the first ANR label, and from that information it switches the frame onto the outbound link for delivery to the next HPR node. The current HPR node will remove the label used prior to sending the frame onto the outbound link queue. The last label in the ANR routing field is always hexadecimal value FF. This indicates that the destination HPR endpoint is found when the label prior to the FF label remains in the ANR routing field. The second to last label is the endpoint of the ANR routing path, and the node that receives this ANR frame is the *Network Connection Endpoint (NCE)*. The NCE may not be the final destination of the data, but it is the final HPR node on the route. The ANR labels are node-specific and, therefore, must be unique within a node. The labels do not have to be unique within the entire network.

3.5.2.2 Rapid Transport Protocol

Rapid Transport Protocol (RTP) is the connection-oriented layer of APPN/HPR using full-duplex protocol. RTP connections transport the LU-LU session or CP-CP traffic across the HPR network. Recall that HPR improves performance by removing processing and error recovery overhead from each intermediate node in the route. RTP provides this service on the two RTP endpoints.

A major component of RTP is the determination of the route at session establishment and dynamic rerouting. The *RTP Transport Header (RTPTH)* is the field within the ANR transport frame immediately following the 1-byte reserved field after the end of the ANR routing field. The RTPTH contains a main header and optional segments. The main header includes:

- Transport Connection Identifier (TCID)—Identifies the RTP connection and an HPR node

- Status Requested Indicator—Used to request an acknowledgment from an RTP endpoint connection

- Retry Indicator—Indicates reliable transport requested

- First|middle|last segment—Identifies the position of the data in the frame when segmentation is used

The optional segments of the RTPTH indicate control information used on the RTP connection. This information may be one or all of the following:

- Connection Setup segment—Used to activate an RTP connection

- Status segment—Acknowledges data when a definite response is requested and may include more data if any exists. This segment is also used (unsolicited) to resend parts of the data stream after a data has been received out of sequence

- Connection Identifier Exchange (CIE) segment—This is used during RTP connection activation for the exchange of TCIDs between RTP connection endpoints

- Routing Information segment—This is used to send routing information for the reverse route to the other RTP endpoint during activation.

- Adaptive rate-based segment—This is used to send congestion control information between RTP connection endpoints.

- Client out of band segment—This segment is used at deactivation of an RTP connection.

- Connection fault segment—Contains sense information when one endpoint detects a protocol violation

An RTP connection is set up either when an HPR node establishes a LU-LU session for the first time or when an RTP connection does not already exist. An existing RTP connection is determined by first finding out whether a Class of Service (COS) name is already in use, and second finding out whether either the RTP connection's RSCV or the HPR network portion of the RSCV is the same. If there is no matching existing connection, the HPR node begins the route setup process.

The route setup protocol determines various pieces of information about the path for use by the RTP connection. This includes:

- The ANR labels of the links to use in both directions

- The maximum frame size of each link along the route to determine the largest frame size to use

- The NCE address if the RTP endpoint does not contain the LU of the session

Figure 3-31 diagrams the RTP activation sequence. After the route setup reply is received, the RTP connection is activated.

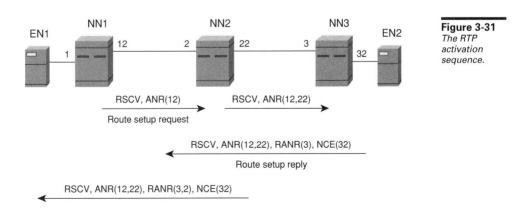

Figure 3-31
The RTP activation sequence.

Probably the most widely hailed feature of HPR is the ability to reroute a connection-oriented session nondisruptively. RTP is responsible for deciding and acting on the selection of a new route. RTP may attempt nondisruptive path switch when an RTP connection endpoint detects either a failure of a local link or a timeout on an RTP connection. Detection of a timeout may mean that an intermediary link along the route has failed or has become heavily congested, or a node along the route is experiencing the same symptoms. The timeout occurs after the alive timer expires between the RTP endpoints and the retry count is exhausted. At this point only one of the RTP endpoints will initiate the nondisruptive path switch process. The decision about which endpoint will begin the process is determined at the initial RTP connection. The new route must use the same HPR network and satisfy the COS used for the original RTP connection. The nondisruptive path switch functions include the following:

- A locate search to determine the latest EN TG vectors

- A new RSCV calculation

- A route setup process

- A new RTP connection activation

In a mixed ISR/HPR network, the NN Route selection Services will only choose a new HPR route (even if the HPR route has a higher cost than a suitable ISR route). At the beginning of the nondisruptive switch process, the HPR node begins a new timer. If the switch does not occur within the desired time period, the HPR node breaks the RTP connection causing the sessions on the RTP connection to fail. After this has occurred, the HPR node will no longer attempt to re-route the RTP connection. The other major functions of RTP are:

- End-to-end error recovery

- Reliable transport

- Segmentation and reassembly (SAR)

- Resequencing

- Adaptive rate-based congestion control

- Adaptive session level pacing in HPR

These functions along with label swapping of ANR have made APPN a viable candidate for the delivery of SNA application data through an enterprise network.

3.6 DLUR/DLUS SUPPORT FOR LEGACY SNA

Although APPN/HPR has made SNA routing a viable contender for the delivery of data in a deterministic, yet dynamic, topology, it did not support the thousands of legacy SNA devices that still require the master/slave relationship for network connectivity and delivery of data. This inability to support legacy SNA devices over APPN led to the creation of Dependent LU Requester/Server (DLUR/S) functionality.

All dependent LUs, and the PUs that support them, require sessions to their own SSCP for transmission of control and management messages. These are the *SSCP-PU* and *SSCP to LU sessions*. Prior to DLUR/S, these sessions could not cross domain boundaries, which meant that any PU serving dependent LUs always be directly connected to either its owning VTAM or to an NCP owned by that VTAM. By encapsulating these flows inside a pair of LU 6.2 sessions between the DLUR and DLUS, the DLUR and dependent PU function can reside anywhere in an APPN network as the DLUR function provides a remote boundary function for dependent LUs. The endpoints of these two LU 6.2 sessions (known as *CP-SVR* or *CPSVRMGR pipe*) are the CPs of the DLUR and DLUS.

The DLUR functionality is implemented in an APPN EN or NN (remote to VTAM), whereas DLUS is implemented in a VTAM APPN NN (version 4.2 or higher).

In addition, DLUR/S overcomes the limitation affecting routing for dependent LUs. Since routing in a subarea network is always done at the subarea level, any session involving a dependent LU must pass through the same adjacent subarea node as the SSCP-LU session. This occurs even if the DLU happens to reside in an APPN node. In the DLUR/S implementation, the LU-LU routing is performed by the APPN function, not the subarea function.

When a PLU requests a search for a DLU, it receives a response from the DLUS indicating that the DLUS is the server for the DLUR, but it shows the CP name of the DLUR as the destination. The route is then calculated directly to the DLUR; this means that the PLU-SLU sessions (BIND and session data) are not required to traverse the same path as the DLUR-DLUS pipe. The result is that the LU-LU sessions are directly routed. It is important to remember that they are not encapsulated and flow "natively" on whichever link is chosen for them by APPN route selection.

Recall that SNA resources require permission from VTAM to connect to the network and then request session establishment. In APPN DLUR/S (as shown in Figure 3-32) a pair of LU 6.2 session pipes are created between the DLUR and the DLUS.

The DLUS sends traditional SNA SSCP commands to the DLUR over these session pipes, and the DLUR, on behalf of the dependent LUs, replies to the DLUS after delivering and receiving the response from the actual SNA legacy device. At this point the SNA legacy LU can request a session with an application residing on VTAM. DLUS and VTAM support cross-domain sessions through an extension of VTAM DLUS called

Figure 3-32
*DLUR/S
session pipes
for
transporting
dependent
legacy SNA
traffic over
APPN
networks.*

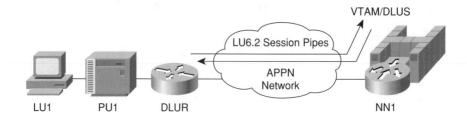

session services extension. VTAM/DLUS receives the BIND requests and sends an SNA CDINIT-LOCATE command to the VTAM that hosts the requested application. After the BIND is received from the destination application, the DLUR session need not flow through the DLUS VTAM. The session flow uses APPN routing techniques (as shown in Figure 3-32) to move the information between the two partners.

The activation of the session pipes that service the DLUR/S function is shown in Figure 3-33. Upon receipt of an XID, the DLUR NN will send the request to the DLUS SSCP by sending an REQACTPU command. The DLUS SSCP responds with an SNA ACTPU command. In the example, the DLUR receives the XID from an attached SNA PU, which in turn requests SSCP services from the DLUS. If a session pipe is not active, the DLUR issues a BIND to the DLUS to start a pipe. The DLUS issues at least one LOCATE for the DLUR node to establish the DLUR-DLUS sessions. After the session pipes have begun, the DLUS returns the REQACTPU +RSP commands followed by the ACTPU command.

SNA VTAM supports a function that allows cross-domain sessions to continue even though the owning VTAM SSCP of the resource in session may fail. This function is called *Automatic Network Shutdown (ANS).* When the parameter ANS=CONT is defined for the resource, it indicates that the LU-LU cross-domain session should continue even though the owning SSCP has failed. In traditional SNA subarea networks, this feature is supported by the NCP. DLUR in APPN supports this continuance of LU-LU sessions even when the session pipes to the DLUS fail. At that point the DLUR rejects any SSCP-PU or SSCP-LU flows from the dependent device and may actually terminate the LU-LU session depending on the definition of the resources.

Another legacy SNA function that was incorporated into DLUR/S is *SSCP takeover and giveback.* The takeover and giveback process is initiated by VTAM commands. *Takeover* is the ability of an SSCP to take ownership of a dependent device if the original SSCP should fail. *Giveback* is the return of ownership to the original owing SSCP.

DLUS supports a similar functionality (as shown in Figure 3-34). The initial DLUS session pipes between the DLUR and the DLUS have failed. A backup DLUS VTAM activates new session pipes to the DLUR of the dependent resources. After the activation sequences have been accomplished and new SSCP-PU and SSCP-LU sessions are established, subsequent LU-LU session requests are satisfied through the new DLUR/S session pipes. The takeover and giveback of the DLUR/S session pipes is nondisruptive to current LU-LU sessions.

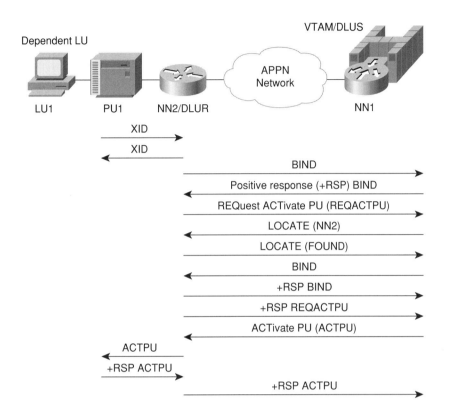

Figure 3-33
Session pipe activation sequence.

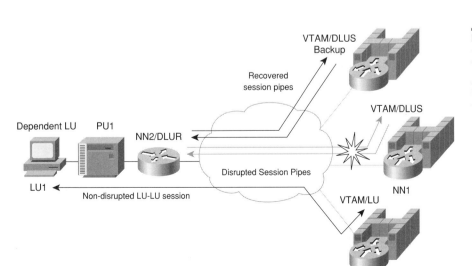

Figure 3-34
DLUR/S support for VTAM ANS and takeover/give back functions.

CHAPTER 4

TCP/IP Networking

Dynamic routing has its foundation in the TCP/IP networking architecture, which was first developed in 1974. The architecture itself did not create a dependence on physical media, nor did it require specific operating systems. TCP/IP's adoption has been very rapid and widespread due to its openness and interoperability. TCP/IP was the first incarnation of a true peer-to-peer protocol. It is the independence from a master control that made TCP/IP so inviting to corporations that they adopted this nonproprietary networking architecture.

4.1 TCP/IP LAYERS

The TCP/IP networking architecture does not implement a full seven-layer stack as found in Open Systems Interconnection (OSI). TCP/IP employs a five-layer networking architecture. Figure 4-1 compares the OSI Reference Model to the TCP/IP networking architecture.

Within the five-layer model employed by TCP/IP, the Internet layer (sometimes compared directly with the Network Layer of the OSI model) comprises the *Internet Protocol (IP)*. This layer is concerned with the details of IP addresses, the datagram format, and the concept of unreliable, connectionless delivery. Where multiple interfaces are bound to the IP protocol, there exists a need for the IP layer to make a decision as to which interface the datagram should be sent to. Therefore, the combination of network interface and IP layers is required to receive, route, and then send datagrams. The TCP/IP protocol suite and the standards that defined it drew a clear delineation between the capabilities of hosts and *gateways,* the latter being hosts with multiple physical interfaces, that are capable of routing.

95

TCP/IP Architecture	OSI Reference Model
Application Layer	Application
File Transfer Protocol (FTP), Simple Mail Transfer Protocol (SMTP), Network File System (NFS), Domain Name System (DNS), Simple Network Management Protocol (SNMP)	Presentation
	Session
TCP and UDP	Transport
IP	Network
X.25, Ethernet, Token-ring Point-to-Point, ATM Frame Relay, ISDN SONET, FDDI	Data Link
	Physical Layer

The intermediate machines that have these multiple interfaces and specialized routing software are now called *IP routers*. Within the IP router, the IP datagram is passed up to the IP layer, which routes it to the correct destination interface. It is not until the datagram reaches its final destination that it is passed up to higher levels of the TCP/IP protocol suite.

The IP router runs software—a *routing* protocol, which at its most basic executes an algorithm using information stored in an IP routing table. This table contains information about possible destinations and how to reach them. The algorithm selects the next machine to which the datagram should be sent. Examples of routing protocols are RIP, OSPF, and EIGRP. A major difference between the TCP/IP layering model and that of SNA and OSI is that TCP/IP bases its layering on the concept that reliability is an end-to-end concern. The architectural philosophy was one that allowed the construction of an internet that was capable of handling the expected load, yet did not burden individual links or machines with the necessity to repeatedly recover lost or corrupt data.

The physical and data link layers supporting the transport of data are actually defined by the various architectures used on a network. Networking media standards such as Token Ring, Ethernet, FDDI, frame relay, ATM, SNA, SONET, and OSI all support the transport of TCP/IP messages based on their individual framing architecture. The TCP/IP messages at this level are, therefore, referred to as *frames*.

The third layer, Network, is the heart of the TCP/IP architecture. At this layer the Internet Protocol (IP) is defined and operates. Transporting information is the primary function of IP. At this layer, information messages are called *datagrams*. IP transports datagrams using connectionless network services without the guarantee of reliable delivery or proper sequence. A *connectionless network service* does not verify that the destination of the datagram is available. This "best-effort" delivery is IP's weakness—a weakness, however, that is circumvented by upper-layer protocols such as Transmission Control Protocol (TCP). The TCP/IP protocol suite's layering model means that this description of a weakness is actually the IP protocol operating as designed. IP's strength is its ability to reroute datagrams dynamically independent of the available connections. This is a valued feature over static traditional SNA networking.

TCP resides in the fourth layer of the TCP/IP architecture. This layer manages the transport of information. The information units at this layer are known as *segments*. TCP guarantees error-free and sequential delivery of segments. This is accomplished through TCP's use of connection-oriented network services. A *connection-oriented service* is one where the delivery of data begins only after an agreed-on connection between the two endpoints is established.

TCP implements the architectural concept of end-to-end reliability as discussed previously. TCP uses the end-to-end capabilities of a transport protocol layer to provide checksums, acknowledgments, and timeouts, to control transmission. TCP wraps the application data into a TCP segment and passes the segment to IP, which routes the ensuing datagram. IP receives datagrams and passes the TCP segment to TCP at Layer 4.

A second protocol is available for use in the architecture. This second protocol is named *User Datagram Protocol (UDP)*, and unlike TCP, it uses connectionless network services. Applications at Layer 5 of the architecture use UDP when the integrity of the information being sent is not crucial. Examples of applications that use UDP instead of TCP are:

- Simple Network Management Protocol (SNMP)

- Domain Name System (DNS)

- Network File System (NFS)

The idea behind using UDP is that the datagrams tend to be small single messages and therefore resending them would not cause network congestion. Contrast this to SNA where every frame is provided with guaranteed delivery.

It's worth noting the different complexities associated with each protocol. UDP are analogous to queues into which incoming datagrams are placed. TCP ports, on the other hand, do not correspond to a single object. They are built upon a connection abstraction in which the objects to be identified are virtual circuit connections, not individual ports. Hence, TCP connections are identified by a pair or endpoints, rather than the individual protocol port.

4.2 INTERNETWORK PROTOCOL (IP)

The third layer of the IP architecture describes the network functions. Internetwork Protocol (IP) resides at this layer. The success of the IP architecture is a result of the simple layered approach. The architecture is viewed as a five-layer architecture when including the physical and data link layers common to all networking architectural models.

4.2.1 IP Addressing

At the heart of the IP networking architecture is the ability to assign a unique address to any device or, for that matter, any network interface that connects to an IP network. This address is a logical address. The IP address can change depending on the attachment of the device or interface to the IP network. This is in contrast to the addressing used for the Data Link layer. Addresses assigned to the network interface on the Data Link layer are considered *physical address assignments*. Every network interface attaching to an IP network can have an IP address assigned.

The IP addressing scheme has gone through some iterations over time. The predominant scheme is defined using IP Version 4 (IPv4). This addressing scheme is based on a 32-bit (4 bytes or octets) length field. The 32 bits provide for a total of 2^{32} addresses. In layman's terms, that's over 4 billion addresses.

The addressing used is in binary but is represented in a decimal form known as *dotted decimal notation*. In the following example, an IP address is shown in dotted decimal notation:

        10.20.30.128

The sample IP address, and for that matter all IP addresses under IPv4, have four dotted decimal positions. Each position is referred to as an *octet*. Each octet in binary form is represented by 8 bits. In binary form, the sample IP address is represented as:

        00001010 00010100 00011110 01100100

You can see why we use the dotted decimal notation over the actual binary values. If all the binary values are 1s, the IP address dotted decimal notation is 255.255.255.255 and is considered a broadcast address, that every IP device will process.

IP address formats are divided into two sections. A *network address* identifies the grouping of many devices into a network, and a *host address* uniquely identifies each device within the network. IP addresses are defined into class formats (as shown in Figure 4-2) identified by the first 4 bits of the first octet. There are five IP address classes. As illustrated in Figure 4-2, the bits set to a 1 in the first four bits of the first octet indicate the potential number of network and host addresses available.

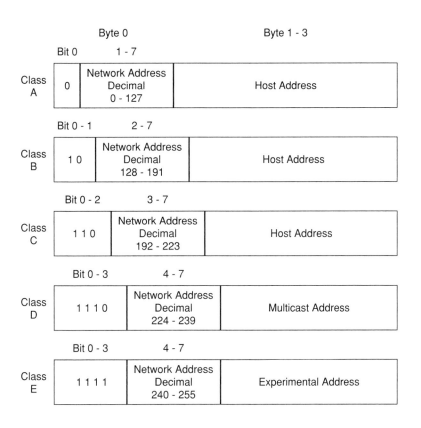

Figure 4-2
The IP address class formats.

The first three classes defined are used for addressing IP networks. Class A network addressing allows for over 16 million addresses, Class B networks can provide just over 65,000 addresses, and Class C networks provide up to 256 addresses per network. Class D network addresses are reserved for an IP service called multicasting. *Multicasting* helps reduce traffic over an IP network by sending one message to many hosts on a network that have elected to receive the multicast address. The Class E address is reserved and used for experimental purposes.

4.2.2 IP Subnet Addressing

The Class A, B, and C network addressing schemes can be further subdivided or subnetted allowing for more network addresses than provided by the standard addressing scheme. This subnetting is accomplished by applying a mask to the first available octet of the host address field within a class. In Figure 4-3 we have subnetted a Class A network of 34 (dotted decimal notation of 34.0.0.0) to include the second and third octets.

Class A network address	34.0.0.0	00100010.00000000.00000000.00000000	34.0.0.0
16-bit subnet mask	255.255.255.0	11111111.11111111.11111111.00000000	0.128.80.0
Class A subnet	34.128.80.0	00100010.10000000.00001000.00000000	34.128.80.0

Figure 4-3
Example of a subnet for a Class A address.

The subnet mask is denoted as 255.255.255.0 in dotted decimal form. The value of a mask sets the bits used as part of the network address to 1s and the part used for host addresses to a 0 value. In our example, the subnet address is 128.80 and the host address is the value found in the last octet. Using this type of subnetting, 253 host addresses are possible for the sample network address. Only 253 host addresses are available versus 255 because the host value of 0 is reserved to represent the network and the value of all 1s is reserved for broadcasting. If we change the subnet mask to 255.255.252.0, the number of available host addresses changes from 253 to 4000 for each subnet. Figure 4-4 illustrates applying a subnet mask to a Class A network address.

Class A network address	34.0.0.0	00100010.00000000.00000000.00000000	34.0.0.0
16-bit subnet mask	255.255.252.0	11111111.11111111.11111100.00000000	0.128.80.0
Class A subnet	34.128.80.0	00100010.10000000.00001000.00000000	34.128.80.0

Figure 4-4
Class A address subnetted using a mask of 255.255.252.0.

4.3 ADDRESS RESOLUTION PROTOCOL (ARP)

Workstations on LANs must use the data link layer protocols specific to the network interface being used. Both Ethernet and Token Ring use the Media Access Control (MAC) sublayer of the Data Link Layer in the OSI Reference Model. The address provided at this layer is commonly referred to as the *MAC address*. The MAC address resides at the Data Link or Layer 2, whereas application-to-application conversations, like those found in client/server environments, communicate at Layer 3 or the Network Layer and are provided the Layer 3 address. For conversations to occur at the Network Layer, the client must determine the MAC address of the server it wants to contact to transport the messages over Layer 2. In an IP network, the MAC address of the server is acquired using the *Address Resolution Protocol (ARP)*, as shown in Figure 4-5.

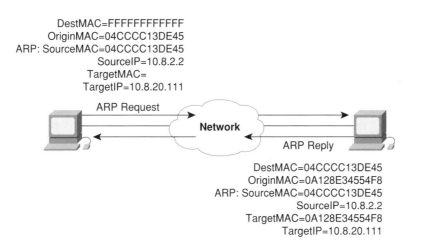

Figure 4-5
*ARP process
on a local LAN.*

When initiating a connection between two IP hosts, the initiator must determine the MAC address of the destination IP host network interface. As illustrated in Figure 4-5, the initiating station sends an ARP request on the LAN using a broadcast MAC address for the LAN protocol. All stations on a LAN adhere to the LAN specification and respond to a MAC broadcast request. The MAC broadcast address in both Ethernet and Token Ring is FFFFFF, or all bits set to 1. As each station receives the broadcast and performs the following functions, it does the following:

   1. Determines if it is using the ARP protocol.

   2. Determines if the target IP address is equal to its own.

   3. If the target IP address does not match, the station discards the request.

   4. If the target IP address does match, the station issues an ARP reply to the initiating station with the target hardware address field completed.

After the initiating station receives an ARP reply with the hardware address of the destination station, it begins conversation setup.

ARP processes that begin and end on the same LAN segment are considered *local ARPs*. All stations use ARP as a means of mapping the known IP and MAC addresses residing on the network. Recall that each station receives and processes the ARP request. During this process, the station builds an ARP table called an *ARP cache*. The station, prior to sending an ARP request, checks its own ARP cache for the destination IP address. If it is in the table, it will use the MAC address associated with the IP address learned from an ARP request. This saves time and bandwidth on the network. An ARP request must be issued each time a new connection is made between stations without the use of an ARP cache.

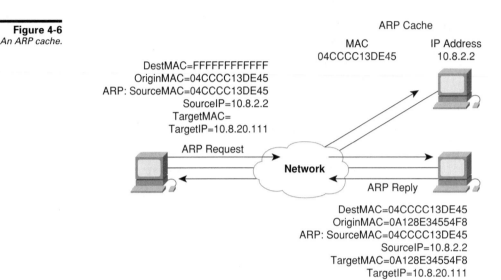

Figure 4-6
An ARP cache.

Figure 4-6 illustrates the use of an ARP cache. Most ARP caches are kept for a period of time. Each entry has a timer. If the IP address associated for the entry has not been processed in the time frame, the entry is removed from the ARP cache.

4.3.1 Proxy ARP

Facilitating the ARP request between different LAN segments is the function of an ARP server. The ARP server becomes a proxy to the ARP requestor and, hence, the process is known as proxy ARP. Routers in an IP network use proxy ARP, illustrated in Figure 4-7. The router maintains its own ARP cache similar to that used by workstations. A station sends an ARP request for an IP host on a different LAN segment, but instead of receiving the actual MAC address of the IP host, the ARP requestor station receives the MAC address of the network interface of the router connecting to the ARP requestor's LAN segment. When the router sends a message from one station to another station between different LAN segments, it inserts its own network interface MAC address as the source address.

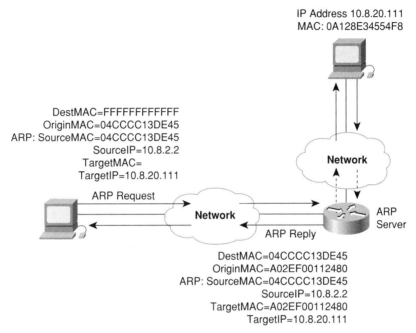

IP Address 10.8.20.111
MAC: 0A128E34554F8

Figure 4-7
Proxy ARP used by routers.

DestMAC=FFFFFFFFFFFF
OriginMAC=04CCCC13DE45
ARP: SourceMAC=04CCCC13DE45
SourceIP=10.8.2.2
TargetMAC=
TargetIP=10.8.20.111

ARP Request

Network

Network

ARP Server

ARP Reply

DestMAC=04CCCC13DE45
OriginMAC=A02EF00112480
ARP: SourceMAC=04CCCC13DE45
SourceIP=10.8.2.2
TargetMAC=A02EF00112480
TargetIP=10.8.20.111

TargetMAC is MAC address of router interface.

4.3.2 Reverse ARP (RARP)

In some cases the workstation knows its hardware address but is not aware of its IP address. This is often found when using diskless workstations or LAN protocols such as Banyan VINES. The format of the RARP request is the same as the ARP request except that the operation code field indicates a RARP reply or request function and the protocol type field identifies RARP instead of ARP.

In a RARP request, as diagrammed in Figure 4-8, the frame is a broadcast with the source IP address field blank. Only stations defined to act as RARP servers respond to the request. If more than one RARP server exists on a network, the requesting station accepts the first RARP reply and discards the rest. The RARP server uses a MAC-to-IP address table and scans it looking for the MAC address that matches the origin MAC address. When the matching address is found, the RARP server places the mapped IP address in the protocol address field of the RARP packet and issues the RARP reply. Then the station has a valid IP address and can use IP services.

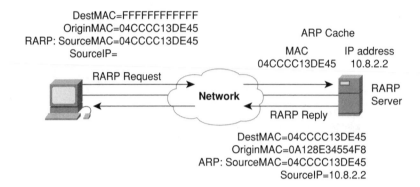

Figure 4-8
Reverse ARP process in use by a workstation.

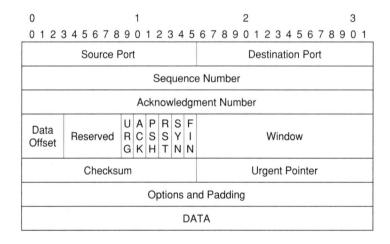

4.4 TRANSMISSION CONTROL PROTOCOL (TCP)

TCP provides applications with guaranteed sequential delivery of messages. The TCP messages are called segments. A *TCP segment* is made up of a header and data field. Figure 4-9 diagrams the TCP segment format.

Figure 4-9
Format of the TCP segment.

A TCP segment begins with a source and destination port identifier. These port numbers are defined to applications as a means for delivering the data to the appropriate TCP application service. Each TCP application uses a port number. There are well-known

TCP applications such as FTP, Telnet, and SNMP, to name a few. Each well-known application is assigned a well-known port number specific to the application. *Ports* are a means for multiplexing different applications over the same TCP connection. You can think of ports as analogous to application interfaces to TCP. For example, FTP uses port 21, Telnet port 23. Each port number field is two octets.

The *sequence number field* follows the port number fields. Like SNA, TCP uses the sequence number of a segment to identify the position of the segment in relation to the outgoing segments of the data stream. The sequence number identifies the position in the byte stream of the data in the segment. Consequently, the numerical value of the sequence number is actually the number of bytes transmitted to date within that session stream.

Likewise, the ACK field contains the number of bytes received by the session partner. The sequence number field is four octets long. The ACK field follows the sequence number field. The ACK field specifies the sequence number of the next expected incoming segment. The ACK indicator field is set to a 1 when the ACK number field contains a value. The sequence and ACK number fields are functionally equivalent to the N(s) and N(r) fields in SNA/SDLC protocol.

The data offset field specifies the length of the TCP header. This field is four bits and measures the TCP header in 32-bit increments. Using this algorithm, the header must end on a 32-bit boundary and must be padded out to meet this boundary. The Options and Padding fields found at the end of the header are used to pad the header to a 32-bit boundary.

NOTES

The Options field can used for more than just padding. As an example, the contents of the Options field can contain the Maximum Segment Size (MSS) that the sender is willing to receive. (Reference TCP Options: RFC 793 Section 3.1.)

TCP provides a mechanism for sending a priority message between stations using the urgent field indicator. When the urgent field indicator is set to a 1, the TCP application goes directly to the point in the segment specified by the urgent pointer field. This pointer identifies the last octet of the urgent data. All data after this point is ignored. An example of urgent data is a terminal break or interrupt.

The Window field contains the number of bytes that can be received by this host. The count begins with the acknowledgment number field. This field is updated on an ongoing basis as the host recalculates the number of bytes it can receive into its available buffer space.

The PSH flag is set to a 1 when the sending application wants the receiving TCP host to deliver the data to the destined application promptly. Applications abort sessions or TCP aborts sessions when there are segment errors by setting the REST flag indicator to a 1. Connections are closed by applications in a normal process by setting the FIN bit to a 1 in disconnect messages.

Like all responsible network protocols, TCP contains a checksum field in the TCP header. The checksum is computed by summing the length of the TCP header and the length of the data. On receiving segments, TCP validates the segment by computing a checksum value and then comparing it against the value found in the checksum field of the TCP header. The segment is discarded if the checksum values do not match. This checksum is performed at the transport layer, IP performs its own checksum at the network layer, and the LAN protocols perform their own checksum at the data link layer.

4.4.1 Sliding Windows

Windows are a means of expressing the number of segments transmitted to a receiver before the sender can expect an acknowledgment that all segments were received intact. TCP uses a mechanism called *sliding window.*

Consider a simple acknowledged transmission sequence. The sender transmits a packet and then waits for an acknowledgment before transmitting another. A consequence of this is that the network will be completely idle during the intervening time. This simple positive acknowledgment protocol wastes bandwidth since the sender must delay sending a new packet until in receipt of the ACK for the previous packet.

TCP uses a window size based on the number of bytes sent versus the number of segments sent. The window field of the TCP header specifies the window size initially determined at connection establishment. ACK messages delivered to the sender from the receiver specify the size of the window for the next transmission. The sender must receive an acknowledgment for each sequence number prior to sliding the window.

An example of the sliding window is depicted in Figure 4-10. The window slides on the outbound buffer until all the data has been sent and acknowledged. Station A in the figure has sent three segments to station B. The initial window size determined at connection time was set to 8. As each segment is sent and an acknowledgment for each segment is received, the sender slides the window forward to include the next segment on the outbound buffer. The window does not slide until each outstanding sequence number has been acknowledged.

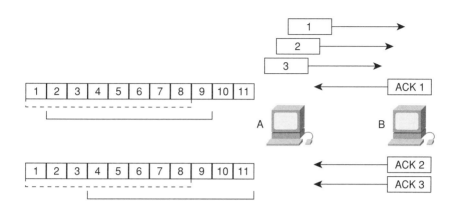

Figure 4-10
*The sliding
window
mechanism.*

This technique also includes a mechanism for ensuring reliable transmission. Lost segments or damaged segments will not allow the window to slide until the retransmissioned sequence number has been acknowledged. This is illustrated in Figure 4-11. Station B received sequence numbers 1,2,4,5,6, missing segment number 3. Station B replies to Station A with an acknowledgment for 4, 5, and 6 but indicates that the last received sequence number was 2. On receiving this, Station A waits for a timeout on the acknowledgment for sequence number 3, and then sends it again. Upon receiving sequence number 3, station B sends an acknowledgment with sequence number 6 in received sequence number field. Station A can now adjust its sliding window with its start at segment 7.

4.4.2 Slow-Start Congestion Avoidance

Although the sliding window ensures delivery, it has issues with timing and congestion. The sliding window is based on indicators from the receiver. This allows a sender to potentially flood the network with messages for specific stations and overrun the station, thereby mismanaging its own output buffers.

The slow-start algorithm was developed primarily to provide a means for TCP to recover from network congestion. As congestion causes a reduction in the sliding window to a value of 1, it is necessary for TCP to have a method of incrementing the window when congestion ends without swamping the network with additional traffic. The algorithm devised for this function is termed the *slow-start algorithm*.

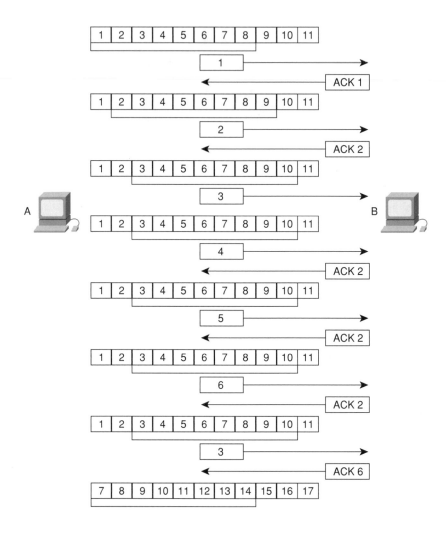

To avoid this possible problem, Van Jacobson in 1988 developed a slow-start avoidance algorithm. The slow-start avoidance algorithm places the responsibility of the sliding window on the sender and not the receiver. At connection establishment, the sender places a value of 1 in the window field. During the progress of the connection, the window size is increased by twice the number of the acknowledgments received. Transmission errors, or statistical processing of acknowledgment delays, governs the doubling. The delay is determined by the round trip time (RTT) for the sender to receive the acknowledgment. The average and standard deviation of the acknowledgments is measured at the beginning of the transmission.

As the RTT increases past the average and standard deviation, the window will decrease to 1 immediately. The sender noting the window size in use prior to the correction thereby determines the optimal window size. The optimal window size is then considered to be half of the window size prior to the correction.

4.5 IPv6

Though IPv4 can provide over four billion IP addresses, the address space on the Internet was being depleted rapidly and required a new addressing scheme. A solution to the addressing problem came about as IP Version 6.

4.5.1 IPv6 Addressing

IP Version 6 uses an addressing scheme based on 128 bits or 16 octets. This addressing scheme allows for 18 billion addresses. There are three addressing schemas used by IPv6.

The first schema is the preferred form of representing the IP address in eight hexadecimal 2-byte (16-bit) pairs. An example is

```
ABCD:1234:A1B2:FED0:5678:C2D3:3344:1232
```

In some cases there will be zeros in the leading characters of each pair. In these cases only a single 0 is required, such as

```
ABCD:0:0:0:0:0:0:1234
```

The standard notation for IPv6 allows for an abbreviation of a long address containing zero bits between populated pairs. For instance, the preceding address may also be represented as follows:

```
ABCD::1234
```

In IPv4 mixed environments, the four rightmost pairs are used as the IPv4 four octet dotted decimal notation as shown following:

```
0:0:0:0:10:20:30:100
```

IPv4 addresses may be embedded into IPv6 schema in two forms. The first is called the *transition mechanism* in which hosts and routers dynamically tunnel IPv6 packets over IPv4 routers. The official term for this address is an "IPv4-compatible IPv6 address" whose form is

```
|                 80 bits           | 16 |      32 bits         |
+-----------------------------------+----+----------------------+
|0000........................0000|0000|    IPv4 address       |
+-----------------------------------+----+----------------------+
```

The second format for embedding IPv4 addressing is used for representing IPv4 only nodes as IPv6 address. This embedded format is called *IPv4-mapped IPv6 address* and has the following format:

```
|             80 bits             | 16 |    32 bits        |
+--------------------------------+--------------------------+
|0000.....................0000|FFFF|   IPv4 address    |
+--------------------------------+----+--------------------+
```

Using these formats, an IPv4 network can coexist with an IPv6 network. Accommodating this new addressing scheme required a new IP packet format.

4.5.2 IPv6 Header

Accommodating the new features of IPv6 also meant backward compatibility with IPv4. To do this, the IP header of the IP packet had to be altered. This change is illustrated in Figure 4-12. The new header allows for a 128-bit address by removing the reserved and optional fields in the IPv4 header. A new field created in the IPv6 header is the *flow label*. This field enables IPv6 to apply a quality of service to a packet.

The flow label field is divided into two areas over 28 bits in length:

- The 24-bit FLOWID subfield provides a unique ID to the flow of sequence packets between stations for the Quality of Service (QoS).

- The 4-bit TCLASS subfield identifies the type of service the packet is to receive based on the IPv6 standard.

Figure 4-13 diagrams the format of the flow label and the breakdown of the TCLASS subfield.

The TCLASS values are listed in ascending order correlating low to high QoS. Network-level messages get the highest QoS possible. IPv6 enables the QoS to be determined on a hop-by-hop basis using the TCLASS bits.

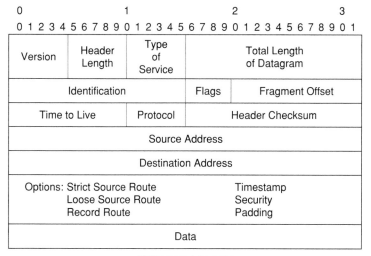

IP Version 4 Header

IP Version 6 Header

Figure 4-12
The IPv6 header format to accommodate the 128-bit address field.

Figure 4-13
*The
FLOWLABEL
field of the IPv6
header.*

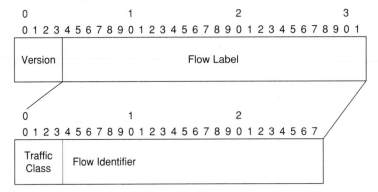

0 - Uncharacterized traffic
1 - "Filler" traffic
2 - Unattended data transfer
3 - Reserved
4 - Attended bulk data transfer
5 - Reserved
6 - Interactive traffic
7 - Internet controller traffic (e.g., SNMP, IGPs)
15 - Highest QoS

CHAPTER 5

Bridging and Routing

As personal computers (PCs) grew in both strength and numbers, the communications environment that supported them also evolved. The advent of local area networks (LANs) allowed for disparate PCs to communicate and exchange information. This interconnection is performed by bridges, routers, and switches.

Let's create some basic understandings up front. There are two separate modes of connection—physical and logical. Bridges connect LANs at the OSI Layer 2 level, whereas routers function at OSI Layer 3, and furthermore, switches can operate at both OSI Layer 2 and 3.

5.1 BRIDGING NETWORKS

The most widely used communications transport protocols (especially for our focused discussions on internetworked SNA) are Ethernet and Token Ring. Figure 5-1 shows a very basic diagram of Ethernet vs. Token-Ring topology.

As you can see, Ethernet uses a bus topology, whereas Token Ring uses a ring topology:

- Bus Technology—The information is housed in a unit called a *packet*. The term for a particular Ethernet LAN is called a *segment*. Functionally, every station will receive a particular packet, even if it is not theirs. When sending information, each station sends when it has information to send.

Figure 5-1
Ethernet and Token-Ring physical topologies.

Bus Topology

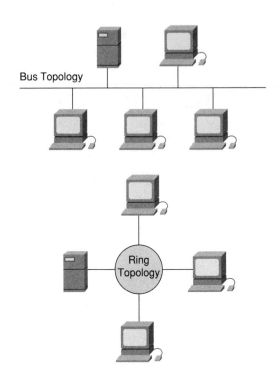

- Token Ring—The information is housed in a unit called a *frame*. The term for a particular Token-Ring LAN is called a *ring*. Functionally, each station will wait until the token is passed to the station to transmit or receive data.

The Data Link Layer (OSI Layer 2) is the area where we find the hardware addresses for the connection for the PC onto every LAN, Ethernet or Token Ring. The specific piece of hardware we are talking about is the *network interface card (NIC)*. The NIC card is the physical device that connects the PC to the network.

The first adaptations of LANs were separate and physically connected by a hardware device called a *bridge*. Bridge is a good name as it connects to separate entities, in much the same way that separate highways and roadways are connected by bridges. LAN bridges operate at the Data Link Layer 2 and use the hardware addressing schema to interconnect multiple physical LANs. They perform this function using the *Media Access Control (MAC) address*.

In some shops, this MAC address is the burned-in address shipped on the NIC card from the vendor, thus using the *universal administered address (UAA)*. Other shops override this burned-in address and define a *locally administered address (LAA)*. Using an LAA can greatly add to the problem determination that always follows. In either case, it is this 12-digit number that will be the hardware address for the physical device on the LAN. Companies that provide NIC interfaces have registered numbers that identify their cards. LAA addresses begin with `x'40'` to identify them as an LAA.

The various LAN topologies dictate the types of bridging. The four different bridging technologies are as follows:

- Transparent Bridging

- Source Route Bridging (SRB)

- Translational Bridging

- Source Route/Translational Bridging (SR/TB)

5.1.1 Transparent Bridging

The basis of transparent bridging is that all stations on the LAN are viewed to be on the same segment. Transparent bridges do not use route information fields; instead they look at the source address of each frame on a segment (see Figure 5-2). The transparent bridge then creates a table that contains the source address of a specific station and the interface it was transmitted over. There is also a timer value placed on the entry that enables old entries to age away.

Bridge 1 receives a frame from Ring A. Bridge 1 inspects the source address field against the table for Ring A. If there is a match, the bridge knows the source station is on Ring A. The destination address field is inspected, but the address is analyzed for both Ring A and Ring B. If the destination address is found on Ring A, the bridge ignores the frame. If, however, the address is found to be on Ring B, the bridge forwards the frame. An intermediate transparent bridge places the source address of a frame whose source and destination address are not in the routing table into the on-ring table and the destination's address into the off-ring table.

Transparent bridging requires that there is only one active connection between LANs. If there are parallel paths, the transparent bridge will assume that all source and destination addresses are on the same physical segment, thus creating an endless loop. To eliminate this, all transparent bridges must employ a single route selection process, also known as *spanning tree*.

Figure 5-2
Transparent bridging.

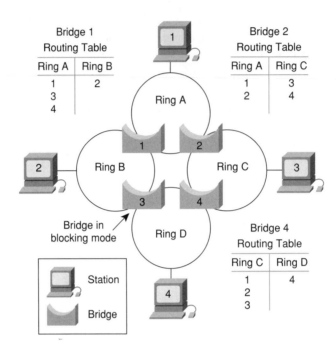

5.1.2 Spanning Tree Algorithm

Multisegment LANs using transparent bridges for their interconnection use the *spanning tree algorithm* to ensure only one active route, thus eliminating possible loops in their networks.

Bridges have incorporated this algorithm for use with source route bridges (we will discuss source route bridges in the next section) to ensure a single active path. There is a difference in the implementations. Transparent bridging and source route bridging use different functional addresses. The result of this is that a single route broadcast configuration will be performed by all transparent bridges and separately by each source route bridge in a network that utilizes both.

In the spanning tree algorithm, there are five possible states a bridge may be in:

- DISABLED—The bridge is *hard down,* completely inaccessible and, therefore, is not functional.

- BLOCKING—The bridge is not actively partaking in frame forwarding, address learning, nor in the spanning tree algorithm. The bridge will ensure that another bridge is forwarding frames onto the segment.

- LISTENING—The bridge cannot forward frames nor learn addresses, but the bridge fully participates in the spanning tree algorithm.

- LEARNING—The bridge learns addresses and participates in the spanning tree algorithm, but does not forward frames.

- FORWARDING—The bridge can learn addresses, participate in the spanning tree algorithm, and forward frames.

The spanning tree algorithm has some key terms that should be discussed, as follows:

- Unique bridge identifier—This is the MAC address of the bridge's lowest port number and 2-byte priority level. This is defined during customization.

- Port identifier—Each port is defined with a unique 2-byte identifier.

- Root bridge—The lowest value of the bridge identifier becomes the root bridge. This device may support a large part of the data due to its posture of connecting two halves of the network.

- Path cost—Preferred routes on a LAN have the least amount of impact on LAN performance. Fast bridges are preferred over slow, and minimally traveled LANs are chosen over heavily utilized ones. These preferences are factors that lead to the decision of a preferred route in the network. Each route is assigned a cost, with the all the factors considered.

- Root port—The bridge port with the least cost path.

- Root path cost—This is the path with the least cost path from each bridge to the root bridge.

- Designated bridge—The bridge that forwards frames on a LAN segment. The others would be in a blocking state.

- Designated port—The least cost path for all traffic from this bridge to all other LANs. This is the port that connects the LAN to the designated bridge.

Bridges transport frames called *bridge protocol data units (BPDU)*. Look at Figure 5-3 for the format of this frame.

In a LAN using the spanning tree algorithms, the tree itself is learned after the passing of these BPDUs. The sending of HELLO BPDUs creates the placement and the roles the bridges will play in the network. For example, the bridge with the lowest bridge identifier will become the root bridge and assume the responsibility to periodically pass the HELLO frames.

Bytes	2	1	1	1	8	4	8	2	2	2	2	2
	Protocol ID	Protocol Version ID	BPDU Type	Flags	Root ID	Root Path Cost	Bridge ID	Port ID	Message Age	Maximum Age	Hello Time	Forward Delay

Figure 5-3
BPDU format.

Spanning tree is a good mechanism to create the stability and automation necessary for transparent bridging. There are some shortfalls, however:

- The single path between two stations is only as fast as the slowest link.

- The root bridge can become a bottleneck as all intersegment traffic must traverse through it.

5.1.3 Source Route Bridging

Source route bridging is an IBM-created architecture. IBM first used this method for bridges to communicate over Token Ring. These practices and definitions have been accepted and adopted and now represent the IEEE 802.5 standard.

When you're creating an SRB network, there are two very important numbers:

- Ring number

- Bridge number

You will create these numbers during the configuration of the bridge. Ring numbers are given to every segment that a bridge connects. In turn, the bridge itself is given a unique identifier.

It is important to note that these two numbers together, ring number and bridge number, must be unique within a network. The result of this newly created number will be the route designator field of the route information field (RIF) in the MAC frame format. Developing a ring-bridge number standard during the architecture and design phase enables a vibrant, robust and manageable network that can systematically grow. Failing to develop a ring-bridge number standard results in a a convention that will last for only this particular life cycle.

NOTES

Spend time planning out the bridge and ring number conventions. Be thoughtful and create a solid standard that can be the foundation of your logical network. The time taken in planning these conventions will be paid back in the reduction of troubleshooting time.

The originating or source station issues a TEST or XID LPDU command. If the response from the destination stations responds with another TEST or XID LPDU, the source station does not set the route information indicator bit to B'1' because the destination station is on the same ring. If the source station does not receive the TEST or XID LPDU response, it determines that the destination station is off the local ring. When a station is not on the local ring, Token-Ring architecture will use an all-routes broadcast or single-route broadcast to determine the location and traverse this Token-Ring bridged network.

Let's look at Figure 5-4 to better explain broadcasts on a Token-Ring LAN.

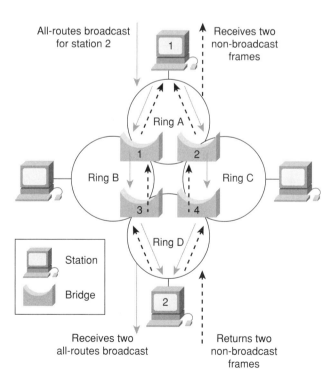

Figure 5-4
All-routes broadcast on a token-ring LAN.

During an all-routes broadcast, the TEST or XID LPDU frames are forwarded to all bridges except for the following conditions:

- The frame originated from that segment.

- The hop count limit is exceeded. (*Hop count* is a parameter that is set during bridge configuration.)

There is a filter on the bridge that stops the forwarding of the frame.

So, how does this work? When a frame is sent to the bridge, the source sets the all-routes indicator. The first bridge then adds the route designator field identifying the source ring number and bridge number of the next ring followed by a null bridge entry. As the frame travels the network, the ensuing bridges will append the bridge number and 2-byte designator field.

Our example in Figure 5-4 shows a small Token-Ring network with four rings. Let's assume that Station 1 wants to communicate with Station 2. There are two possible routes to get from 1 to 2. Station 2 will receive two frames. One route will be A to B to D and the other will be A to C to D. Station 2 will respond to both of them with a non-broadcast frame, flipping the direction bit, and house a completed RIF field. These responses are sent back, over the reverse RIF ring designations. Usually the first response received will be the path chosen for all communications to and from these stations. Sometimes variables, such as number of hops and frame sizes, can determine the best path.

NOTES

The chosen path is the only path used for the connection between the source and destination partners when employing SRB. It will be the only route to and from the source and destination partners. If there is a problem on the intermediate connected rings, the session will break and need to go through the session startup process from the beginning.

During single-source routing, the source station sends a TEST or XID LPDU command, but sets the single route broadcast indicator. Now only one copy of the broadcast will be sent to each LAN segment. This frame is sent when the bridge is configured to forward single-route broadcast frames, the router designator field indicates that this frame was already on the next segment, and there are no filters for this frame.

Figure 5-5 shows the single-route broadcast in more detail.

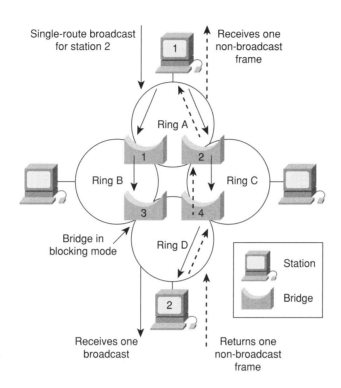

Figure 5-5
*Single-route
broadcast
detail.*

The destination station receives the single-route broadcast and in turn responds with an all-routes broadcast frame with the destination being the source station. The source station will receive the responses and choose the desired route.

A weakness of an SRB network is the volume of broadcasts in the network. Most corporate networks have parallel and redundant paths in the design to protect from outages. The single-route process cuts down some of the broadcast traffic in the network, however, bridge options and capabilities will determine their applicability. The best way to run an efficient network is to derive better payloads on the bandwidth for data, not network overhead.

5.1.4 Translational Bridging

Translational bridging is used to communicate between dissimilar LANs, that is, Ethernet and Token Ring. This is a short topic but an important one for users making the transition from Token Ring to Ethernet or those who have frozen Token-Ring expansion and will be implementing Ethernet on all LANs going forward. The absolute key to success is to understand that the MAC address bits are reversed (see Figure 5-6).

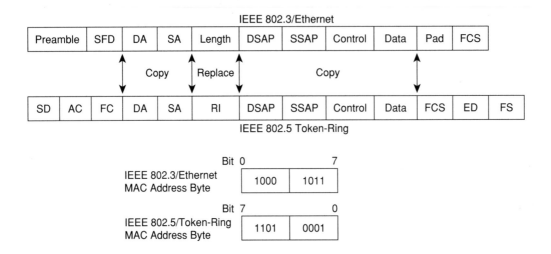

Figure 5-6
Token Ring–to–Ethernet translational bridging and MAC address manipulation.

Remember this: the key to Ethernet–to–Token Ring translation is the reverse order of the significant bits for the MAC address in the destination and source address fields. Ethernet uses the most significant bit first of each byte, and Token Ring uses the least significant bit first of each byte.

5.1.5 Source Route Translational Bridging

Now we move on to the problem of marrying the varied bridging methodologies onto the same LAN. IBM proposed to the IEEE a new standard to do just this: 802.1—*source route translational bridge (SR/TB).*

The problem arises when two stations, one on an SRB network and one on a transparent network, want to communicate with another station that does not (depending on transparent bridging) understand SRB RIFs. The benefit of SR/TB is to provide interoperability between source-route bridged stations (Token Ring–attached) and transparent bridged stations (Ethernet-attached).

The idea is based on the transparent bridge with a tower of functionality for the SRB clients. SR/TB bridges form a single spanning tree with other SR/TB bridges in a pure translational bridge method. SRB stations will use the source-route path, if one exists. If not, they will use the spanning tree path. SR/TB bridges forward single on-segment route explorer frames; as a result, single-route broadcast frames are received by the destination.

5.2 ROUTING NETWORKS

With the advent of routers, LAN networking as we knew it changed. Not only LAN networking, but LAN applications, and thus client/server applications, are forever the application trends of the future.

Routers perform the same store-and-forward procedures as bridges perform, but they can also look at the entire frame and perform protocol analysis—a powerful distinction.

Routers were once concerned with only Network Layer 3 of the OSI model. Routers were a means of transportation of TCP/IP networks; they move information from hardware address on one wire, or LAN segment, to another using IP.

Routers have grown to encompass many other functions of networking. The first move was to engulf the functions of bridging. In fact the first incarnation of this new device was called a *brouter*. Thankfully, that term grew into a more aptly named device as a *multiprotocol router*. In today's networking, a router can even perform functions of a classical pure SNA network.

5.2.1 LAN Networking with Routers

Routers open up a whole new universe of design for the network architects of today. We can construct LAN segments based not only on proximity, but upon functionality. We can protect other LAN segments from chatty applications and protocols (see Figure 5-7).

Figure 5-7 shows disparate LANs using different protocols. LAN A and LAN D use Novell IPX, LAN B uses IP only, and LAN C requires SNA. Although each of the aforementioned LAN protocols have methodologies for transportation, they do not share them with all of the separate LANs. For example, the IPX SAPs do not flood the local IP LAN, and the broadcasts from SRB to support the SNA from LAN C are not sent across all of the segments.

Routers can also act as translational bridges to connect dissimilar LAN structures. Figure 5-8 shows routers connecting a Token-Ring LAN to a Ethernet LAN over an FDDI backbone.

Figure 5-7
*LAN
segmentation
with routers.*

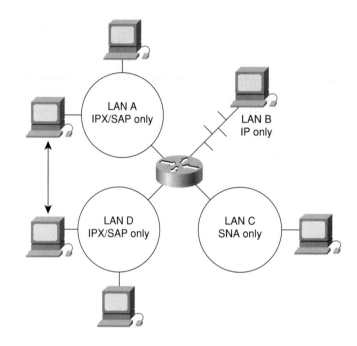

Figure 5-8
*Translational
bridging with
routers.*

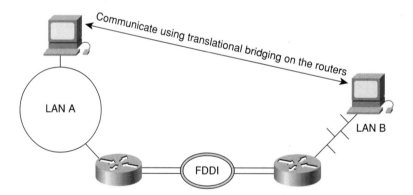

As the Token-Ring station puts a frame out on the ring, the LAN A router takes it in and looks at the destination field and protocol header. He sees that it is on the Ethernet and translates the Token-Ring IEEE 802.5 to Ethernet IEEE 802.3 and further encapsulates the newly formed frame with the FDDI frame for transport over its backbone

LAN segment. The LAN B router receives the frame, strips off the FDDI envelope, and sends the translational Ethernet frame to the device.

5.2.2 WAN Networking with Routers

As corporate networks adopted routers as the cornerstone device, they affect not only LAN design, but also Wide Area Network (WAN) design. The evolution of applications drove the needs of the WAN network. Applications were being written in client/server methodologies and needed to reach remote offices across the company. Routers were able to meet these goals. Figure 5-9 depicts a typical corporate network using routers for WAN connectivity.

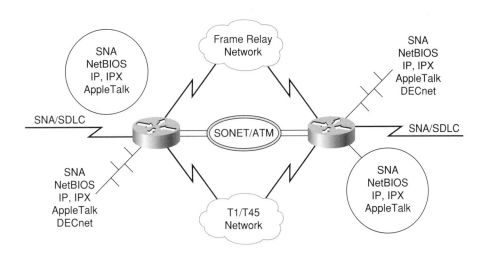

Figure 5-9
Typical WAN network.

Figure 5-9 shows many varied connections to and from a router. Routers can be the answer to all corporate networking needs. This depends on application and operational requirements. The router can transport data over a WAN that originates as SNA, SDLC, IPX, NetBIOS, AppleTalk, DECnet, and of course IP. Routers encapsulate bridged protocols such as SNA and NetBIOS in TCP or IP prior to transporting over the links. IBM's classic SDLC traffic can be encapsulated in TCP, or it can be converted to LLC-2 Token-Ring format and then encapsulated into TCP or IP for transport over the WAN. IP, IPX, AppleTalk, and DECnet are all routable (Network Layer 3) protocols and thus do not need special handling. Routers can also be used to help protect lower-speed lines from traffic broadcasts.

5.2.2 Routing Techniques

The three most widely used routing methodologies are:

- Source routing
- Label swapping
- Destination routing

5.2.2.1 Source Routing

Much akin to the notion of bridging, *source routing* works on the idea that each frame contains the complete route needed for the transport of the data from the source to the destination station. The process is: The source, through some broadcast, finds the destination and the destination responds, thus, creating the route for the connection. This is an efficient technique for RIFs, but it comes with an overhead cost.

5.2.2.2 Label-Based Routing

This technique is often referred to as *address swapping* and is the dominant method of switched network models. Switched networks operate at Layer 2, and routed networks use label swapping at Layer 3. The *label*, or address, is an index into the switch table at each intermediate routing node in the network. This table determines the port or link the information frame should be sent out on and provides a new label for the next node on the route to use.

5.2.2.3 Destination Routing

Based on Layer 3 information, the destination and source addresses are provided without the exact path to use. Each node along the way, after interpreting current network topology information, congestion, and other metrics, will make a decision on which path to route the frame.

5.2.3 Routing Algorithms

Each of the aforementioned routing techniques require routing algorithms to determine the best route. These algorithms are *distance vector* and *link state*. The physical path a data frame takes through the network is calculated to run over the optimal path. This information is calculated and stored in route tables that reside inside the router.

5.3 DISTANCE VECTOR ROUTING PROTOCOLS

As the name implies, this metric is based on the distance or hops between the origin routing node and the destination routing node and the vector or direction in which the data is sent. The routing tables have entries on each known destination in the network. As the router determines its network topology, it exchanges the entire table with the adjacent routers. These routers in turn update their tables and send them to their adjacent routers, and so on, and so on.

A router running a distance vector protocol sends update information periodically to its neighbors, who in turn process the messages and send messages of their own, if needed. RIP broadcasts routing updates every 30 seconds. The update messages contain pairs of IP network addresses and an integer distance to that network. This information is extracted from the advertising router's route table. Upon receipt of the RIP update, another RIP router will compare the contents of its own routing table with the information it has just received. This comparative process and any subsequent changes to the routing table are computed using the distributed Bellman-Ford algorithm.

RIP also affords the ability to broadcast an update immediately upon detection of a change in network reachability, without waiting for the next periodic update. This is called a *triggered update*. The use of triggered updates can reduce the time that a given router or set of routers is in possession of incorrect information, and potentially forwarding packets along paths that no longer exist.

IGRP's operation is similar, with the exception that its update time is 90 seconds, and the topology updates contains additional metric information.

The advantage in using distance-vector routing is its simplicity. The cost of this simplicity is the long convergence time in large routed networks. The common routing protocols based on the distance-vector algorithm is Routing Information Protocol (RIP) and Cisco's Interior Gateway Routing Protocol (IGRP).

5.3.1 RIP and RIP2

Routing Information Protocol (RIP) is a very basic protocol that provides connectivity with minimal configuration and processing overhead. As outlined in RFC 1058, now including split horizon and triggered updates, it is known as RIP-1.

RIP-1 is best used inside a single network. Figure 5-10 shows the message format.

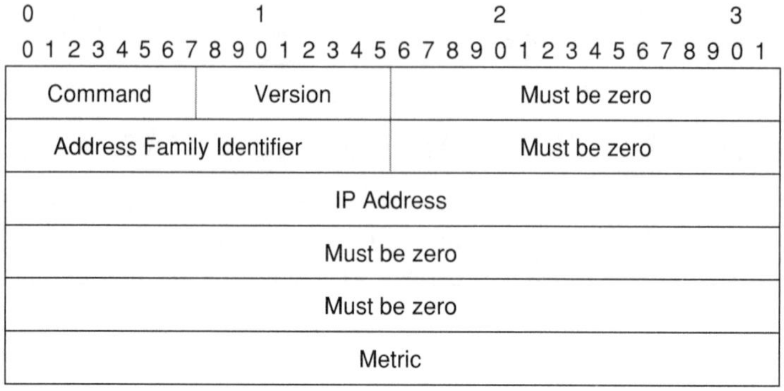

Figure 5-10
*RIP-1 frame
format.*

```
0                   1                   2                   3
0 1 2 3 4 5 6 7 8 9 0 1 2 3 4 5 6 7 8 9 0 1 2 3 4 5 6 7 8 9 0 1
```

Command	Version	Must be zero
Address Family Identifier		Must be zero
IP Address		
Must be zero		
Must be zero		
Metric		

The command field is 8 bits in length. Many values are defined; consider only two values:

- 1 for a RIP request
- 2 for a RIP response

The version field for RIP-1 must be 1. The next field must be all zeros. The address Family Identifier is a 2-byte field. The only valid value for RIP-1 is 2. The next field is all zeros. This field is the IP address. The IP address in RIP-1 represents either the network, subnet, or IP host address. In RIP-1, the subnet mask is not passed in the message format. The routing node must analyze the IP address to determine its specific value. Remember that IP addresses are broken down into three classes, A, B, and C. When determined, RIP-1 code in the routing node analyzes the subnet and host fields by applying the defined subnet mask for use with this autonomous system.

RIP-1 reserves three types of IP addresses:

- 127.0.0.0 is reserved to provide loopback functionality utilizing the PING program.
- 0.0.0.0 is reserved as the default address.
- 255.255.255.255 is reserved as a broadcast address.

The last field in the RIP-1 message format is the metric. The simple hop count metric is used to determine the value. RIP-1 uses 1 to 15, and 16 is used to represent infinity.

RIP-1 is supported on both point-to-point links and local networks of Token Ring and Ethernet. The RIP messages are transported using the connectionless best effort User Datagram Protocol (UDP) of IP. Routing tables are sent every 30 seconds.

RIP-1 was a longtime true standard and was not improved until recently. RIP-2 improvements were documented in RFC 1037 and RFC 1388. Areas added were subnet masking in support of variable-length subnet masks, authentication, and support for multicasting.

Take a look at the RIP-2 message format shown in Figure 5-11.

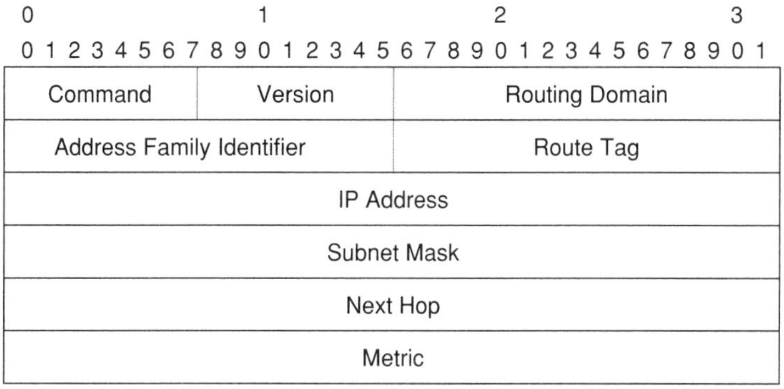

Figure 5-11
RIP-2 message format.

One big improvement is the insertion of the subnet mask field in the message format. In this manner, RIP-2 can support multiple networks that have different subnet masks.

RIP-2 utilizes the must-be-zero fields in the RIP-1 message format to include the functionality of RIP-2 routing protocol.

5.3.2 Cisco IGRP

RIP is universal and supported by all routing vendors and thus enables interoperability. But, as discussed, RIP has some shortcomings for today's networking. One such shortcoming is the ability to create a more robust tunable distance vector routing protocol. Cisco developed a proprietary protocol called *Interior Gateway Routing Protocol (IGRP)*.

The goals of IGRP were to address the many shortcomings apparent in RIP. These goals can be summarized as follows:

- Stable routing even in very large and complex networks. No routing loops should occur, even as transients.

- Fast response to changes in network topology (convergence).

- Low overhead. That is, IGRP itself should not use more bandwidth than what is actually needed for its task.

- Splitting traffic among several parallel routes when they are of roughly equal desirability.

- Taking into account error rates and level of traffic on different paths.

- The ability to handle multiple "types of service" with a single set of information.

In IGRP, the general Bellman-Ford algorithm was modified in three major areas:

- First, instead of a simple metric, a vector of metrics was used to characterize a path.

- Second, instead of picking a single path with the smallest metric, IGRP introduced the ability for traffic to be split among several paths, whose metrics fall into a specified range.

- Third, it added the provision for greater stability in situations where the topology is changing.

The result was a routing protocol that performs what amounts to a distributed algorithm. Each router only needs to solve part of the problem, and it only has to receive a portion of the total data.

IGRP's enhancements come from expanding the distance vector protocols to include four additional values, instead of just hop count:

- Delay

- Bandwidth

- Reliability

- Load

Delay and bandwidth are determined through network link type (that is, point-to point line speed, Ethernet, Token Ring, and so on) or through network definitions. A value of all 1s indicates that the destination is unreachable. Using 24 bits allows for representation in bandwidth style values from 1200 bps to 10 gigabits. The bandwidth value has the greatest effect on the metric.

Figure 5-12 shows an example of how the bandwidth value has greater weight in the metric than does hop count. If you compare RIP to IGRP in this example, the two would produce different results.

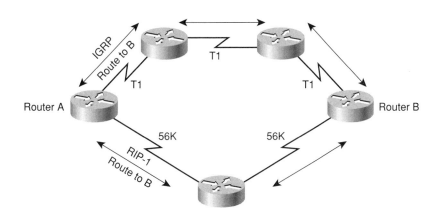

Figure 5-12
*RIP vs. IGRP
route selection
metric
example.*

NOTES

Reliability and load are determined by statistics taken from the router itself. Be careful that the load parameter is taken directly from the bandwidth value defined from the router code. Great care should be used when defining values because their definition, either positive or negative, affects the flows of your network.

IGRP sends its route updates every 90 seconds. Again, with distance vector-based routing, the updates can produce large convergence delays in the network. We have seen networks that can take up to 15 minutes to converge. With huge downtimes like this, for normal ebbs and flows in a network, the industry addressed this issue with the advent of link state routing protocols.

5.4 LINK STATE ROUTING PROTOCOLS

Link state routing protocols were created to reduce the convergence time of routing table updates. In a link state algorithm, each router is responsible for connecting to its direct neighbors. The great advantage to this is that only the connections available from each link to its neighbors will be sent in the routing update and not the entire network topology. Also, updates are exchanged as the event occurs, not on a timed basis. Convergence time is drastically reduced and new changes are recognized on a very timely basis.

Examples of routing protocols based on this methodology are as follows:

- IBM's APPN/HPR

- OSI's Intermediate-System to Intermediate-System (IS-IS)

- Cisco's Enhanced Interior Gateway Routing Protocol (E-IGRP)

- IP Open Shortest Path First (OSPF)

Let's look at two of the most popular adaptations, OSPF and Cisco E-IGRP.

5.4.1 OSPF

The IETF developed a link state protocol to support the large IP networks that were cre-ated over the past several years. The standard is the IETF RFC 1247, also known as *Open Shortest Path First (OSPF)*.

OSPF uses IP as its network layer protocol. As such, the OSPF implementation uses IP addressing to provide many of its services. Each router participating in an OSPF net-work has a *unique router identifier*. This is an elected IP address associated with the router. OSPF networks designate routers as the source for authoritative routes to sub-nets in broadcast networks.

Routers that are not designated routers are referred to as *nondesignated routers*. Non-designated routers use a Class D IP multicast address of 224.0.0.6, which is the stan-dard IP multicast address defined as "all-designated-routers." *Designated routers* use the multicast IP address 224.0.0.5 for contacting "all-OSPF-routers" when flooding a broadcast network with link state information.

Besides support for designated router and flooding, OSPF offers many other features that make it the preferred open-standard link state routing protocol:

- Type of Service routing

- Load balancing

- Partitioning large networks into smaller more manageable networks called areas

- Authentication for information exchange

- Host-specific and network-specific route support

- Designated router and backup designated router

- Flood protocol support

- May use virtual links to noncontiguous areas

- Variable-length subnet mask support

- Imports routing information from RIP and EGP networks

In supporting large networks, OSPF divides a network into areas, as shown in Figure 5-13. Each area is identified with its own unique number.

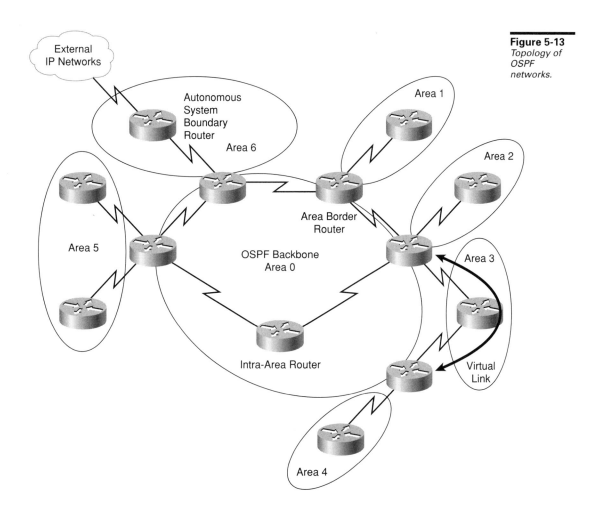

Figure 5-13
Topology of OSPF networks.

5.4.1.1 Backbone Area

The OSPF backbone area always uses 0.0.0.0 as the area number. All other networks are simply considered areas and assigned unique numbers. OSPF nomenclature has specific terms for a router based on its position in an area:

- *Intra-area routers*—Routers that function specifically within their area.

- *Area border router (ABR)*—A router that connects two areas.

- *Autonomous system boundary routers*—A router that joins autonomous systems OSPF networks.

OSPF areas minimize the topology information necessary in each router. This reduces CPU processing, memory requirements, and the amount of link state information being flooded into the network.

OSPF backbone routers are usually directly connected, forming a contiguous network. Each backbone router contains the full network topology for distributing routing information to attached areas. In some cases, however, a backbone router must be connected through a nonbackbone router. This configuration is possible by using an OSPF virtual link.

Each backbone pair defines the virtual link. However, the packets actually traverse non-backbone routers. The nonbackbone routers are defined to forward out-of-area packets to a backbone router that can then deliver the packet to destined backbone router defined on the virtual link.

OSPF intra-area (IA) routers use the flooding protocol to OSPF link state advertisements (LSAs) to other IA routers found in the area. If the IA router is on a broadcast link, it will also send LSAs identifying all the routers on the broadcast network. Each IA router contains a network map of only the topology for that area.

Area Border routers (ABRs) connect two or more areas and maintain a topology database describing all interconnected areas. Flooding of summary link state advertisements in these areas allows IA routers to learn of inter-area routes.

Autonomous system boundary routers (ASBRs) flood the network with external link advertisements with information about the external networks connected. RIP, HELLO, and EGP route information may also be imported to OSPF for redistribution suing OSPF LSAs to the OSPF network.

5.4.1.2 External Network Routes

External network routes increase the size of the network topology database considerably. An area called a *stub area (SA)* is used by OSPF to control the size of the database topology. An SA contains only a default route to all the external routes. The SA is usually a small OSPF area with one or two AB routers connecting it to the backbone area. Figure 5-14 diagrams stub areas.

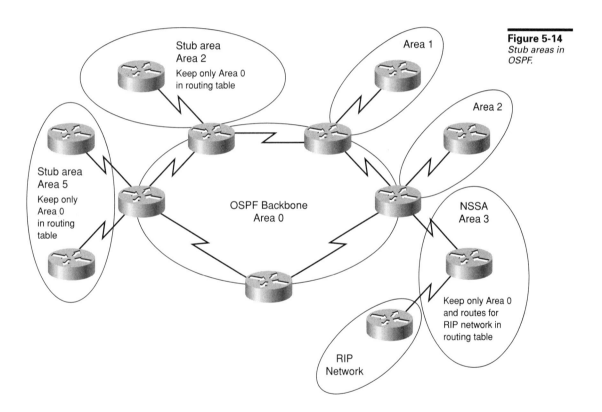

Figure 5-14
Stub areas in OSPF.

Keeping the link state database small places certain restrictions on stub areas:

- ASB routers in a stub area cannot connect to external networks.
- An ABR cannot be chosen for sending packets outside of the area.
- Virtual links cannot traverse a stub area.

The final area specified for OSPF is an area called *not-so-stubby-area (NSSA)*. These areas that allow the connection of an external network to a stub area. This configuration is usually used when migrating from a RIP-based network to OSPF. The NSSA replaces these external routers with a single default route to the external network. In Figure 5-14, an NSSA is represented by Area 3.

5.4.1.3 HELLO Protocol

OSPF routers use the HELLO protocol to discover neighboring routers. Within the HELLO packet, the router will identify itself as to whether it can be a designated, backup, or nondesignated router. A priority field within the HELLO packet indicates the desire of the router to be a designated backup router. The value may range from 0–255. A value of 0 indicates that the router is a nondesignated router. If all the priority fields of particpating routers is is equal 0 then the router with the highest router ID value becomes the designated router.

5.4.1.4 Link State Types

The OSPF flooding protocol is used by OSPF to send out link state advertisements. OSPF has defined five link state types:

- Router links (Type 1)
- Network links (Type 2)
- Summary links for IP (Type 3)
- Summary links for boarder routers (Type 4)
- External links (Type 5)

All OSPF routers describing the state of the links assigned to an area send router link advertisements. Router link advertisements are flooded intra-area only and include a Type of Service (TOS) metric value for calculating the cost of the link.

Network link advertisements are also intra-area only. The network link advertisement lists all the known adjacent routers to the designated router on a broadcast and non-broadcast network.

Area border routers send summary advertisements describing IP network link summaries with TOS metrics for each.

AS boundary routers send external link advertisements describing external routes to this OSPF network. These advertisements include TOS metrics; however, they are not comparable to the metrics in the OSPF network.

The OSPF algorithm uses the TOS metrics in its route computation. Each route is first computed for the default TOS 0. This default metric is normal service. The five OSPF TOS values that match the TOS field for IP are listed in Table 5.1. Routers indicate their ability to participate in TOS routing by setting a support for TOS bit in the LSA. Routers advertising lack of TOS support for links may result in unreachable destinations for some TOS routes. In this case, the metrics used are those for the default TOS 0. Each TOS can be assigned a metric based on bandwidth, delay, reliability, or cost, as shown in Table 5-1.

Table 5-1   *OSPF TOS values.*

OSPF Value	RFC 1349	TOS Values
0	0000	Normal service
2	0001	Minimize monetary cost
4	0010	Maximize reliability
8	0100	Maximize throughput
16	1000	Minimize delay

5.4.2 Cisco E-IGRP

E-IGRP's aim is to remove transient loops and is based on the *diffusing algorithm (DUAL)*. E-IGRP uses information on the distance from the destination from distance vector advertisements and the cost of the link used. The router will select one of its neighbors as the best route. If new updates are sent, they evaluate them to see if the new cost is lower than their original value. If it is lower, the router will use this path.

The complexity of OSPF is removed when using E-IGRP as the link state protocol for routing IP. Shown in Figure 5-15, an E-IGRP network does not denote areas within the network for determining routes. Instead it has kept the simplicity of a RIP network but with the enhanced metrics available in OSPF. Instead of area numbers, E-IGRP uses autonomous system numbers to designate the routing domains. The simplicity of E-IGRP and its robustness for metric routing has made E-IGRP the dominant routing protocol for Cisco router-based networks.

The autonomous systems in E-IGRP communicate by using autonomous system numbers assigned to multiple autonomous E-IGRP networks within a router. Through redistribution of routes, the individual autonomous systems learn the routes between the systems. There is no designated or backup designated router in E-IGRP because each router contains the information for determining the best path to any destination.

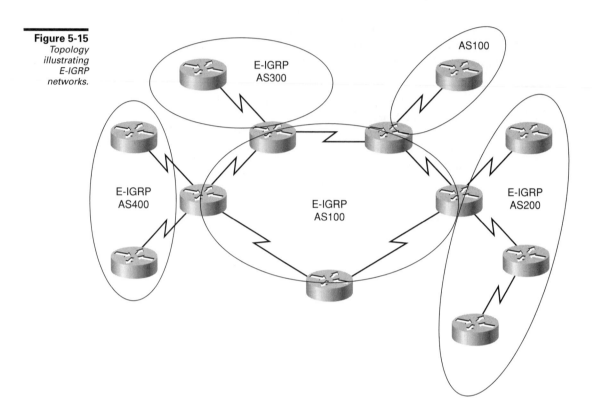

Figure 5-15
*Topology
illustrating
E-IGRP
networks.*

The multiple E-IGRP autonomous systems configured on a single router cause a default action of the IOS to redistribute default information between these autonomous systems. A single E-IGRP process is analogous to an area of a link state protocol. However, within the process, information can be filtered and aggregated at any interface boundary. If you want to restrict the propagation of routing information, multiple routing processes can be configured to achieve a hierarchy.

There are five packet types used by E-IGRP:

- Neighbor discovery
- Update
- Query
- Reply
- Requests

In Neighbor discovery, the use of a HELLO packet is similar to a multicast broadcast. E-IGRP also uses these HELLO packets to test the links for connectivity.

The Update and Query messages are transmitted with expected acknowledges through multicasting.

Replies and Requests are unicast messages.

NOTES

E-IGRP also has support for variable-length subnet masking and support for Classless Inter-Domain Routing (CIDR). E-IGRP can summarize routes and handle external gateways by using route tag support.

CHAPTER 6

Network
Topology

We have spent the last few chapters discussing the higher layers of the network stack. In this chapter, we discuss some of the physical media that the logical network rides upon. Our discussion will include both LAN and WAN technologies.

6.1 LAN CABLES

The LAN network that reaches out to the end user is connected by physical cables. There are four types of LAN cables, as follows:

- Coaxial cable—This cable media has good attenuation, minimal loss of signal over distance, and high data rates over long distances.

- Telephone twisted pair—Also known as *unshielded twisted pair (UTP)*. This wire does not contain an outer metal shield to cut down on unwanted radio frequencies. UTP also suffers from crosstalk.

- Shielded twisted pair (STP)—Unlike UTP, this wire has an outer covering that handles the radio frequency problems. With good attenuation, STP can carry data rates in the 32 Mbps range and higher.

- Fiber optics—Unlike the aforementioned media types that are copper wire, fiber optics uses glass and light impulses to transmit data. This glass and light mechanism launches fiber away from radio frequency problems. Fiber optics can produce speeds of terabits per second.

6.1.1 Cable Classification

First and foremost, cables must be installed according to local and state electrical codes. The Electronics Industry Association (EIA) and the Telecommunications Industry Association (TIA) define the cable categories.

There are five categories for UTP, as follows:

- Category 1 (CAT1)—This category is undesirable for data transmission due to the wide range of impedance.

- Category 2 (CAT2)—Again, like CAT1 cables, not good for LAN traffic. However Category 2 can be used for IBM 3270 data transmission.

- Category 3 (CAT3)—Can transmit LAN traffic. This was fine for early LANs that had speeds of 4 Mbps Token Ring and 10Mbps Ethernet.

- Category 4 (CAT4)—Just like CAT3, but with extra megahertz, it brings it closer for 16Mbps Token Ring. Although it can run 16Mbps Token Ring, it is not certified for production usage.

- Category 5 (CAT5)—The preferred UTP cable standard for LAN networking. This wiring can support speeds up to 100Mbps. CAT5 has made the aforementioned cable types obsolete.

6.2 ETHERNET

Ethernet was a product of the famous Palo Alto Research Center (PARC) of Xerox Corporation. The final appearance that we see today had additional development from Digital Equipment Corporation (DEC) and Intel. The IEEE documented a standard frame format in 802.3. Ethernet and IEEE 802.3 frames are very similar, but most vendors deploy the 802.3 standard. Ethernet runs over a bus-based architecture.

6.2.1 Ethernet Bus Topology and CSMA/CD

In a bus architecture, all stations attached to the LAN can talk at the same time. Due to this method, it is very conceivable that two or more stations could talk at exactly the same moment. If this does occur—and it does—it is termed a *collision*. A technology was developed to respond to this condition. The standard is called *Carrier Sense Multiple Access/Carrier Detect,* or *CSMA/CD.* Each station on the segment analyzes the destination frame address to see if it is theirs; if yes—the frame is copied.

In the carrier sense function, each station listens on the wire. If the wire is busy, the station will wait. If there are two stations that want to send simultaneously, and the wire is silent, both stations sending will result in a collision. As part of the carrier detect functionality, collisions will cause the station to abort the send and send a jamming signal to the other stations on the LAN. Remember, the aim for CSMA/CD is to listen before you send.

6.2.2 Ethernet MAC Frame Format

Figure 6-1 shows the Ethernet frame format.

Ethernet Frame

8 bytes	6 bytes	6 bytes	2 bytes	46-1500 bytes	4 bytes
Preamble	Destination Address	Source Address	Type	Data and Pad	Frame Check

Figure 6-1
Ethernet frame format.

NOTES

This is the Ethernet frame format and not the 802.3 frame that was later developed.

The various parts of the Ethernet frame format include the following:

- The Preamble—The first field, an alternating pattern of bits, is 8 bytes in length and used to provide synchronization.
- The Destination Address—Six bytes in length; this is the physical address of the target device.
- The Source Address—Six bytes in length; this is the physical address of the sending device.
- The Type—A 2-byte address that indicates the upper-layer protocol. Some common examples are: x'805D' for IBM SNA over Ethernet, x'8183' for Novell IPX, and x'0800' for IP.

- The Data and Pad—This is a variable-length field that can range from 46 to 1500 bytes.

- The Frame Check Sequence (FCS)—A 4-byte field used for validity checking. A valid Ethernet frame is from 64 to 1518 bytes in length.

NOTES

Frames smaller than 64 bytes in length are called *runts,* and frames larger than 1518 are called *giants.*

6.2.3 IEEE 802.3/Ethernet Mac Frame Format

Figure 6-2 shows the IEEE 802.3 frame format.

Figure 6-2
IEEE 802.3
frame format.

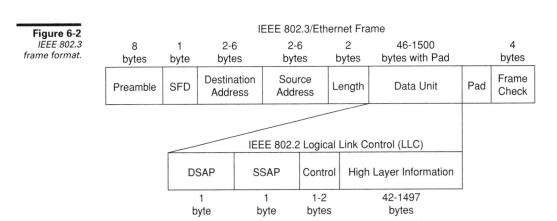

The various parts of the IEEE 802.3 frame format include:

- The Preamble—The first field which is only 8 bytes in length. This alternating pattern of bits is used to provide synchronization.

- The Start Frame Delimiter (SFD)—A single-byte field. The preamble and the SFD together create the same function as the preamble did for the plain Ethernet frame.

- The Destination Address—From 2–6 bytes in length, this is the target address.

- The Source Address—From 2–6 bytes in length, this is the address of the sending station.

NOTES

The destination and the source must match in size.

- The Length—This is the length of the data as represented in bytes (replaces the plain Ethernet frame type section).

- The Data Unit—The IEEE 802.2 LLC protocol data unit. The minimum is 46 bytes; if the data is smaller, this field will be padded. The maximum size of this field is 1500 bytes.

  Within the data unit is the *Logical Link Control (LLC)* information. The DSAP field is the Destination Service Access Point (DSAP) and the SSAP is the Source Service Access Point (SSAP) field. The Control field indicates the function of the LLC and the High Layer Information field is the end-user data.

- The FCS—This is a validity checking frame based on CRC calculations of the total fields.

6.2.4 10Mbps Ethernet

There are four ways to transmit Ethernet at 10Mbps. The nomenclature is 10Base2—10Mbps, baseband transmission, over a maximum cable length of 200 meters—in this case coaxial cable. Another example is 10BaseT: 10 megabits transmission speed, baseband signaling over twisted pair cabling. Further examples are shown following:

- 10Base5—As the name already tells us, the speed is 10Mbps, on a baseband network, and the 5 means that the segment length is 500 meters and can support only 100 connections. Its nickname was *Thicknet* due to the 10mm size cable.

- 10Base2—10Base2 uses thinner coaxial cable than did the early 10Base5 and as such costs less to install. It had a distance of 200 meters and reduced the number of connections to 30. With the installation of repeaters, it could be extended to 925 meters. Its nickname was *Thinnet,* due to the thinner coaxial cable run needed to support the network.

- 10Base-T—Using 2 UTP twisted pairs for Ethernet, requires at least CAT3, can create networks of 500 meters and 10Mbps speeds. With 10Base-T, Ethernet moved from bus technology to a star-wired LAN. Each station is physically wired back to a central hub. Physical LAN management was improved with the advent of 10Base-T.

- 10Base-F—Fiber for Ethernet. You can use either two strands of single mode or multimode fiber, and it is further broken down into three substandards:

  10Base-FP—Uses a passive star topology with a one-segment length of 1000 meters. This can create a network diameter of 2500 meters.

  10Base-FB—This standard is for backbone and repeater fiber networks. A single segment can be 2000 meters with a network diameter of 2500 meters.

  10Base-FL—Used to connect repeaters. Segments between repeaters are 1000 or 2000 meters long and a network diameter of 2500 meters.

All in all, Ethernet's numerous options and ability to run effectively at relatively high rates of 10Mbps on relatively low-cost, already-installed media has made Ethernet the LAN of choice. Ethernet's rich and robust older architecture has led to 100Mbps Ethernet (*Fast Ethernet*). Fast Ethernet has already virtually replaced 10Mbps Ethernet in corporate LANs. *Gigabit Ethernet* (1 billion bits per second), in its early phase of implementation, shows the ability of Ethernet to meet networking demands through the years.

6.3 FAST ETHERNET

As an extremely smart move to leverage the very great installed base of 10Mbps Ethernet, the creation of 100Mbps Ethernet was accomplished. IEEE 802.3 is the standard for 100Base-T. 100Base-T requires a star-wired topology with wiring of UTP or fiber.

The IEEE kept the 802.3 standard frame and parameters as close as possible for 10 to 100Mbps. The only change was in the InterFrameGap (IFG) time changed from 9.6 to 0.96 microseconds. There are three types of Fast Ethernet deployed over the physical media:

- 100Base-TX

- 100Base-T4

- 100Base-FX

6.3.1 100Base-TX

100Base-TX uses two pairs of CAT5 UTP. There is a distance of 100 meters from hub-to-station limitation.

6.3.2 100Base-T4

100Base-T4 uses four pairs of CAT3 wire. Three pairs are used for transmission and one pair is used for receiving data. Again, there is a distance limitation of 100 meters from hub to jack.

6.3.3 100Base-FX

This standard uses two strands of multimode or single-mode fiber. In the past we have seen this design deployed as backbone networks, not to the desktop. Distance between stations can be 412 meters and with the use of repeaters can go up to 2000 meters.

6.4 TOKEN RING

In Token Ring, each physical device is wired back to a central hub for communication. So, in essence, this is only a logical ring and not a physical one.

The word *token* is used because each station will speak only when it is their turn and the "token" or microphone has been passed to them. The notion of a *ring* comes from the closed unidirectional path of data being transmitted to and from the end stations. When data is received, the station looks at the destination address to see if it is theirs. If it is, it copies the frame into its receive buffers and sends a response back to the originating host to remove the frame from the LAN.

6.4.1 Star-Wired Ring Topology

A pure ring technology has each station physically connected to the ensuing station. Inherently, this can cause problems; when one station has an error, the entire group of attached devices fail. To compensate for some of the potential weak points, a star-wired ring topology is a nice combination of a star and ring design. In the star-wired design (see Figure 6-3), there is a relay center that acts as a go-between partner on the segment. The transmit path of one station is connected to the receive path of the other. This connection on the relay station is called a *lobe*.

Figure 6-3
*Star-wired
LAN.*

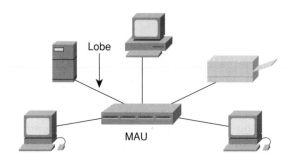

Typically, each station in a star-wired Token Ring is connected directly to the relay. If the relay is passive, it is called a *multistation access unit (MAU);* if the relay is active, it is called an *intelligent hub.* Intelligent hubs also provide protection to the LAN from runaway devices and can also provide much-needed network management to the network staff.

6.4.2 Token Passing

The length of the token is 24 bits and the shortest MAC frame is 200 bits. Data flows on a Token Ring by the station reading the frame and sees that it is a data frame and not a free token. The header is then updated with the destination and source MAC address, data, a new FCS value, an end delimiter, and a frame status field.

As the frame goes around the ring, each station looks to see if it is theirs, and if not, retransmits the frame back on the ring. If the frame is at its true destination, it receives the frame, goes through some error processing, and sends a free token on to the ring for processing. This special process of capturing and releasing tokens is called *single token protocol.*

6.4.3 Token Claiming

Token claiming determines which device is the active monitor. To claim a token, one of the following conditions must exist:

- A loss of signal
- Expiration of the active monitor receive notification timer
- Expiration of the ring purge timer

If one of the conditions exist to enable token claiming, a station transmits a broadcast claim token MAC frame. When a station encounters this broadcast, it will respond in one of the following ways:

- If the source address is greater, it enters claim token repeat mode.

- If the source address is less, it transmits a claim token MAC frame.

- If the station receives the same address three times, it assumes that it is inserted onto a sound ring and can add the token on to the ring, purge the ring, start active monitors, and issue a new token.

6.4.4 Active Monitor

The *active monitor* is the station on the ring that performs error detection and recovery. The active monitor station sets the B'1' on access control field and interrogates the field. If it has already seen the frame, it assumes that the frame has circled the ring and removes it.

It also keeps a good *token timer*. This is the time it takes for the longest frame to encircle the ring. If the timer pops, the station assumes the frame was lost.

6.4.5 Neighbor Notification

Stations on a Token Ring recognize an Active Monitor Present MAC frame and start a neighbor notification process. This process enables ring stations to learn their *nearest active upstream neighbor (NAUN)* and to give it its active downstream neighbor.

6.4.6 Access Priority

Priority of tokens on the ring are determined by the values of the first 3 bits of the access control field.

6.4.7 Ring-Attachment Process

The ring attachment process is the procedure for station insertion on a Token Ring. The process is as follows:

1. Lobe Testing—The station sends a lobe media test MAC to the MAU. The MAU loops the frame back, creating a closed circuit between the two.

2. Duplicate address checking—The station sends a duplicate address test MAC. If it receives a B'1' in the address recognition bit, it will detach from the ring.

3. Monitor Check—This station starts its insert timer. It is looking for the active monitor, standby monitor, or ring purge MAC within the timer. If it does not receive them, it will initiate the token claiming process and become the active monitor on the ring.

4. Neighbor Notification—The station sends its NAUN address to its downstream neighbor.

5. Request Initialization—The station sends a request initialization MAC to the bridge. The response is information that will set its physical location, soft error report timers, ring number, ring authorization values, and potential LAN manager information.

6.4.8 IEEE 802.5/Token-Ring MAC Frame Format

The Media Access Control sublayer is a unique addressing schema that ensures receipt and delivery of data on the LAN. There are nine main functions of the MAC layer:

- Addressing—The MAC address is the physical address of the station adapter on the LAN.

- Frame copying—When the frame has been recognized as its address, it must copy it into its adapter buffers.

- Frame recognition—This function determines the type of frame being read, that is, system or user.

- Frame eliminator—The beginning and ending of the frame.

- Frame status and verification—Performs the FCS validation.

- Priority management—Participates in the processing of frames and the recognition of the use of priority transmission.

- Routing—Determines which function in a node should process the frame.

- Timing—Keeps track of all the timers utilized by the MAC layer.

- Token management—Handles error conditions and participates in LAN management.

The MAC Token-Ring frame is shown in Figure 6-4.

The MAC frame is the basic transmission unit (BTU) for the IBM Token Ring network. The frame is broken up into two portions, the *physical header* and the *physical trailer*. Other parts include the following:

- The start delimiter—A single-byte field, with only a finite number of valid combinations.

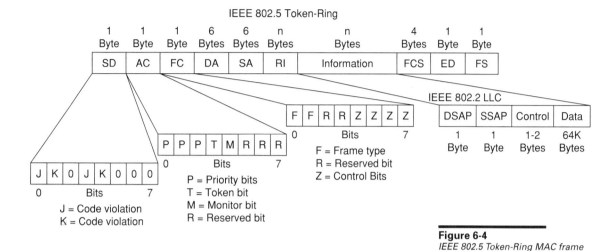

Figure 6-4
IEEE 802.5 Token-Ring MAC frame format.

- The access control field—A 1-byte field denoting the access required, that is, frame or token.

- The frame control—Identifies the frame type.

- Destination address—A 6-byte field that houses the receiving stations MAC address. If it's FFFFFF, it is an all-stations broadcast.

- Source address—A 6-byte field that identifies the routing information, either provided by the manufacturer, or the LAN administrator.

- Routing Information Field—Used when the frame is leaving the originating ring (see Figure 6-5). The station then becomes part of a source route bridging process to determine the physical path through the network. This process was outlined in Chapter 5, "Bridging and Routing."

- The Information Field—Contains MAC control information.

- The Frame Check Sequence (FCS)—A 4-byte value created by an algorithm that creates a CRC value to maintain data integrity.

- The Ending Delimiter—Used to indicate code violations or that the frame is one of many being associated together.

- The Frame Status—Indicates that the frame was copied, or that the destination address (DA) has been matched or an error has occurred.

Figure 6-5
RIF field within the Token Ring MAC frame.

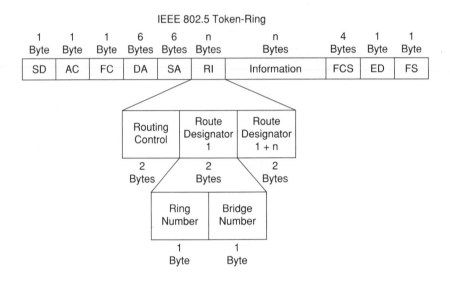

IEEE 802.5 Token-Ring

1 Byte	1 Byte	1 Byte	6 Bytes	6 Bytes	n Bytes	n Bytes	4 Bytes	1 Byte	1 Byte
SD	AC	FC	DA	SA	RI	Information	FCS	ED	FS

Routing Control	Route Designator 1	Route Designator 1 + n
2 Bytes	2 Bytes	2 Bytes

Ring Number	Bridge Number
1 Byte	1 Byte

6.4.9 Token-Ring MAC Addressing

Unique addressing is a necessity for MAC layer communications. Addresses have both form and function:

- Individual and group addressing—Either unique for a specific station, or a group address that can refer to a number of stations.

- Universally and locally administered addresses—The *universally administered address (UAA)* is assigned by IEEE. This address is found on all Token-Ring cards. It is set in the card's ROM memory and is commonly referred to as its *burned-in address (BIA)*. This UAA can be overridden by the *locally administered address (LAA)*. The LAA is an assigned address given to LAN administrators from the design team. This address, if used properly, can aid in network management.

NOTES

Ethernet cards also contain a BIA. The majority of Ethernet cards only use UAAs. However, some devices, such as Cisco routers, allow LAAs for Ethernet and Token-Ring interfaces.

- Null Address—In a Token-Ring network, a value of all zeros. When a station recognizes a null frame, it strips the frame of its data and sends a new frame.

- All Stations Broadcast—A value of all x'FFFFFFFFFFFF' or x'C000FFFFFFFF' are all stations broadcasts.

- Functional Address—There are currently 14 such addresses as defined in the access protocol level.

6.4.10 4Mbps Token Ring

The dynamics of 4Mbps Token Ring are defined within a transmission measurement as follows:

- The length of 1 bit is 50 meters.

- A 24-bit token is 1200 meters.

- A 200-bit MAC is 10000 meters.

The result: a 4Mbps Token Ring will maintain high-bandwidth utilization at high traffic levels.

6.4.11 16Mbps Token Ring

At 16Mbps, the transmission measurement is as follows:

- 1 bit measured at 12.5 meters

- A token at 300 meters

- The 200-bit MAC at 2500 meters

16Mbps Token-Ring networks have options to better use the media. They allow for the release of a free token while information frames are being circulated. This is a default on all 16Mbps Token-Ring cards.

6.4.12 32Mbps Token Ring

As with the push for greater speed in the LAN, Token Ring answered with 32Mbps. This was accomplished by implementing "full duplex" Token Ring on the LAN, thus allowing for sending and receiving data at the same time.

With sending and receiving at the same time, the Token Ring functions of token access, recovery protocols, frame repeating, frame stripping, and end of frame processing are no longer necessary. This is accomplished by having the LAN device directly connected to a hub or switch usingfull duplex transmission.

NOTES

100Mbps Token Ring is on the horizon.

6.5 FIBER DISTRIBUTED DATA INTERCHANGE

Fiber Distributed Data Interface (FDDI) was the powerhouse LAN protocol of the 1980s. FDDI was architected to run at 100 Mbps and still has presence as some backbone LANs. FDDI uses two counter rotating rings and operates similarly to Token Ring.

6.5.1 FDDI Dual Ring Topology

In FDDI, the counterclockwise ring is the primary and the clockwise ring is the secondary (see Figure 6-6). The primary ring transports all of the data and the secondary ring is used for backup. Stations are attached in the following manner—class A to both and class B only to the primary.

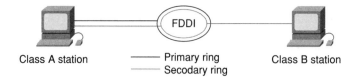

Figure 6-6
FDDI dual counter rotating rings.

Class A station   —— Primary ring   Class B station
                   .... Secodary ring

6.5.2 FDDI Access Protocol

FDDI uses a token just like Token Ring, but FDDI relies on timers rather than events to determine ring availability and function. The three timers are as follows:

- Token rotation timer (TRT)—Used to determine the time elapsed since the station last received the token.

- Target token rotation timer (TTRT)—This value indicates the target maximum time between sends from a particular end station. This value is station-defined and is negotiated at ring initialization; also, the lowest value on the entire ring is used.

- Token hold timer (THT)—Maximum amount of data a station can transmit during its transmit time with the token.

FDDI requires fiber, not CAT3 or CAT5. Most companies are turning to Fast Ethernet for speed at the lowest deployable cost.

6.6 FRAME RELAY

Frame relay is an interface definition that had its origins in Integrated Services Digital Network (ISDN). But there are no requirements for any forms nor usage of ISDN components.

The concept of frame relay is that the network provides logical/virtual circuits over a physical link. These virtual circuits can be defined into *private virtual circuits (PVC)*. Each of these PVCs is deliminated by a *Data Link Connection Identifier (DLCI)*. The marvel of frame relay is that the network can bypass outages to ensure end-to-end connectivity. Figure 6-7 shows a typical frame setup.

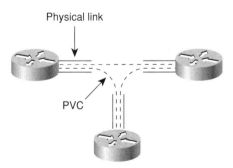

Figure 6-7
Typical frame relay connection.

A PVC exists from endpoint to endpoint across a given network. Many PVCs share a physical connection, thus, saving money on each additional connection. Frame relay also does not poll and therefore yields additional savings with less network-generated traffic.

6.6.1 Frame Relay Frame Format

Frame relay discards any frames that are found to be in error. Frame relay does not perform error recovery because that is the job of the link control protocol; as a result, this too saves bandwidth and adds to efficiency.

The most common link level protocol that is implemented is *High-level Data Link Control (HDLC)*. Frame relay does not implement a class-of-service notion as is customary in classical SNA. Each packet goes into the network with the same priority. Frame relay networks monitor network congestion through a signal notification. These terms are called *Forward Explicit Congestion Notification (FECN)* and *Backward Explicit Congestion Notification (BECN)*. Figure 6-8 shows the frame relay frame format.

Figure 6-8
Frame relay format.

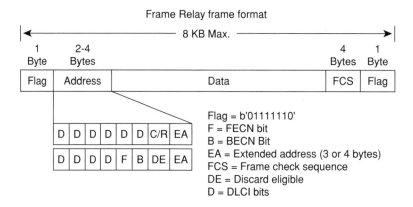

- The Flag—This value starts the frame in HDLC and is equal to x'7E'.

- The Address Field—Here the meat of the frame relay information is housed: the DLCI, FECN, BECN, and discard eligibility (DE) bit.

- The Data—Self-explanatory.

- The Frame Check Sequence (FCS)—Again, as in the aforementioned protocols and frame layouts, it is an algorithm that ensures the integrity of the frame.

- The Flag—The same x'7E' that denotes the end of the frame.

Let's highlight some of the functionality of FECN and BECN. The FECN bit is set when the nodes along the path, in front of the packet, are congested. BECN, in turn, is set when the nodes behind the packet are experiencing congestion. *Congestion* can be found in the form of a slow link or even large frames pulsating through the network.

Frame relay networks can support frames up to 8KB in size, and the most common maximum support is 2KB. Remember, supporting multiple and variable frame sizes can result in unpredictable and erratic response times.

Frame relay nodes in a network act as switches as they transport packets across their links. The proper term for such devices is *Frame Relay Switching Equipment (FRSE)*. The devices that these connections are attached to are termed *Frame Relay Terminal Equipment (FRTE)*. In other words, the PVCs connect the FRTEs. Also, the FRSE map the DLCIs to the FRTE endpoints.

Frame relay networks are often referred to as *meshes*. The mesh topology does not necessarily mean a physical mesh but a logical mesh based on the PVC configurations. These configurations are generally called *partial* and *full mesh*.

6.6.2 Partial Mesh

Frame relay networks are capable of providing many different options for the WAN. In a partial mesh configuration, shown in Figure 6-9, we see that the remote locations all connect to the host site. However, communication between remote sites must take place by having the data routed through the host router and then to the destined remote location. Typically, a partial mesh is employed when remote-to-remote communication is not required or when the traffic is occasional.

Partial Frame Relay Mesh

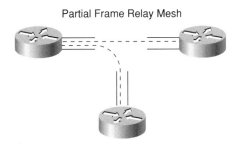

Figure 6-9
Partial mesh frame relay topology.

A variation of the partial mesh is called a *dual-homed* or *dual-star partial mesh*. As shown in Figure 6-10, a dual-star partial mesh configuration utilizes two PVCs from each remote site. One PVC connects to one of the host site routers. This type of configuration is generally used when high availability is a requirement for access to the central location.

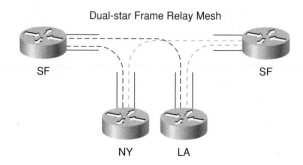

6.6.3 Full Mesh

A *full mesh configuration* for frame relay calls for a PVC from each location to connect to all the locations (see Figure 6-11). Although this configuration gives you full connectivity to any location in the network, it requires careful planning when engineering the router configurations.

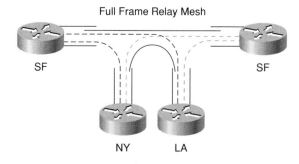

CHAPTER 7

Cisco SNA Support

Cisco has a strategic plan in place that provides a roadmap for internetworking IBM SNA with TCP/IP networks. The plan takes into account various features and functions of SNA implementing them on Cisco router platforms. Cisco's approach is a simple one: If an IBM front-end processor is involved and the network requires enhanced through-put, a Cisco Channel Interface Processor (CIP) can replace it. If an IBM interconnect controller is used, a CIP can be used. If an IBM cluster controller serves a function, a router can also perform the same function. The outline of this simplistic approach is published as a blueprint called *CiscoBlue*.

7.1 CISCO BLUEPRINT FOR TRANSPORTING SNA

The dominance IBM SNA once had on delivering vital corporate information dictated a strategic approach for transporting SNA over internetworks. Cisco delivered such an approach called CiscoBlue in 1991. This five-phased strategy focused on delivering SNA over LANs and WANs to and from the mainframe computers. Table 7-1 outlines a table of the initial five phases outlined for CiscoBlue.

Table 7-1   *Initial five-phased approach for transporting SNA over internetworks.*

Phase	LAN Extensions	WAN	Management	Delivery	Extensions
1	4/16-Mbps SRB/RSRB	Private Packet-Switched	SNMP	1990	Enhanced VR Scalability, Dynamic Spanning Tree
2	IGS Token-Ring Cisco 3000	SDLC Transport	NetView-SNMP	1991	SDLC TWS, SDLC Broadcast
3	Token Ring Ethernet	SDLLC Local Termination	LAN Network Manager	1992	QLLC Conversion, DLSw Standard
4	IBM Chipset 4-Port Token	Cisco4000	SNA PU Type 4 Ring Properties	1993	Custom Queuing, 250,000-pps SRB
5	Channel Attach	Cisco 7000	APPN SNMPv2	1994/95	TCP Offload, Channel, APPN

The first five phases enabled Cisco routers to transport SNA using standards developed by IBM and others. The first phase, for instance, enabled Cisco to transport SNA from Token-Ring networks over Cisco router backbone networks using traditional IBM source-route bridging techniques. The following phases enabled direct SDLC connection as well as SDLC-to-LLC2 conversion for transporting SNA from a serial-line connection as if it were generated originally from a LAN. The final phase culminates in direct connectivity to the mainframe with the CIP card for the Cisco 7000 series routers in 1995. This final phase in the original strategy enabled Cisco to carry SNA traffic directly from the mainframe to the end station on a LAN as IP traffic over a non-SNA backbone using Cisco routers at the source and destination locations.

NOTES

Cisco does not promote a Cisco-only network. It may be stated that a single-vendor network is the easiest to maintain/support, but Cisco equipment complies with standards/RFCs and will work with other vendors.

The initial five-phase strategy was quickly outdated, however, as new technology forced the requirements for delivering data on different media and using different protocols to deliver the data. As part of Cisco's view on integrating all types of network traffic under the CiscoFusion strategy, CiscoBlue has been enhanced to further support routing, LAN switching, and Asynchronous Transfer Mode (ATM) switching networks. Table 7-2 details the enhancements to the 1991 CiscoBlue roadmap strategy.

Table 7-2 *Phases 6–10 of the CiscoBlue road map strategy.*

Phase	CiscoBlue	Cisco IOS Software	CiscoWorks Blue	Delivery
6	Ethernet Switch, Catalyst Family, 1600, Token-Ring Switch, LightStream 2020 ATM Switch	LAN Frame Relay Access Devices (FRADs), DLSw Lite	Native Service Point	1995/96
7	LightStream 1010 ATM Switch, Stackable Token-Ring Switch	TN3270 Server, SNA Backbone Enhancements	SNA Maps SNA Views	1996
8	Multiservice WAN, Token-Ring LAN Emulation, Catalyst 5000 Token-Ring Module	NCIA Enhancements, Channel-Attached HPR	Token Ring VLANs, Connectivity Toolkit, Response Time Reporter	1996/97
9	Service Interworking, Token-Ring Switched Access Unit	SNA session Switching Protocol Servers	Performance Solver	1997
10	Multiprotocol over ATM (MPOA), Standards-Based VLANs	COS/TOS/QOS Mapping, HPR, Native ATM Support	Distributed Management	1997/98

The second set of phases for internetworking IBM SNA supports a variety of enhancements generated by international committees for delivering SNA over internetworks. These standards are:

- RFC 1483 for transporting APPN over ATM
- RFC 1661 for transporting SNA over SMDS, PPP, and ISDN
- RFC 1490 for transporting SNA over Frame-Relay networks
- RFC 1795 for transporting SNA using Data-Link Switching

NOTES

Although network management is not discussed in this book, it is important to realize that Cisco has always maintained and delivered on the requirement for managing SNA over internetworks. Cisco's product line offering called CiscoWorks Blue enables network managers to manage SNA PUs and LUs over internetworks as if they were native SNA networks.

Recently, Cisco has completed the CiscoBlue roadmap and now promotes a migration path from centric SNA to IP-centric networking. Figure 7-1 shows this.

Figure 7-1
The new migration strategy path for SNA to IP-centric networking.

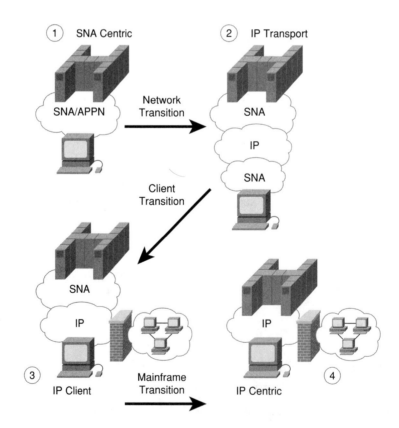

This new strategy illustrates the first stage as moving from an all SNA/APPN network to one where SNA is pushed to the edges of the network and IP is used as the transport between the edges of the network. The next phase is one of creating a single protocol at the client's edge to the network while keeping SNA at the connection to the main-frame. The final phase migrates mainframe access from SNA to IP. At this point, the net-work and access to the mainframe applications have been migrated to employing IP as the transport of vital corporate data. Although this can serve as a migration path, it does not necessarily mean that this is the definitive strategy. In reality, sections of a cor-porate network may be in any one or more of the quadrants shown. What the diagram does indicate is that:

- The diagram represents the different positions that a client's network would be in at any one point in time.

- The goal of the diagram is to show a stepped approach to an IP network (ready for VoIP) or to show how to move and skip a step.

7.2 SERIAL TUNNELING

Serial tunneling (STUN) is a Cisco implementation for delivering IBM SDLC and High-level Data Link Control (HDLC) device communication over TCP/IP multiproto-col networks using routers. STUN is a mechanism for encapsulating the SDLC frame in IP packets for transmission over the multiprotocol network. The SDLC frame is untouched and remains intact during the process. Cisco implements STUN in several flavors. Each flavor enables all SNA PU types to communicate over a multiprotocol router-based network. The router configurations used for supporting STUN resemble traditional SNA/SDLC configurations.

7.2.1 Direct STUN

This is the simplest of the STUN configurations. Shown in Figure 7-2, a cluster control-ler is serially attached to a router, which is directly attached to an IBM front-end pro-cessor channel attached to an IBM mainframe. From an SNA perspective, this cluster controller is directly attached to the front end. The router delivers the SDLC frame from the front end to the cluster controller. The router appears as a modem to the two SNA devices. The bus within the router actually transfers the frame from the front-end port to the cluster controller port, hence direct tunneling.

Figure 7-2
*Direct SNA
serial
tunneling
configuration.*

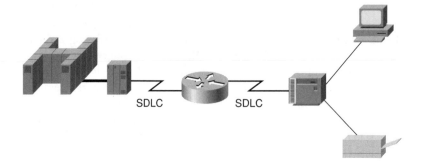

SDLC   SDLC

7.2.2 Point-to-Point

In a configuration where there is only one router and one way to the front-end router, a point-to-point configuration may be used. In such a configuration, the SDLC frame is encapsulated or enveloped on the outbound serial port into the serial-frame data field. The outbound serial line is usually using HDLC as the link-level protocol between the routers. Figure 7-3 illustrates the placement of the SDLC frame into the HDLC frame data field.

Figure 7-3
*Simple serial
encapsulation
of an SDLC
frame into the
HDLC data
field.*

SDLC Frame

LH	TH	RH	RU	LT

LH	Address	Control	Data	LT

Cisco HDLC Frame

Advantages to using simple serial encapsulation for point-to-point configurations like that shown in Figure 7-4 are:

- Reduced cycle time on router for encapsulating the frame
- The encapsulation technique minimizes the frame overhead
- Increased performance and throughput

However, the HDLC implemented on Cisco is proprietary to Cisco based on the ISO 3309 specification. Although the Cisco HDLC is fast, it does cause problems with delivering SDLC frames. Recall that SDLC is very deterministic and protective of the data being delivered. The Cisco HDLC implementation is efficient, but does not ensure frame integrity. The following weaknesses result from using simple serial encapsulation:

- Frame is not routable.

- Availability to front-end router is diminished due to single line connection.

- Cisco HDLC does not support frame check sequencing and acknowledgement.

- HDLC does not perform retransmission of frames.

Recovery of improperly delivered SDLC frames lies with the SNA devices connected at the far ends of the router connection.

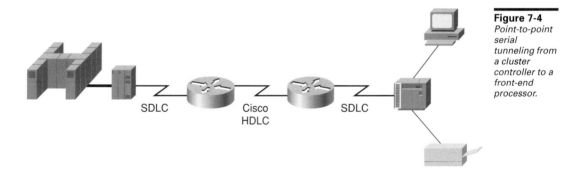

Figure 7-4
Point-to-point serial tunneling from a cluster controller to a front-end processor.

7.2.3 WAN Point-to-Point

The majority of networks use wide area network (WAN) router backbones as a means of connecting remote locations to the data center. Having the capability to route SDLC frames through this backbone serves as an advantage in providing reliable transport of the SDLC frame by encapsulating the frame in TCP. Using TCP, the frame is not only routable, but TCP will guarantee integrity and sequence of the data. Figure 7-5 illustrates the use of TCP/IP as the encapsulation technique for transporting SDLC frames over a router WAN.

Note that the TCP/IP encapsulation places the SDLC frame into the data area of the TCP segment. The TCP segment is then placed into the data area of the IP datagram, which is then placed into the data area of the data link frame used for connecting the router to the WAN.

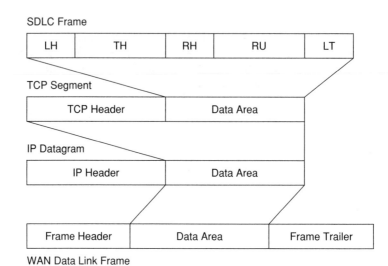

Figure 7-5
*SDLC TCP/IP
encapsulation.*

This encapsulation technique ensures that the SDLC frame is routed through the WAN. The WAN connectivity can be any of the various WAN configurations available. These may be serial, Frame Relay, ATM, ISDN, or even SONET. Although it is an advantage to be able to reliably route the STUN traffic through the WAN, the encapsulation technique is costly in processor cycles and frame overhead.

Figure 7-6 shows a typical configuration of a remote location with an attached cluster controller connecting to a router. At the data-center side, an IBM AS/400 rather than a front-end processor, is attached to the data-center router. The serial links attaching the SNA devices carry only SDLC frames. The serial lines connecting the routers over the WAN can transport multiple protocols as well as the STUN traffic. This capability to carry traditional SDLC traffic intermingled with routable protocols such as TCP/IP, Novell IPX, and AppleTalk enable merged networks rather than two disparate networks.

Figure 7-6
*Wide area
network
point-to-point
STUN
configuration.*

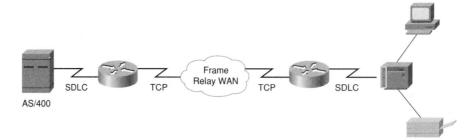

7.2.4 Virtual Multidrop/Multipoint

Traditional IBM SNA/SDLC configurations have used a single line to connect multiple locations to save money on the network design. Cisco STUN implementations allow for the connection of these multiple locations via a virtual multidrop over the routed network. Shown in Figure 7-7, the IBM front end attaches a line configured for five remote cluster controllers. The front-end router will send the SDLC frames encapsulated in TCP/IP to the remote routers over the WAN router backbone. Note that one of the remote sites is also using a line splitter to connect the cluster controllers. This configuration is often referred to as *virtual multidrop-multipoint*.

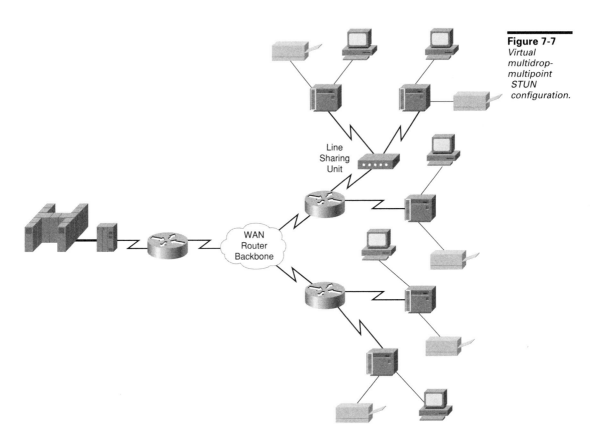

Figure 7-7
Virtual multidrop-multipoint STUN configuration.

7.2.5 Proxy Polling and Local-Acknowledgement

Part of the SNA/SDLC protocol is the capability to recognize that a resource attached to a link has disconnected or is not ready for accepting frames or has rejected frames. This "polling" in SNA is performed by SNA supervisory frames Receiver-Ready (RR), Receiver-Not-Ready (RNR), Frame Rejects (REJ). This polling occurs constantly and uses CPU cycle time and bandwidth through the router backbone network. Cisco routers reduce this overhead of polling over the WAN by using either proxy polling or local-acknowledgement.

Figure 7-8 illustrates why you should use these methods and how they affect the WAN. When using proxy polling, the router responds back to the attached SNA device for RRs, RNRs, and REJs. Cisco's STUN implementation further gains back bandwidth and CPU cycles by employing a feature that locally acknowledges the delivery of SDLC information frames (frames carrying end-user data) and supervisory frames at the router port attaching the SNA device. This feature is called local-acknowledgement. As seen in Figure 7-8, local-acknowledgement keeps the supervisory frames on the local links and only transports frames with user data over the WAN. Local-acknowledgement is used only when implementing TCP encapsulation. Analogous to NCP slowdowns, a Cisco router will send RNRs to a secondary SDLC device when the TCP queue buffers reach 90 percent full when using local-acknowledgement. Proxy polling and local-acknowledgement cannot be used at the same time. They are mutually exclusive.

Figure 7-8
Proxy polling and local-acknowledgement with STUN.

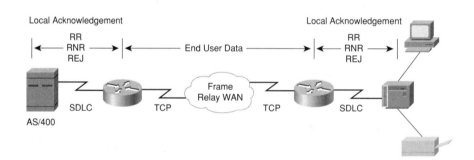

7.2.6 PU and LU prioritization

Enhancing network performance to the remote SNA devices attached to the serial links of a router can be directed at the PU and/or the LU resources. This capability allows the router to send frames destined for different cluster controllers and the LUs attached to each controller preference over other LUs specifically in a virtual multidrop configuration. As seen in Figure 7-9, this prioritization is only taking place at the remote router serial interface and does not affect the delivery of frames over the router WAN. As an example, prioritization of terminals over printers is possible, and thus diminishes the effect of print traffic on interactive terminal response time.

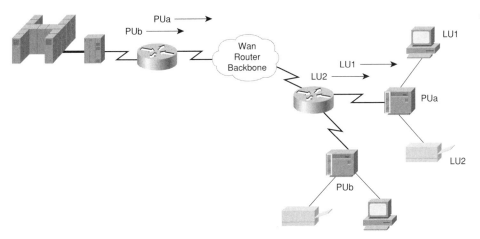

Figure 7-9
Prioritization of traffic to SNA devices on a virtual multidrop configuration.

7.2.7 SNA PU—PU Support

FEP-to-FEP connectivity through routers can also use STUN. Shown in Figure 7-10, traditional FEP-FEP connectivity may use multiple links logically defined as one and called a *transmission group (TG)*. Cisco routers using STUN can also associate the multiple serial lines attached from the FEPs into a TG by associating them with the same STUN connection that defines the STUN as an SDLC transmission group.

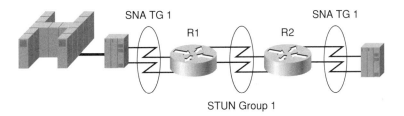

Figure 7-10
FEP-FEP TG support using STUN.

7.2.8 Class of Service

An enhanced feature of STUN when connecting FEP-FEP is the capability to use the SNA Class of Service (COS) assigned by VTAM on the IBM host computer during session establishment with the downstream PUs. The STUN router code distinguishes the COS for the SDLC frame by interpreting the COS bits, the TPF (Transmission Priority Field), found in the transmission header (TH) of the FID4 sent between the FEPs. Each frame is sent in the sequence order received to ensure proper sequence on the downstream SNA device. If a link is lost, the routers will attempt to reroute the SDLC frames over a remaining link in the TG based on sequence number and not COS. The routers have the capability to exert backward pressure on the sending SNA device by using the built-in limit of sending RNRs to the device at 90% TCP queue buffer utilization. Keeping the TCP queue buffer at 70 or higher will force more frames queued in the NCP, and thereby base delivery of frames on COS more than on sequence number.

7.3 REMOTE SOURCE-ROUTE BRIDGING (RSRB)

The advent of LANs and the requirement for workstations attached to these LANs to access mainframe applications and servers over a Token-Ring network called for a technique to send Token-Ring nonroutable traffic over a router backbone network. The LAN (in this case Token Ring) frames contain a protocol (SNA) carried directly within the MAC frames, and MAC frames cannot be dynamically routed by any dynamic routing protocol. Source-route bridging (SRB) determines the path, or route, to be used for the life of a session through the use of an exploration process. These frames use a "sourced" routing field embedded in the frame itself to determine the route to the destination device. Because these frames are not routable, they must be bridged between two segments on a LAN. This bridging between routers over serial-line connections is accomplished by using a virtual ring segment assigned to represent the LAN segment between the routers. Because the routers connected by a line are remote to each other, the technique used is Remote Source-Route Bridging (RSRB).

RSRB is nothing more than another technique to tunnel nonroutable protocols over a router backbone network. Each RSRB tunnel is treated as a virtual Token-Ring segment. The RSRB segments can be associated as a group, and can therefore have multiple connections on the same virtual Token-Ring segment. Each router participating in a RSRB ring group defines the remote routers also participating in the group as peers. As with STUN, the nonroutable frames are encapsulated into a frame that can be sent by a router to the WAN or directly to another router.

7.3.1 Direct RSRB

Direct RSRB encapsulation is very much like that used in STUN. The Token-Ring frame is placed in total into the data field of the data link frame. As depicted in Figure 7-11, the data link frame may be HDLC for serial-line connectivity, Ethernet, Token-Ring, or FDDI encapsulations. Note that direct RSRB is used only when no intermediate routers are involved with the connection. Direct encapsulation uses the least amount of CPU cycles and frame overhead because it is switching the frame from one port to another.

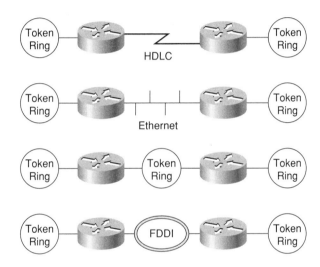

Figure 7-11
The four connectivity options for direct RSRB encapsulation.

7.3.2 TCP Encapsulation

Using TCP encapsulation for the transport of nonroutable protocols over RSRB ensures that the frames are received by the far-end device in sequential order. This ensures that the SNA session riding on this RSRB connection does not disconnect its session with VTAM because of out-of-sequence frames—a very important factor when dealing with the sensitivity of SNA and its basis on point-to-point connections. TCP encapsulation, shown in Figure 7-12, requires the frame received from the LAN be placed in the TCP segment data area. The TCP segment, including the frame received from the LAN, is placed into the data area of the IP datagram which is then finally placed in the data area field of the data link frame used for connecting the SNA device to the destination router. This encapsulation technique ensures in-sequence delivery of SNA frames, but increases CPU cycles on the router and increases frame overhead due to the TCP and IP header information required.

The increase in CPU requirement is due in part to the process of mapping an LLC session (an acknowledged and sequenced protocol) to a TCP session. The direct correlation between protocol sessions allows for resequencing and resending of frames/packets when necessary. Frame overhead can be reduced through the use of TCP header compression, which can reduce the TCP header from 20 bytes to as little as 8 bytes. Although TCP header compression reduces bandwidth requirements, it too increases CPU.

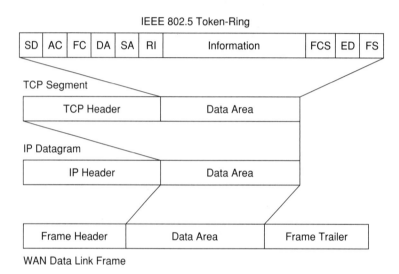

Figure 7-12
RSRB TCP encapsulation.

7.3.3 Fast Sequenced Transport (FST) Encapsulation

Cisco routers can send frames encapsulated in IP datagrams, and can thereby reduce frame overhead and CPU cycles for RSRB encapsulation. This technique is known as *Fast Sequenced Transport (FST)*. Actually, a better name for this would be Fast Out-of-Sequenced Transport. Why is this a better name? Because IP does not ensure sequenced delivery of frames. As shown in Figure 7-13, frames between the RSRB peers may arrive out of sequence and thereby cause the destination router to drop the out-of-sequenced frames; the SNA session would then disconnect. Care should be taken when employing the FST technique. FST should only be used when you can guarantee that the frames will not be received out of sequence.

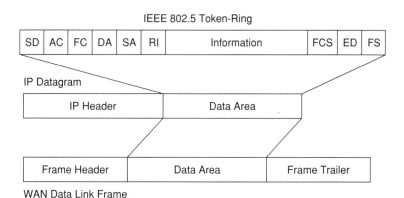

Figure 7-13
*RSRB
encapsulation
using FST.*

Currently, there are two ways to set up remote source-route bridging. One way is to encapsulate the source-route bridged traffic inside IP datagrams passed over a TCP connection between two Cisco routers. TCP is used to ensure the reliable and ordered delivery of bridged traffic. Token-Ring networks may be connected across arbitrary media. Another way is to use only a MAC layer encapsulation over a single serial line, Ethernet, Token Ring, or FDDI ring connected between two routers attached to Token-Ring networks.

FST offers a third method to set up remote source-route bridging. This method encapsulates the bridged traffic inside IP datagrams, without having a TCP connection. The reliability of bridged traffic is left to end stations to ensure because IP does not guarantee datagram delivery. Although this way does not have the flexibility of the TCP approach, it offers better performance because there is less overhead. An advantage that this way has over MAC encapsulation is that it can route IP datagrams over arbitrary networks.

To support this feature, two fields in the IP header are of significant importance: protocol and identification. The IP protocol field specifies which high-level protocol is used to create the message being carried in the data area of a datagram. Cisco's IOS software maps a unique integer value in this field to FST. Because this value is Cisco proprietary, the datagrams will only be further processed by Cisco routers upon receipt. The other vendors' routers will just route the datagrams.

The identification field contains a unique integer that identifies a datagram. Cisco's IOS software keeps a counter to increment it each time a new datagram is created, and assigns the result as the datagram's identification field. The receiving Cisco router also keeps a counter so that it knows which sequence number to expect next. If the identification field is received out of sequence, the datagram will be discarded by the router without notifying the sender or receiver. The higher-level protocol of the two communicating end stations must detect such error conditions and request retransmission. Upon retransmission, new datagrams with higher identification value are generated.

7.3.4 Virtual Ring

SRB has a restriction on the number of "hops" allowed between origin and destination resources. The IBM Token-Ring specification calls for a maximum of eight rings and seven bridges. The IEEE 802.5 Token-Ring specification allows for a maximum of 14 rings and 13 bridges. This hop limitation is due to the size of the RIF field in the LLC2 frame. Cisco allows an SRB to circumvent the hop-count restriction by implementing a virtual ring between routers that any number of routers can attach. Figure 7-14 shows the use of multiple virtual rings for connecting RSRB traffic from peer routers. The concept is quite simple: For each router, a virtual ring number is defined. Multiple virtual-ring numbers may be assigned to a router; however, customarily only one virtual ring may be assigned to a router. Although there are no limits on the number of peers associated with a virtual ring, it is best to keep the number of peers to a minimum. Router 1 in the figure has peer definitions for both Router 2 and Router 3. Only Router 1 is defined as a peer in Routers 2 and 3. Note that the two remote routers do not require peering. This is because there are no destination applications from either remote router for resources attached to each router. Peering is needed when communication between network resources occurs between routers.

Figure 7-14
Virtual-ring concept depicted for RSRB.

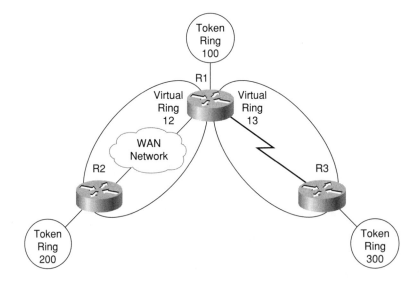

7.3.5 Proxy Explorer

For source-route bridged protocols such as SNA, an explorer packet is sent by the SNA device to discover the best route to the destination. As stations come on and off the LAN, connecting to a destination resource using an SRB protocol such as SNA, the explorer packets can cause bandwidth constraints (particularly at the beginning of the day when users power on their SNA sessions for connectivity to the mainframe). This sudden explorer burst can cause excessive delay in the network and can cause end users to repeatedly retry their connection because of timeouts on the receipt of the explorer packet. Reducing the explorer bursts on the network can be accomplished by using the proxy explorer function. Proxy explorer establishes a RIF cache in the router for all destined MAC addresses that have been used by resources attached to the router.

As shown in Figure 7-15, Device B sends out an explorer packet for connecting to the mainframe. Device A has already established a connection with the same mainframe, and, as such, the router has cached the destination MAC address from the receipt of the explorer packet sent back to Device A from the mainframe. Therefore, instead of the router forwarding the explorer packet over the WAN to discover the RIF of the route, the router responds back to Device B with the cached RIF for the destination MAC address. This process reduces explorer broadcasts over the WAN for known MAC address RIFs and reduces the response time considerably for session establishment. Proxy explorer, however, is not useful when duplicate MAC addresses are used on different front ends for connecting to the mainframe. This is because after the first requesting station receives a RIF field for the mainframe MAC address, all stations on the router will use the same RIF and thereby reduce the load-balancing effect of having active duplicate MAC addresses for mainframe connectivity.

7.3.6 Local-Acknowledgement

In STUN, we can reduce supervisory frame polling and acknowledgement of frame delivery; we can also locally acknowledge using RSRB. LLC2 frames rather than SDLC frames are acknowledged by the router, and only frames carrying end-user data between the session partners traverse the WAN links. RSRB requires TCP encapsulation to use local-acknowledgement.

7.3.7 Local LU Prioritization

RSRB allows for local LU prioritization much like that used for STUN. LAN-attached SNA PUs can have their LUs prioritized within the router. Again, this can enable you to provide better service to terminals over printers. Local LU prioritization requires the use of TCP encapsulation and local-acknowledgement. A more detailed discussion of how prioritization takes place is found in Chapter 8, "STUN Design and Configuration."

Figure 7-15
*Use of proxy
explorer on
RSRB
connections.*

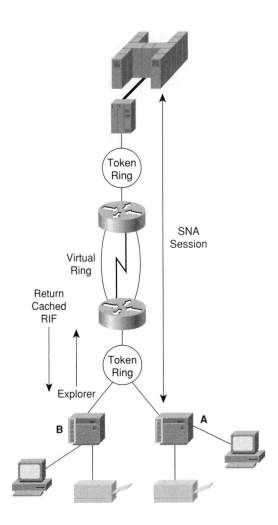

7.3.8 SNA FEP-FEP and COS Support

FEP-FEP communications using RSRB are also supported. Two Token-Ring segments attached to the same FEP may be defined in the FEP as a single transmission group. The router will treat these as a single LAN. Along with the capability to support TGs, RSRB also interprets the COS bits in the FID4 TH to determine the priority of the frame for scheduling delivery over the link. COS requires the use of TCP encapsulation and local-acknowledgement.

7.3.9 Source Route/Translational Bridging

In today's networking environment, there will be many different flavors of LAN connectivity. Some devices may be attached to Ethernet, for example, and others to Token Ring. Predominantly, you will see that the SNA host device—be it a front-end processor or an AS/400—will typically be attached using a Token-Ring LAN connection. This is not to say that this LAN connection cannot be Ethernet; it is just an assumption because IBM developed Token-Ring interfaces for these devices first. A means of delivering SRB protocols over these two different LAN architectures is required. Source Route Translational Bridging (SR/TLB) accomplishes this for you.

Take a look at Figure 7-16. This figure shows an Ethernet-attached SNA controller with connectivity requirements to a Token-Ring–attached mainframe. For the session to establish, a special bridging function must take place to bridge the Ethernet frame to a Token-Ring frame. Ethernet, by design, uses transparent bridging; Token Ring uses source-route bridging. When the frame enters the router, the router examines the frame for a RIF field. If a RIF field is present, the frame is source-route bridged. If the RIF is not present, the frame is transparently bridged. The bridging takes place using a pseudo ring defined for the transparent bridging. This pseudo ring is bridged to the virtual ring that connects the mainframe host to the network.

Another special feature employed by using the SR/TLB technique is the translation of the MAC address from Ethernet format to Token-Ring format. This translation is often referred to as *bit-flipping*. Ethernet frames place the least significant bits (LSB) first in each nibble (half byte) of a byte and reverse the byte. Token-Ring places the most significant bit (MSB) in order from left to right. These two competing forms of MAC address format are known as canonical and non-canonical. The importance of this is as follows: SNA devices that connect to the mainframe often have the destination MAC address defined for use by the explorer packets. If an Ethernet SNA device places the Token-Ring non-canonical address (MSB order) of the mainframe in the destination field, the router will translate the MAC address as an LSB to MSB address and place this address in the destination MAC field of the Token-Ring frame. This MAC address will not be found, and the Ethernet SNA device will never get a session with the mainframe. What should be placed in the Ethernet SNA device destination MAC address field is the LSB format of the Token-Ring MAC address for the mainframe.

Figure 7-16
SR/TLB
configuration
connecting an
SNA controller
to the
mainframe.

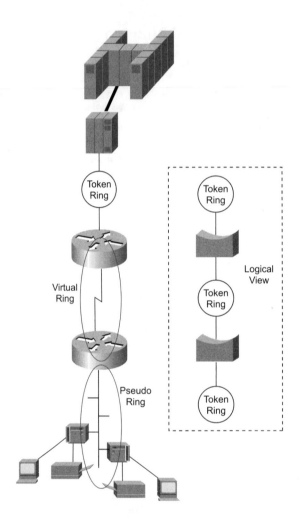

7.4 SDLC—LLC2 (SDLLC)

SNA devices serially attached to a router may also be enveloped by an LLC2 frame. Cisco employs this media translation as SDLLC. Simply put, this allows serially attached devices to a router to communicate to LAN-attached mainframe hosts. As shown in Figure 7-17, a cluster controller needs to communicate with a Token-Ring–attached front-end processor. The front end may also be Ethernet attached. In between the host and cluster controller is a router WAN backbone. Frames are transported from the remote location to the mainframe using RSRB encapsulation. Direct SDLLC is also possible through the router that is LAN attached to the FEP.

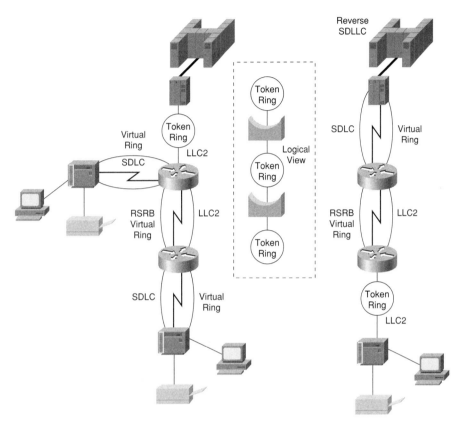

Figure 7-17
*SDLLC
connectivity
between a
cluster
controller and
a mainframe
FEP.*

The WAN backbone can be any number of WAN supported media, such as the following:

- Frame Relay
- Serial
- X.25
- FDDI
- ATM

It is also possible to use the reverse topology; in which case, the FEP is serially attached to a router and the cluster controller is LAN attached to the remote router. Connectivity between the front-end processor and the cluster controller is accomplished by mapping the SDLC information to LLC2 fields.

7.4.1 SDLC-to-LLC2 Mapping

Configuration in the remote router attached to the cluster controller defines the mapping between the SDLC frame and the LLC2 frame. The mapping is based on associating the cluster controller station address with a virtual MAC address assigned to the serial interface of the router. The serial interface of the router is associated with a virtual ring, and thus completes the LAN connectivity mapping. The station address of the cluster controller is also mapped to the exchange identification defined on the mainframe for the cluster controller. This final mapping completes the information required for making the connection. Figure 7-18 illustrates the SDLC frame information mapped to the LAN frame format.

Figure 7-18
*SDLC-to-LLC2.
configuration
and key
mappings.*

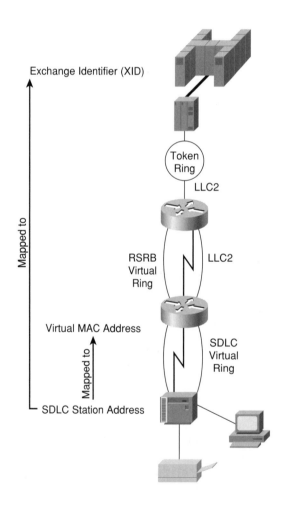

7.4.2 Virtual Ring

Again, we find virtual rings being used to connect remote SNA devices over a router WAN backbone. In this instance, shown in Figure 7-19, the serial line attached to the router is defined as a virtual Token Ring—or it may even be an Ethernet connection defined as a virtual Token Ring. The figure shows that the path for connectivity from the serially attached cluster controller to the front-end processor is using the following RIF in the LLC2 frame:

```
VirtualRing100 - Bridge1 - VirtualRing200 - Bridge1 - Ring1
```

In Figure 7-19, an Ethernet-attached cluster controller from a different remote location is also connecting to the same front-end processor. Instead of using Virtual Ring 200, it is using Virtual Ring 300. The remote routers both use the common backbone Virtual Ring 200 for connecting to the front-end Token-Ring Ring 1. The front-end router also connects a serially attached cluster controller to the front end using direct SDLLC encapsulation, using Virtual Ring 400 for the RIF sequence.

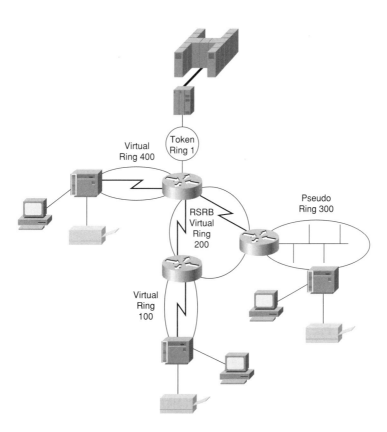

Figure 7-19
Use of virtual rings in connecting non-Token-Ring attached SNA devices.

7.4.3 Local-Acknowledgement

Acknowledging frames on the local connections and leaving the WAN for transport of end-user data are goals of all these various transport techniques. Enabling local-acknowledgement for SDLLC reduces backbone bandwidth overhead, but at the same time may incur CPU cycles and buffer use on the routers. It is not uncommon with SDLLC to see the router CPU cycles and buffer usage fluctuating when the delivery of end-user data is at a minimum due to the local-acknowledgement of frames. TCP encapsulation is required for using local-acknowledgement with SDLLC. Again, the advantages of using TCP encapsulation rather than FST for RSRB are reliable and sequenced delivery of data. Here again, we must be aware that TCP encapsulation costs frame overhead as compared to direct or FST encapsulation. Table 7.3 lists the encapsulation overhead usage with SDLLC. This table may also be used as a guideline for general overhead costs that result from these encapsulation techniques.

Table 7-3   *Encapsulation overhead usage with Direct, FST, and TCP.*

		Media header	IP header	TCP header	RSRB header
Direct Encapsulation					16
	Serial	4			
	Ethernet 802.3	22 + padding			
	Ethernet Type II	18 + padding			
	Token-Ring 802.5	Maximum 39			
	FDDI	18			
FST Encapsulation		Same as direct	20		10
TCP Encapsulation		Same as direct	20	20	16

7.5 FRAME RELAY

Support for the transport of SNA over Frame Relay is based on RFC 1490. This RFC is an end-to-end standard for defining multiprotocol over multiplexed links using a single line interface. Although many vendors say they support RFC 1490 for the transport of SNA data, be sure they adhere to the RFC 1490 extension that specifically describes the SNA encapsulation. This extension is the Frame Relay Forum document FRF.3 authored by IBM for SNA-specific encapsulation over Frame Relay. The RFC 1490/FRF.3 describes only the encapsulation technique used. Each vendor adhering to the technique applies vendor-specific algorithms for local-acknowledgement, dynamic rerouting of the SNA data, SNA prioritization, and Frame Relay Private Virtual Circuit (PVC) prioritization.

7.5.1 RSRB Direct

When using RSRB as the encapsulation and transport mechanism for SNA traffic over Frame Relay, a mapping is required. The mapping associates the Frame-Relay DLCI number for use by RSRB. Recall that RSRB requires router peers for transporting encapsulated SNA data. Figure 7-20 illustrates a configuration using RSRB as the transport for SNA data over Frame Relay.

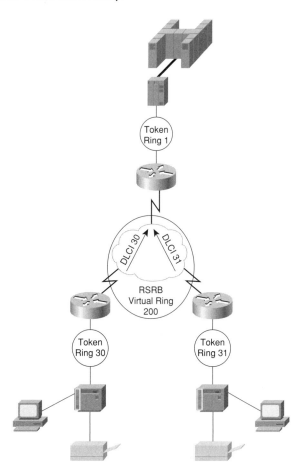

Figure 7-20
RSRB direct encapsulation over Frame Relay.

7.5.2 Boundary Network Node (BNN)

The RFC 1490/FRF.3 specification defines a means for connecting downstream SNA PUs directly to the FEP without using an intermediate Frame-Relay device. Cisco routers using LAN-attached or SDLC-attached SNA resources can send SNA data directly to the FEP without the use of a data-center–based router. This is supported by NCP V7.1 Boundary Network Node (BNN) functions. The advantage to such a configuration is the elimination of hardware and software changes at the remote locations. Using the router, these SNA devices can partake in the Frame-Relay network. Figure 7-21 illustrates a BNN connection to a mainframe front-end processor using Cisco routers at the remote location. The mapping for LAN devices is the associating of the downstream PU MAC address with the DLCI of the PVC being used for transporting the data to the FEP. SDLC-attached devices map the SNA device SDLC station address and serial port number to the Frame-Relay DLCI. The router assigns a dedicated PVC to each downstream SNA PU being connected over the Frame-Relay line. Additional PVCs may be defined in the router to support non-SNA traffic. Cisco routers can use the custom queuing techniques available to prioritize the SNA traffic over non-SNA traffic.

Figure 7-21
Boundary Network Node connectivity using Frame Relay for downstream SNA PUs.

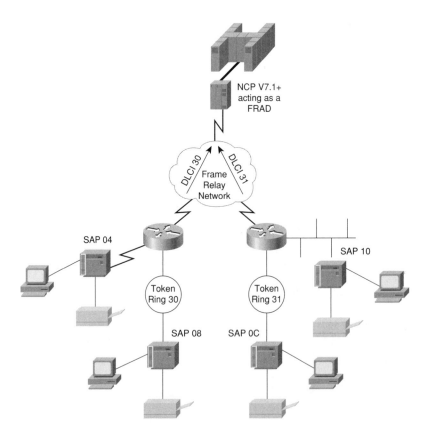

NCP V7.1 supports up to 997 concurrent PVCs on each high-speed physical link. The slow-speed scanners on the front end support up to 238 concurrent PVCs. The NCP does not associate a PU with a DLCI until the connection is active. Therefore, more than 1,000 PUs can be connectable, but not all can be active at the same time. To overcome the high cost associated with a single PVC for each downstream PU connected over Frame Relay, Cisco implements the use of service access point (SAP) addresses to multiplex multiple PUs over a single PVC connection for downstream PUs at a single location. AS/400 systems require OS/400 V2R3 or higher to accommodate the BNN functions described.

Cisco implements local-acknowledgement and custom queuing to ensure SNA service levels. Using local-acknowledgement, SNA connections will be preserved at times of network congestion. The custom queuing mechanism will provide the SNA traffic with a degree of guaranteed bandwidth for the access links between the router and the FEP.

7.5.3 Boundary Access Node (BAN)

The Boundary Access Node (BAN) function of RFC1490/FRF.3 enhances Frame-Relay connectivity directly to the FEP by including the IEEE 802.5 MAC header in every frame. This allows the mapping of unlimited SNA devices on a single Frame-Relay PVC. Using BAN reduces complex definition requirements for both VTAM/NCP and router definitions of the downstream SNA PUs by eliminating the need to use SAP addresses for multiplexing the SNA connections over a single Frame-Relay PVC. A second enhancement to using BAN is the capability to have duplicate DLCI-MAC address mappings on the FEPs for load balancing and redundancy. These functionalities require that the FEP be running NCP V7.3 or higher and the router must be using IOS 11.1 or greater. Figure 7-22 illustrates the use of BAN connectivity. Each downstream PU is mapped to a PVC. Each PVC is given a virtual MAC address that associates the DLCI to a virtual ring over the backbone Frame-Relay network. The FEPs also associate a virtual MAC address with the Frame-Relay interface.

Although both BNN and BAN accomplish SNA connectivity over Frame Relay directly to the FEP, they do have the following meaningful differences:

- At remote locations where there are no multiple SNA PU requirements, BAN does not greatly reduce router configuration over BNN. If this very same site has LAN-attached devices and their MAC address changes, however, BNN requires a router configuration change as opposed to the dynamic use of MAC addresses employed by BAN.

- BAN has more WAN overhead than BNN because of the inclusion of the MAC information in every frame.

- BNN is more efficient for SDLC-attached devices than BAN is. At locations that have both SDLC attached and LAN attached, a combination of BNN and BAN is prudent.

- BAN may require an NCP upgrade to V7.3.

- Only BAN supports load balancing and dynamic redundancy.

Figure 7-22
BAN
connectivity to
the SNA FEP.

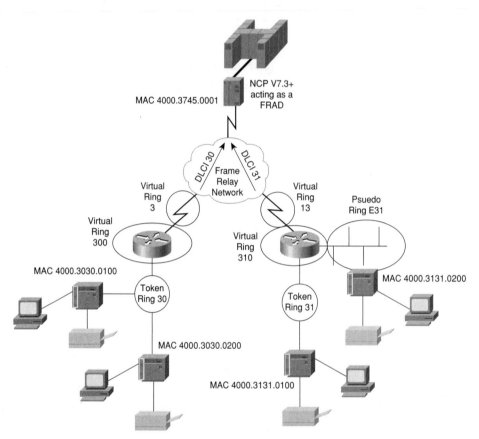

7.6 APPN

As discussed earlier, APPN is a peer-to-peer networking architecture that dynamically locates session-level partners. Along with this, APPN now dynamically defines and reroutes sessions through an APPN network without disrupting the session. These dynamics are provided by a distributed directory service with network topology mappings available on every network node in the APPN network. Cisco routers can function as an APPN network node and thereby route SNA data based on SNA Class of Service (COS) parameters.

APPN deployment must be considered carefully. APPN functionality should be used when considering the following network criteria:

- Granular transmission prioritization down to the application running on an end-user station is required.

- The majority of the network traffic is SNA based.

- The network infrastructure and skill set is primarily SNA.

- LU6.2 applications are being deployed for SNA client/server business solutions between mainframes, AS/400s, and SNA emulated on UNIX servers.

- Peer-to-peer SNA routing is required between SNA hosts without mainframe connectivity—for example, AS/400–AS/400 connectivity over the common enterprisewide network infrastructure.

- VTAM V4R1 or higher is being implemented or in use.

7.6.1 Cisco Strategic APPN Direction

Cisco is the dominant platform for implementing APPN through multiprotocol internetworks. As such, Cisco has committed to providing APPN solutions for internetworks around the world. The strategy for Cisco APPN is as follows:

- Availability on the following hardware platforms: 2500, 4x00, 70x0, 75xx

- APPN support over multiple media types: T1/T3, ATM, Frame Relay, SMDS, SONET

- Legacy SNA device support using DLUR/DLUS

- High Performance Routing (HPR)

- Direct mainframe connectivity through channel-attached routers

- Guaranteed service levels for applications through the use of protocol prioritization and custom queuing

Cisco's implementation of APPN is not derived from reverse engineering. Cisco has licensed the APPN code for implementation in their routers, and thus ensure interoperability to non-Cisco APPN network nodes. Cisco has committed to continued support and enhancing the APPN networking architecture and functionality.

7.6.2 HPR Support

High-performance routing is APPN's second generation of routing protocol. Using HPR, SNA APPN sessions can be rerouted over the backbone network without disruption to the SNA session. HPR support includes the following:

- Reduced processing at intermediate nodes by moving the error processing, flow control, and segmentation to end node

- Nondisruptive rerouting of data due to path failures

- Use of Adaptive Rate-Based (ARB) flow control providing an optimal method for high-bandwidth environments

HPR support on Cisco routers is found in IOS V11.3. Figure 7-23 illustrates the use of Cisco routers in an APPN HPR network.

Figure 7-23
APPN HPR with Cisco routers.

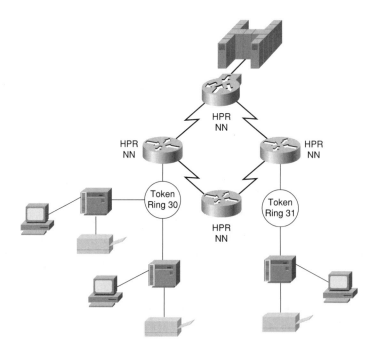

7.6.3 DLUR/DLUS Support

Support for transporting legacy SNA traffic over APPN is implemented on Cisco routers by using Dependent LU Requestor (DLUR) in concert with VTAM V4R2 or higher implementing Dependent LU Server (DLUS) function. The support on VTAM V4R2 or higher is also referred to as Session Services Extension. Using DLUS and DLUR legacy, SNA devices attached to a router implementing DLUR can have their session and data transported over an APPN HPR network and thereby gain all the advantages of a dynamic transport. Figure 7-24 diagrams a DLUR/DLUS connection supporting legacy SNA PU devices. Note that there is no need for the legacy SNA PU to have an owning VTAM (SSCP-PU) session to enable LU-LU sessions. This function is emulated by the DLUR feature defined on the Cisco router.

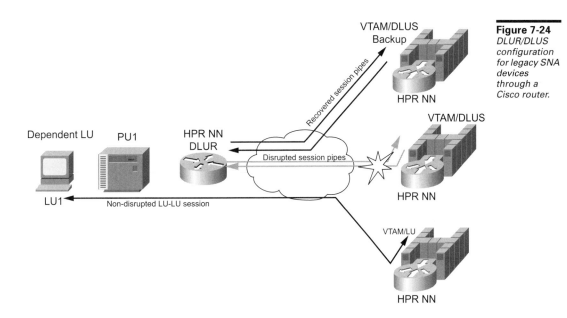

Figure 7-24
DLUR/DLUS configuration for legacy SNA devices through a Cisco router.

7.7 DATA LINK SWITCHING (DLSW)

IBM defined DLSw when introducing the IBM 6611 router as a means of transporting SNA and NetBIOS traffic across TCP/IP-based backbone networks. The definition was submitted by IBM to become a standard and was accepted as RFC 1434. This first incarnation of DLSw included TCP encapsulation with local-acknowledgement for transporting data. RFC 1434 also overcame the hop limits of source-route bridging by massaging the RIF field of the packet to emulate one hop to the destination.

Since RFC 1434, a second RFC that makes RFC 1434 obsolete was introduced and accepted. RFC 1795 enhances DLSw by including prioritization of packets and terminating the RIF field at the virtual ring. Termination of the RIF at each router's virtual ring allows the RIF to extend to its fullest implementation of 7 hops or 13 hops (IEEE 802.5) on the downstream side of the router. Finally, RFC 1795 enabled the DLSw partners to exchange information for divulging the capabilities of each DLSw partner, alleviating configuration errors.

A third iteration of DLSw has been introduced by Cisco into the RFC standards. This iteration enables DLSw networks to scale into large networks, provides enhanced availability, reduces configuration requirements, and increases performance through custom queuing and load balancing. This iteration is commonly called DLSw+. Table 7-4 lists the functional comparisons of RSRB and DLSw versions.

7.7.1 DLSw+ Modes of Operation

At the outset of DLSw+, it was imperative that it be compatible with RSRB. Cisco IOS Release 11.0 supports both RSRB and DLSw+ concurrently. A main reason for this compatibility is to allow large RSRB networks to methodically migrate to DLSw+. The peers used in the connections must be configured as either RSRB or DLSw+ peers. For DLSw+ to be compatible with RSRB, the peer is defined as an RSRB peer. This allows DLSw+ to use the RSRB peers as well as RSRB to function.

Using the capabilities exchange feature of DLSw+ allows the Cisco router to detect whether the peer is using DLSw+ or is a DLSw router. If the capabilities exchange indicates that the peer is a non-DLSw+ peer, the Cisco router using DLSw+ will communicate in the RFC 1795 standard mode of operation with that peer. However, enhanced features of DLSw+ are still allowed for the locally controlled options. These enhanced options are location learning, explorer firewalls, and media conversion. If the peer indicates that it indeed supports DLSw+, the router will operate in enhanced mode for DLSw traffic supporting all the features of DLSw+. Cisco DLSw+ routers will not interoperate with routers using RFC 1434 DLSw.

Table 7-4 *DLSw and RSRB compared.*

	Feature	RSRB	RFC1434	RFC1795	DLSw+
Transport	TCP with local acknowledgement	•	•	•	•
	FST	•			•
	Direct	•			•
Performance	Custom queuing	•			•
	Prioritization	•		•	•
	Load Balancing	•			•
Administrative	Capabilities exchange			•	•
	Peer Costs				•
	Dynamic Peers				•
	Ring Lists				•
Scalability	Caching	•			•
	Hop reduction	Passthru	•	Terminates	Terminates
	Peer/border groups				•
	On-demand peers				•
	Broadcast firewall				•
Availability	Local termination	Optional	Required	Required	Optional
	Backup peers				•
	Directed verify				•
Management	Standard MIB/per circuit management			•	•

7.7.2 DLSw+ Scalability

RSRB and the RFC 1434 version of DLSw had a scalability problem in large SNA networks. The scaling problem was due to the fully meshed networking environment requirement of these techniques. By using DLSw+ enhanced feature sets, very large DLSw networks are possible. This is accomplished by using the following:

- *Peer groups and border peers* optimize transmission of DLSw explorers (CANUREACH and NAMEQUERY frames) by ensuring that duplicate frames are not sent over the same link. Peer groups address the replication of broadcasts in a fully meshed network. A group of routers is defined into a peer group. One or more routers are defined as the border peer for the group. When explorer packets are generated within the group, only the border sends the explorer to the other peer group. This eliminates the multiple broadcasts that would be found in a fully meshed network. Figure 7-25 diagrams the peer group and use of border peers.

Figure 7-25
Peer group and border peer DLSw+ topology.

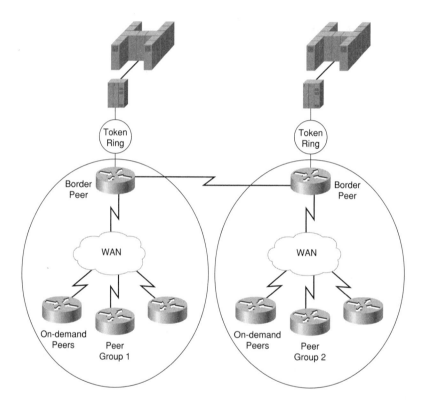

- *On-demand peers* can be used to establish DLSw+ sessions with peers that have not been configured in the requesting routers. This dynamic DLSw+ session enables casual and any-to-any connections without preconfiguring the peers in advance. These casual connections reduce the configuration requirements in the routers. Session establishment takes longer, however; therefore, on-demand peering may be a preferred configuration for use with casual connections.

- *Explorer firewalls* reduce the broadcasts realized in an SNA or NetBIOS network across the WAN by sending only one broadcast message for each destination MAC address or NetBIOS name. These broadcasts are most prevalent at the start of the day when SNA devices are searching for the MAC address of the mainframe front-end processor or SNA gateway. Any duplicate requests for broadcasts that have already been sent across the WAN are cached. Upon receipt of the response to the explorer at the originating DLSw+ peer, all cached explorer requestors are sent an immediate response.

- *Border Peer caching* allows DLSw+ peers to cache destinations found on the first explorer frame for the destination. Using this method, broadcast traffic is further reduced through the border peers preserving bandwidth and reducing replicated explorers from the border peers. Subsequent explorers for cached partners are forwarded to the cached address instead of using a broadcast.

- *Multiple bridge groups* allow the definition of more than one bridge group associated with a physical Ethernet segment. This makes it possible to transport Ethernet traffic to multiple segments over the LAN segregated by bridge groups.

7.7.3 DLSw+ Availability

Cisco's DLSw+ enhances availability of SNA networks by caching multiple paths for a discovered MAC address or NetBIOS name. Multiple paths are very useful in an SNA network that employs the use of duplicate MAC addresses for connection to the main-frame. In mainframe lingo, this is often referred to as duplicate Token-Ring Interface Coupler (TIC) addressing. The TIC is the LAN interface from the IBM front-end pro-cessor (FEP). DLSw+ will cache the duplicate TIC path as long as more than one DLSw+ peer can be used to reach the FEP. This availability feature is called Border Peer caching.

The cached paths are categorized as preferred or capable. The preferred peer is usually the peer that first responded positivly to the initial explorer frame. This can be overrid-den, however, if a peer cached in the table has a lower cost than the first responder. If the preferred peer becomes unavailable, the next capable peer becomes the new pre-ferred peer for connections to the cached destination. Using this methodology, rapid reconnects are possible without additional broadcast traffic. This technique is therefore designed to support a fault-tolerant topology.

7.7.4 DLSw+ Performance

The RFC 1795 DLSw standard supports only TCP for transporting between DLSw routers. In DLSw+, the following traditional encapsulation techniques used by Cisco for all other SNA solutions are possible:

- TCP encapsulation across WANs. This is primarily used when bandwidth is a premium and termination of data-link control sessions is mandatory. TCP encapsulation is also a requirement when DLSw+ routers are to operate in RFC 1795 compliance mode.

- Fast Sequenced Transport (FST) encapsulation over the WAN where ample bandwidth is available to ensure the delivery of the frames in a timely sequenced order.

- Encapsulating directly into the data link frame format used on point-to-point connections. This encapsulation will provide the least-intensive router resources, but will restrict the available configurations for fault tolerance and load balancing.

In fact, load balancing is achieved using Border Peer caching by distributing the traffic between destination points using the capable router cache table in a round-robin technique. This will load balance the network traffic, and thereby improve SNA performance to the mainframe or SNA gateway.

SNA Class of Service (COS) is the foundation for performance in a pure SNA or APPN network. Router priority queuing provides link scheduler prioritization, but does not carry the priority over the intermediate WAN routers. DLSw+ enables COS functionality with a feature called SNA Type of Service (SNA TOS). Using SNA COS, the DLSw+ sets the IP precedence bits in the IP header to high or by building multiple pipes for different priorities and setting each one to a different priority. If APPN is transported over DLSw+, SNA TOS can use weighted fair queuing to reduce response time for the APN sessions by ensuring DLSw+ bandwidth. This prioritizes DLSw+ traffic while characteristically ensuring APPN COS over the WAN. Table 7-5 lists the IP precedence bits mapped to the SNA COS.

Table 7-5 *IP precedence mapping for SNA COS in DLSw+ SNA TOS.*

TCP Ports	Priority Queue Level	IP Precedence APPN Value	IP Precedence DLSw+ Value
2065	High	Network	Network control
1981	Medium	High	Internetwork control
1982	Normal	Medium	Critical
1983	Low	Low	Flash override

DLSw+ uses the Network Control IP precedence value as the default when priority queuing is not specified on the DLSw+ definition. Configuring priority queuing indicates to DLSw+ that the four TCP ports used for connectivity to the remote peer are assigned traffic based on the table listed in Table 7-6.

Table 7-6 *DLSw+ priority assignment to TCP ports.*

TCP Ports	DLSw+ Queue Priority	Type of Traffic (default)
2065	High	Circuit administration frames
		Peer keepalives
		Capabilities exchange
1981	Medium	None
1982	Normal	Information frames
1983	Low	Broadcast traffic

Port 2065 is the default port when not configuring priority queuing. The TOS settings are modifiable by the use of policy routing features applied to the TCP ports. Caveats specific to using the SNA TOS feature include the following:

- Mapping of APPN COS to IP TOS is only viable when both DLSw+ and APPN are operating in the same router and the priority keyword is specified on the remote peer statement.

- The SNA TOS functions only when using TCP or FST encapsulation types.

- If using FST encapsulation, all DLSw+ traffic is marked as IP precedence "network."

7.7.5 Compared to RSRB

In RSRB networks, the RIF is passed through the WAN, providing full RIF visibility at any point in the connection. Although this is an advantage for troubleshooting using tools such as a SNIFFER, it limits the size of the connection to the 7 or 13 hop limit depending on which standard is being implemented for RSRB. Using a terminated configuration—like that used with DLSw+, shown in Figure 7-26—the RIF ends at the virtual-ring number attaching the routers. This allows the network to scale better than RSRB, providing the full 7 or 13 hop-count limit on the end-user side of the routers involved. The downfall to termination is the inability to view the entire RIF used for the complete connection using trace analysis tools such as Network Associates SNIFFER.

Figure 7-26
RSRB RIF passthrough compared to terminating the RIF.

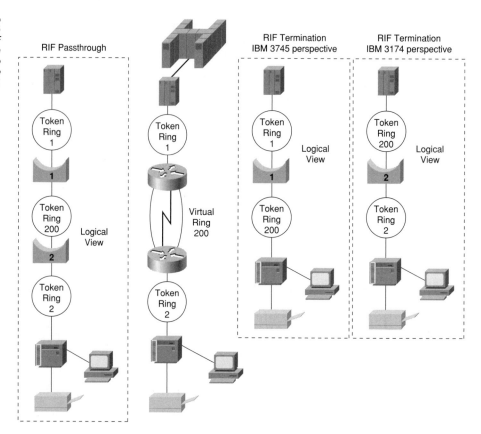

The two encapsulation techniques for reliably transporting SNA data have the following features in common:

- TCP, FST, and direct encapsulation
- FST and direct for Token Ring-to-Token Ring only

- Access-list filtering on LAN and WAN

- WAN prioritization and custom queuing

RSRB has some features not found in DLSw+, however. These as the follows:

- FST and direct encapsulation for SDLLC

- DLC passthrough for TCP encapsulations

- End-to-end RIF passthrough

7.8 NATIVE CLIENT INTERFACE ARCHITECTURE (NCIA)

NCIA is an implementation of an encapsulation technique that begins at the end-user workstation. SNA frames, for the most part, are sent from the station to an SNA gateway using Novell IPX or NetBIOS for the delivery mechanism. From the server, the data is then sent to the IBM mainframe as a pure SNA frame. NCIA is a software architecture that describes the delivery from the end station to a server using TCP/IP encapsulation. Using TCP/IP as the encapsulation technique on the end station is an important factor when considering the expense of supporting multiple protocols on the end station in software costs and memory required for implementing multiple protocol stacks. Using TCP/IP allows flexible use of multiprotocol networks for SNA enterprises.

NCIA has been implemented in two phases. The first phase, NCIA I, solely used Cisco RSRB encapsulation for transporting the SNA-encapsulated data to the mainframe host. The second phase, recently introduced, uses a client/server model and allows either RSRB or DLSw as a transport mechanism to the mainframe.

7.8.1 NCIA Phase I

As with all Cisco SNA encapsulation techniques, and NCIA I is no exception, a virtual ring is used to set up the connection. As shown in Figure 7-27, a virtual ring is associated with all the end-station segments connected to the router. This allows NCIA to view all the end-station connections as if they are on the same Token-Ring segment. Associating multiple LAN segments connected to the router as a virtual ring constitutes a ring group. Using NCIA, a ring group number is assigned to designate the ring number for use in the RIF for bridging. The ring number assigned must be unique to the entire network.

An end station using NCIA I acts like an RSRB router and an end station. A virtual ring number and virtual bridge number specific to this end station are defined at the end station. These "fake" ring and bridge numbers are used by the RSRB router and the NCIA station. In addition, LLC2 is required for establishing LLC2 sessions.

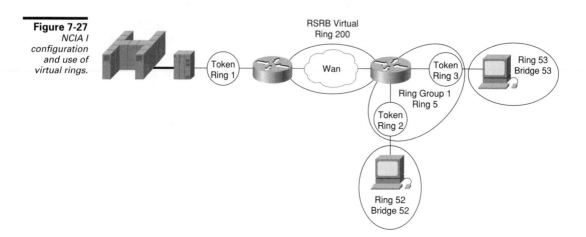

Figure 7-27
NCIA I configuration and use of virtual rings.

7.8.2 NCIA Client/Server Model

Enhancements to NCIA I resulted in the client/server model for NCIA. These enhancements allow NCIA client/server to be installed on RSRB and DLSw+ networks. Cisco has based NCIA client/server on RFC 2114 Data Link Switch Access Protocol. Configuration and functionality enhancements include the following:

- No "fake" ring and bridge numbers need be defined on the client.

- The requirement to define each NCIA station on the router is removed.

- The MAC address used for the connection may be dynamically defined by the NCIA server.

- SNA is encapsulated directly into TCP/IP without the LLC2 frame at the end station.

- NCIA server interacts with RSRB APPN, DLSw+, and DSPU components.

- End station supports unsolicited (connect-in) and solicited (connect-out) session establishment. From a server perspective, the reverse is true: The end station supports solicited (connect-in) and unsolicited (connect-out) session establishment.

- Server model is independent of upstream topology.

- End station is no longer considered a router peer.

- NCIA uses efficient NCIA Data Link Control (NDLC) protocol for communicating with the server.

7.8.3 NCIA Client/Server Model Architecture

The NCIA client must first establish a TCP-to-NDLC session for sending and receiving data. NCIA server uses the Cisco Link Services Interface (CLSI) for communication to and from NDLC and other components such as APPN, DLSw+, and DSPU. Figure 7-28 diagrams the NCIA usage of CLSI. NDLC is used for establishing the peer connection between the client and the server and is used for supporting the end-to-end circuit connection between the client and its destination partner.

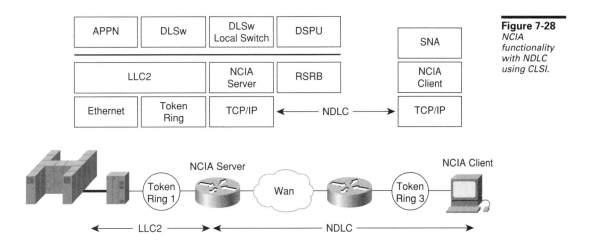

Figure 7-28
NCIA functionality with NDLC using CLSI.

The NCIA server is actually functioning as a data-link provider, much like Token Ring and Ethernet do in the router. NCIA server can interface directly with APPN, DLSw+, and DPSU as long as they are configured on the router. For all other types on data-link providers, Ethernet, Token Ring, ATM, FDDI, Frame Relay, and Channel, the NCIA server must employ the services of DLSw+ locally on the router.

Before an SNA end station can establish an end-to-end circuit with the mainframe, it must create a session with the NCIA server. The peer session associates the client MAC address with the peer session. The client can provide the MAC address. The NCIA server provides the MAC address should the client not have one. After providing a MAC address, a client can initialize sessions using NCIA server connect-in functions. NCIA connect-out functions will only work if the registered client has not disconnected its peer session and is listening for incoming connection requests. Session requests with explorers containing registered MAC addresses will immediately be delivered to clients with established peer sessions. Clients without peer sessions will automatically be connected to the NCIA server as long as the client is in listening mode. The NCIA server sends keepalive messages on the peer session only to determine the presence of active clients. The NCIA server establishes a circuit between the client and server and then the server and destination partner to establish the end-to-end circuit.

The use of NCIA greatly extends the scalability of a RSRB or DLSw+ network. NCIA clients are defined on the host as SNA PUs, and therefore each must have a peer connection to a central site router—also known as the data-center router. Using NCIA server, these clients attach locally and then a single peer connection is used for connecting to the central site router. As an example, 500 clients attaching to four NCIA servers would only require four peer connections on the central site router. Note that the central site router must still maintain connectivity to the mainframe and therefore respond to mainframe data traffic. However, NCIA can use Downstream Physical Unit (DSPU) functions of SNA to minimize the number of polls and supervisory frames that will traverse the connection.

7.9 DOWNSTREAM PHYSICAL UNIT (DSPU)

Cisco routers can concentrate multiple downstream SNA PUs attached to the router using SNA Downstream Physical Unit (DSPU) features. The PU concentration is represented to the VTAM as a single PU, and thus simplifies VTAM definitions while providing flexibility at the remote location. The router defines the downstream PUs, isolating the mainframe host from remote topology changes. The representation of one PU for multiple PUs by the router also assists in reducing network traffic over the WAN. Figure 7-29 illustrates the use of DSPU on a Cisco router.

Each DSPU representation on a Cisco router can handle up to 1,024 physical units with each physical unit supporting a maximum of 255 logical units. The router defines the upstream PU representing the DSPU on VTAM and each downstream PU connected. The LUs defined in the router representing the DSPU LUs may be dedicated or pooled. Dedicated LUs require careful mapping so that each LU on activation consistently receives the same SNA configuration parameters as before. Pooled LUs are assigned sequentially as LUs become active to the router.

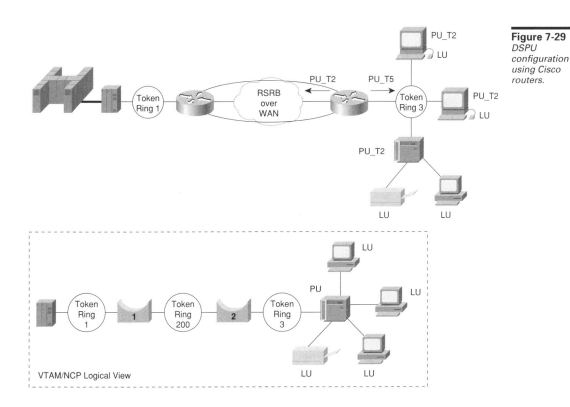

Figure 7-29
DSPU configuration using Cisco routers.

7.9.1 SNA PU Type 5 Services

The DSPU router emulates the SSCP functions of an SNA PU Type 5 node when communicating with the downstream PUs. Viewing the connection from an SNA perspective, the router appears to the mainframe host as an SNA PU Type 2 node and to the downstream PUs as an SNA PU Type 5. Assuming SSCP functionality, the router assumes all the SSCP-PU and SSCP-LU functions between the router and the downstream SNA resources. These SSCP-PU and SSCP-LU sessions are established between the router and the downstream resources independently of the SSCP-PU session connecting the router to the mainframe host computer. The DSPU feature of Cisco routers uses a routing algorithm that maps the downstream LUs to the upstream LUs.

7.9.2 Supported Data-Link Controls

DSPU supports the majority of data-link controls available on Cisco routers. These include the following:

- Token Ring
- Ethernet
- FDDI
- X.25
- DLSw+
- RSRB
- VDLC
- SDLC

7.9.3 SNA Service Point Support

Support for the SNA Service Point function enables the router to be managed by IBM's NetView or Sterling Software's Solve:NetMaster SNA network-management products. Using this feature, NetView can receive alerts about connection problems or disconnects from downstream LUs and PUs attached to the router. In turn, an operator on NetView can issue commands to the Cisco router using the SNA Service Point RUNCMD function specifying Cisco commands for displaying router information. This is a very helpful tool for a predominantly SNA network operations center with responsibility for managing the SNA devices attached to Cisco routers.

7.10 CHANNEL INTERFACE PROCESSOR (CIP)

The Cisco CIP was first introduced in 1994, and has been growing since its introduction. The first CIP was later superseded by the second generation CIP. The Cisco Channel Interface Processor-2 (also referred to as CIP) provides direct LAN device access to the mainframe through a Cisco 7000 or 7500 series router. The CIP uses mainframe fiber-optic Enterprise System Connection (ESCON), and bus-and-tag Parallel Channel Adapter (PCA) support. Using this connectivity, the Cisco router with a CIP interface can replace all the functions of an IBM 3172 Interconnect Controller, enabling complete mainframe application communication to LAN-attached workstations. It also replaces many of the functions of the FEP. The CIP interface card can provide two ESCON or PCA interfaces or one ESCON and one PCA or a combination of both on a single card. This flexibility allows for varied configurations and also provides for an easy migration to ESCON from PCA.

7.10.1 CIP Overview

The CIP is for use on the Cisco 7000 and 7500 series routers. Its sibling—the Channel Port Adapter (CPA)—is available on the Cisco 7200 series routers. Each establish connections in various ways to the mainframe. Shown in Figure 7-30, the CIP may use multiple or single subchannels for communicating to the mainframe. When using Cisco Systems Network Architecture (CSNA) functions for transporting SNA data to the mainframe, the CIP uses a single half-duplex subchannel. This subchannel can only send or receive at any given time. CSNA cannot concurrently send and receive. When connecting to the mainframe for TCP/IP traffic, the CIP will use an even/odd pair of subchannel addresses—the even numbered subchannel for sending to the mainframe and the odd numbered subchannel for receiving data from the mainframe. Using Cisco MPC (CMPC) for connecting APPN nodes using HPR to the mainframe, the CIP will allocate a pair of subchannels for each adjacent SNA node connecting to the mainframe.

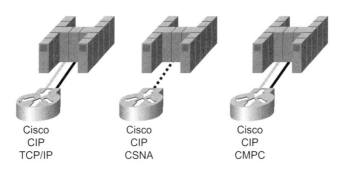

Figure 7-30
CIP subchannel allocations to the IBM mainframe.

Cisco CIP TCP/IP

Cisco CIP CSNA

Cisco CIP CMPC

Read Channel
Write Channel
Read/Write Channel

7.10.2 Capabilities and Functions

The CIP and associated router software can provide the following many different flavors of communications to the mainframe:

- TCP/IP using CLAW

- TCP/IP Offload

- SNA Connectivity

- TN3270 Server for SNA Connectivity

7.10.2.1 TCP/IP Using CLAW

Common Link Access to Workstation (CLAW) channel protocol is used to provide a dedicated pair of even/odd channel unit addresses for sending and receiving data traffic to the mainframe. This protocol supports the entire TCP/IP suite of applications including terminal emulation (Telnet), File Transfer Protocol (FTP), Simple Mail Transfer Protocol (SMTP), Network File System (NFS), Domain Name System (DNS), Internet Control Message Protocol (ICMP), and User Datagram Protocol (UDP). The CLAW protocol is used to communicate to the host TCP/IP applications such as IBM's TCP/IP for MVS, Interlink's TCP/Access, and Cisco's IOS for S/390. Figure 7-31 illustrates the use of a CIP router for connecting TCP/IP traffic to the mainframe.

Figure 7-31
TCP/IP mainframe connectivity using Cisco CIP connectivity.

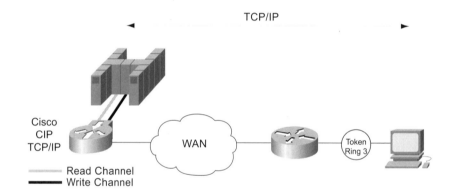

CLAW supports 256 concurrent addressable devices and 128 concurrent connections per interface adapter. The number of IP connections through the router to the mainframe is unlimited. The limit for these connections depends on the capabilities of the TCP/IP application residing on the mainframe.

7.10.2.2 TCP Offload

This feature moves the responsibility of interpreting each IP packet for its destination to the router, and thereby reduces TCP mainframe cycle overhead. The TCP Offload facility requires definitions on the TCP application residing on the mainframe as well as the router. This feature uses CLAW protocol in support of this function. The host TCP/IP application will still remain on the host, and the CIP will offload the TCP processing using the standard APIs provided by the host.

7.10.2.3 SNA Connectivity

The majority of connectivity to an IBM mainframe uses IBM's Systems Network Architecture (SNA) protocol. The CIP interface card provides a robust set of features and functions to facilitate this communication. This feature of the CIP is known as Cisco SNA (CSNA) and Cisco Multipath Channel (CMPC). Figure 7-32 diagrams the use of CSNA and CMPC for SNA connectivity. CSNA supports all the traditional SNA connections: PU Type 2.0, PU Type 2.1 (dependent) connectivity, as well as downstream PU connections and Advanced Peer-to-Peer Network (APPN) communications. CMPC functionality enhances the availability and throughput of the CIP along with the traditional SNA feature support. Support for SNA through the CIP to applications residing on the mainframe requires CIP router definitions and Virtual Telecommunications Access Method (VTAM) definitions on the mainframe. The CIP supports the following maximums for mainframe and SNA connectivity:

- Maximum number of concurrent channel-attached hosts is 64.

- Maximum number of internal LANs is 32.

- Maximum number of internal adapters is 32.

- Maximum number of opened SAPs is 256.

- Maximum number of LLC2 sessions is 4,000.

NOTES

Recent updates to VTAM allow it to support upwards of 1.6 million SNA elements. The Cisco CIP has no restriction on SNA elements, and will support as many as VTAM supports.

7.10.2.4 TN3270 Server for SNA Connectivity

The function of TN3270 Server is to maintain the 3270 applications and 3270 data stream requirements that exist on many mainframes while at the same time providing IP connectivity to the client's desktop. TN3270 Server meets both these requirements by acting as the gateway that translates the user's IP address into an SNA LU and then passes the user through to the host.

Figure 7-32
*CIP CSNA and
CMPC
connectivity to
the mainframe.*

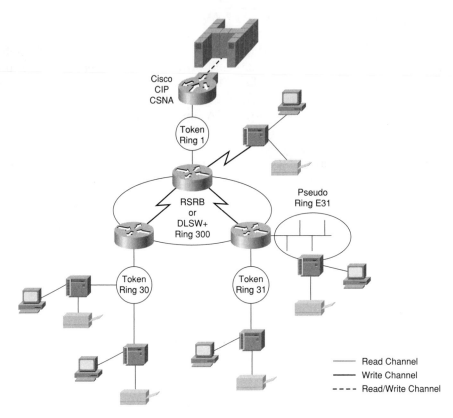

Figure 7-32 *CIP CSNA and CMPC connectivity to the mainframe.*

7.10.2.4.1 SNA Features of TN3270 Server

The TN3270 Server function of the CIP appears to the mainframe host VTAM as an SNA physical unit supporting up to 255 logical units. Multiple TN3270 PUs are supported. The logical units (LUs) supported are LU types 1, 2, and 3. The current architected limitation is 30,000 LUs. From the SNA VTAM perspective, these devices are pure SNA resources.

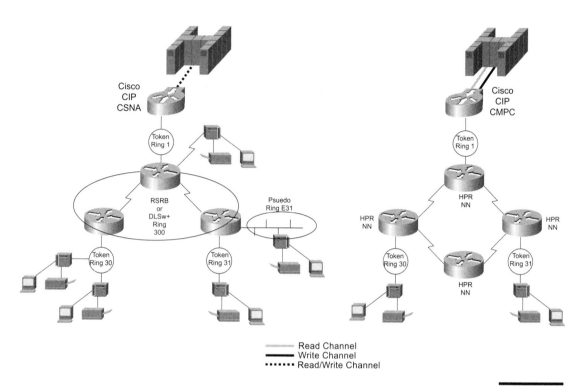

Read Channel
Write Channel
Read/Write Channel

Figure 7-32
Continued

The TN3270 Server also supports dependent LUs with the capability to implement end-node dependent LU requestor (DLUR) services. DLUR with TN3270 Server enables the CIP to switch the SNA sessions to the appropriate VTAM host using APPN links to the primary LUs on the hosts directly instead of using SNA sub-area routing to the destination. This feature is optional to support APPN functions to levels lower than VTAM V4.2.

7.10.2.4.2 Telnet 3270 Functions

Recent tests indicate the TN3270 Server supports up to 30,000 concurrent Telnet sessions. The CIP TN3270 Server supports TN3270 client access using Telnet negotiation and data format for traditional TN3270 (RFC 1576) and TN3270E (RFC 1647), extended TN3270 function where the client specifies then LU characteristics.

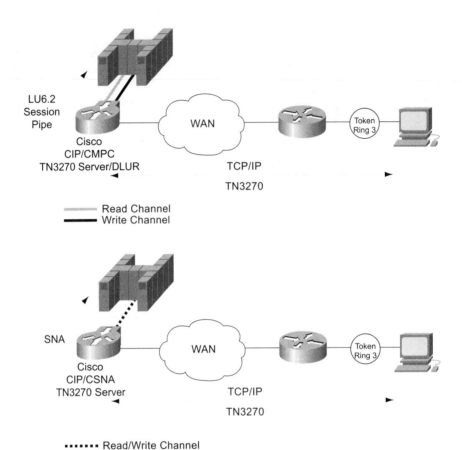

Figure 7-33
*CIP TN3270
Server
connectivity
scenario to the
mainframe.*

The architected value of supporting 30,000 concurrent Telnet sessions is not a viable real-world solution. In such a situation, where extremely large numbers of TN3270 connections are required to the mainframe through the CIP, it is best to divide the connections over two or more routers. In this way, if each router were defined to support 30,000 TN3270 connections, the other could provide a level of backup for a reasonable amount of time during an outage on one of the CIP routers.

Further availability to the mainframe is accomplished by utilizing the mainframe's capability to parallel process. In this configuration, a single CIP interface using ESCON can be actively attached to all the logical partitions (LPARs) defined on the mainframe. Figure 7-34 illustrates a single ESCON CIP connection to four LPARs on a mainframe.

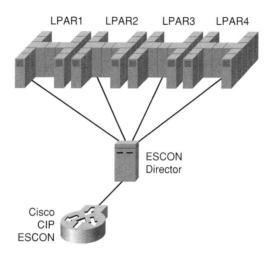

Figure 7-34
CIP configuration in a parallel sysplex mainframe environment.

The high availability is actually the capability of the IBM ESCON Director and the CIP microcode residing on the router to determine which LPAR is being addressed on the subchannel. A future release of VTAM will include a feature called Multi-Node Persistent Session (MNPS). This feature will enable mainframe applications (that is, CICS) to dynamically take over processing of sessions from a downed CICS region on one of the other LPARs. This feature, along with the CIP's capability to communicate to all LPARs concurrently, provides for a very effective, high-availability, fault-tolerant configuration.

PART II

Implementation

CHAPTER 8

STUN Design and Configuration

STUN is the basic encapsulation technique for transmitting SDLC-connected SNA devices to an IBM SNA host computer. STUN enables a single network to carry both SNA data and multiprotocol LAN data across a WAN.

Figure 8-1 illustrates the advantage of using STUN for combining the two networks into one. The SDLC frames may be encapsulated using direct HDLC encapsulation, TCP, and Frame Relay. All SDLC traffic is passed through the WAN over the STUN connection, including all supervisory and control frames between the end SNA devices.

Figure 8-1
*Traditional
SNA and
non-SNA
networks with
and without
STUN.*

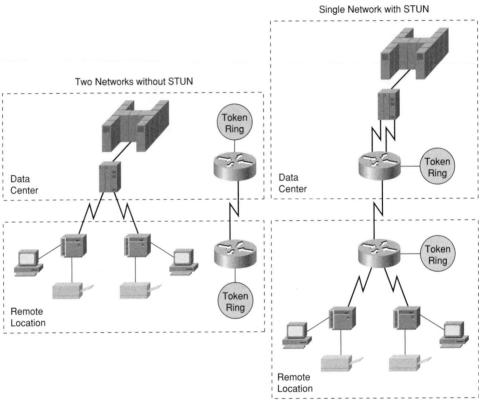

8.1 DESIGN CRITERIA

Connecting STUN to a Cisco router platform is possible for many of the different router flavors available. STUN can be used to connect SNA PU Type 1, 2, 4, and 5. For STUN networks, a list of answers must be obtained prior to configuring the routers. The design criteria for STUN involves the following:

- Evaluating the current SDLC network configuration

- Understanding the current configurations defined for the SDLC-attached devices as specified in VTAM and NCP

- Identifying which IBM router-based services apply to your configuration

- Possible NCP changes due to IBM features used in the router

- Possible end-station controller configuration changes

8.1.1 Evaluating the Current SDLC Network Configuration

In evaluating the current SNA SDLC network configuration, it is important to understand not only the topology of the network, but also how the different types of SNA devices specify their connections to the network. The following are some of the criteria for understanding the current network configuration:

- What types of host controllers are used to connect to the downstream SNA devices?

  Host controllers may be IBM 3745, IBM 3172, IBM 3174, IBM AS/400, or IBM ES/9000.

- What are the end-station controllers connecting to the host?

  End-station controllers may be IBM 3274/3174, IBM 5395/5494, SNA gateways, or PCs with serial lines.

- How are the end stations connecting to the host location?

  Does the end-station controller connect to the network using Token Ring or Ethernet, while the host connects using SDLC?

  Does the host connect using Token Ring or Ethernet, and the end station use SDLC?

  Do both the host and end station use SDLC?

- What is the serial line configuration?

  Determine the line speed of the attached SDLC devices.

  Identify the serial interface types used—that is, V.24, RS-232, V.35, or X.21.

  Is the line a multipoint connection through a public telephone network?

  Is the end-station site using a multipoint connection by virtue of a modem-sharing or line-sharing device?

  Determine the type of modem or data service unit/channel service unit (DSU/CSU) being used.

  Does the line use half-duplex or full-duplex signaling?

  Does the equipment on the line employ Non-Return to Zero (NRZ) or Non-Return-to-Zero Inversion (NRZI) line encoding?

- Determine current performance and planned performance considerations.

  Monitor and record the current line utilization.

  Monitor and record the current response time for the critical applications, specifically during peak load periods.

Identify character traffic patterns.

Determine the number of end-station PUs to be supported.

How many PUs are attached to a multipoint line, if there are any?

How many PUs are planned for the future?

How many LUs does each PU service?

How many LUs are planned for each PU in the future?

What type of traffic is supported by each LU—that is, interactive terminal or batch print?

Diagram the network topology.

8.1.2 Current SDLC Configuration Definitions in VTAM and NCP

In this part of design criteria, the network designer must get a complete understanding of how VTAM and NCP represent the remote SNA devices. This information may be gathered from the following:

- The VTAM major node definitions for the devices

- The NCP GROUP, LINE, PU, and LU definition statements

- The SNA device configuration parameters

8.1.3 Identify IBM Services Used in the Routers

The various encapsulation techniques and delivery of the data will make a difference in the definition of the SNA resources and their performance. Some of the criteria to be considered include the following:

- Full-duplex transmission for multipoint configurations

- The use of half-duplex or full-duplex signaling on the SDLC line

- Prioritization of PUs and LUs for enhanced performance

- Local acknowledgement

- Encapsulation techniques: direct HDLC, TCP, and Frame Relay

8.1.4 VTAM and NCP Changes Needed to Support IBM Features on Routers

In support of some of the IBM features employed on the router, VTAM and NCP definitions may need reconfiguration. Some of these features include the following:

- Point-to-point SDLC lines may need reconfiguration to multipoint

- PU prioritization requires a change on the station address of the PU in VTAM/NCP.

- The Token Ring or Ethernet T1 timer must be increased to support delays in the network if local acknowledgement is not enabled.

- The NCP Retries parameter should be adjusted for longer retry sequences.

8.1.5 End-Station Controller Configuration Changes

In deciding on how to implement STUN, try to avoid having to make changes on the remote controllers whenever possible. If changes are to be made, they are usually due to some of the following factors:

- End-station controller PU address change due to virtual multidrop function on the router.

- End-station controller PU address change due to PU prioritization in the router.

- NRZ versus NRZI is defined on the router due to the interface being used.

- The use of full-duplex signaling versus half-duplex signaling for controller connectivity may need analysis.

8.2 DESIGN EXAMPLES

The examples shown in the following sections have been chosen to represent the most-often-seen types of STUN configurations. For the most part, STUN is the least-preferred configuration for encapsulating SNA/SDLC traffic. In some instances, however, STUN may not be avoided when implementing a multiprotocol network. The first example, connecting an SNA PU Type 1 controller to an AS/400, is such an instance.

8.2.1 SNA PU Type 1 Connection to AS/400

In the sample configuration diagrammed in Figure 8-2, we find PU Type 1 controllers requiring connectivity to an AS/400 host. The PUa is directly attached to R1, which connects to the AS/400 serial port. PUb connects to remote router R2, which connects to R1 over a serial-line connection.

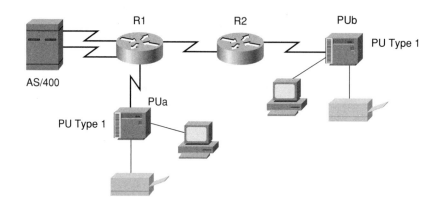

Figure 8-2
PU Type 1 connectivity to AS/400 using STUN.

8.2.2 SNA PU Type 2 Connection to AS/400

Figure 8-3 illustrates a multipoint PU Type 2 STUN connection to the AS/400. Here we see two types of multipoint connection. Remote router R2 has a direct attached 5494 controller and two 5494 controllers connected to a second serial port using a line-sharing device. This type of configuration is a multipoint, virtual-multidrop configuration.

8.2.3 SNA PU Type 2 Connection to FEP

In the configuration shown in Figure 8-4, we find that PU Type 2 devices connect to an IBM 3745 through a serial line attached to a Cisco router named R1. R1 connects to two remote routers, R2 and R3. The IBM 3174 controller attached to R2 requires more service than the controller attached to R3. The terminal LU1 on the IBM 3174 controller attached to R3 requires a higher level of service than the printer LU LU2. Figure 8-4 also includes a topology using the Cisco CIP for connecting SNA/SDLC devices to the mainframe.

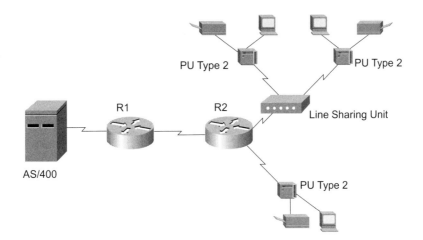

Figure 8-3
A multipoint PU Type 2 connection to an AS/400.

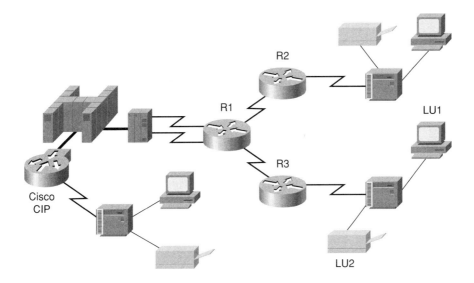

Figure 8-4
PU Type 2 connectivity using STUN virtual multidrop with prioritization.

8.2.4 SNA PU Type 4 – PU Type 4 Connection

In this configuration, two IBM 3745 controllers are communicating over a router WAN. The multiple lines connecting the 3745s to the routers constitute an SNA INN transmission group (TG). The configuration illustrated in Figure 8-5 uses STUN as the delivery mechanism supporting INN TGs.

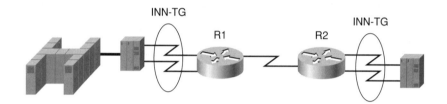

Figure 8-5
IBM 3745-3745 using INN TGs over STUN between two Cisco routers.

8.3 ENABLING STUN

Defining STUN on a router is accomplished using a global router command. This command is not associated with any particular interface. It specifies that the feature is available to any interface on the router. The command is entered as follows:

```
stun peer-name ip-address
```

The `ip-address` value used for the `stun peer-name` global command specifies the IP address this router will use to establish STUN connections with the other routers in the network.

NOTES

To ensure the IP address selected is always available, it is best to use a loopback interface IP address. Using this address, especially when having more than one serial link to the WAN, will guarantee STUN peer connections even if LAN interfaces go inactive.

To remove STUN support on a router, enter the : `no stun peer-name` *ip-address* global command. If `stun peer-name` is not specified, it is disabled.

After the `stun peer-name` is defined, the following commands must be specified to complete STUN configurations:

1. Define a protocol group that will be associated with a specific interface.

2. Specify `stun` encapsulation on the interface.

3. Associate the interface with a specific `stun` group.

8.3.1 Defining STUN Protocol Groups

STUN protocol groups restrict STUN packets from being delivered to the wrong peers. Transport of STUN packets occurs only between STUN interfaces defined in the same stun protocol group. The following four types of STUN groups can be specified:

- Basic

- SDLC

- SDLC transmission group

- Schema

The format of the `stun protocol-group` command is this:

```
stun protocol-group group-number frame-format
```

The `stun protocol-group` is a global command that identifies the group by a number ranging from 1–255 for the *group-number* parameter. The type of frame format used for transmitting frames on the stun group is defined by the *frame-format* parameter, which can be one of the following:

- `basic`

- `schema`

- `sdlc`

- `sdlc sdlc-tg`

The basic value for *frame-format* allows the STUN transport to default to the frame format used by default for the serial link associated with this group. A value of `basic` usually indicates the use of HDLC or some other non-SDLC protocol.

The value `schema` is used for defining a unique protocol to use for the STUN group.

When using STUN for SNA connectivity of PU Type 1 or PU Type 2 SNA nodes, the value of sdlc is used for the *frame-format* parameter.

If connecting IBM 3745-type controllers (SNA PU Type 4 nodes), the sdlc sdlc-tg value is used to indicate FID. Type 4 processing is required on the STUN connection. The STUN connections used in an SNA transmission group must use the same IP address peers. The sdlc sdlc-tg frame format requires the use of SNA local acknowledgement. Local acknowledgement is enabled using the stun route address tcp command. Specifying, the sdlc frame-format negates the use of the stun route all command on the associated interface. Including no in front of the stun protocol-group command disables the command, which is the default if never specified.

8.3.2 Specify stun Encapsulation on the Interface

The serial interface that has been chosen for supporting STUN connections must be defined to use STUN. This is done with the interface command encapsulation stun specified for the serial interface. After encapsulation stun is defined on a serial interface, it can only serve as a multiprotocol link if one of the following encapsulation techniques is used:

- HDLC without local acknowledgement
- TCP without local acknowledgement
- TCP with SDLC local acknowledgment and priority queuing
- Local acknowledgment for direct Frame Relay

8.3.3 Associate the Interface with a Specific STUN Group

The final step in enabling STUN on a router is to associate the SDLC link connecting the SNA device to the router with a stun group. The command for this association is this:

```
stun group group-number
```

The group-number parameter must match a global stun group. As with the other commands, prefacing no in front of the stun group group-number command disables the mapping from the interface.

8.4 DEFINE SDLC BROADCAST

SDLC broadcasts are sent by the IBM host to end-station controllers. The hexadecimal value FF is the broadcast PU station address used by all SNA PUs. To enable the capability of a host router to broadcast the hexadecimal FF to all remote STUN peers, the following interface command is used:

```
sdlc virtual-multidrop
```

The `sdlc virtual-multidrop` interface command is specified on the serial link attaching to the host computer. This serial interface is often referred to as the *SNA secondary link station.*

To allow the host router to forward the hexadecimal FF PU address to the remote STUN peers, the `stun route address tcp` interface command must be specified on the host serial interfaces that connect to the remote STUN peer routers and on the remote router serial interfaces that attach to the end-station SNA devices. The format of the `stun route address tcp` interface command is as follows:

stun route address *address-number* tcp *ip-address* [local-ack] [priority] [tcp-queue-max *value*]

The `stun address tcp` interface command enables TCP encapsulation of the SDLC frame received on the serial interface; may optionally use SDLC local acknowledgement for STUN. The `address-number` parameter is the hexadecimal value of the SNA PU station address. The `ip-address` parameter defines the IP address of the remote STUN peer using TCP encapsulation for STUN. The optional parameters are as follows:

- `local-ack` enables SDLC local acknowledgement for the STUN connection.

- `priority` establishes the use of the four priority queues: low, medium, normal, and high.

- `tcp-queue-max` optional parameter specifies the maximum size of the outbound TCP queue on the SDLC link. The default for the `tcp-queue-max` value is 100.

8.5 SPECIFY ENCAPSULATION METHOD

The encapsulation techniques mentioned earlier enable the serial link used for STUN connections to also transport multiple protocols over the same link. The three encapsulation techniques—direct HDLC, TCP, and Frame Relay—have features specific to their usage.

8.5.1 Direct HDLC

Recall the earlier discussion that HDLC encapsulation is used only when a dedicated point-to-point link exists between the two routers participating in the STUN connection or when the same router is used as the connection. Direct HDLC encapsulation can be defined using the following four different formats of the stun route interface command:

```
stun route all interface serial number

stun route all interface serial number direct

stun route address address-number interface serial number

stun route address address-number interface serial number direct
```

The stun route all interface serial number interface command is specified for the serial interface connecting to another appropriately configured router at the other end of the serial line. The number parameter value is the interface number of the outbound serial link used for forwarding the SDLC frames.

When the command is specified as stun route all interface serial number direct, the direct keyword indicates that this router is routing the SDLC traffic internally without sending the frame out of the router to another router.

Using the stun route address address-number interface serial number interface command on the outgoing serial link forwards all SDLC frames for the specified SNA PU station address defined by the address-number parameter value using the serial interface identified by the number value. Adding the direct keyword to the end of this command indicates to the router that the STUN connection is made without sending the data to a remote router.

8.5.2 TCP

Using TCP encapsulation enables you to provide prioritization and SDLC local acknowledgement of SDLC frames sent to a STUN peer. Encapsulation in TCP facilitates the transmission of SDLC frames across a disparate medium, and is useful when transmitting the SDLC frames with STUN over a multiprotocol WAN backbone. Two forms of the stun route command can be used to encapsulate SDLC frames in TCP. These interface command forms are as follows:

```
stun route all tcp ip-address

stun route address address-number tcp ip-address [local-ack] [priority] [tcp-queue-max value]
```

stun router all tcp commands the router to forward all STUN traffic to the specified ip-address value in the command. The ip-address value is the IP address of the remote STUN peer connected to the serial interface over the WAN. Note here that the SNA PU station address is irrelevant for forwarding to the STUN peer. All SDLC frames, regardless of the SNA PU station address, are forwarded to the STUN peer specified by the ip-address value.

The second form of the TCP encapsulation interface command for STUN identifies the exact SN PU station address with the *address-number* value and also identifies which STUN peer, specified by the *ip-address* value, connects to the SNA device involved in the STUN connection. The `priority` and `local-ack` keywords are discussed in the sections "Local Acknowledgment" and "Define Prioritization."

8.5.3 Frame Relay

STUN using direct Frame-Relay encapsulation is made possible by using the following interface command:

```
stun route address sdlc-addr interface frame-relay-port dlci number localsap local-ack
```

Frame-Relay encapsulation with STUN must be used with local acknowledgement. The *sdlc-addr* value is the SNA PU station address found at the remote end of the Frame-Relay connection. The interface connecting to the Frame-Relay connection is specified by the *frame-relay-port* value, which identifies the serial port on the router.

Frame Relay has virtual connections on a single link. Each virtual connection, called *permanent virtual circuits* (PVC), is identified by a number. The number is the *Data Link Control Identifier* (DLCI). Mapping the STUN connection to a DLCI is accomplished by specifying the *number* value after the `dlci` keyword. Each end-to-end connection will use a Local Service Access Point (LSAP) port for transmitting the encapsulated SDLC frame over the DLCI. The *localsap* value defines the SAP number in use for this SNA controller.

Finally, the `local-ack` keyword is required for Frame-Relay encapsulation. This ensures that the far-end SNA devices will not time out their SNA sessions due to delays in the Frame-Relay network.

8.5.4 Local Acknowledgment

Preserving valuable WAN bandwidth is always a goal for network design. *Local acknowledgement* allows the routers to respond to far-end SNA devices attached to the router, reducing the chatter created by SNA polls found in SNA/SDLC networks. These supervisory control frames are the following:

- Receiver Ready (RR)

- Receiver-Not-Ready (RNR)

- Reject (REJ)

Local acknowledgement actually terminates the SNA session at the router serial interface ports instead of at the SNA far-end devices. Enabling local acknowledgement is accomplished through adding the local-ack keyword on the following interface commands:

```
stun route address sdlc-addr interface frame-relay-port dlci number localsap local-ack
```

```
stun route address address-number tcp ip-address [local-ack] [priority] [tcp-queue-max value]
```

Establishing local acknowledgement requires the SDLC interfaces on the router to participate as either a SNA primary or secondary link station. A primary SNA link station sends and receives supervisory SDLC frames to the PU Type 1 or PU Type 2 SNA controller. A secondary SNA link station receives and sends supervisory SDLC frames to SNA PU Type 4 or PU Type 5 resource.

Figure 8-6 illustrates the use of a SDLC STUN connection through routers connecting an IBM 3745 and an IBM 3174 controller. The router attached to the IBM 3745 acts as a secondary link station, and the router attaching to the IBM 3174 acts as a primary link station. This link station role allows the routers to locally acknowledge the SNA supervisory frames. The rule is this: Attaching a router to a PU Type 4 or PU Type 5 results in the router acting as a secondary link station. Routers attaching to a PU Type 1 or PU Type 2 perform the function of a primary link station.

Figure 8-6
Primary and secondary link station assignments for a STUN connection.

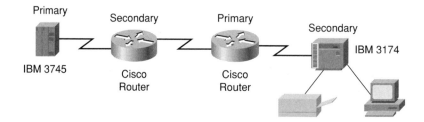

Specifying the primary or secondary link station role is accomplished by entering one of the appropriate interface commands for the SDLC interface that connects to the SNA device:

```
stun sdlc-role primary
```

```
stun sdlc-role secondary
```

Use the stun sdlc-role primary command on the SDLC interface of the router connecting SNA PU Type 1 or PU Type 2 devices. The router in primary mode will poll the devices in the order they are defined on the interface. When the router acts as a secondary link station, it will send back any outgoing data it may have to the primary link station (that is, IBM 3745). The outbound data is sent based on first-in first-out (FIFO), or based on the prioritization assigned to the PU or LU associated with the frame.

8.6 DEFINE PRIORITIZATION

Prioritization of PUs and LUs is possible by including the `priority` keyword on the `stun route address tcp` interface command. When `priority` is specified, the router uses up to four levels of priority for the TCP-encapsulated SDLC frame. The `priority` keyword must be used in conjunction with the `local-ack` keyword. The `priority` keyword affects the priority of outgoing TCP frames on the serial interfaces. The four priority levels are as follows:

- Low
- Medium
- Normal
- High

Priority queuing can be assigned to the serial interface address or TCP port and LU addresses.

8.6.1 Serial Link Prioritization

Serial link prioritization is most useful when prioritizing individual SNA SDLC station addresses for the PUs attached to the serial connection. STUN traffic may be prioritized for serial interfaces by specifying the SNA SDLC station address along with the TCP port number associated with the priority level. Prioritization on the serial link allows traffic destined for a specific PU to be prioritized over another PU, especially on a multidrop connection.

The format of the global configuration commands for establishing prioritization on the serial links are as follows:

```
priority-list list-number stun queue address group-number address-number

priority-list list-number protocol ip queue tcp tcp-port-number
```

Using the priority-list stun address *list-number* value specifies a number ranging from 1–10, identifying the priority list being defined. The *queue* parameter specifies the type of queue being defined for the priority definition. The possible values for queue are high, medium, normal, and low. The *group-number* parameter value identifies the stun group associated with this priority definition. Finally, the address-number is the SNA SDLC station address being assigned the priority.

The priority-list stun address command must be defined prior to using the priority-list protocol ip tcp global command. The *list-number* and *queue* parameter values have identical meanings to the priority-list stun address command. The *tcp-port-number* parameter of the priority-list stun address command allows the assignment of a priority list to a TCP port defined for a queuing priority. In support of SDLC traffic, the *tcp-port-number* assignments are as follows:

- STUN port 1994 - High priority
- STUN port 1990 - Medium priority
- STUN port 1991 - Normal priority
- STUN port 1992 - Low priority

The default priority for all traffic on an interface is normal (FIFO queuing). When using these two priority-list commands together, the STUN traffic receives the highest service of all traffic out of the serial interface using the defined priority-list.

The priority-list is specified for a serial interface by including the priority-group interface command when configuring the definition for the serial interface. The format of the command is as follows:

```
priority-group list-number
```

The *list-number* parameter of the priority-group interface command identifies which priority-list to apply to the traffic traversing the interface.

8.6.2 Local LU Prioritization

Further prioritization of SNA traffic to the LU is possible through *local LU prioritization commands*. Use of these command LUs on a point-to-point or even a multidrop connection can result in higher priority for transmission than other LUs. Prioritization of LUs is possible for both STUN and SRB configurations. This is important for connections that support both interactive and print traffic. Using the local LU prioritization feature allows interactive traffic to take precedence over print traffic. We use the following locaddr-priority-list command:

```
locaddr-priority-list list-number address-number queue-keyword
```

The `list-number` parameter value identifies the `locaddr-priority-list` being defined. The `address-number` is the LU's address on the SNA PU to which the LU is owned. The LU address is obtained from the `LOCADDR` operand on the LU macro definition of the PU definition statement in the NCP configuration or the VTAM major node describing the PU. The value is a 1-byte hexadecimal value in the range of 01-FF.

The `queue-keyword` is the type of priority this LU is to receive. The `queue-keyword` may be valued as high, medium, normal, or low.

The `locaddr-priority-list` must be associated with the serial interface that attaches the end-to-end connection. This association is through the interface command `locaddr-priority`, with the following format:

```
locaddr-priority list-number
```

The `list-number` parameter is the number associated with the predefined `locaddr-priority-list` global command. Using this sets up the queuing policies for the LUs connected to this serial link.

8.7 DEFINE MULTILINK TRANSMISSION GROUP

Multilink transmission groups are multiple physical lines connecting two IBM 3745 communications controllers as a single logical connection. As noted earlier, the `stun protocol-group sdlc-tg global` command defines the use of SNA transmission groups. Using `sdlc-tg` allows multilink transmission groups to be collapsed on a single WAN link.

The STUN connections used for setting up the transmission group must be using local acknowledgement. This will ensure that the SDLC supervisory traffic remains local to the SDLC line connection, and thereby ensure available bandwidth for the delivery of data between the front ends. Each serial interface used for the STUN connection must use the same STUN peer address, mapping the one-to-one relationship between the multiple TGs and the WAN link connecting the routers.

8.7.1 Design Considerations

Several factors influence the implementation of connecting IBM 3745s using STUN in a multilink TG configuration. These design considerations include the following:

- The WAN link connecting the routers used for the end-to-end PU Type 4-to-PU Type 4 session must be larger than the aggregate bandwidth of the multiple SDLC serial line connections of the router connecting to the IBM 3745s. If the WAN link is also being used for multiprotocol traffic, the bandwidth should be at least double the aggregate SDLC bandwidth requirement.

- It is advisable to not use a configuration where one link of an SNA TG is connected through the routers, and the other is connected directly between the IBM 3745s. The routed TG frames may not arrive in the expected time allowed and may cause SNA session outages. It is best to keep all your multilink TG connections using routers directly connected on a point-to-point connection. This will provide a higher level of reliable transport.

- Customers frequently come to grief over INN SDLC addresses. Each direction has a different SDLC address because of the echo defeat support. The address is dynamically generated and is an internal address. It was introduced in 1985 for 3705 and 3725 by providing Program Temporary Fixes; this code was incorporated with NCP V4R2. During the contact phase, NCP will use its SDLC address; after the NCP is contacted, NCP will use a specific address from range of 01 to 7E in order of line generation in an NCP. If this is the sixth line, for instance, NCP will use 06 for primary and 86 for secondary. The FEP with the highest sub-area address becomes the primary link statoin. Therefore, the router on that side must be set up to behave as a secondary link station.

8.8 STUN CONFIGURATION EXAMPLES

Now that we have discussed the essential commands for defining STUN functionality on Cisco routers, let's look at some configuration scenarios.

8.8.1 SNA PU Type 1 Connection to AS/400

In the sample configuration shown in Figure 8-7, we find PU Type 1 controllers requiring connectivity to an AS/400 host. The PUa is directly attached to R1, which connects to the AS/400 serial port. PUa connects to a remote router R2, which connects to R1 over a serial-line connection.

This configuration shows the use of the initial STUN commands:

```
stun protocol-group

stun group

stun peer-name

encapsulation stun
```

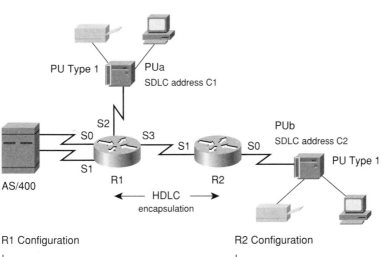

Figure 8-7
*Cisco router
configuration
for a PU Type 1
connecting to
an AS/400
using STUN.*

R1 Configuration

!
stun protocol-group 2 sdlc
stun protocol-group 3 sdlc
!
interface serial 0
encapsulation stun
stun group 2
stun route address C1 interface serial 2 direct
!
interface serial 1
encapsulation stun
stun group 3
stun route address C2 interface serial 3
!
interface serial 2
encapsulation stun
stun group 2
stun route address C1 interface serial 0 direct
!
interface serial 3
no shutdown

R2 Configuration

!
stun protocol-group 3 sdlc
!
interface serial 0
encapsulation stun
stun group 3
stun route address C2 interface serial 1
!
interface serial 1
no shutdown

8.8.2 SNA PU Type 2 Connection to AS/400

Figure 8-8 illustrates a multipoint PU Type 2 STUN connection to the AS/400. Here we see two types of multipoint connection. Remote router R2 has a direct-attached 5494 controller, and two 5494 controllers connected to a second serial port using a line-sharing device. This type of configuration is a multipoint, virtual-multidrop configuration.

This configuration emphasizes the use of the following commands:

```
stun route address tcp

priority-group

priority-group list
```

Figure 8-8
*Cisco router
configuration
for a multipoint
PU Type 2
connection to
an AS/400 with
STUN.*

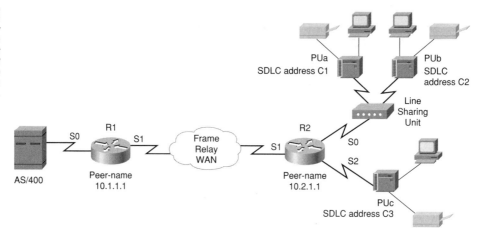

R1 Configuration

```
stun peer-name 10.1.1.1
stun protocol-group 1 sdlc
!
interface loopback 0
ip address 10.1.1.1 255.255.0.0
!
interface serial 0
encapsulation stun
stun group 1
stun route address C1 tcp 10.2.1.1 local-ack
stun route address C2 tcp 10.2.1.1 local-ack
stun route address C3 tcp 10.2.1.1 local-ack
stun sdlc-role secondary
sdlc address C1
sdlc address C2
sdlc address C3
!
interface serial 1
ip address 10.4.1.1 255.255.0.0
encapsulation frame-relay
frame-relay lmi-type Annex D
frame-relay map ip 10.4.1.2 30 broadcast
```

R2 Configuration

```
stun peer-name 10.2.1.1
stun protocol-group 1 sdlc
!
interface loopback 0
ip address 10.2.1.1 255.255.0.0
!
interface serial 0
encapsulation stun
stun group 1
stun route address C1 tcp 10.1.1.1 local-ack
stun route address C2 tcp 10.1.1.1 local-ack
stun route address C3 tcp 10.1.1.1 local-ack
stun sdlc-role primary
sdlc address C1
sdlc address C2
sdlc address C3
!
interface serial 1
ip address 10.4.1.2 255.255.0.0
encapsulation frame-relay
frame-relay lmi-type Annex D
frame-relay map ip 10.4.1.1 30 broadcast
!
interface serial 2
encapsulation stun
stun group 1
stun route address C3 tcp 10.1.1.1 local-ack
stun sdlc-role primary
sdlc address C3
```

8.8.3 SNA PU Type 2 Connection to FEP

In the configuration shown in Figure 8-9, we find that PU Type 2 devices connect to an IBM 3745 through a serial-line attached to a Cisco router named R1. R1 connects to two remote routers, R2 and R3. The IBM 3174 controller attached to R2 requires more service than the controller attached to R3. The terminal LU1 on the IBM 3174 controller attached to R3 requires a higher level of service than the printer LU LU2. The Cisco IOS configuration uses the following STUN commands:

```
sdlc virtual-multidrop

stun route address tcp

locaddr- priority

locaddr- priority-list

priority-group

priority-group list
```

8.8.4 SNA PU Type 4 – PU Type 4 Connection

The configuration illustrated in Figure 8-10 uses STUN as the delivery mechanism supporting INN TGs. Specifying TG support is accomplished by using the stun proto-col-group sdlc sdlc-tg global command.

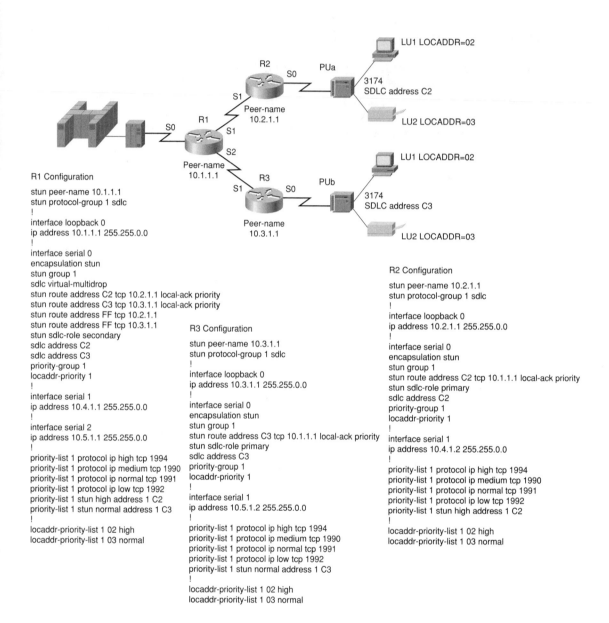

R1 Configuration

stun peer-name 10.1.1.1
stun protocol-group 1 sdlc
!
interface loopback 0
ip address 10.1.1.1 255.255.0.0
!
interface serial 0
encapsulation stun
stun group 1
sdlc virtual-multidrop
stun route address C2 tcp 10.2.1.1 local-ack priority
stun route address C3 tcp 10.3.1.1 local-ack priority
stun route address FF tcp 10.2.1.1
stun route address FF tcp 10.3.1.1
stun sdlc-role secondary
sdlc address C2
sdlc address C3
priority-group 1
locaddr-priority 1
!
interface serial 1
ip address 10.4.1.1 255.255.0.0
!
interface serial 2
ip address 10.5.1.1 255.255.0.0
!
priority-list 1 protocol ip high tcp 1994
priority-list 1 protocol ip medium tcp 1990
priority-list 1 protocol ip normal tcp 1991
priority-list 1 protocol ip low tcp 1992
priority-list 1 stun high address 1 C2
priority-list 1 stun normal address 1 C3
!
locaddr-priority-list 1 02 high
locaddr-priority-list 1 03 normal

R3 Configuration

stun peer-name 10.3.1.1
stun protocol-group 1 sdlc
!
interface loopback 0
ip address 10.3.1.1 255.255.0.0
!
interface serial 0
encapsulation stun
stun group 1
stun route address C3 tcp 10.1.1.1 local-ack priority
stun sdlc-role primary
sdlc address C3
priority-group 1
locaddr-priority 1
!
interface serial 1
ip address 10.5.1.2 255.255.0.0
!
priority-list 1 protocol ip high tcp 1994
priority-list 1 protocol ip medium tcp 1990
priority-list 1 protocol ip normal tcp 1991
priority-list 1 protocol ip low tcp 1992
priority-list 1 stun normal address 1 C3
!
locaddr-priority-list 1 02 high
locaddr-priority-list 1 03 normal

R2 Configuration

stun peer-name 10.2.1.1
stun protocol-group 1 sdlc
!
interface loopback 0
ip address 10.2.1.1 255.255.0.0
!
interface serial 0
encapsulation stun
stun group 1
stun route address C2 tcp 10.1.1.1 local-ack priority
stun sdlc-role primary
sdlc address C2
priority-group 1
locaddr-priority 1
!
interface serial 1
ip address 10.4.1.2 255.255.0.0
!
priority-list 1 protocol ip high tcp 1994
priority-list 1 protocol ip medium tcp 1990
priority-list 1 protocol ip normal tcp 1991
priority-list 1 protocol ip low tcp 1992
priority-list 1 stun high address 1 C2
!
locaddr-priority-list 1 02 high
locaddr-priority-list 1 03 normal

Figure 8-9
*Cisco router configuration for
a PU Type 2 connection using
a STUN virtual multidrop with
prioritization.*

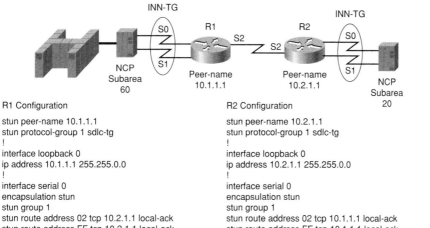

Figure 8-10
*A Cisco router
configuration
supporting
IBM 3745-3745
using INN TGs
over STUN.*

R1 Configuration

stun peer-name 10.1.1.1
stun protocol-group 1 sdlc-tg
!
interface loopback 0
ip address 10.1.1.1 255.255.0.0
!
interface serial 0
encapsulation stun
stun group 1
stun route address 02 tcp 10.2.1.1 local-ack
stun route address FF tcp 10.2.1.1 local-ack
! NCP with higher subarea is primary link station for TG
stun sdlc-role secondary
sdlc address 02
sdlc address FF
!
interface serial 1
encapsulation stun
stun group 1
stun route address 04 tcp 10.2.1.1 local-ack
stun route address FF tcp 10.2.1.1 local-ack
! NCP with higher subarea is primary link station for TG
stun sdlc-role secondary
sdlc address 04
sdlc address FF
!
interface serial 2
ip address 10.3.1.1 255.255.0.0

R2 Configuration

stun peer-name 10.2.1.1
stun protocol-group 1 sdlc-tg
!
interface loopback 0
ip address 10.2.1.1 255.255.0.0
!
interface serial 0
encapsulation stun
stun group 1
stun route address 02 tcp 10.1.1.1 local-ack
stun route address FF tcp 10.1.1.1 local-ack
! NCP with higher subarea is primary link station for TG
stun sdlc-role primary
sdlc address 02
sdlc address FF
!
interface serial 1
encapsulation stun
stun group 1
stun route address 04 tcp 10.1.1.1 local-ack
stun route address FF tcp 10.1.1.1 local-ack
! NCP with higher subarea is primary link station for TG
stun sdlc-role primary
sdlc address 04
sdlc address FF
!
interface serial 2
ip address 10.3.1.2 255.255.0.0

CHAPTER 9

SRB/RSRB Design and Configuration

Cisco routers connecting Token-Ring–to–Token-Ring LAN segments attached to the same router use source route bridging (SRB). Remote SRB (RSRB) is Cisco's first encapsulation technique for transporting Token-Ring frames over non–Token-Ring media.

Cisco's SRB features enable the configuration and use of multiport Token-Ring bridges. Previously, this required multiple chassis, each supporting only two ports. This is subsequently noted in this chapter. SRB implementation supports the following features:

- Configurable fast-switching software for source-route bridging
- A local source-route bridge that connects two or more Token-Ring networks
- Multiple Token-Ring interfaces in one or more routers that collectively represent a virtual ring
- Support for both all-routes and spanning-tree explorer packets
- Dynamic RIF cache along with manual RIF entries
- Filtering by MAC address, link service access point (LSAP) header, and protocol type
- Translation between Token-Ring bridge frames and transparently bridged frames (typically Ethernet frames)
- Source-route bridging that is supported over FDDI on Cisco 7000, 7200, 7500, and 4000 series routers

RSRB, in contrast to SRB, enables Token-Ring media to bridge over non–Token-Ring media. The early remote SRB implementations provided connection between two SRB devices typically on a slow link that had to be dedicated to Token-Ring traffic. The remote connection could be considered an extension of the bus of the bridge itself, because no intermediate ring number existed. This was IBM's initial WAN solution for connecting Token-Ring bridged networks using "half-bridge" configurations. Cisco's implementation of remote SRB removes the restriction of dedicating the link to Token-Ring–only traffic by allowing multiple protocols to traverse a given link or links in tangent with the SRB traffic.

In concert with the support of multiport SRB bridges at either end of the network, RSRB enables designers to build SRB backbones across WAN environments. Implementing RSRB enables the use of the following techniques:

- Encapsulating the Token-Ring traffic in TCP segments inside IP datagrams passed between two routers

- Using Fast-Sequenced Transport (FST) (IP encapsulation) to transport RSRB packets to their peers without TCP or User Datagram Protocol (UDP) header or processor overhead

- Direct encapsulation on point-to-point connections, a single serial line, Ethernet, Token Ring, or FDDI ring connected between two routers attached to Token-Ring networks

- Configuring limits to the size of the TCP backup queue

9.1 DESIGN CRITERIA

As we implement Cisco routers into a network, we need to understand many things about the current structure and future vision. Carrying SNA data will always be a protocol that multiprotocol networks need to transport. There are so many options for transmitting legacy data; SRB/RSRB is only one option. SRB/RSRB is the simplest form of transporting source-route bridge traffic over router networks. DLSw+ is the preferred and strategic choice due to its capability to scale to larger networks. However, SRB/RSRB may be appropriate for small, bridged networks migrating to a router backbone configuration. This migration path enables network personnel to learn the routers and to gain technical knowledge of transporting SNA data connections over routers.

Building a reliable and predictable network using SRB takes careful planning. Understanding the following criteria will assist in the design:

- *How large is the network?*—There are size limitations as to how large the virtual ring can grow. It is very difficult to give an exact number to the limit. Check with the local technical staff if you feel your network may approach sizable amounts.

- *What is the speed of your network?*—If you have a network comprised of T1-type speeds, the power of the links can reduce traffic to and from some routers and aid in requirement of maintaining SNA timers.

- *Do you need to connect traditional SNA or NetBIOS as well?*—When designing an SRB network, you need to understand that if you have mostly SNA up to a Front End Processor (FEP) or a Cisco router with a CIP, you need not connect every ring to every other ring. You can implement a partially meshed configuration that connects every user ring to the FEP ring, and thus increase the scalability of the network.

- *Are you running any other protocol on this network?*—The answer is almost always yes. This is the most critical question of all. You need to determine how to control the burst of a routable protocol to protect the SNA traffic. You can handle this balance via the use of prioritization.

Keep in mind a basic axiom while designing SRB hierarchical networks. We can think of them in three layers:

- *Core*—The core routers should be used to transport IP over the WAN links. In this measure, they can dedicate their speed and processing to putting packets out on the circuit and receiving packets from the circuit. These routers can then be tuned for optimal performance based on this important task.

- *Distribution*—The distribution router function is to perform the CPU-intensive functions found in a multiprotocol network. With our focus on RSRB here, we would peer our local and remote routers, and thus have this layer perform the encapsulation into IP. (We discuss further the hows and whys of IP encapsulation in section 9.5).

- *Access*—The access router is the device that connects the local LAN segment into the remote network for access on to a different subnet.

Look at Figure 9-1 for an example of a layered approach to hierarchical networking.

Another important design point for SRB networks is the notion of the *virtual ring*. We will speak often about virtual ring number, and you will need to specify this number many times during IOS configurations. It is important to understand this because it will dramatically impact network design.

Figure 9-1
*Hierarchical
networking.*

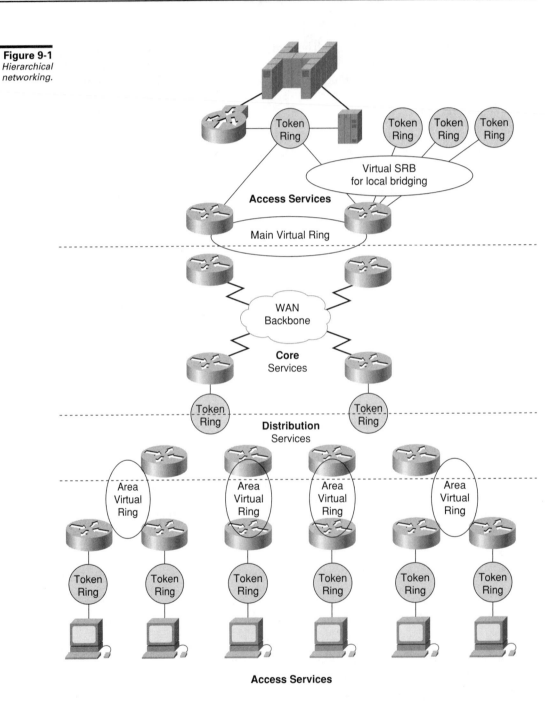

The virtual ring is a logical representation of a combination of physical ones. *Remote virtual rings* can be partially meshed or fully meshed. The routers provide virtual ring connectivity through peer connections using TCP, FST, or direct encapsulation techniques. We can apply the virtual ring concept to the physical hierarchy through a combination of virtual and physical Token Rings, as shown in Figure 9-2. In this figure, we have taken the physical hierarchy diagrammed in Figure 9-1 and applied the hierarchy of virtual rings. In addition, the virtual ring is used in multiport local configurations. As such, the virtual ring is a representation of the bus complex of the router.

A hierarchical virtual ring network as shown in Figure 9-2 functions well for small SRB networks. A true hierarchical network such as the one depicted may limit the capability for connectivity, however, because of the SRB hop count restriction placed in the RIF field. In the example given, the hop count stands at five, allowing for only two more hops for growth based on the initial standard of seven hops. A hierarchical SRB virtual ring network is appropriate for 15–100 peer connections. For local SRB using virtual rings, multiple Token-Ring interfaces are bridged together by using the virtual ring as the connecting ring.

Partially meshed virtual rings can be used when you are running a traditional SNA network where the destination of the sessions are to a FEP or a Cisco CIP and any-to-any connectivity is not the goal. Implementing a fully meshed topology provides any-to-any connectivity. A fully meshed network topology is not suitable for SNA networks due to the anomaly of explorer broadcast storms. Partially meshed virtual rings are advantageous for creating large RSRB networks with multiple virtual rings connecting to the SNA data-center Token Ring. Figure 9-3 illustrates a scalable, partially meshed virtual Token-Ring network.

Partially meshed virtual ring networks overcome the hop count constraint because only one virtual ring is adding to the count. This allows for ring growth at the remote locations. However, due to the partial mesh design the physical hierarchical layered services of core, distribution and access are compromised. Access routers are now providing distribution and core services. This impacts the performance of the router. Due to this performance impact, a data-center router must be added to support 15–100 peers. This design criterion is recommended to guard the performance level of the routers in a partially meshed, multiple-peer environment.

Figure 9-2
Hierarchical virtual ring networking.

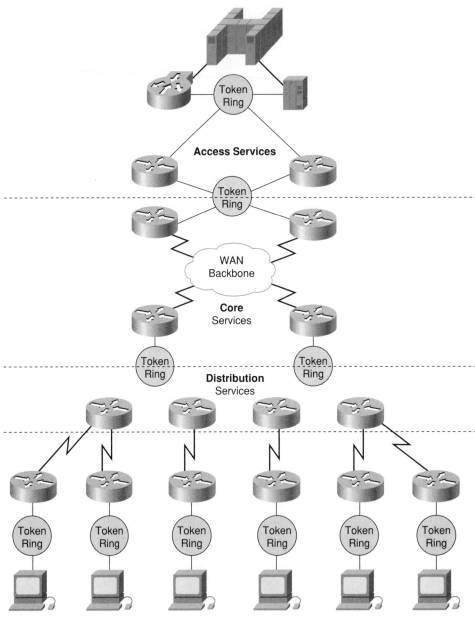

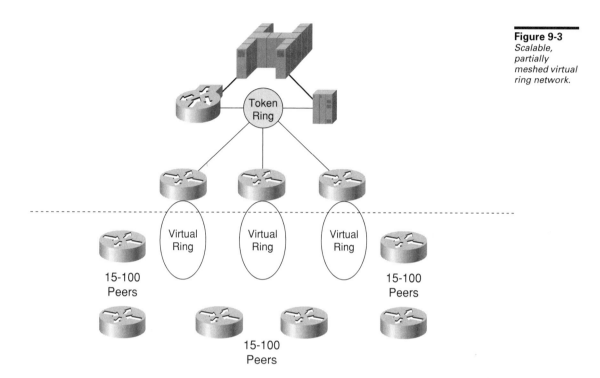

Figure 9-3
Scalable, partially meshed virtual ring network.

Token Ring

Virtual Ring

Virtual Ring

Virtual Ring

15-100 Peers

15-100 Peers

15-100 Peers

Much of the SNA data transported over the SRB network is destined for the mainframe. The access point for Token-Ring connections to the mainframe via an FEP is known as the *Token-Ring interface coupler* (TIC). This nomenclature is also used for the Cisco CIP Token-Ring representation to the mainframe. The destination address of the remote stations can be either the MAC address of an FEP or Cisco CIP Token-Ring adapter. Duplicate MAC addresses are often used for facilitating high availability to the mainframe. Use of duplicate MAC addresses also provides a migration path from the Token-Ring interface of an FEP to a Cisco CIP. It is important to note that when designing SRB networks, you need to pay appropriate attention to the amount of backup and detail during the configuration of the data-center portions of the network. In most cases, multiple routers will be necessary to provide redundancy to the network components.

> **NOTES**
>
> Although there may be multiple paths to the destination MAC address on a source route bridge network in the local router's RIF cache, all the connections are made using the first entry for the destination MAC in the RIF cache. No round-robin balancing is performed. DLSw+ provides this feature.

9.2 DESIGN EXAMPLES

We have compiled the most common examples of implementing an SRB/RSRB network. The simplest is using a Cisco router Token Ring attached to two or more ring segments for connecting to an IBM 3745 FEP or a Cisco CIP.

9.2.1 Local SRB Connection to Mainframe TIC

In this scenario, we have PU1 connected to ring number 2. Router R1 Token-Ring interface 2 connects to ring number 2. The IBM 3745 Token-Ring segment connects to Token-Ring interface 0 on router 1. This configuration employs pure SRB connectivity between the two Token-Ring LAN segments. This same configuration is possible using the Cisco CIP. Figure 9-4 illustrates the topology for both these examples.

9.2.2 Multiport Local SRB Connections to the Mainframe

In this example, we build on Figure 9-4 by adding multiple Token-Ring segments to the same router, R1. We still employ local SRB because the destination ring is the same for all the downstream SNA devices. The router acts as a multiport bridge for connecting the FEP ring to the downstream rings. Again, replacing the FEP with a Cisco CIP provides the same capabilities. Figure 9-5 illustrates the topology for this example.

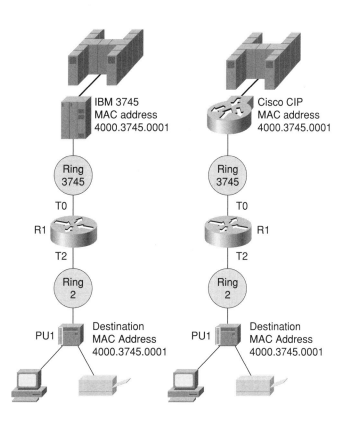

Figure 9-4
*Two
Token-Ring
segments
connecting
using local
SRB to an FEP
and a Cisco CIP.*

IBM 3745
MAC address
4000.3745.0001

Cisco CIP
MAC address
4000.3745.0001

Ring
3745

Ring
3745

T0

T0

R1

R1

T2

T2

Ring
2

Ring
2

PU1   Destination
MAC Address
4000.3745.0001

PU1   Destination
MAC Address
4000.3745.0001

9.2.3 High Availability to Mainframe Using Local SRB

Duplicate TIC MAC addresses on the same or different mainframe gateways attached to different Token-Ring segments increase SNA availability. The Cisco routers feeding these Token Rings implement virtual rings to distinguish different physical paths to the mainframe. In Figure 9-6, a Cisco router, R1, connects two of its Token-Ring interfaces to ring segments attached to different mainframe gateways. Each gateway is using the same MAC address for the TIC. Local SRB can still be used by employing the virtual ring concept in the router. The virtual ring within the router is used for bridging the downstream devices to both gateway rings.

As shown in Figure 9-6, a second router, R2, is also used for connecting the downstream devices to the FEP rings. The R1 and R2 routers use different virtual ring numbers to distinguish the RIF paths. Both the IBM 3745 and the Cisco CIP provide the SNA connectivity to the mainframe and back each other up should the other become inoperative.

Figure 9-5
*Multiple
Token-Ring
segments
connecting to
the mainframe
Token-Ring
segment.*

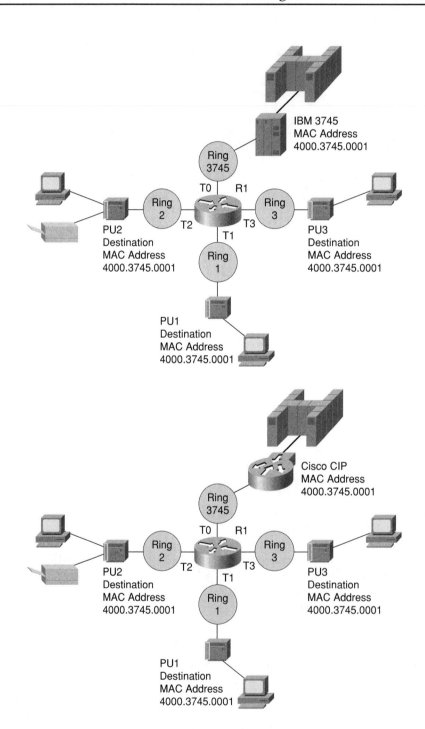

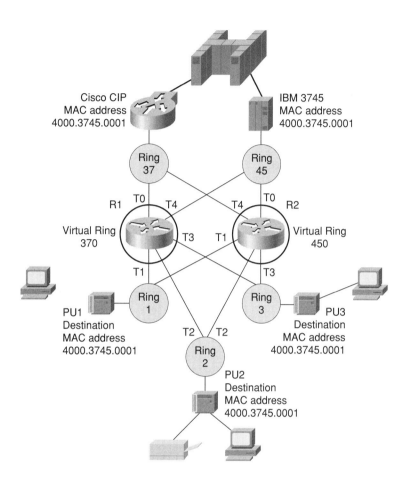

Cisco CIP
MAC address
4000.3745.0001

IBM 3745
MAC address
4000.3745.0001

Ring
37

Ring
45

R1 T0 T4 T4 T0 R2

Virtual Ring
370

Virtual Ring
450

T3 T1

T1 T3

Ring
1

Ring
3

PU1
Destination
MAC address
4000.3745.0001

PU3
Destination
MAC address
4000.3745.0001

T2 T2

Ring
2

PU2
Destination
MAC address
4000.3745.0001

Figure 9-6
High availability using duplicate MAC addresses and local SRB.

9.2.4 Remote SRB Connection to Mainframe

Let's build on the prior examples and place our users not in the same building as the gateway, but rather somewhere out in our remote network. We can still connect to this station through the WAN using RSRB. Look at how PU1 connects via router R2 over the WAN to router R1 and then finally on to the Token-Ring segment connecting the FEP TIC in Figure 9-7. This illustrates the use of local acknowledgement on both routers to reduce SNA RR, RNR, and REJ supervisory frames from traversing the WAN.

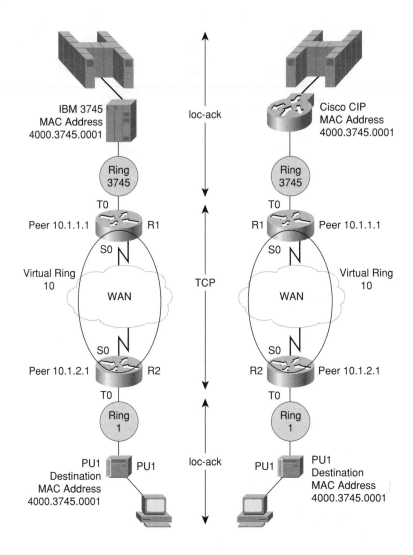

Figure 9-7
Remote SRB connection to a mainframe.

9.2.5 High Availability Mainframe Connection with RSRB

At the data center—the recipient of the bulk of the SNA sessions—we like to have redundancy and backup. Let's expand on our prior RSRB diagram to include high availability. Look at Figure 9-8; all remains the same except for the additional router and Token Ring to support the additional gateway. In this case, with two gateways running duplicate MAC addresses—one an IBM 3745 FEP, and the other a Cisco CIP—we can have a measure of redundancy if SNA session traversing the R1 connection were broken due to a connection problem. The SNA devices can reestablish their SNA session to the same MAC address; however, they would flow over the R2 connection.

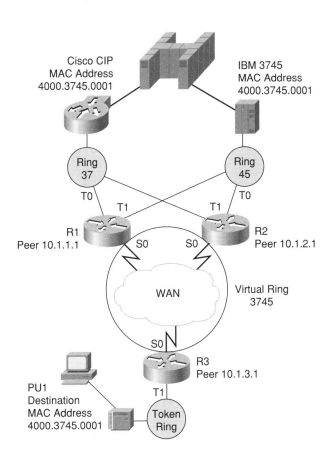

Figure 9-8
High-availability connection using RSRB.

9.2.6 Direct RSRB Connectivity

As was demonstrated with STUN connections, RSRB connectivity supports direct serial encapsulation of SNA frames over point-to-point connections. In Figure 9-9, we see a remote location connected by an HDLC serial interface between two routers. Both R1 and R2 in the figure define the virtual ring group 10 as the connection between the two locations. The SNA Token-Ring frame is encapsulated into the HDLC frame without the overhead of the TCP or IP datagram.

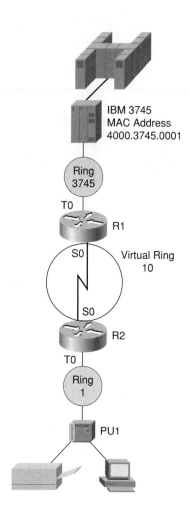

Figure 9-9
Direct RSRB
connectivity
over HDLC
serial line.

IBM 3745
MAC Address
4000.3745.0001

Ring
3745

T0

R1

S0   Virtual Ring
               10

S0

R2

T0

Ring
1

PU1

9.2.7 SR/TLB Between Ethernet and Token Ring

In many installations, Ethernet has become the dominant LAN media. As such, a typical data-center topology may look like that found in Figure 9-10. The Ethernet segment off of router R1 provides connectivity to the Token-Ring–attached gateway for the downstream SNA device named PU2.

In a source-route translational bridge configuration, keep in mind the following things: the assignment of a virtual ring group, a pseudo-ring group representing the Ethernet, and the MAC address translation between canonical and non-canonical format.

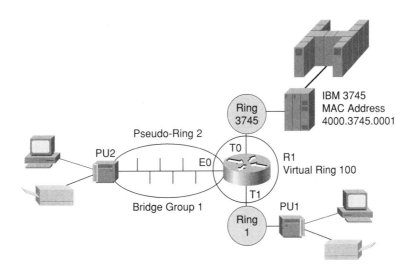

Figure 9-10
Source-route translational bridge example.

9.3 SRB SWITCH PROCESSING

When implementing an SRB network, we need to evaluate the impact of the environment on the network. Processes need to be performed in the delivery of the packets in the network. Four switching methods can be employed for tuning the performance of data from one router interface to another:

- Process switching

- Fast switching

- Autonomous switching

- Silicon switch engine

9.3.1 Process Switching

In *process switching*, each frame is sent to the route processor CPU. The CPU will encapsulate or de-encapsulate the data. In addition, route selection and filtering would be performed during process switching. Section 9.5 discusses different ways for remote routers to peer together while creating an RSRB network; one of the configuration options, TCP peering, will cause process switching. Process switching is CPU intensive and will slow down packet throughput. Process switching is available on all Cisco router platforms.

NOTES

If you use priority queuing, custom queuing, or filtering, frames become process switched. There is no special parameter or command to enable process switching.

9.3.2 Fast Switching

Fast switching refers to a method used on Cisco routers when a Cisco cbus interface processor is installed. Fast switching enables the passing of a frame destined for a port on another cbus Token-Ring interface processor directly over the router cbus backplane at the interrupt level without copying the frame to the system memory first. This bypasses the involvement of the router processor CPU, and therefore provides better performance. Fast-switching support provides for high performance in SRB environments. Fast switching removes the requirement for the CPU to process each and every SRB frame by allowing a cache entry to specify a destination interface. Fast switching is available on all Cisco router platforms. Fast switching is enabled on a Token-Ring interface using the following configuration interface command:

```
source-bridge route-cache
```

Fast switching is the default when SRB is enabled.

NOTES

A *bus* is the common electrical connection used by all the interface processors on a router. The *Cisco cbus architecture* is a high-speed backplane for connecting the routers' interface processors.

9.3.3 Autonomous Switching

Autonomous switching occurs without an interrupt or the route processor CPU intervening. Autonomous performs better than fast-switch processing. Autonomous switching is advantageous for local SRB traffic between cbus Token-Ring interfaces and functional for two-port or multiport bridging. Autonomous switching is available only on the Cisco 7000 and 7500 series routers. Enabling autonomous switching is accomplished by entering the following configuration interface command:

```
source-bridge route-cache cbus
```

9.3.4 Silicon Switch Engine

The switching of packets using a *silicon switching engine (SSE)* is a software solution versus the previous switching methods that use a hardware bus handler processor. This speeds the switching of packets through the cbus because the SSE is a programmable cache. SSE switching is available only on the Cisco 7000 and 7500 series routers. To enable SSE, the following configuration interface command must be entered:

```
source-bridge route-cache sse
```

9.4 DEFINING SRB/RSRB

In our initial discussions, consider a local SRB scenario as a single router that has two Token-Ring LAN ports that connect a "user" ring to the FEP ring. To define this communication, we need to define the SRB environment as well as the concepts of virtual rings, and the use of explorer packets.

9.4.1 Specifying SRB

Each Token-Ring interface being used with source-route bridging requires SRB. SRB is enabled on the interface using the source-bridge interface command. To do so, use the following command:

```
source-bridge local-ring bridge-number target- ring
```

The *local-ring* parameter is the ring number of the attached Token-Ring segment connected to the router Token-Ring interface port. This is a decimal number ranging from 1–4095.

The *target-ring* is the ring number assigned to the Token-Ring segment attached to a router Token-Ring interface port used in local SRB. In an RSRB configuration, the *target-ring* value is the virtual ring number assigned through the `source-bridge` `ring-group` global command. The *target-ring* value ranges from 1–4095.

The *bridge-number* is the number of the bridge that connects the *local-ring* to the *target-ring*. The *bridge-number* ranges from 1–15.

9.4.2 Explorer Packet Definition

When defining SNA networks to run over router backbones, we can take advantage of the proxy explorer feature to limit the amount of explorer traffic. This feature enables the router to cache the RIF entries it receives for destination addresses. This is useful in the SNA network that has end users destined for a MAC address of an FEP. In this fashion, we are saving all the cycles and bandwidth to process this unnecessary data flow. Here is the command:

```
source-bridge  proxy-explorer
```

9.4.3 Determine Ring Groups

When you are designing and planning your SRB/RSRB network and have determined your virtual ring methodology, as mentioned in the design section of this chapter, you need to configure your network. Here is the command to implement your SRB/RSRB ring group:

```
source-bridge ring-group ring-group
```

The *ring-group* is the unique virtual ring number you have chosen to link the bridged rings in your network. The *ring-group* value ranges from 1–4095 and must be unique in the network.

9.5 Defining Remote SRB

A good method to connect SNA sessions over any media type is remote source route bridging (RSRB). To invoke the use of RSRB within the routed network, you need to define the environment in which the packets are following. This includes defining the relationship between the local and remote routers—thus forming peers. We also need to define the links that connect these routers and the types of communication that flows between them. When connecting routers in an RSRB cloud, there are quite a few choices for the types of logical connections that can be defined. We can directly connect one router to the other—thus *direct encapsulation*. If we must traverse a link, we can encapsulate in IP over an FST or TCP connection. The following sections speak to these topics with more detail and focus.

9.5.1 Direct Encapsulation

The option to define direct connections for RSRB is a good choice if the connection is a single hop away and is a relatively simple connection. A real-life example of a good use for direct encapsulation would be connecting two routers in the same building that communicate for backup and load balancing. The following parameters are necessary in the definitions.

Here is the IOS configuration command:

```
source-bridge remote-peer ring-group interface interface-name [mac-address]
```

The `ring-group` is your network wide virtual ring number specified on a `source-bridge ring-group` global command. The `mac-address` value is the MAC address of the remote interface directly connected to the router. The `mac-address` value is optional. The `interface-name` value is any valid interface on the router that supports direct encapsulation, which include:

- Serial
- Ethernet
- FDDI
- ATM
- Tokenring

Direct encapsulation in Frame Relay is accomplished using the following command:

```
source-bridge remote-peer ring-group frame-relay interface interface-name
[mac-address] [dlci-number] [lf-size]
```

The `ring-group`, `interface-name`, and `mac-address` values are entered just as with the `source-bridge ring-group interface` command. The `dlci-number` value is the valid DLCI number assigned to the RSRB peer associated with the connection. The `lf size` is the largest frame that can be expected on the connection. The possible values (representing bytes) are 516, 1500, 2052, 4472, 8144, 11407, and 17800.

9.5.2 TCP Encapsulation

When transporting the bridged traffic over the WAN, we encapsulate the data in a routable shell, in this case TCP. The advantage of TCP encapsulation is the reliable characteristics of the transport mechanism. The benefits include the following:

- Possible packet reordering
- Timers for retransmission
- Acknowledgements

As a result, you must pay careful attention to the drain on the CPU. In some cases, with TCP encapsulation you may have two layers of protocols managing the life of the session—one protocol, TCP, reordering packets and setting timers, and the underlying SNA devices performing the SNA reordering and timer checks. We have found no hard and fast rule for peering encapsulation. We can suggest that if your CPU is high, and your lines are close to being heavily utilized, FST may be a better choice.

Here are the specifics for TCP encapsulation peer definitions:

```
source-bridge remote-peer ring-group tcp ip-address
```

where the *ring-group* is the network wide virtual ring number, and the *ip-address* value is the IP address of a router acting as a remote peer for the connection.

9.5.3 FST Encapsulation

A less taxing form of encapsulation for bridge peers is *Fast Sequenced Transport (FST)*. FST uses the basic IP datagram, with a sequence number, as its mechanism. The router will interrogate the sequence number to see whether it is greater than the last one received. If the sequence number is greater, the router places the frame on the ring; if the sequence number is less, the router discards the frame. FST relies on the underlying protocol, in this case Token Ring's LLC2, to retransmit the packet. This has cost savings on the router CPU and works well in WAN networks with multiple hops. The logical connection must be that of a point-to-point single path, however, to avoid packets arriving out of order.

```
source-bridge remote-peer ring-group fst ip-address
```

where the *ring-group* is the network wide virtual ring number, or partial network, and the *ip-address* is the address of the router on the remote end of the link.

9.5.4 Proxy Explorer Definition

As part of the SRB process for finding stations, explorer packets are generated by the originating end station and responded to by the destination station. This can generate chatty and repetitive data flows over the network. The router can cache the path from each request and save the RIF entry in its table. To this end, the router saves needless packets from crossing the network to satisfy an SRB activation flow.

```
source-bridge proxy-explorer
```

9.5.5 SAP Prioritization

We can prioritize one particular protocol over another as the packets are transported over the network. To do this, we use the *Service Access Point (SAP)* of the particular application. When talking about straight SNA protocols, you may want to prioritize SNA-SAP 04 over NetBIOS SAP F0. Remember that prioritization can be based on priority queuing or custom queuing. For our example, we will base it on priority queuing.

```
sap-priority-list list-number queue-keyword [dsap ds] [ssap ss] [dmac dm] [smac sm]
```

where the *list-number* is a decimal number between 1–10 used to enumerate the list, and *queue-keyword* is the priority queue name or remote RSRB TCP port name. *ds* is an optional function that represents the destination service access point hexadecimal address. *ss* is an optional function that represents the source service access point hexadecimal address. *dm* is an optional function that represents the destination MAC address. *sm* is an optional function that represents the source MAC address.

9.6 SPECIFYING LOCAL ACKNOWLEDGMENT FOR LLC2

SNA, on the whole, does much work in the area of fortifying the connection and checking that stable communication is in progress. To ensure this, SNA performs checking to see whether packets have arrived intact and in order. These flows can impinge on WAN bandwidth. The router can respond to these messages on behalf of the destination device, the mainframe gateway. This cuts the amount of traffic in the network. More importantly, however, the routers respond within the specified timeout value of the local device. The router network will deliver the packet, and TCP guarantees it (but perhaps not in the timeframe of the LLC2 timeframe). With the SRB peer defined as TCP, you can use the TCP protocol to deliver the packet and let the router handle the "local acknowledgement" to the end user device.

```
source-bridge remote-peer ring-group tcp ip-address local-ack
```

where the *ring-group* is the network wide virtual ring number, and the *ip-address* is the IP address of the router being peered with this router. The local-ack keyword enables the aforementioned function on the router, and thereby protects the WAN from transporting SNA RR, RNR, and REJ supervisory frames. Both peers must have local-ack defined for local acknowledgement to function properly.

9.7 SNA Local LU Prioritization

This topic was already explained in our discussion on STUN in Chapter 8, "STUN Design and Configuration," but we can also utilize its functionality with regard to RSRB. We can give priority to a particular LU. The first command identifies the SNA local address of the LU using the SRB/RSRB connection:

```
locaddr-priority-list list-number address-number queue-keyword
[dsap ds] [dmac dm] [ssap ss] [smac sm]
```

where the *list-number* is a decimal number between 1–10 used to map to a priority list defined on the router. The *address-number* is the address of the LU. In addition, the *queue-keyword* is the priority queue name or remote RSRB TCP port name. Usually they are assigned as follows:

- High -TCP port 1996

- Medium - TCP port 1987

- Normal - TCP port 1988

- Low - TCP port 1989

dsap *ds* is an optional function that represents the destination service access point hexadecimal address. ssap *ss* is an optional function that represents the source service access point hexadecimal address. dmac *dm* is an optional function that represents the destination MAC address. smac *sm* is an optional function that represents the source MAC address.

The next command sets the priority:

```
priority-list list-number protocol protocol-name queue-keyword
```

where the *list-number* is a unique identifier and the *protocol-name* is the protocol you are using (in most cases, it is IP). Again, the priority *queue-keyword* is high, medium, normal, or low.

The locaddr-priority interface command is used to assign a priority to the interface. The command format is as follows:

```
locaddr-priority list-number
```

The `list-number` is an identifier that points to a defined `priority-list` command.

9.8 SR/TLB BRIDGING

The Cisco IOS software supports media translation from a source-router bridged network to a transparent bridged network. Typically, this translation is used when communicating between an Ethernet segment and a Token-Ring segment. Routers configured to support source-route translational bridging (SR/TLB) have fast-switch mode enabled by default. Disabling fast-switch mode is accomplished by using the global command:

```
no source-bridge transparent fastswitch
```

Entering this command forces the packet to process switching.

9.8.1 Defining SR/TLB

The transparent bridge domain is viewed by the SRB domain as a ring using the Cisco IOS software virtual ring feature. A ring and bridge number are associated with the entire transparent bridge domain. From the transparent bridge domain, the SRB domain is viewed as another port on the transparent bridge domain.

When bridging from the SRB domain to the transparent domain the RIF fields are cached by the router for use in the return frame. Bridging from transparent to SRB, the router first determines whether the packet is a multicast, broadcast, or a unicast packet. When the received packet is a multicast or broadcast, the router forwards the packet as a spanning-tree explorer. For unicast packets, the router first determines whether a RIF is cached for the destination MAC address in the packet. If a path is not found, the router sends the packet as a spanning-tree explorer.

Remember the following caveats when defining SR/TLB:

- Spanning-tree packets are not forwarded to SRB domains. Therefore, multiple paths between the SRB and transparent domains may lead to loops.

- The maximum frame size of SRB devices may need manual configuration to limit the largest frame size to that allowed for by Ethernet networks. Typically this is 1500 bytes.

- MAC address access filtering must be applied to both the SRB and transparent bridge domain interfaces. This is because the filter is applied to the frame as it exists on the interface.

SR/TLB is enabled by entering the following global command:

```
source-bridge transparent ring-group pseudo-ring bridge-number bridge-group [oui]
```

The *ring-group* variable is the virtual ring number assigned to the `source-bridge ring-group` global command used for connecting SRB networks by the router. The *pseudo-ring* is the virtual ring number assigned to the transparent bridging domain. The *bridge-number* variable is the virtual bridge connecting the transparent bridge domain *pseudo-ring* to the *ring-group* virtual SRB ring. Finally, the *bridge-group* variable is the transparent bridge group number for which frames may be passed to through to the SRB network.

Note that all interfaces assigned to the transparent bridge domain using the interface command bridge-group have the potential for sending frames on to the SRB network. Usually, it is best to assign a unique *bridge-group* number, if possible, to the interface that requires connectivity to an SRB attached station.

9.8.2 Translation Types

SR/TLB supports two types of translation:

- Token Ring LLC2-to-Ethernet Type II (0x80d5 processing)
- Token Ring LLC2-to-Ethernet 802.3 LLC2 (standard)

The first translation type is not commonly found anymore, however, support still exists in the Cisco IOS software. The Token Ring LLC2 (IEEE 802.5) format translates to the Ethernet Type II frame format whose type is specified as 0x80d5 in hexadecimal. This is a nonstandard format, and therefore must be specified to allow the translation to take place. The following global command is required for this translation:

```
source-bridge enable-80d5
```

For the majority of SR/TLB configuration, the standard Token Ring IEEE 802.5-to-Ethernet IEEE 802.3 LLC2 frame translation is applicable. If there is a requirement to mix the two translation types on the same SR/TLB, however, it is done using the *destination SAP (DSAP)* as a qualifier for targeting only that frame for 0x80d5 translation. The remaining IEEE 802.3 LLC2 frames will use standard translation.

The format for qualifying specific 0x80d5 frame translation to identified stations through the use a DSAP is the following global command:

```
source-bridge sap-805d dsap
```

The `dsap` value is the DSAP of the nonstandard Ethernet station. Each such station requires a specific `source-bridge sap-805d` command.

9.9 SRB/RSRB CONFIGURATION EXAMPLES

Let's take a closer look and see some of the IOS configurations necessary to define the concepts covered in this chapter.

9.9.1 Local SRB Connection to FEP

In this scenario, we have PU1 connected to ring number 2. Router R1 Token-Ring interface 2 connects to ring number 2. The IBM 3745 Token-Ring segment connects to Token-Ring interface 0 on router R1. The ring number used for Token-Ring interface T0 is ring number 3745. This configuration employs pure SRB connectivity between the two Token-Ring LAN segments. Figure 9-11 illustrates the topology for this example.

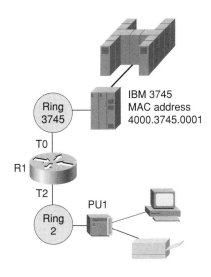

R1 Configuration

interface tokenring 0
no ip Address
source-bridge 3745 1 2
!
interface tokenring 1
no ip address
source-bridge 2 1 3745

IBM 3745
MAC address
4000.3745.0001

Ring 3745

T0

R1

T2

PU1

Ring 2

Figure 9-11
Local SRB connectivity to a FEP between two Token-Ring segments on a single router.

9.9.2 Multiport Local SRB Connections to a Mainframe TIC

Support for multiport local SRB is possible using the Cisco virtual ring feature. In Figure 9-12 three end-user Token-Ring segments connect to the IBM 3745 Token-Ring segment over a virtual ring defined on router R1. Each Token-Ring interface enables source-route bridging with a connection to the common virtual ring. The router acts as a multiport bridge for connecting the FEP ring to the downstream rings.

Figure 9-12
Implementing SRB using a multiport bridge configuration with a virtual ring.

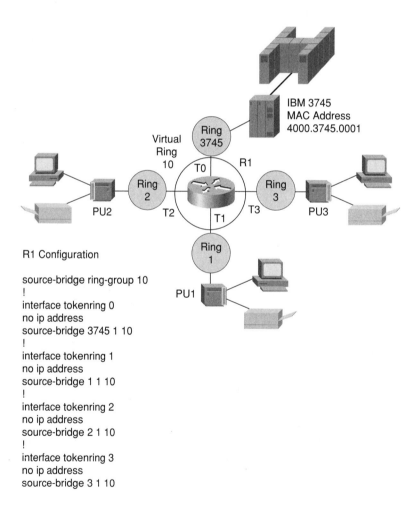

R1 Configuration

```
source-bridge ring-group 10
!
interface tokenring 0
no ip address
source-bridge 3745 1 10
!
interface tokenring 1
no ip address
source-bridge 1 1 10
!
interface tokenring 2
no ip address
source-bridge 2 1 10
!
interface tokenring 3
no ip address
source-bridge 3 1 10
```

9.9.3 High Availability to FEP Using Local SRB

Duplicate TIC MAC addresses on the same or different IBM 3745 FEPs attached to different Token-Ring segments increases SNA availability. In Figure 9-13, two Cisco routers using unique virtual ring numbers attach to the downstream rings 1, 2, and 3 along with the FEP rings 37 and 45. Local SRB can still be used by employing the virtual-ring concept in the router. The virtual ring within the router is used for bridging the downstream devices to both FEP rings.

9.9.4 Remote SRB Connection to Mainframe TIC

Connecting remote SNA devices over WANs is possible through the use of RSRB implementation. Figure 9-14 highlights the configurations used for connecting a remote SNA device attached to a Token-Ring segment on router R2 to the FEP router R1. The configurations used the `loopback interface` command as the RSRB peer for establishing the TCP encapsulation connection. The `source-bridge remote-peer tcp` command used in the sample configurations employs the local-acknowledgement feature for reducing the SNA RR, RNR, and REJ supervisory frame from traversing the WAN.

9.9.5 WAN High-Availability Connection

Two FEPs using duplicate TIC MAC addresses ensure a measure of redundancy if SNA session traversing the R1 connection is broken because of a connection problem. The SNA devices can reestablish their SNA session to the same TIC MAC address; they would flow over the router R2 connection, however. The sample configuration uses FST as the encapsulation method.

9.9.6 Direct RSRB Connectivity

Figure 9-16 shows a remote location connected by an HDLC serial interface between two routers. Both R1 and R2 in the figure define the virtual ring group 10 as the connection between the two locations. The SNA Token-Ring frame is encapsulated into the HDLC frame without the overhead of the TCP or IP datagram.

9.9.7 SR/TLB Between Ethernet and Token Ring to TIC

Figure 9-17 illustrates the configuration used for defining a SR/TLB local SRB connection. The Ethernet segment off router R1 provides connectivity to the Token-Ring–attached FEP for the downstream SNA device named PU2. The pseudo-ring number 2 is used by the router for bridging the SRB to transparent domains.

Figure 9-13
Duplicate MAC address configuration for high-availability to mainframe.

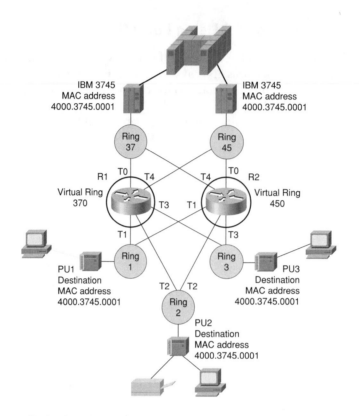

R1 Configuration

source-bridge ring-group 370
!
interface tokenring 0
no ip address
source-bridge 37 1 370
!
interface tokenring 1
no ip address
source-bridge 1 1 370
!
interface tokenring 2
no ip address
source-bridge 2 1 370
!
interface tokenring 3
no ip address
source-bridge 3 1 370
!
interface tokenring 4
no ip address
source-bridge 45 1 370

R1 Configuration

source-bridge ring-group 450
!
interface tokenring 0
no ip address
source-bridge 45 1 450
!
interface tokenring 1
no ip address
source-bridge 1 1 450
!
interface tokenring 2
no ip address
source-bridge 2 1 450
!
interface tokenring 3
no ip address
source-bridge 3 1 450
!
interface tokenring 4
no ip address
source-bridge 37 1 450

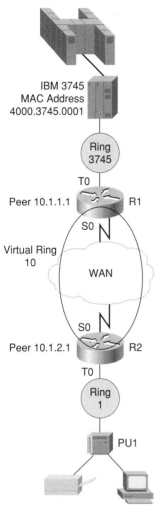

IBM 3745
MAC Address
4000.3745.0001

Ring
3745

T0

Peer 10.1.1.1   R1

S0

Virtual Ring
10

WAN

S0

Peer 10.1.2.1   R2

T0

Ring
1

PU1

R1 Configuration

source-bridge ring-group 10
source-bridge remote-peer 10 tcp 10.1.1.1
source-bridge remote-peer 10 tcp 10.1.2.1 local-ack
!
interface tokenring 0
no ip address
source-bridge 3745 1 10
!
interface serial 0
ip address 10.254.1.1 255.255.255.0
!
interface loopback 0
  ip address 10.1.1.1 255.255.255.0

R2 Configuration

source-bridge ring-group 10
source-bridge remote-peer 10 tcp 10.1.2.1
source-bridge remote-peer 10 tcp 10.1.1.1 local-ack
!
interface tokenring 0
no ip address
source-bridge 1 1 10
!
interface serial 0
ip address 10.254.2.1 255.255.255.0
!
interface loopback 0
  ip address 10.1.2.1 255.255.255.0

Figure 9-14
RSRB connection employing TCP encapsulation with local-acknowledgement enabled.

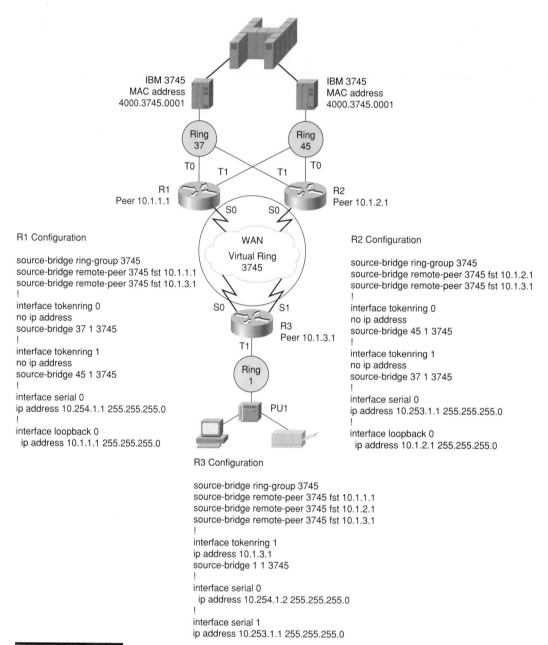

IBM 3745
MAC address
4000.3745.0001

IBM 3745
MAC address
4000.3745.0001

Ring
37

Ring
45

T0   T1   T1   T0

R1
Peer 10.1.1.1

R2
Peer 10.1.2.1

S0   S0

WAN
Virtual Ring
3745

S0   S1

R3
Peer 10.1.3.1

T1

Ring
1

PU1

R1 Configuration

source-bridge ring-group 3745
source-bridge remote-peer 3745 fst 10.1.1.1
source-bridge remote-peer 3745 fst 10.1.3.1
!
interface tokenring 0
no ip address
source-bridge 37 1 3745
!
interface tokenring 1
no ip address
source-bridge 45 1 3745
!
interface serial 0
ip address 10.254.1.1 255.255.255.0
!
interface loopback 0
  ip address 10.1.1.1 255.255.255.0

R2 Configuration

source-bridge ring-group 3745
source-bridge remote-peer 3745 fst 10.1.2.1
source-bridge remote-peer 3745 fst 10.1.3.1
!
interface tokenring 0
no ip address
source-bridge 45 1 3745
!
interface tokenring 1
no ip address
source-bridge 37 1 3745
!
interface serial 0
ip address 10.253.1.1 255.255.255.0
!
interface loopback 0
  ip address 10.1.2.1 255.255.255.0

R3 Configuration

source-bridge ring-group 3745
source-bridge remote-peer 3745 fst 10.1.1.1
source-bridge remote-peer 3745 fst 10.1.2.1
source-bridge remote-peer 3745 fst 10.1.3.1
!
interface tokenring 1
ip address 10.1.3.1
source-bridge 1 1 3745
!
interface serial 0
  ip address 10.254.1.2 255.255.255.0
!
interface serial 1
ip address 10.253.1.1 255.255.255.0

Figure 9-15
*FEP high-availability connection using
RSRB over a WAN.*

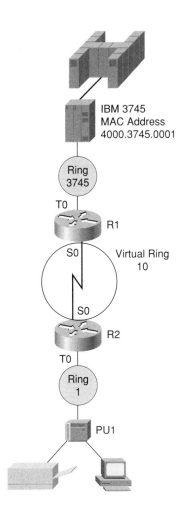

Figure 9-16
Direct HDLC encapsulation with RSRB over a point-to-point serial line.

R1 Configuration

source-bridge ring-group 10
source-bridge remote-peer 10 interface serial 0
!
interface tokenring 0
no ip address
source-bridge 3745 1 10
!
interface serial 0
  encapsulation HDLC
  no ip address

R2 Configuration

source-bridge ring-group 10
source-bridge remote-peer 10 interface serial 0
!
interface tokenring 0
no ip address
source-bridge 1 1 10
!
interface serial 0
  encapsulation HDLC
  no ip address

Figure 9-17
*SR/TLB
configuration
from an
Ethernet
segment to a
Token-Ring–
attached IBM
3745 FEP.*

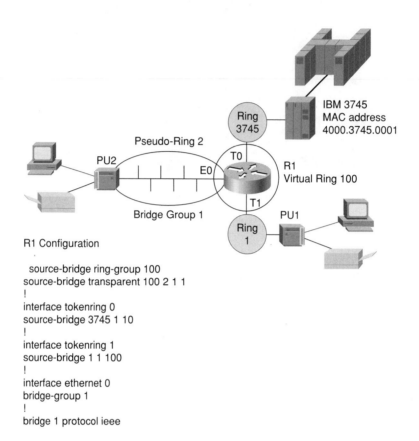

R1 Configuration

```
  source-bridge ring-group 100
source-bridge transparent 100 2 1 1
!
interface tokenring 0
source-bridge 3745 1 10
!
interface tokenring 1
source-bridge 1 1 100
!
interface ethernet 0
bridge-group 1
!
bridge 1 protocol ieee
```

CHAPTER 10

SDLLC Design and Configuration

SDLLC enables SNA SDLC-attached devices to communicate to LAN-attached SNA devices through the use of LLC2 protocol. The Cisco IOS SDLLC features perform the following functions:

- Terminate SDLC sessions

- Translate SDLC to LLC2

- Translate LLC2 to SDLC

- Forward the LLC2 frame over RSRB or DLSw+ across a point-to-point or IP WAN backbone

Figure 10-1 diagrams various SDLLC topologies. Within Figure 10-1, we see that the remote SNA PUs can be attached to the Cisco router using SDLC, Token Ring, or Ethernet. The WAN supporting the connection from the IBM mainframe data center to the remote locations supports all the possible WAN technologies employed by Cisco routers. The connection on the data-center router to the mainframe is through a LAN-attached or serial-attached IBM 3745 FEP. The connection to the mainframe can also be made using a Cisco CIP connection. This configuration is explored in Chapter 16, "CIP Design and Configuration."

Because connectivity from the remote PUs is encapsulated in TCP/IP, we use three methods for SDLC connectivity. Serial-attached SNA devices use *SDLC*. When the remote PU is SDLC attached to a router and the IBM 3745 FEP is LAN attached, however, the topology is viewed as *traditional SDLC-to-LLC2* translation. If the IBM 3745 FEP is SDLC attached to the router and the remote PU is LAN attached, the topology is termed *reverse SDLLC*.

Figure 10-1
SDLLC
topology for
connecting
SDLC-attached
SNA PUs with
LAN-attached
SNA PUs.

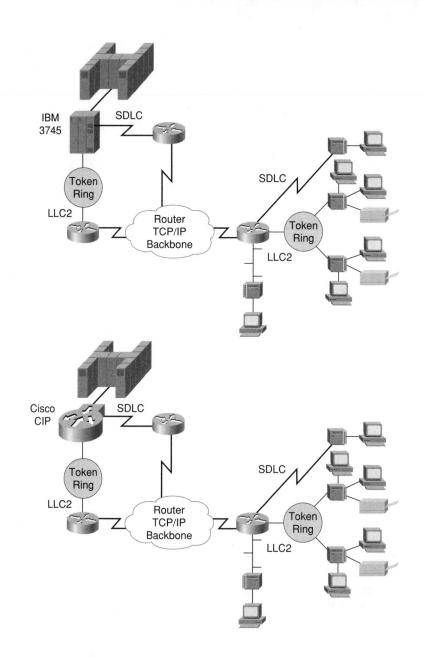

10.1 DESIGN CRITERIA

Many factors must be considered when implementing SDLLC over Cisco routers. The majority of these factors revolve around reducing WAN bandwidth requirements while increasing throughput and meeting response-time performance objectives. The following list identifies some of the design criteria that meet the aforementioned goals by implementing an SDLLC network on Cisco routers:

- *Locally terminate LLC2 sessions*—This reduces WAN bandwidth usage by as much as 10% by eliminating acknowledgement and keep-alive traffic from traversing the backbone. From the SNA PU perspective, intermittent loss of WAN connectivity is unperceived because local-acknowledgement retains the SNA sessions. Locally terminating LLC2 sessions requires the use of TCP encapsulation.

- *FEP frame sizes*—LAN-attached FEPs set frame size to the largest allowed by the FEP for the LAN media. This is usually 1510 for Ethernet and 4095 for Token Ring. The router attaching the SDLC PU will segment the frame to a size acceptable by the SDLC-attached PU. With SDLC-attached FEPs, the frame size is set to the maximum allowed for the PU device type. Typically, this is either 521 or 1033.

- *PU frame sizes*—LAN-attached PUs set the frame size to the largest allowed by the PU device for the attached LAN media. The router SDLC attached to the FEP will segment the frames to the allowed maximum frame size for the SDLC connection to the FEP.

- *Window size* (MAXOUT)—VTAM sets the window size for the umber of unacknowledged frames sent to the PU using the MAXOUT parameter of the PU statement in VTAM's switched major node definition for the PU. A MAXOUT of 1 is recommended for LAN-attached PUs. SDLC-attached PUs can see performance improvement by setting the MAXOUT value to 7.

- *SDLC line speed*—The SDLC-attached devices directly attached to the router should use the maximum line speed capable for the SNA device. For older IBM 3274 devices, this is 19.2Kbps. The newer 3174 devices can be clocked at 64Kbps. Direct attachment to the router causes the router to maintain the clocking, however, and thereby eliminates a point of failure by removing the need for a modem.

- *SDLC role*—Routers attached to the FEP using an SDLC serial line must have their serial interface set as a secondary link station. Routers attached to a PU (that is, IBM 3174) using an SDLC serial line must have the serial interface set as a primary link station.

- *Point-to-point line control*—On SDLC-attached devices connecting to the router over a point-to-point line set the Request-to-Send (RTS) line control to permanent (high). This eliminates the RTS toggling normally found on serial-line connections. Setting RTS to high reduces modem turnaround delays that may result in a 10% reduction in link utilization. Setting RTS to toggle is required for multipoint line configurations.

- *NRZ/NRZI*—Set the router SDLC serial interface to be compatible with the attached SNA PU definition for *non-return-to-zero (NRZ)* or *non-return-to-zero-inversion (NRZI)*. If the router serial interface does not match the SNA PU definition for this value, the SDLC line will not activate.

- *VTAM/NCP mappings*—Verify that the corresponding SNA values defined on the routers map one-for-one with the VTAM/NCP definitions. Failing to map accurately will either cause failed connectivity or unplanned session characteristics. In addition, the appropriate transmission properties of Token-Ring–connected PUs differ from those of SDLC-connected PUs. VTAM/NCP definitions must be configured for the characteristics of the downstream device.

10.2 DESIGN EXAMPLES

The examples discussed here depict the most widely used topologies and configurations you are likely to encounter. The examples discuss local data-center router connectivity to the SNA PUs as well as WAN SNA PU connections.

10.2.1 Direct to FEP with Local SRB

SDLC connectivity of remote PUs can be serviced by a data-center Cisco router using SDLLC. Local SRB SDLLC supports only SNA PU 2.0 devices, however. In Figure 10-2, we see the use of a virtual ring applied to the SDLC serial interface on the router. This established the SRB connection for building a RIF field in the Token-Ring frame to the IBM 3745 FEP.

10.2.2 Direct to FEP with Local RSRB

Note that the configuration shown in Figure 10-3 looks almost exactly like that for direct connection using SRB. The difference here is the use of RSRB as the encapsulation method versus direct LLC2 encapsulation. Note the virtual ring used by the router R1 is now used for RSRB encapsulation. Using RSRB requires the specification of RSRB peers.

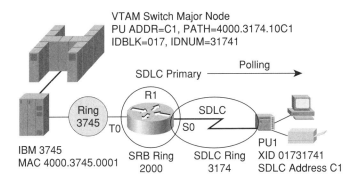

Figure 10-2
Direct SDLLC connection to FEP using local SRB.

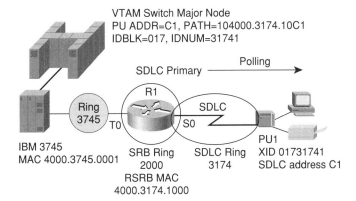

Figure 10-3
Direct SDLLC connection to FEP using local RSRB.

10.2.3 Direct to FEP with Local DLSw+

In Figure 10-4, we again see a similar topology. Here, however, the the encapsulation method is changed to DLSw+. DLSw+ requires the use of a virtual MAC address on the virtual SDLLC ring, representing the SDLC link because DLSw+ terminates the RIF at the DLSw+ ring.

10.2.4 Direct to FEP with Local RSRB Reverse SDLLC

In this configuration, we see that the IBM 3745 NCP PU definition for the Token-Ring–attached PU is accessed by the NCP through the use of the SDLC station address rather than the Token-Ring MAC address. The Cisco router performs the connection and mapping between the two mediums and data-link control functions.

Figure 10-4
*Direct SDLLC
connection to
FEP using local
DLSw+.*

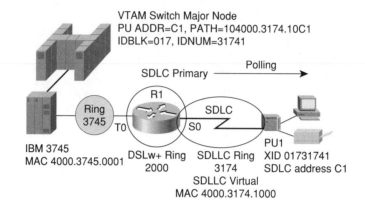

VTAM Switch Major Node
PU ADDR=C1, PATH=104000.3174.10C1
IDBLK=017, IDNUM=31741

SDLC Primary ──── Polling ────▶

R1

Ring
3745 T0   SDLC
              S0

IBM 3745
MAC 4000.3745.0001

PU1
XID 01731741
SDLC address C1

DSLw+ Ring   SDLLC Ring
2000   3174
       SDLLC Virtual
       MAC 4000.3174.1000

Figure 10-5
*Direct SDLLC
connection to
FEP using
RSRB with
reverse SDLLC.*

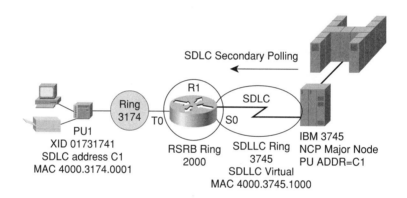

SDLC Secondary Polling
◀────

R1

Ring
3174 T0   SDLC
              S0

PU1
XID 01731741
SDLC address C1
MAC 4000.3174.0001

IBM 3745
NCP Major Node
PU ADDR=C1

RSRB Ring   SDLLC Ring
2000   3745
       SDLLC Virtual
       MAC 4000.3745.1000

10.2.5 Direct to FEP with Local DLSw+ Reverse SDLLC

DLSw+ removes the virtual ring requirement for the SDLC link to the FEP because of
DLSw+ terminating the RIF at the router. However, DLSw+ local encapsulation
requires a virtual MAC address to be assigned to the image of the FEP residing on the
DLSw+ ring.

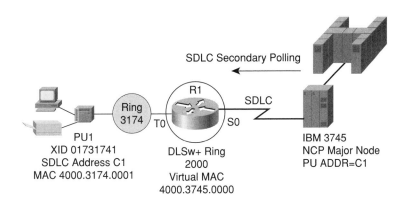

Figure 10-6
Direct SDLLC connection to FEP using DLSw+ with reverse SDLLC.

10.2.6 Remote RSRB to LAN-Attached FEP with Local-Acknowledgement

Defining remote RSRB over a WAN for SDLLC is accomplished by just extending the virtual ring across the WAN interfaces. From the FEP perspective, the configuration is the same as if it were using the direct RSRB connection. Figure 10-7 illustrates the remote RSRB SDLLC topology.

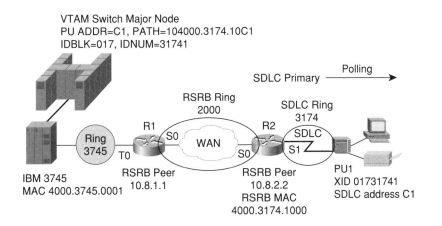

Figure 10-7
Remote SDLLC connection to FEP using RSRB.

10.2.7 Remote DLSw+ to LAN-Attached FEP

Figure 10-8 shows the use of DLSw+ over the router WAN for delivering SDLLC traffic. The SDLC-attached PU named PU1 is represented to the FEP by a virtual MAC address representing the SDLC link.

Figure 10-8
Remote SDLLC connection to FEP using DLSw+.

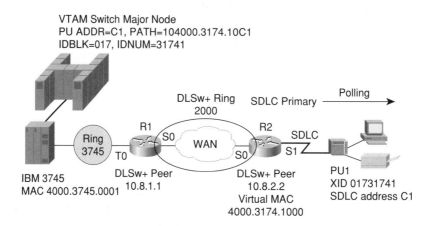

10.2.8 SDLLC over Frame Relay

You may encounter two types of configurations when using Frame Relay to connect legacy SDLC-attached devices. These are *direct router-to-FEP connections* and *router-to-router connections*. Router-to-FEP connections use a remote router connecting SDLC devices directly to the IBM 3745 FEP over a Frame-Relay connection. Figure 10-9 depicts this. In Figure 10-9, the Frame-Relay connection maps the SDLC address of PU1 directly to the Frame-Relay interface. The Frame-Relay access support (FRAS) feature of Cisco IOS encapsulates the SDLC frame in an LLC2 frame for delivery over Frame Relay.

Figure 10-9
SDLLC over Frame Relay directly to the IBM 3745 FEP.

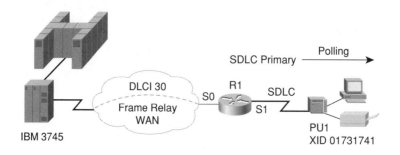

Figure 10-10 illustrates SDLLC connectivity using two Cisco routers. The remote router R2 connects to data-center router R1 over a Frame-Relay network. The router R1 connects to the IBM 3745 FEP over a Token-Ring interface. The SNA PU PU1 is SDLC attached to Cisco router R2.

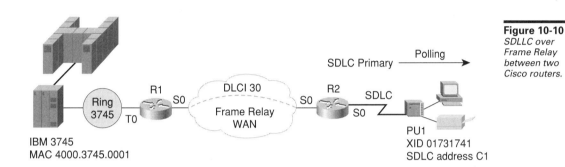

10.2.9 SR/TLB Bridging to FEP

In this example, we use DLSw+ as the transport mechanism for delivering SNA data from an Ethernet-attached PU over the WAN to an SDLC-attached IBM 3745 FEP. Figure 10-11 illustrates this topology. DLSw+ is the preferred mechanism because it provides the automatic MAC address conversion between the Ethernet MAC address format and the Token-Ring MAC address format. This conversion is needed because of the use of a virtual ring by DLSw+. Figure 10-11 also illustrates the use of reverse SDLLC with DLSw+ while using SR/TLB.

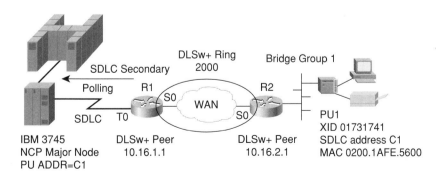

10.3 DEFINING SERIAL INTERFACE ENCAPSULATION

SDLLC requires the serial interface being used for connectivity to the SNA device to IBM SDLC link layer protocol. This is performed using one of the following three interface commands:

```
encapsulation sdlc

encapsulation sdlc-primary

encapsulation sdlc-secondary
```

SNA SDLC devices may act as either a primary or secondary node. Primary nodes poll the secondary nodes for data. If the secondary node has data, it will then send it to the polling primary node. SNA PU 2.0 resources are defined as secondary nodes; therefore, the SDLLC router connecting to the SNA PU 2.0 node over SDLC defines its encapsulation mode as primary using the `encapsulation sdlc-primary` interface command. The IBM 3745, a PU 4 device, acts as a primary node when communicating to the attached Cisco router. In this case the serial interface connecting to the IBM 3745 is defined as a secondary node using the `encapsulation sdlc-secondary` command. The `encapsulation sdlc` command is used when either RSRB, DLSw+, or FRAS is used as the underlying transport. In this case, the `sdlc role` command is used on the serial interface connecting to the SDLC device.

10.4 DEFINING THE ROLE OF THE ROUTER WITH RSRB OR DLSW+

The role of the serial interface attaching the SDLC device is specified by using the `sdlc role` interface command when RSRB or DLSw+ is used for transporting the SNA data. The format of the `sdlc role` interface command is as follows:

```
sdlc role {none | primary | secondary | prim-xid-poll}
```

The primary or secondary role of the router is specified by including either the `primary` or `secondary` keyword on the `sdlc role` interface command. If the router is attached to a PU 2.0 device, it must be defined as a primary node. If the router is SDLC attached to a PU 4 (IBM 3745 FEP), it must be defined as a secondary node. The none keyword is used to enable dynamic determination of the role when the attached SNA device uses a negotiable link connection. Typically, this is found when using SNA Type 2.1 nodes as primary nodes. If the attached SNA PU 2.1 device is set to negotiate and prefers a primary role, the router will assume the secondary role. If the attached SNA PU is a PU 2.1 secondary device, the `prim-xid-poll` keyword must be specified.

10.5 DEFINE SDLC ADDRESS

Under the serial interface supporting the SDLC connection, the secondary SDLC station address(es) of the attached SNA PUs must be defined. This value must match the SDLC station defined on the PU 2.0 configuration. The format for specifying the SDLC station address is as follows:

```
sdlc address hexbyte
```

The *hexbyte* variable is any valid SNA/SDLC station address in hexadecimal ranging from 1–FE. If the SDLC interface supports a multidrop configuration, an sdlc address command is required for defining each SDLC station address of the attached SDLC devices. If the SDLC interface connects to a FEP, the sdlc address value must match the NCP major node PU ADDR= definition.

10.6 DEFINE TOKEN-RING ADDRESS OF SDLLC CONNECTION

The SDLC interface connecting the SDLC PU is mapped to a virtual ring and associated with a virtual MAC address on the virtual ring. This is done using the sdllc traddr command:

```
sdllc traddr xxxx.xxxx.xx00 lr bn tr
```

The first parameter of the sdllc traddr command is the virtual MAC address used to represent the SDLC-attached PU device. The value used must have the last two hexadecimal digits as 00. These two digits are replaced by the router with the value defined from the SDLC address interface command. Together these values create a unique MAC address for mapping the SDLC-attached PU to the LLC2 protocol used for connecting to the IBM 3745 FEP.

The *lr* variable is the SDLLC virtual ring number to which the virtual MAC address attaches. The *tr* variable is the SDLLC target ring. This value is typically the virtual ring defined by the source-bridge ring-group global command. In direct connection topology, the target ring is the Token-Ring number used that attaches the IBM 3745 FEP. The *bn* variable is the virtual bridge used to connect the SDLLC virtual ring to the target ring.

10.7 IDENTIFY THE SDLLC MAC PARTNER ADDRESS

The SDLLC router must have the destination MAC address of the LAN attached to initiate connectivity. The sdllc partner interface command defines the FEP MAC address and maps it to an SDLC station address attached to the SDLC serial line on this router. The format of the sdllc partner interface command is as follows:

```
sdllc partner mac-address sdlc-address
```

The *mac-address* variable is the LAN MAC address of the IBM FEP or the Cisco CIP internal LAN adapter. In most installations, this is a Token-Ring MAC address. However, it can be an Ethernet MAC address. The *sdlc-address* variable must match a sdlc address value previously defined on this interface definition. There must be one sdllc partner command for each attached SDLC end station on the SDLC serial interface.

10.8 DEFINE THE SNA PU XID VALUE

VTAM on the IBM host issues an XID request to the SNA device because the connection is seen as a switched (temporary) connection. The VTAM XID request will interpret the 4-byte XID response from the SNA PU as the PU IDBLK and IDNUM parameter values for the PU definition in VTAM's switch major node. The XID for SDLLC is defined using the sdllc xid interface command. The format of the command is as follows:

```
sdllc xid address idblkidnum
```

The *address* variable is the SDLC station address defined on a previous sdlc address interface command. The *idblkidnum* variable is the 4-byte hexadecimal XID value. The first three hexadecimal digits (*idblk*) must match the IDBLK value defined in VTAM. Likewise, the remaining five digits (*idnum*) must match the IDNUM parameter of the VTAM PU switch major node.

10.9 ADDING LOCAL-ACKNOWLEDGMENT

Local-acknowledgement for SDLLC requires the use of RSRB transport. To enable local-acknowledgement when using SDLLC, the following source-bridge command must be entered in global configuration mode:

```
source-bridge sdllc-local-ack
```

This command is required for the SDLLC router to use local-acknowledgement with RSRB.

10.10 DLSw+ VIRTUAL MAC ADDRESS DEFINITION

When using DLSw+, a virtual MAC address must be assigned to map the SDLC-attached device to the DLSw+ virtual ring. The format of the command is as follows:

```
sdlc vmac mac-address
```

The `sdlc vmac` *mac-address* command value is the 12-digit hexadecimal value used as the MAC address of the SDLC-attached device. The last two digits must be `00`. These digits are replaced by the SDLC station address to provide a unique MAC address for this interface. The virtual MAC address is presented to the LAN-attached FEP and should match the `PATH` parameter value used on the PU definition in VTAM's switch major node.

10.11 ATTACHING SDLC DEVICES TO DLSw+

The SDLC-attached devices must be mapped to DLSw+. This is done using the interface command `sdlc dlsw`. The format of the command is as follows:

```
sdlc dlsw sdlc-address
```

The *sdlc-address* variable is a previously defined SDLC `address` value used on this serial interface. Multiple *sdlc-address* values may be specified to map multiple SDLC devices to DLSw+ with the single `sdlc dlsw` command.

10.12 SETTING THE LARGEST INFORMATION FRAME SIZE

SNA PUs set their information frame size in their configuration. The SDLC-attached router can segment received information frames down to the size accepted by the SDLC device. To set the largest information frame, use the following interface command:

```
sdlc sdlc-largest-frame address size
```

The *address* variable is a value previously defined on an SDLC `address` command used on this serial interface. The *size* variable defaults to 265. Typically, use 265 or 521 for older IBM 3274-type controllers. The newer IBM 3174-type controllers and SNA PU 2.0 gateways can use larger frame sizes of 521, 1033, and 2057.

10.13 SDLLC CONFIGURATION EXAMPLES

This section provides the Cisco IOS configuration specific to supporting SDLLC connectivity.

10.13.1 Direct to FEP with Local SRB

In this configuration, we see the use of a virtual ring as the bridging medium between the SDLC line and the LAN-attached FEP. In Figure 10-12 the router R1 acts as the primary node to the PU 2.0 device.

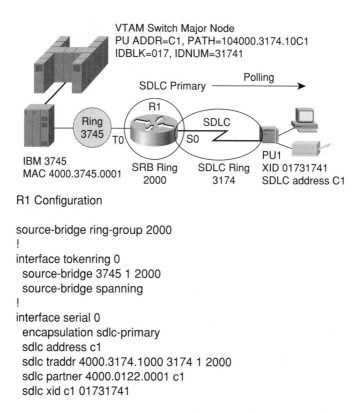

Figure 10-12
Direct SDLLC Cisco IOS configuration for FEP connectivity using local SRB.

VTAM Switch Major Node
PU ADDR=C1, PATH=104000.3174.10C1
IDBLK=017, IDNUM=31741

SDLC Primary ——— Polling →

R1

Ring 3745   T0   SDLC   S0

IBM 3745
MAC 4000.3745.0001

SRB Ring 2000

SDLC Ring 3174

PU1
XID 01731741
SDLC address C1

R1 Configuration

```
source-bridge ring-group 2000
!
interface tokenring 0
  source-bridge 3745 1 2000
  source-bridge spanning
!
interface serial 0
  encapsulation sdlc-primary
  sdlc address c1
  sdlc traddr 4000.3174.1000 3174 1 2000
  sdlc partner 4000.0122.0001 c1
  sdlc xid c1 01731741
```

10.13.2 Direct to FEP with Local RSRB

Figure 10-13 shows the inclusion of RSRB source-bridge remote-peer statements for establishing RSRB on the same router. In this configuration, we utilize the interface loopback 0 definition to identify the IP peer address used for RSRB.

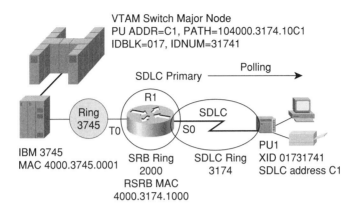

Figure 10-13
*Direct SDLLC
Cisco IOS
configuration
for connecting
an FEP using
local RSRB.*

R1 Configuration

```
source-bridge ring-group 2000
source-bridge remote-peer 2000 fst 10.8.1.1
source-bridge remote-peer 2000 fst 10.8.2.2
!
interface tokenring 0
  ip address 10.8.1.1 255.255.255.0
  source-bridge 3745 1 2000
!
interface serial 0
  encapsulation sdlc-primary
    ip address 10.8.2.2 255.255.255.0
  sdlc address c1
  sdlc traddr 4000.3174.1000 3174 1 2000
  sdlc partner 4000.3745.0001 c1
  sdlc xid c1 01731741
```

10.13.3 Direct to FEP with Local DLSw+

The encapsulation method used in Figure 10-14 illustrates the use of DLSw+ local switching. Note that the DLSw+ function requires you to define a virtual MAC address for the SDLC device for attachment to the virtual ring defined on the `source-bridge ring-group` command.

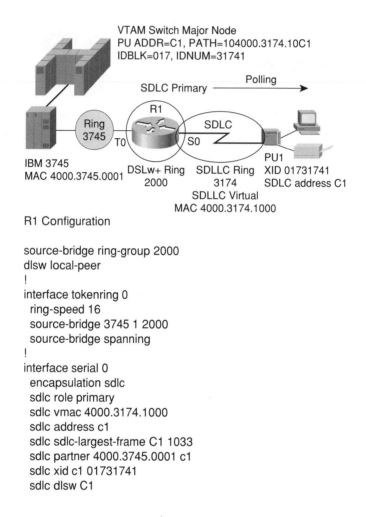

Figure 10-14
*Direct SDLLC
Cisco IOS
configuration
for connecting
to a FEP using
local DLSw+.*

R1 Configuration

```
source-bridge ring-group 2000
dlsw local-peer
!
interface tokenring 0
  ring-speed 16
  source-bridge 3745 1 2000
  source-bridge spanning
!
interface serial 0
  encapsulation sdlc
  sdlc role primary
  sdlc vmac 4000.3174.1000
  sdlc address c1
  sdlc sdlc-largest-frame C1 1033
  sdlc partner 4000.3745.0001 c1
  sdlc xid c1 01731741
  sdlc dlsw C1
```

10.13.4 Direct to FEP with Local RSRB Reverse SDLLC

In Figure 10-15 we see that the IBM 3745 NCP PU definition for the Token-Ring–attached PU is accessed by the NCP through the use of the SDLC station address rather than the Token-Ring MAC address. The Cisco router performs the connection and mapping between the two mediums and data-link control functions.

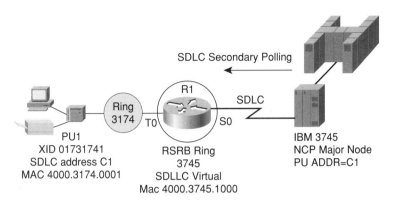

Figure 10-15
*Direct SDLLC
Cisco IOS
configuration
connecting a
FEP using
RSRB with
reverse SDLLC.*

R1 Configuration

```
source-bridge ring-group 2000
source-bridge remote-peer 2000 tcp 10.8.1.1
source-bridge remote-peer 2000 tcp 10.8.2.2
!
interface tokenring 0
  ip address 10.8.2.2
  ring-speed 16
  source-bridge 3174 1 2000
  source-bridge spanning
!
interface loopback 0
  ip address 10.8.1.1
!
interface serial 0
  encapsulation sdlc-secondary
  sdlc address c1
  sdlc sdlc-largest-frame c1 1033
    sdlc traddr 40000.3745.1000 3745 1 2000
  sdlc partner 4000.3174.0001 c1
```

10.13.5 Direct to FEP with Local DLSw+ Reverse SDLLC

DLSw+ removes the virtual-ring requirement for the SDLC link to the FEP because of DLSw+ terminating the RIF at the router. However, DLSw+ local encapsulation requires a virtual MAC address to be assigned to the image of the FEP residing on the DLSw+ ring.

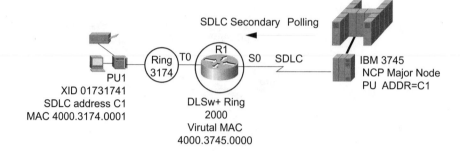

Figure 10-16
Direct SDLLC
Cisco IOS
connection to a
FEP using
DLSw+ with
reverse SDLLC.

R1 Configuration

```
source-bridge ring-group 2000
dlsw local-peer
!
interface tokenring 0
  ip address 10.8.2.2
  ring-speed 16
  source-bridge 3174 1 2000
  source-bridge spanning
!
interface serial 0
  encapsulation sdlc
   sdlc role secondary
  sdlc address c1
  sdlc sdlc-largest-frame c1 1033
   sdllc vmac 4000.3745.0000
  sdlc xid c1 01731741
   sdllc partner 4000.3174.0001  c1
   sdlc dlsw c1
```

10.13.6 Remote RSRB to LAN Attached FEP with Local-Acknowledgement

In this configuration, we see the employment of the local-acknowledgement feature. Enabling this feature for SDLLC is accomplished using the `source-bridge sdllc local-ack` global command. Figure 10-17 illustrates the remote RSRB SDLLC topology with local-acknowledgement.

R1 Configuration

```
source-bridge ring-group 2000
source-bridge remote-peer 2000 tcp 10.8.1.1
source-bridge remote-peer 2000 tcp 10.8.2.2 local-ack
!
interface tokenring 0
  source-bridge 3745 1 2000
!
interface loopback 0
  ip address 10.8.1.1. 255.255.255.0
!
interface serial 0
  ip address 10.254.1.1 255.255.255.0
```

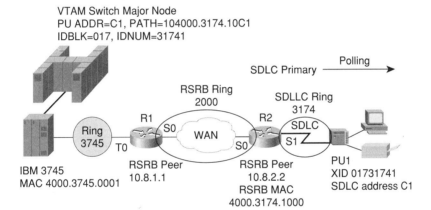

Figure 10-17
Remote SDLLC Cisco IOS configuration connecting a FEP using RSRB.

R2 Configuration

```
source-bridge ring-group 2000
source-bridge remote-peer 2000 tcp 10.8.1.1 local-ack
source-bridge remote-peer 2000 tcp 10.8.2.2
    source-bridge sdlc local-ack
!
interface loopback 0
  ip address 10.8.2.2 255.255.255.0
!
interface serial 0
  ip address 10.254.2.1 255.255.255.0
!
interface serial 1
  encapsulation sdlc-primary
  sdlc address c1
  sdlc traddr 4000.3174.1000 3174 1 2000
  sdlc partner 4000.3745.0001 c1
sdlc xid c1 01731741
```

10.13.7 Remote DLSw+ to LAN Attached FEP

Figure 10-18 shows the use of DLSw+ over the router WAN for delivering SDLLC traffic. The SDLC-attached PU named PU1 is represented to the FEP by a virtual MAC address representing the SDLC link.

Figure 10-18
Remote SDLLC Cisco IOS configuration connecting a FEP using DLSw+.

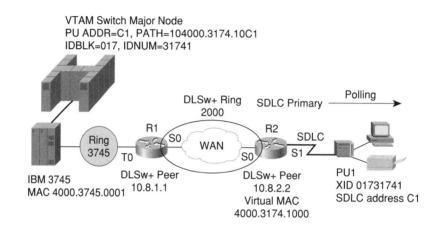

R1 Configuration

```
source-bridge ring-group 2000
dlsw local-peer peer-id 10.8.1.1
dlsw remote-peer 0 tcp 10.8.2.2
!
interface tokenring 0
  source-bridge 3745 1 2000
!
interface loopback 0
  ip address 10.8.1.1 255.255.255.0
!
interface serial 0
  ip address 10.254.1.1 255.255.255.0
```

R2 Configuration

```
source-bridge ring-group 2000
dlsw local-peer peer-id 10.8.2.2
dlsw remote-peer 0 tcp 10.8.1.1
!
interface loopback 0
  ip address 10.8.2.2 255.255.255.0
!
interface serial 0
  ip address 10.254.2.1 255.255.255.0
!
interface serial 1
  encapsulation sdlc
    sdlc role primary
  sdlc address c1
  sdlc vmac 4000.3174.1000
  sdlc partner 40000.3745.0001 c1
  sdlc xid c1 01731741
    sdlc dlsw c1
```

10.13.8 SDLLC over Frame Relay

Figure 10-19 displays the Cisco IOS configuration requirements for connecting an SDLC-attached device over Frame Relay directly to an IBM 3745 FEP. For more information of the FRAS commands used in this configuration, consult Chapter 11, "Frame-Relay Design and Configuration."

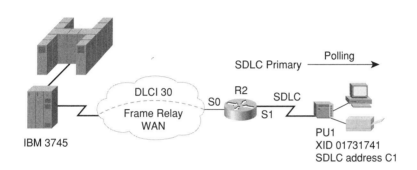

Figure 10-19
SDLLC over Cisco IOS configuration for Frame Relay direct to the IBM 3745 FEP.

R1 Configuration

```
interface serial 0
  encapsulation frame-relay ietf
  frame-relay lmi-type ansi
  frame-relay map llc2 30
!
interface serial 1
  encapsulation sdlc
  sdlc role primary
  sdlc address c1
  sdlc xid c1 01731741
  fras map sdlc c1 serial 0 frame-relay 30 4 4
```

Figure 10-20 illustrates SDLLC connectivity over Frame Relay using two Cisco routers. The remote router R2 connects to data-center router R1 over a Frame-Relay network. The router R1 connects to the IBM 3745 FEP over a Token-Ring interface. The SNA PU PU1 is SDLC attached to Cisco router R2.

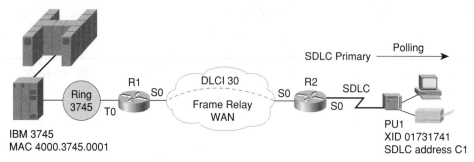

Figure 10-20
SDLLC Cisco IOS configuration for Frame Relay between two Cisco routers.

IBM 3745
MAC 4000.3745.0001

PU1
XID 01731741
SDLC address C1

R1 Configuration

```
interface serial 0
  encapsulation frame-relay ieft
  frame-relay lmi-type ansi
  frame-relay map llc2 30
!
interface tokenring 0
  fras map llc 4000.3745.0001 4 4 serial 0 frame-relay 30 4 4
```

R2 Configuration

```
interface serial 0
  encapsulation frame-relay ieft
  frame-relay lmi-type ansi
  frame-relay map llc2 30
!
interface serial 1
  encapsulation sdlc
  sdlc role primary
  sdlc address c1
  sdlc xid c1 01731741
  fras map sdlc c1 serial 0 frame-relay 30 4 4
```

10.13.9 SR/TLB Bridging to FEP

The configuration shown in Figure 10-21 depicts the use of DLSw+ for connecting an Ethernet-attached SNA PU to an SDLC-attached FEP using reverse SDLLC. The Ethernet bridge group must be mapped to DLSw+ for transport over the virtual ring 2000 between the DLSw+ peers.

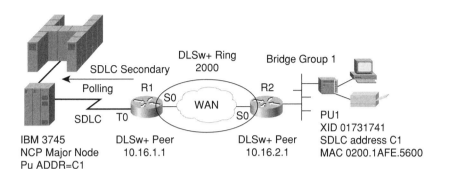

Figure 10-21
SDLLC using SR/TLB from Ethernet PU to SDLC-attached FEP.

R1 Configuration

source-bridge ring-group 2000
dlsw local-peer peer-id 10.16.1.1
dlsw remote-peer 0 tcp 10.16.2.1
!
interface loopback0
ip address 10.16.1.1 255.255.255.0
!
interface serial 0
ip address 10.254.1.1 255.255.255.0
!
interface serial1
no ip address
encapsulation sdlc
no keepalive
clockrate 56000
sdlc role secondary
sdlc vmac 4000.3745.1000
sdlc address C1
sdlc partner 0020.1AFE.5600 C1
sdlc dlsw C1

R2 Configuration

source-bridge ring-group 2000
dlsw local-peer peer-id 10.16.2.1
dlsw remote-peer 0 tcp 10.16.1.1
dlsw bridge-group 1
!
interface serial 0
ip address 10.254.2.1 255.255.255.0
!
interface loopback0
ip address 10.16.2.1 255.255.255.0
!
interface Ethernet0
bridge-group 1

CHAPTER 11

Frame-Relay Design and Configuration

Frame-Relay networks have quickly become a dominant network infrastructure in the 1990s. This is due mostly to the cost savings realized through using public switched Frame-Relay networks instead of private, corporate-owned networks. Through a single physical connection, multiple locations may be connected using Frame Relay. This reduces the number of physical router serial interfaces required at each location to communicate with multiple locations. These logical connections, called *permanent virtual circuits (PVCs)*, allow for many types of different network topology configurations. Each configuration type has its advantages and disadvantageous and must be weighed against system requirements for availability, accessibility, performance, and throughput. Balancing between cost and system requirements requires special design considerations.

11.1 DESIGN CRITERIA

Frame-Relay networks are shared public networks. Therefore, data from your SNA resources is transmitted over a public network infrastructure to which management and control of the throughput is not fully available to corporate network managers. Frame-Relay architecture, however, provides a means for allowing some type of minimal control and management using *committed information rates (CIR)*. Requesting a minimum CIR for your SNA traffic over a Frame-Relay network enables the network designer and engineer to guarantee minimal performance characteristics deemed necessary for deterministic SNA traffic.

It is always best, no matter what your Frame-Relay provider insists, to have a CIR defined for each of your Frame-Relay PVCs used for delivering SNA data. If a CIR of zero is used, it will indicate to all the Frame-Relay switch nodes that every packet carrying SNA is eligible for discarding. Frame-Relay switches will discard or drop frames if the Frame-Relay network becomes congested and needs to relieve congestion by dropping frames. Dropped SNA frames will result in retries by the end devices participating in the SNA session and potentially allow for frames received out of sequence. Out-of-sequence frames will force the SNA session to fail, and thereby, disrupt connectivity for the end user or SNA application.

Guidelines for designing an SNA Frame-Relay network are as follows:

- Limit the number of PVCs on a single physical interface to between 10 and 50. The number of supported PVCs is dictated by the type of protocols used over the Frame-Relay connections and the bandwidth allocated to each PVC on the Frame-Relay connection. Limiting the number of PVCs will reduce broadcast storms and frame replications, both of which consume valuable bandwidth.

- Strive for a partially meshed network design. Full-meshed networks require a larger number of PVCs, and therefore increase the potential for broadcast and replication storms. Star-mesh configurations contain the minimal number of PVCs for supporting system requirements, but fall short on availability and accessibility. The combination of a full- and star-meshed network, resulting in a partially meshed network configuration, provides the best of both Frame-Relay network topologies.

- Segregate SNA from other protocols by using dedicated PVC for SNA. This gives SNA minimal competition for bandwidth over the physical Frame-Relay connection.

- Is connectivity for SNA through an IBM 3745 FEP, AS/400, or a channel-attached router? Each type of connection may dictate the Frame-Relay configuration used on the Cisco routers.

- Determine attachment of the downstream SNA devices. LAN-attached devices may be defined using static or dynamic BNN definitions. SDLC-attached devices must be defined using static definitions.

- Determine the Cisco Frame Relay Access Support (FRAS) feature that best meets the network requirements. Using FRAS BNN static definitions provides complete mapping control and management of SNA device connectivity to a FEP, AS/400, or the mainframe through a channel-attached router. Static BNN requires a definition for each LAN-attached SNA device mapping the device MAC and SAP address pairs to a Frame-Relay PVC DLCI. Dynamic BNN enables the FRAS feature to learn the MAC/SAP pairs defined to a Frame-Relay PVC DLCI, and therefore simplifies definitions and allows for dynamic changes of SNA-device attachments to the network without reconfiguring the routers. All SDLC-attached devices must have their SDLC station address mapped using static mapping to the Frame-Relay PVC DLCI.

• For LAN-attached SNA devices, the FRAS *Boundary Access Node (BAN)* feature enables complete multiplexing of all MAC/SAP pairs defined to a single DLCI. This occurs because the MAC address is included in every frame, uniquely identifying the LLC session. BAN allows for the greatest flexibility of adding and deleting downstream SNA devices without requiring router configuration changes.

11.2 DESIGN CONFIGURATIONS

Support for SNA Frame Relay over Cisco routers comes in two flavors: the *Boundary Network Node (BNN)* and the *Boundary Access Node (BAN)*. Remote routers can communicate directly to an IBM 3745 to establish SNA connections to VTAM on the mainframe using Frame Relay. The Cisco router feature that enables SNA connectivity over the Frame-Relay network is Frame Relay Access Support (FRAS). Both BNN and BAN support SNA connectivity between a remote router attaching SNA devices with a SDLC, Token-Ring, or Ethernet connection.

A Cisco router channel attached to a mainframe or LAN attached to an AS/400 can also take on the functions of BNN and BAN Frame-Relay services through a Cisco feature named *Frame Relay Access Support (FRAS) Host*. The FRAS Host support enables the Cisco router to respond to LLC2 using pass-through mode or local termination. *Pass-through mode* is the recommended feature when connecting a mainframe using a Cisco *Channel Interface Processor (CIP)* connection. *Local termination* is the recommended approach when connecting using a LAN-attached IBM FEP channel connected to the mainframe or LAN-attached AS/400. FRAS Host employs features of source-route bridging, DLSw+, and a virtual Token-Ring interface. Consult Chapter 7, "Cisco SNA Support," for more information on pass-through mode and local termination.

11.2.1 Boundary Network Node (BNN)

There are two types of support for BNN. The first is a direct mapping of SNA devices and the associated Service Access Port (SAP) address used by the Frame-Relay feature of the router for mapping the connection over a PVC Data Link Connection Identifier (DLCI). Figure 11-1 illustrates a sample configuration.

BNN supports both LAN-attached and serially SDLC-attached SNA devices for transport over the Frame-Relay network. A mapping between the SNA device address pair and the Frame-Relay DLCI is required for each downstream SNA device using the Frame-Relay connection. The router Frame-Relay interfaces connect directly to the IBM 3745 FEP using DLCIs. Each SNA connection supported over a Frame-Relay interface identifies the downstream SNA device using a unique SAP that maps to the SNA device MAC/SAP or SDLC station address of the SNA device.

These static definitions require detailed knowledge of the downstream SNA device configuration and consequently require configuration changes on the routers should an end station be moved, added, changed, or deleted. This address pair mapping allows multiple SNA PUs to use a single DLCI connection. This SAP multiplexing function incurs high configuration overhead, however, and increases the chances of misconfiguration.

Figure 11-1
FRAS configuration employing a static BNN definition.

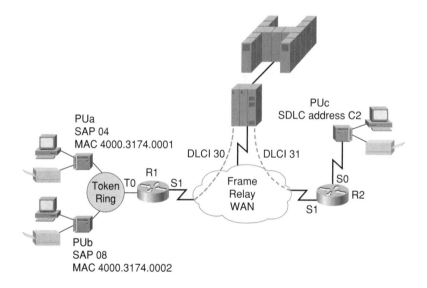

With the introduction of Cisco IOS 11.3, dynamic BNN connectivity is possible. *Dynamic BNN* enables the router to "learn" the MAC/SAP pairing based on the incoming frames from the downstream LAN-attached SNA devices. Dynamic BNN is available only for LAN-attached SNA devices. SDLC serially attached SNA devices must use the static BNN configuration. Typically, SNA devices use a SAP address of 04 for connecting via an LAN to an IBM 3745 FEP. Using dynamic BNN, we need only define one instance for mapping over the Frame-Relay DLCI.

As depicted in Figure 11-2, a mapping between the SAP 04 used by both SNA devices and the Frame-Relay DLCI 30 enables transport of the SNA data to the IBM 3745 FEP. The benefits of dynamic BNN, as compared to static BNN, are as follows:

- Reduces or eliminates reconfiguring routers to support end-station topology and configuration changes

- One mapping definition supporting multiple downstream SNA devices

- The router "learns" the address mapping of MAC/SAP address pairs through normal communications between the SNA device and the mainframe

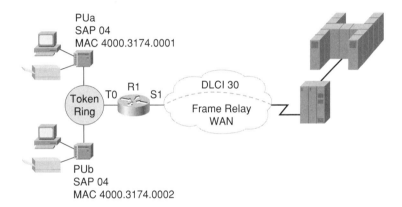

Figure 11-2
FRAS configuration employing a dynamic BNN definition.

11.2.2 Boundary Access Node (BAN)

The chief difference between BNN and BAN is the inclusion of the MAC address within the frame over the Frame-Relay connection. BAN uses a virtual Token Ring to identify the Frame-Relay interface mapping to the DLCI used for transporting the SNA data. In the sample configuration shown in Figure 11-3, the Frame-Relay DLCI 30 maps to a virtual Token-Ring number 200. BAN also employs the use of a ring group for establishing the LLC connection to the IBM 3745 FEP.

Serially attached SDLC devices can also use the BAN feature through the virtual MAC address feature used in SDLC connectivity. Seen in Figure 11-4, PUc uses a virtual MAC address of 4000.3174.00C2 to establish its connection using BAN. PUd, likewise, uses a virtual MAC of 4000.3174.00C3 for its connectivity mapping.

Figure 11-3
FRAS
configuration
employing a
BAN definition
for
LAN-attached
SNA devices.

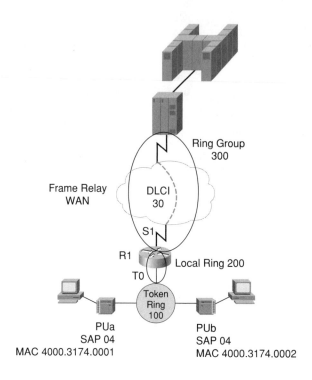

Ring Group
300

Frame Relay
WAN

DLCI
30

S1

R1

Local Ring 200

T0

Token
Ring
100

PUa
SAP 04
MAC 4000.3174.0001

PUb
SAP 04
MAC 4000.3174.0002

Figure 11-4
SDLC serial
connection
using BAN for
SNA PU Type
2.0 and 2.1
devices.

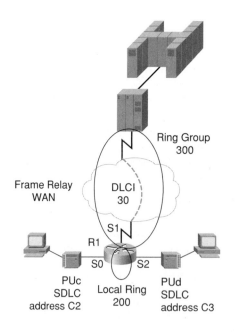

Ring Group
300

Frame Relay
WAN

DLCI
30

S1

R1

S0   S2

PUc
SDLC
address C2

Local Ring
200

PUd
SDLC
address C3

11.2.3 Source-Route Bridging (SRB) over Frame Relay

Connectivity using SRB over Frame Relay for LAN-attached devices is also possible through the use of a feature specific to Frame Relay called *conserve-ring*. Using this feature allows the multiple Frame-Relay DLCIs to map to the same ring number for connecting the upstream router at the data center. Figure 11-5 illustrates the use of the conserve-ring feature.

The virtual ring 3031 on router R1 is the target ring for both the remote routers in the configurations. This conserves ring numbers and reduces explorer packet overhead by eliminating the need for the DLCI ring number in the packet for the PVC. This feature is only allowed for Frame-Relay subinterface definitions. *Frame-Relay subinterface definitions* allow for the autonomous definitions of DLCIs on a PVC with their own specific configuration requirements. The DLCI 30 on router R1 uses the virtual ring 3031 for the PVC and connects over the Frame-Relay network to virtual ring 330 at router R2. Likewise, router R3 configures its virtual ring as 431 and connects to the PVC virtual ring 3031.

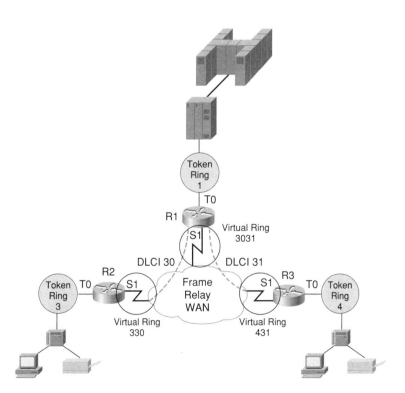

Figure 11-5
SRB Frame-Relay connectivity.

11.2.4 FRAS Host Connectivity

The introduction of Cisco IOS 11.3 establishes the capability of a Cisco router to act as the destination Frame-Relay device for connecting to an IBM host rather than an IBM 3745 FEP or AS/400 directly. FRAS host connectivity enables the use of a Cisco router channel attached to a mainframe using the Cisco Channel Interface Processor (CIP) interface or a Cisco router LAN attached to an AS/400 or IBM 3745.

FRAS Host connectivity provides two methods for communications:

- LLC2 pass-through
- LLC2 local termination

Cisco suggests using LLC2 passthru for channel-attached routers to an IBM mainframe. This enables the router to pass through LLC2 session functions to the mainframe instead of terminating the LLC2 requests in the router. LLC2 local termination is the suggested configuration where the mainframe or an AS/400 is LAN attached or the use of DLSw+ is being employed for delivery of the SNA data. LLC2 passthru is the default when using the FRAS Host connectivity feature.

Figure 11-6 shows a LLC2 passthru configuration using a Cisco router with a CIP interface connecting over a channel to an IBM mainframe. In this configuration, the SNA feature of the CIP is used for communicating to the mainframe, enabling the CIP LLC2 stack on the router to manage session timeout, as well as to manage the LLC2 window and timer parameters independently of the CIP SNA stack. This combination provides enhanced performance and a robust solution for connecting SNA to the mainframe over a Frame-Relay router network.

The Cisco CIP interface employs a virtual Token-Ring LAN and virtual adapter on that LAN to represent the connection to the mainframe. All the Cisco IOS LLC2 parameters available to any LAN interface are available to the virtual LAN adapter of the CIP. This allows for fine-tuning of the LLC2 stack on the CIP, and thereby, proactively manages congestion and transmit window sizes so important to reducing dropped frames (which will render an SNA session over a LLC2 connection inoperable).

LLC2 local termination using FRAS Host feature employs DLSw+ for terminating the LLC2 sessions locally. Again, LLC2 tuning parameters are used to prevent LLC session timeouts and to manage window sizes. An advantage to using LLC2 local termination is the router's ability to dynamically adjust the LLC2 transmit window size based on Frame-Relay BECN messages.

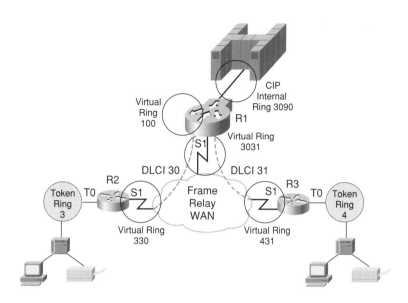

Figure 11-6
FRAS Host feature configuration employing LLC2 passthru using a Cisco CIP connection to an SNA mainframe.

Using LLC2 local termination with a Token-Ring–attached IBM 3745 removes Frame-Relay responsibilities from the NCP operating in the IBM 3745. In this case, the Cisco router sends the SNA data to the IBM 3745 over the LAN. This avoids interface, memory, and possibly, NCP software upgrades. Likewise, when using LLC2 local termination for connecting to an AS/400 over a LAN, the Cisco router protects the AS/400 from using valuable processor cycles on managing the Frame-Relay connection. Figure 11-7 illustrates the use of LLC2 local termination for an Ethernet-attached AS/400 through a Cisco router.

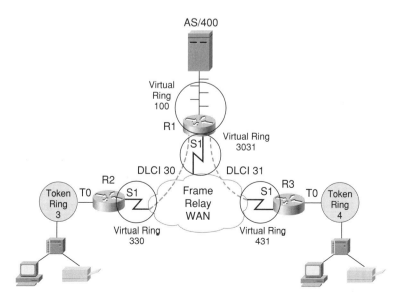

Figure 11-7
FRAS Host feature configuration employing local termination of LLC2 sessions to an Ethernet-attached AS/400.

11.3 ENABLING FRAME RELAY

Defining Frame Relay to the router requires several different commands. These commands specify the following:

- The physical location of the Frame-Relay connection on the router

- Use of Frame-Relay encapsulation for communicating to the network

- The type of Local Management Interface (LMI) protocol being used for communicating to the Frame-Relay switch

- The mapping used on this Frame-Relay interface

- Defining the use of virtual subinterfaces for the physical port

Defining the Frame-Relay Physical Interface

As with all connections to the network from a router, it is necessary to define which physical port on the router is being used for the connection. This is accomplished by using the `interface` IOS configuration router command. The standard `interface` command for defining a Frame-Relay connection is as follows:

```
interface serial slot/port
```

The `slot/port` parameter on the `interface serial` command is used to specify the physical location of the interface processor board and which port on the board is connecting to the network. If the serial interface processor board is installed in slot 1 of the router and port 2 of the board is used for connecting to the network, for example, the command identifying this location is as follows:

```
interface serial 1/2
```

All characteristics relating to the Frame-Relay network connected to this location are defined under this `interface` command. Some Cisco routers do not support slots, however. In this case, the `interface` command identifies only the port being used for connecting to the network. The `interface` command for such a router would appear as follows:

```
interface serial port
```

The `port` parameter, in this case, specifies the physical location on the router of the port being used for connecting to the network. Following our example, the interface supporting the Frame-Relay connection on a Cisco router that does not use slots for identifying the location of the interface processor board is entered as follows:

```
interface serial 2
```

The 2, in this case, represents that port number 2 on the router is used for connecting to the physical network.

11.3.1 Specifying the Encapsulation Type for the Interface

When connecting to Frame Relay it is important to identify the type of encapsulation being used, mainly when the Cisco router is connecting to non-Cisco routers at the other end of the Frame-Relay network. The `encapsulation` command used to identify this is as follows:

```
encapsulation frame-relay [ietf]
```

It is the `encapsulation frame-relay` command under the `interface` command that indicates to the Cisco router IOS that this connection is using Frame Relay. The `ietf` parameter on this command identifies the use of a non-Cisco device at the receiving end of this connection. The `ietf` parameter is used when connecting the Cisco router to an IBM 3745 FEP over Frame Relay.

11.3.2 Selecting the Local Management Interface Support

Frame relay uses a protocol specification called *Local Management Interface (LMI)* for communicating Frame-Relay switch configuration to the Cisco router or any other type of Frame-Relay end device. The LMI is used for confirming connectivity with the proper PVC and DLCI along with congestion-management frames such as BECN and FECN. The format of the command for describing to the Cisco router Frame-Relay interface the type of LMI support on the Frame-Relay switch is as follows:

```
frame-relay lmi-type {ansi | cisco | q933a}
```

The command identifies the three different types of LMI support available on the Cisco IOS software. Connecting to a switch that supports the American National Standards Institute (ANSI) flavor of LMI communications is entered as follows:

```
frame-relay lmi-type ansi
```

Entering the `lmi-type` in this way requires information from the Frame-Relay provider on the type of LMI supported on the switch connecting to the router. Autosensing the LMI type used on the switch connecting to the Cisco router was introduced in the Cisco IOS 11.2 software release.

The feature known as *LMI autosense* is the default when the `frame-relay lmi-type` command is left out of the configuration. The LMI autosense feature sends out a full status request to the attached switch in the three flavors supported by the Cisco IOS 11.2 software. The status requests are sent out in the order of ANSI, q933a (ITU), and Cisco. If the switch supports any of these LMI types, it will respond with the appropriate status message reply.

The Cisco IOS 11.2 software will decode the message and automatically configure the `frame-relay lmi-type` command for the interface. If the switch sends more than one valid status message reply to the Cisco router, the router will use the last valid reply received. The LMI autosense feature is disabled if the `frame-relay lmi-type` command is explicitly defined.

NOTES

The `frame-relay lmi-type` values are not kept between power-on restarts or router reloads. Therefore, it is important to note that after the Frame-Relay connection is active the configuration must be written to memory—otherwise known as *Non-volatile Random Access Memory (NVRAM)*. To save the configuration with the changed `lmi-type` value, use the Cisco enable mode command `WRITE MEMORY`.

11.3.3 Defining SNA Support on the Frame-Relay Port

Frame Relay is not a reliable transport, and therefore, does not have the capability to resequence, acknowledge, or provide flow control for time-sensitive SNA frames. The RFC 1490 FRF.3 SNA support overcomes these requirements for delivering SNA using LLC2 as part of the encapsulation method. The Cisco router IOS software is made aware of this encapsulation technique with the following `interface` subcommand:

```
frame-relay-map llc2 dlci-number
```

The `dlci-number` parameter identifies to the Cisco IOS software that RFC 1490 FRF.3 encapsulation techniques are used for transporting SNA data on the specified DLCI. If DLCI 30 is being used for connecting to an IBM 3745 FEP, for example, the command is coded as follows:

```
frame-relay-map llc2 30
```

This indicates to the router software that SNA-type data sent over DLCI 30 is encapsulated using RFC 1490 FRF.3 standards.

11.3.4 Defining Subinterfaces for the Physical Port

Subinterfaces enable a router supporting the transmission of SNA frames using SRB over Frame Relay by defining a specific DLCI to the subinterface. Subinterfaces create virtual physical ports under the true physical interface connecting to the Frame-Relay network. This also provides the engineer with greater flexibility for tuning each individual DLCI on the PVC. The format for defining a subinterface is as follows:

```
interface serial slot/port.subinterface-number point-to-point
```

The same rules—as for the `interface` command discussed earlier—hold true when specifying the `slot/port` parameter for subinterfaces. However, the `subinterface-number` parameter is the part of the command that identifies this interface definition as a subinterface. The `point-to-point` parameter defines this DLCI connection between two Frame-Relay devices rather than a multipoint connection. Using the preceding interface definition example, a subinterface is defined as follows:

```
interface serial 1/2

encapsulation frame-relay ietf

interface serial 1/2.30 point-to-point

encapsulation frame-relay ietf
```

It is customary to use the DLCI number being used for the connection as the `subinterface-number`. In our example, therefore, the subinterface 30 is indicating that the DLCI being used is 30. Identify the DLCI number used on a Frame-Relay interface by using the following command:

```
frame-relay interface-dlci dlci-number
```

The `dlci-number` parameter defines the number assigned to the DLCI used for the subinterface. To complete our example, we add the following command to the `subinterface` commands:

```
frame-relay interface-dlci 30
```

In this example, we specifically define to the router IOS software that DLCI 30 is used for the subinterface 1/2.30 on the router.

11.4 DEFINING STATIC BNN CONNECTION

FRAS BNN supports two types of SNA connectivity:

- LAN-attached devices
- Serially attached SDLC devices

Support for LAN-attached SNA devices is provided by the `fras map llc` command. The `fras map llc` command is specified on the LAN interface connecting the LAN-attached SNA devices. The format of the command is as follows:

```
fras map llc mac-address lan-lsap lan-rsap serial port frame-relay dlci fr-lsap fr-rsap
[pfid2¦afid2¦fid4]
```

The `fras map llc` command sets up the MAC/SAP address pair mapping between the downstream SNA device and the upstream SAP address of the IBM SNA host computer. The `mac-address` parameter value is the Medium Access Control (MAC) 48-bit, dotted-triple decimal address of the LAN-attached SNA device. An example of a MAC address is as follows:

```
4000.3174.1000
```

The next parameter, `lan-lsap`, identifies the SAP address used by the downstream SNA device being mapped. SNA devices use SAP addresses in multiples of four, starting with the value 04. The value is a hexadecimal number. For the most part, only the SAP address 04 is used. Typical values used in SNA networks are as follows:

```
04, 08, 0C, 10, 14
```

The `lan-rsap` parameter defines the destination SAP address of the IBM SNA host from the perspective of the downstream SNA device. Because the `fras map llc` command maps the downstream SNA device to the DLCI, which is mapped to the destination SAP, the `lan-rsap` value does not necessarily have to match the true destination SAP address. For clarity and ease of configuration, however, the best practice is to have the local and remote SAP addresses match. The value for the `lan-rsap` parameter follows the same definition rules as that described for the `lan-lsap` parameter.

The `port` parameter following the `serial` keyword of the `fras map llc` command identifies which serial port on the router connects to the Frame-Relay network. The `dlci` parameter of the `frame-relay` keyword identifies the DLCI number used for this mapping over the Frame-Relay network. The `fr-lsap` parameter is the local SAP address used by the router for identifying the DLCI in the LLC2 frames. The `fr-rsap` parameter defines the actual SAP address of the SNA host found on the other end of the Frame-Relay connection. If the downstream SNA device were connecting to an IBM 3745 using SAP 04 over DLCI number 30, for example, the `fras map llc` command is entered as follows:

```
fras map llc 4000.3174.1000 4 4 serial 1/2 frame-relay 30 4 4
```

The three remaining optional parameters reduce router processor overhead by indicating the only type of SNA format identifier (FID) to expect from the downstream SNA device. Entering a value of pfid2 at the end of the command identifies traditional SNA PU Type 2 device connectivity. A value of afid2 indicates that APPN Node Type 2.1 FID2 transmission headers are in use. A value of fid4 indicates that an SNA subarea connection is being used over this Frame-Relay configuration.

Supporting serial SDLC-attached devices requires the use of the fras map sdlc command on the serial interface connecting the SDLC-attached SNA device. The format of the fras map sdlc command is as follows:

```
fras map sdlc sdlc-address serial port frame relay dlci fr-lsap fr-rsap
[pfid2|afid2|fid4]
```

The key in mapping the serial-attached SDLC SNA device is the use of the SNA SDLC station address in the command. The sdlc-address parameter defines the actual SNA SDLC station address defined on the SNA device. This value must be unique for all serial-attached SDLC SNA-attached devices using the same DLCI on this router.

The remaining parameter values on the fras map sdlc command are entered following the same rules found on the fras map llc command. If we use the preceding fras map llc command example and replace it with a serial-attached SDLC SNA device using an SDLC station address of C1, the following command is entered:

```
fras map sdlc c1 serial 1/2 frame-relay 30 4 4
```

11.5 DEFINING DYNAMIC BNN CONNECTION

The coding of the MAC address and the destination SAP address for the frame need not be defined in the router configuration because dynamic BNN learns the mapping of MAC/SAP pairs through analyzing the frames as they enter the router LAN interface port. The format for using dynamic BNN fras map llc is as follows:

```
fras map llc lan-lsap serial interface frame-relay dlci dlci fr-rsap
```

Here only the lan-lsap parameter is defined to identify the SAP address used for communicating to the downstream SNA device. Also, note that in this command, the fr-lsap parameter used in the static BNN definition is not required. The DLCI number and the destination SAP address on the opposite Frame-Relay connections are required, however. These values are defined by the positional parameters dlci and fr-rsap, respectively. All the parameters in the dynamic BNN fras map llc command are defined using the same rules as found on the static BNN fras map llc command.

11.6 DEFINING BAN CONNECTIVITY

BAN support for Cisco FRAS requires the coding of the source-bridge ring-group global command prior to defining the fras ban interface command. For a discussion on the use of the source-bridge ring-group global command, consult Chapter 9, "RSRB Design and Configuration."

Using BAN requires the definitions of the Token-Ring logical connectivity along with a logical MAC address representing the DLCI used for the transport of the SNA frames. The format of the fras ban command is as follows:

```
fras ban local-ring bridge-number ring-group ban-dlci-mac dlci dlci#1
[dlci#2-dlci#5] [bni-mac-addr]
```

The local-ring parameter is used to define the actual ring number assigned to the LAN interface being used for connecting the downstream LAN-attached SNA devices. The local-ring value ranges from 1 through 4095, and is in decimal format. The bridge-number parameter is the number of the logical bridge connecting the physical LAN Token Ring to the logical virtual ring defined by the ring-group parameter. The ring-group parameter must match the virtual ring number defined on the source-bridge ring-group global command used for this connection. The valid range for values used on the local-ring parameter is 1 through 15 (in decimal format). The ring-group value is a valid decimal number from 1 to 4095, matching the source-bridge ring-group value.

The ban-dlci-mac parameter represents the BAN PVC MAC address used in the frame sent to the receiving BAN device. This value is coded in accordance with the 48-bit, triple-dotted decimal address as noted in the discussion on defining static BNN.

The dlci parameter following the dlci keyword specifies one or more DLCI numbers used for the BAN connection. Each DLCI number must be unique and range between 16 and 1007. Defining more DLCI numbers, up to a maximum of five, allows the router to perform load balancing over the DLCIs for connectivity to the destination SNA device.

The final optional parameter bni is used to define the MAC address used by the IBM SNA host for connecting to the network. The Boundary Node Identifier (BNI) value uses the 48-bit, triple-dotted decimal representation of the MAC address. Using the BNI value allows the IBM 3745 NCP or AS/400 to be configured without the need for the BAN DLCI MAC address. With this in mind, it is good practice to have the ban-dlci-mac value equal to the bni-mac-addr values. The following example uses the fras ban command:

```
fras ban 200 1 100 4000.3745.0001 dlci 30 bni 4000.3745.0001
```

In this example, the physical Token-Ring interface is attached to ring number 200. We have defined bridge number 1 as the connection from ring 200 to the ring-group ring number

100. The DLCI MAC address is defined to equal the actual IBM 3745 MAC address, and the connection is using Frame-Relay DLCI number 30 to make the connection.

11.7 DEFINING SRB OVER FRAME RELAY

Cisco's implementation of SRB over Frame Relay using RFC 1490 bridged 802.5 encapsulation is interoperable with SRB over Frame Relay from other vendors. SRB over Frame Relay is implemented by the inclusion of the `source-bridge` interface command using the `conserve-ring` keyword. The format of the command is as follows:

```
source-bridge source-ring-number bridge-number target-ring-number conserve-ring
```

The `conserve-ring` keyword is valid only on Frame-Relay subinterface definitions. Cisco's implementation of SRB over Frame Relay does not support the following features of Cisco IOPS for SNA support:

- Proxy explorer

- Automatic spanning tree

- LAN Network Manager

The `source-ring-number` value is the virtual ring representing the Frame-Relay DLCI for the subinterface on the router. The `bridge-number` is the logical bridge being used to connect the source-ring to the target-ring. The `target-ring-number` is the value matching the global `source-bridge ring-group` number defined for the router. The `conserve-ring` keyword indicates to the router to use SRB over Frame Relay encapsulation specifications.

11.8 DEFINING FRAS HOST CONNECTIVITY

The FRAS Host feature of Cisco IOS 11.3 enables Cisco routers to be the Frame-Relay connection point to the LAN-attached IBM SNA host. Both BNN and BAN techniques are available for use by the Cisco host-attached router. The Cisco router attached to the host computer can use either LLC2 passthru or LLC2 local termination functions to enable LLC2 transport.

11.8.1 LLC2 Passthru Configuration Commands

The LLC2 passthru functions of the FRAS Host feature are most useful when combined with the Cisco router attached to the IBM SNA mainframe using a CIP for connecting to the mainframe. LLC2 passthru requires the use of the following `interface` command:

```
interface virtual-tokenring number
```

The use of the `interface virtual-tokenring` command along with the `fras-host bnn` or `fras-host ban` interface commands enables the use of LLC2 pass-through mode. This virtual ring is used as the connection point for transporting LLC2 traffic over the Frame-Relay connection between the SNA host and the downstream SNA device. The *number* parameter of the `interface virtual-tokenring` command identifies the virtual port associated with the `fras-host` definitions. Under the virtual ring definition, the `source-bridge` command is also defined to associate the virtual ring number of the `virtual-tokenring` to the global ring-group number. An example of using the virtual-tokenring interface definition is as follows:

```
interface Virtual-TokenRing0

source-bridge 200 1 100
```

In this example, ring number 200 is being identified with the `virtual-tokenring` interface and is being bridged to the ring-group number 100.

11.8.2 LLC2 Local Termination Configuration Commands

Enabling LLC2 local termination function of the FRAS Host feature is possible using the following commands:

```
dlsw local-peer

fras-host dlsw-local-ack
```

The first command, `dlsw local-peer`, enables the router to use Data Link Switching (DLSw) as the means for delivering LLC2-type traffic through the `virtual-tokenring` interface defined on the router. The `dlsw local-peer` command is a global command and is not specific to any particular interface. Couple the `dlsw local-peer` command with the `fras-host dlsw-local-ack` defined on the `virtual-tokenring` interface and LLC2 Local termination function is enabled for the router.

LLC2 local termination is most appropriate for connectivity to a LAN-attached SNA host. The SNA host may be directly attached to the LAN or it may be channel attached to an IBM 3745 FEP.

11.8.3 FRAS Host BNN Configuration Command

To configure a router to use the FRAS Host BNN feature, the following command must be issued on the virtual-tokenring interface:

```
fras-host bnn (sub)interface fr-lsap sap vmac virt-mac hmac hmac [hsap hsap]
```

The fras-host bnn command enables the service on the interface defined by the value set for the positional parameter (sub)interface. The sap parameter following the fr-lsap keyword defines the SAP address used by the LLC2 as the destination SAP address for inbound BNN frames on the Frame-Relay connection. A virtual MAC address is used along with the DLCI number to create a unique MAC address for the BNN connection. The virt-mac value is a full 48-bit, dotted-triple decimal value (6 full bytes) whose last 2 bytes must be 0. These last 2 bytes are replaced with the DLCI number associated with the BNN connection. Examples of an invalid and valid virtual MAC address are as follows:

```
Valid VMAC: 4000.7500.0000

Invalid VMAC: 4000.7500.0101
```

The hmac value following the hmac keyword is the actual MAC address defined on the Cisco router CIP internal adapter or the MAC address of the AS/400 or IBM 3745 LAN interfaces. The final optional parameter, hsap, indicates the host SAP address used for connecting to the SNA host. Not coding the hsap value and keyword defaults this SAP address to the one used for the fr-lsap keyword. The following is an example of a composed command:

```
fras-host bnn serial 1/2 fr-lsap 04 vmac 4000.7513.000 hmac 4000.3745.0001
```

The command indicates that serial 1/2 is the Frame-Relay interface with a virtual MAC address of 4000.7513.000 using the SAP address of 04 for connecting LLC2 sessions with the SNA host at MAC address 4000.3745.0001 and IBM 3745 FEP.

11.8.4 FRAS Host BAN Configuration Command

The BAN configuration for the FRAS Host function is simpler in form. The format for the fras-host ban command is as follows:

```
fras-host ban (sub)interface hmac hmac [bni bni-mac]
```

Again, the command identifies the interface used for connecting the virtual Token Ring to the Frame-Relay network using the (sub)interface positional parameter. The hmac value is the MAC address of the destination IBM SNA LAN-attached host computer.

The *bni-mac* value is the BNI MAC address of the Frame-Relay connection to the host computer. An example of using this command is as follows:

```
fras-host ban serial 1/2.30 hmac 4000.3745.0001
```

In the example, we are defining BAN support for the subinterface 30 on port 2 of the serial interface board installed in slot 1. The MAC address of the SNA host computer is 4000.3745.0001.

11.9 FRAME-RELAY CONFIGURATION EXAMPLES

The examples included for SNA using Frame-Relay networks show the various types of Frame-Relay topologies discussed and the with the Cisco IOS configuration commands for defining connectivity.

11.9.1 Boundary Network Node

Figure 11-8 diagrams the use of static BNN for LAN- and SDLC-attached SNA devices. Note that in the sample configurations we have coded no IP address for the serial interfaces and the Token-Ring interface definitions. Although not coding an IP address is valid, it does not preclude that IP traffic be prohibited from these interfaces while using SNA. It is not coded here for clarity when defining the SNA-only commands.

The configurations connecting to the IBM 3745 use the IETF form of RFC 1490 FRF.3 encapsulation because the destination Frame-Relay device is a non-Cisco Frame-Relay device. The fras map llc commands defined on router R1 specify the mapping for PUa and PUb Token-Ring–attached SNA 3174 controllers.

Besides the MAC address for each being unique, they also use different SAP addresses for communicating to the IBM mainframe. The SNA IBM 3174 controller SDLC attached to router R2 is defined using the SDLC address of the controller in the fras map sdlc command. Note that the IBM 3745 communicates over a single physical Frame-Relay interface to both router R1 and router R2. The IBM 3745 uses DLCI 30 for communicating with R1 and DLC31 for communicating with R2. This is also reflected in the router configurations and the fras map commands.

Figure 11-9 shows dynamic BNN configuration. Here, we see that a single fras map llc is used to map both PUa and PUb to the Frame-Relay network connected over serial 1.

R1 Configuration

interface serial 1
ni ip address
encapsulation frame-relay IEFT
frame-relay lmi-type ansi
frame-relay map llc2 30
!
Interface tokenring 0
no ip address
ring-speed 16
fras map llc 4000.3174.0001 4 4 serial 1 frame-relay 30 4 4
fras map llc 4000.3174.0002 8 8 serial 1 frame-relay 30 8 8

Figure 11-8
Static BNN
`fras map`
*configuration
example for
LLC2 and SDLC
connections.*

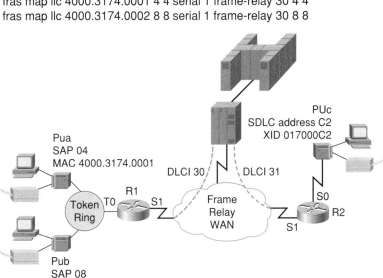

R2 Configuration

interface serial 0
no ip address
encapsulation sdlc
no keepalive
clockrate 56000
sdlc address C2
sdlc xid C2 017000C2
sdlc role primary
fras map sdlc C2 serial 1 frame-relay 31 4 4
!
interface serial 1
no lp address
encapsulation frame-relay lmi-type ietf
frame-relay lmi-type ansi
frame-relay map llc2 31

Figure 11-9
Dynamic BNN
`fras map`
`llc`
configuration
example.

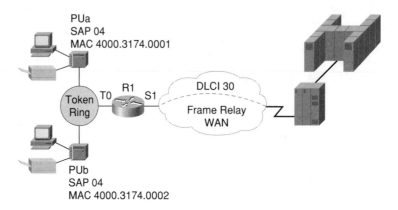

PUa
SAP 04
MAC 4000.3174.0001

R1
T0   S1   DLCI 30
Token Ring   Frame Relay
WAN

PUb
SAP 04
MAC 4000.3174.0002

R1 Configuration

interface serial 1
no ip address
encapsulation frame-relay ieft
frame-relay lmi-type ansi
frame-relay map llc2 30
!
interface tokenring 0
no ip address
ring-speed 16
fras map llc 4 Serial 1 frame-relay dlci 30 4

11.9.2 Boundary Access Node

In the BAN configuration shown in Figure 11-10, we see the use of virtual ring groups for establishing the LLC2 connectivity over the Frame-Relay network. Ring group 300 represents the Frame-Relay connection and bridges to the virtual ring 200, representing the DLCI to destination MAC address mapping. The Token-Ring interface bridges to the ring group 300 from its own ring number 100.

Figure 11-11 illustrates support for SDLC-attached devices over a router using BAN. Here, we see two SNA IBM 3174 controllers attached over serial connections to the same router. The device attached to serial interface 1 is an SNA PU 2.1 device, and the SNA device attached to serial interface 2 is an SNA PU 2.0 device. Each uses a virtual MAC address to represent itself on the virtual ring assigned to the Frame-Relay DLCI ring number 200. For more information on the SDLC definitions used in this example, consult Chapter 8, "STUN Design and Configuration," and Chapter 10, "SDLLC Design and Configuration."

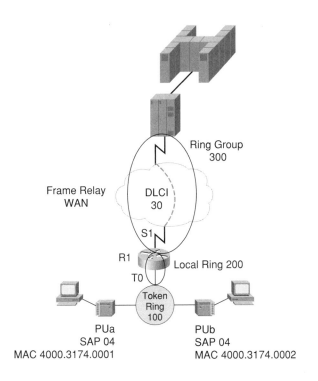

Figure 11-10
*BAN
connectivity
example for
Token-Ring–
attached SNA
devices.*

R1 Configuration
source-bridge ring-group 300
!
interface serial1
  encapsulation frame-relay ietf
  frame-relay lmi-type ansi
  frame-relay map llc2 30
    fras ban 200 1 300 4000.3745.0001 dlci 30
!
interface tokenring 0
  source-bridge 100 1 300

Figure 11-11
*BAN
connectivity
example for
SDLC-attached
SNA devices.*

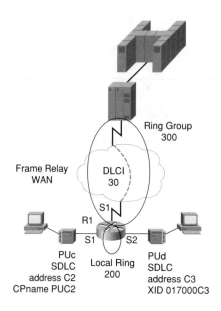

R1 Configuration

```
interface serial 0
encapsulation frame-relay ietf
  frame-relay lmi-type ansi
  frame-relay map llc2 30
  fras ban 200 1 300 4000.3745.0001 dlci 30
!
interface serial 1
  description SDLC line PUc PU2.1
  no ip address
  encapsulation sdlc
  clockrate 19200
  sdlc role prim-xid-poll
  sdlc vmac 4000.0000.C230
  sdlc address C2
  sdlc partner 4000.3745.0001 C2
  fras ban frame-relay serial0 4000.3745.0001 dlci 30
!
interface serial2
  description SDLC line PUd PU2
  no ip address
  encapsulation sdlc
  clockrate 19200
  sdlc role primary
  sdlc vmac 4000.0000.C330
  sdlc address C3
  sdlc xid C3 017000C3
  sdlc partner 4000.3745.0001 C3
    fras ban frame-relay serial 0 4000.3745.0001 dlci 30
```

11.9.3 SRB over Frame Relay

In the example depicting SRB over Frame Relay in Figure 11-12, we see the use of the subinterface on router R1. A key to this configuration is the bridging of all LANs to the `source-bridge ring-group` number 3031. Ring 3031 serves as the Token Ring that all other Token Rings in this configuration are using as the intermediate connecting ring for the end devices. Each subinterface on router R1 uses the virtual ring associated with the partner Frame-Relay router connected over the DLCI assigned to the subinterface. Router R2 uses DLCI 30 and builds its SRB connection over the virtual ring assigned to the DLCI, which is ring 330. Likewise, router R2 uses DLCI 31 on subinterface 1.2 and bridges to the partner Frame-Relay router using virtual ring 431.

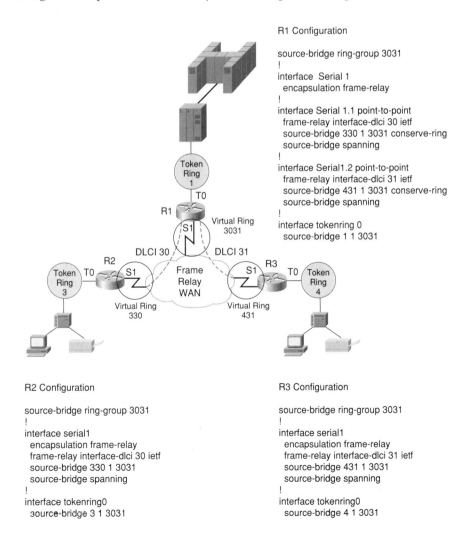

R1 Configuration

source-bridge ring-group 3031
!
interface Serial 1
  encapsulation frame-relay
!
interface Serial 1.1 point-to-point
  frame-relay interface-dlci 30 ietf
  source-bridge 330 1 3031 conserve-ring
  source-bridge spanning
!
interface Serial1.2 point-to-point
  frame-relay interface-dlci 31 ietf
  source-bridge 431 1 3031 conserve-ring
  source-bridge spanning
!
interface tokenring 0
  source-bridge 1 1 3031

Figure 11-12
*SRB over
Frame-Relay
configurations.*

R2 Configuration

source-bridge ring-group 3031
!
interface serial1
  encapsulation frame-relay
  frame-relay interface-dlci 30 ietf
  source-bridge 330 1 3031
  source-bridge spanning
!
interface tokenring0
  source-bridge 3 1 3031

R3 Configuration

source-bridge ring-group 3031
!
interface serial1
  encapsulation frame-relay
  frame-relay interface-dlci 31 ietf
  source-bridge 431 1 3031
  source-bridge spanning
!
interface tokenring0
  source-bridge 4 1 3031

11.9.4 FRAS Host Connectivity

FRAS Host connectivity to a channel-attached mainframe, shown in Figure 11-13, is made possible using the Cisco SNA feature on the CIP board installed in Cisco 7000/7500 series routers. As shown in the figure, the router R1 CIP interface on interface channel 6/0 enables SNA connectivity support over the channel using the csna command. A requirement to this connectivity is the use of an internal LAN and internal LAN adapter associated with the channel. This internal LAN is defined under the channel interface definition labeled 6/2 using the lan tokenring command. An internal adapter is assigned to the internal ring using the adapter subcommand of the lan tokenring command. It is the MAC address assigned to this internal LAN adapter that is used as the destination MAC address for SNA devices connecting to the mainframe using LLC2 communication. You can find an in-depth discussion of the use of SNA over a Cisco CIP in Chapter 16, "CIP Design and Configuration."

Router R2 is using dynamic BNN for connectivity to the channel-attached mainframe. Note the absence of a virtual ring definition for the R2 router. The R3 router is employing the BAN function of Cisco FRAS. The fras ban command on the R3 router identifies the destination MAC address of the mainframe as 4000.7513.4200 over DLCI 31. This MAC address matched the internal LAN adapter address defined for the Cisco CIP on router R1. The use of the virtual token-ring definition in router R1 defines the SNA host MAC address as 4000.7513.4200 matching its own internal LAN adapter MAC address. These definitions are not specifically defining LLC2 local termination and, therefore, the router defaults to using LLC2 passthru for the LLC2 communications.

Figure 11-14 illustrates a configuration using LLC2 local termination for SNA connectivity to an Ethernet-attached IBM AS/400 host computer. You will see that the main difference between the LLC2 passthru configuration and the LLC2 local termination is the inclusion of the dlsw local-peer and the fras host dlsw-local-ack commands. These two commands defined together enable the fras-host LLC2 local termination feature. The dlsw bridge-group 1 command is required in this configuration—not for LLC2 local termination, but rather to enable connectivity over Ethernet 0 to the AS/400 SNA host computer.

R2 Configuration

```
interface serial 1
  encapsulation frame-relay ietf
  frame-relay map llc2 30
!
interface tokenring0
  fras map llc 4 serial 1 frame-relay 30 4
```

R3 Configuration

```
source-bridge ring-group 3031
!
interface serial 1
  encapsulation frame-relay ietf
  frame-relay map llc2 31
  fras ban 431 1 3031 4000.7513.4200 dlci 31
!
interface tokenring0
  source-bridge 4 1 3031
```

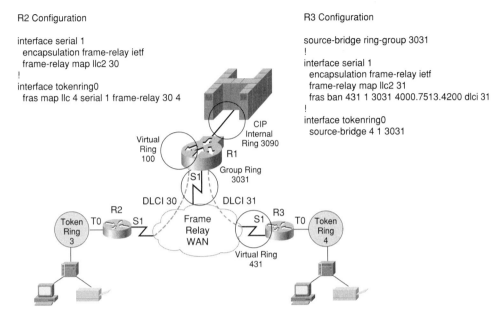

Figure 11-13
Dynamic BNN and BAN connectivity to a channel-attached mainframe using the FRAS Host feature using LLC2 passthru.

R1 Configuration

```
source-bridge ring-group 3031
!
interface serial 1/10
  encapsulation frame-relay IETF
  frame-relay map llc2 30
  frame-relay map llc2 31
!
interface Channel 6/0
  no ip address
    csna E210 02
!
interface Channel 6/2
  no ip address
  lan tokenring 0
    source-bridge 3090 1 3031
    adapter 0 4000.7513.4200
!
interface Virtual-tokenring0
  source-bridge 100 1 3031
  source-bridge spanning
  fras-host bnn serial 1/0 fr-lsap 04 vmac 4000.7513.0000 hm ac 4000.7513.4200
  fras-host bnn serial 1/0 hmac 4000.7513 .4200
```

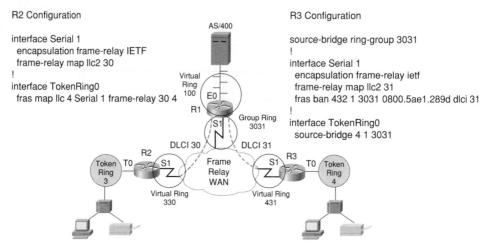

Figure 11-14
*Dynamic BNN
and BAN
connectivity to
an Ethernet-
attached
AS/400 SNA
host using
LLC2 local
termination.*

R2 Configuration

interface Serial 1
  encapsulation frame-relay IETF
  frame-relay map llc2 30
!
interface TokenRing0
  fras map llc 4 Serial 1 frame-relay 30 4

R3 Configuration

source-bridge ring-group 3031
!
interface Serial 1
  encapsulation frame-relay ietf
  frame-relay map llc2 31
  fras ban 432 1 3031 0800.5ae1.289d dlci 31
!
interface TokenRing0
  source-bridge 4 1 3031

R1 Configuration

source-bridge ring-group 3031
dlsw local-peer
dslw bridge-group 1
!
interface Ethernet0
  bridge-group 1
!
interface Serial1
  encapsulation frame-relay ietf
  frame-relay map llc2 30
  frame-relay map llc2 31
  frame-relay lmi-type ansi
!
interface virtual-tokenring0
  no ip address
  ring-speed 16
  source-bridge 100 1 3031
  fras-host dlsw-local-ack
  fras-host bnn Serial 1 fr-lsap 04 vmac 4000.4700.0000 hmac 0800.5ae1.289d
  fras-host bnn Serial 1 hmac 0800.5ae1.289d

CHAPTER 12

DLSw+ Design and Configuration

Data Link Switching Plus (DLSw+) is an encapsulation technique and protocol that uses TCP for transporting SNA frames and NetBIOS traffic. The discussion in this chapter focuses on the transport of SNA. The hierarchical design of DLSw+ networks provides for a great degree of scalability. This chapter focuses on the most commonly used DLSw+ configurations and discusses some of the enhanced features that have made DLSw+ the preferred mechanism over source-route bridging (SRB) in IP-based backbone router networks.

12.1 DESIGN CRITERIA

DLSw+ uses peer-to-peer communications. The connection enabling the communication is referred to as a *peer connection*. DLSw+ supports the following SNA physical unit connections:

- PU1-to-PU4

- PU2/2.1-to-PU4

- PU2.1-to-PU2.1

- PU4-to-PU4

Connectivity support between these SNA PUs is specific to the type of SNA session. PU4-to-PU4 connectivity over DLSw+ supports only a single path between the IBM 3745 FEPs. This is due to the inability of an FEP to handle source-route bridged paths.

Figure 12-1 lists the individual SNA sessions and the supported data-link control when using DLSw+ as the transport.

Figure 12-1		PU2/PU2.1-PU4	PU1-PU4	PU2.1-PU2.1	PU4-PU4
Data-link support for transport SNA PU sessions using DLSw+.	Token Ring	•		•	•
	Ethernet	•		•	
	SDLC	•	•	•	
	FDDI	•		•	
	Frame Relay	•		•	

The end-to-end SNA connection between the DLSw+ partners is called a *circuit*. A single DLSw+ connection can support multiple circuits. Figure 12-2 illustrates a simple DLSw+ connection supporting two circuits.

Figure 12-2
A simple DLSw+ connection.

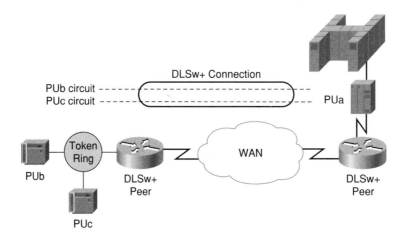

The DLSw+ circuit encompasses all the connections between the two SNA end points. These are:

- The data-link connection between the source SNA PU and its attached router
- The TCP connection supporting the DLSw+ peer connection between the source router and the destination router
- The data-link connection between the destination router and its attached SNA PU

Circuits are identified by unique circuit identifiers. The circuit IDs are comprised of the following:

- Destination and source MAC address

- Destination and source-link service access points (LSAP)

- Data-link control port ID

Many Cisco router-based networks transporting SNA frames were first established using Cisco remote source-route bridging (RSRB) connectivity. Cisco DLSw+ has incorporated many of the enhanced features of RSRB into the base DLSw+ configuration. If you are migrating the transport of SNA frames from an RSRB-based topology to one using DLSw+, it is important to remove the following functions from your IOS configuration to avoid conflict with the inherent functions of DLSw+:

- Proxy Explorer

- NetBIOS name caching

- SDLC-LLC2 conversion (SDLLC)

- Source-route/translational bridging (SR/TLB)

12.1.1 Minimize Explorer Traffic with DLSw+ Border Peers, Peer Groups, and On-Demand Peers

Using peer groups, DLSw+ reduces broadcast replications in a full-meshed network. These broadcasts are typically LLC2 test frames for a destination MAC or the NetBIOS Name Query. A *peer group* is a logical clustering of DLSw+ routers. Within this peer group, one or more DLSw+ are defined to act as a border peer to another logical peer group.

Standard DLSw design dictates that all routers must peer with each other to establish a broadcast search. However, DLSw+ routers within a peer group establish persistent peer connections only with the border peer router. The border peer router of each individual peer group establishes peer connections with all peers defined in the group and a border peer of another peer group.

Figure 12-3 illustrates a logical full-meshed DLSw network and a DLSw+ peer group topology using border peers of the same network. LLC2 test frames are only sent from the requesting router (R1) to a border router (R2), which may then pass on the single broadcast to a peered border peer router (R3) in another peer group. If R3 in our example does not have the destination in its cache, it will broadcast the request to the peer group and other border peers connecting different peer groups than the originating peer group. As you can see, this greatly reduces the broadcasts in a full-meshed network.

Figure 12-3
*Use of DLSw+
peer groups
and border
peers for
reducing
explorer
broadcasts.*

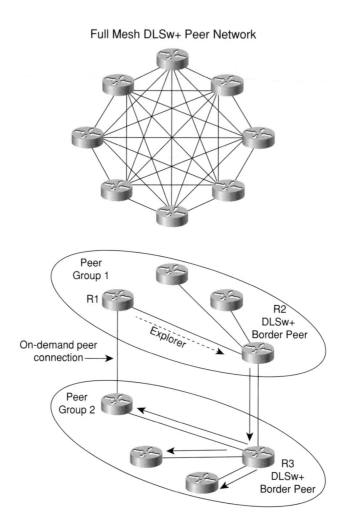

After the destination resource is found, the two DLSw+ peers involved set up a direct DLSw+ connection. This direct connection bypassing the border peers involved in the search is called *peer-on-demand connections*. Peer-on-demand connections occur only when peer connections are established through border peers without preconfiguring the peers in the participating routers.

12.1.2 Reduce Explorer Traffic Using an Explorer Firewall

For many large networks, the start-of-the-day connections cause explorer storms that may hinder network throughput and response time for established non-DLSw+ communications. A feature of DLSw+ that greatly reduces this phenomenon is the use of an explorer firewall. The *explorer firewall* permits only one single explorer across the WAN in search of a destination MAC address. As the explorer traverses the WAN searching for the destination MAC address, subsequent explorer packets searching for the same MAC address are prohibited from the WAN. After the explorer response is received, the DLSw+ router acting as the firewall will reply back to all the outstanding explorer requests searching for the same MAC address. A typical example of this is the morning startup of an SNA session to the destination MAC address of the mainframe.

12.1.3 Explorer Control Using Port Lists

DLSw+ contains a feature for creating broadcast domains within the DLSw+ network. This is performed using the port list feature. *Port lists* enable the engineer to control the forwarding of broadcasts. Port lists allow differentiation between Token Rings and serial ports to establish the broadcast domains. All Ethernet ports are treated as a single domain because of the Ethernet bridge group definitions required. Figure 12-4 illustrates the use of port lists for establishing broadcast domains.

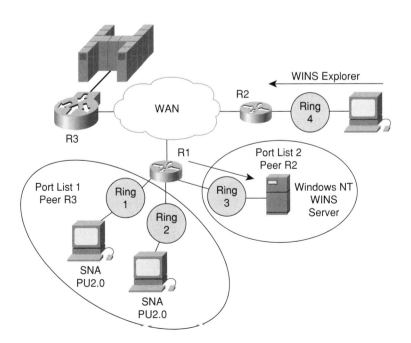

Figure 12-4
Use of port lists to establish broadcast domains within a DLSw+ network.

Route R1 in Figure 12-4 has defined Token Ring 1 and 2 as a broadcast domain supporting SNA devices. Ring 3 on R1 is a broadcast domain of its own supporting Windows NT Servers using WINS protocol. The workstation on R2 needs only to communicate with the WINS server on Ring 3 R1. The port list on R1 will keep all WINS broadcasts from the workstation off Ring 1 and 2 on R1. The port lists can also stop all communications to any devices on Ring 1 and 2 from the workstation on R2.

12.1.4 Backup and Multiple Active Peers

Multiple active peers is the standard DLSw+ connectivity for peering as well as for providing for alternate peering. This is not always prudent in design, however. The use of multiple active peers is not recommended when the alternate peer is at a disaster recovery location or at a secondary data center, for example, or when two DLSw+ routers feed a single channel-attached router. These scenarios are better serviced using the *backup peer feature* of DLSw+. The backup peer feature requires the use of TCP or FST encapsulation. Figure 12-5 diagrams the use of backup peers.

In Figure 12-5 the mainframe is channel-attached to a Cisco CIP router. The CIP router connects via token-ring to routers R1, R2 and R3. The remote routers R4 and R5 peer with routers R1 and R3 respectively. Router R2 is the backup router for both R4 and R5. If the connection between R4 and R1 were to fail, R1 would re-establish the SNA sessions to the mainframe through router R2. Once connectivity is restored between R1 and R4 any new sessions to the mainframe are established over the DLSw+ connection between R1 and R4. Sessions already established through R2 remain active through R2 until they end or until a specified amount of time has expired at which point the R2 router will terminate the active remaining sessions.

12.1.5 Load Balancing and Redundancy

DLSw+-enabled routers maintain a cache of multiple paths. The paths define the reachability of destination MAC addresses and NetBIOS names. If there are multiple paths to a resource, the least-cost path is the preferred path and the remaining paths are labeled capable. Should the preferred path become unavailable, the next path in the reachability path table for the resource becomes the new preferred path. The path entries are stored for remote peers as capable and for local resources as ports. The status capable indicates that the peer associated with the entry at one time was able to reach the destination resource. Entries using ports identify that the destination resource is directly attached to he originating router through one of the communications ports. The multiple paths available for establishing connections are categorized as either *fault tolerant* or *load balancing*.

DLSw+ defaults the path as a fault-tolerant path. Using fault-tolerant mode the originating DLSw+ router will send a response back to the requesting end station from its

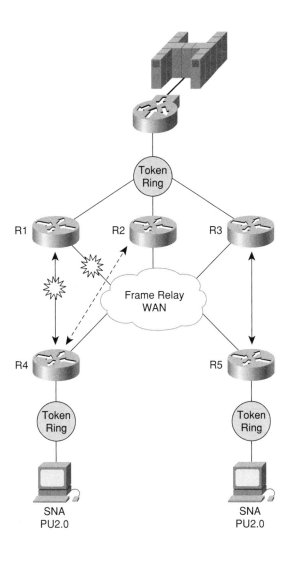

Figure 12-5
*DLSw+ backup
peer
configuration.*

cache if the entry has not timed out. If the cached entry has timed out, the originating DLSw+ router sends a CANUREACH request to each of its DLSw+ peers. Any of the peers not responding are removed from the cache. The destination DLSw+ router will respond to a CANUREACH request immediately if the entry in the cache has not timed out. If the cache entry in the destination DLSw+ router has timed out, it will forward a single route broadcast test frame over all the ports known to the cache. If any of the ports reply to the test frame the destination DLSw+ router replies back to the originating DLSw+ router with an ICANREACH response. The originating DLSw+ router then updates its cache and establishes the circuit for the requesting end station.

Duplicate paths to destination resources allow DLSw+ to be configured for load balancing. This is particularly advantageous for connectivity to IBM hosts that use duplicate MAC addresses for connecting to the same IBM host. The duplicate MAC address is assigned to a LAN interface of an IBM FEP or Cisco CIP internal LAN. The LAN adapters represented by the MAC address must be connected to different Token-Ring segments, however, for them both to be active at the same time. DLSw+ will recognize duplicate MAC addresses and load balance the circuits from the end stations requesting connectivity to the mainframe using a round-robin schema based on the cached entry list in the originating DLSw+ router. Figure 12-6 illustrates the load-balancing feature of DLSw+.

Figure 12-6
*Load-balancing
SNA sessions
using duplicate
MAC addresses
with an IBM
3745 FEP and a
Cisco CIP.*

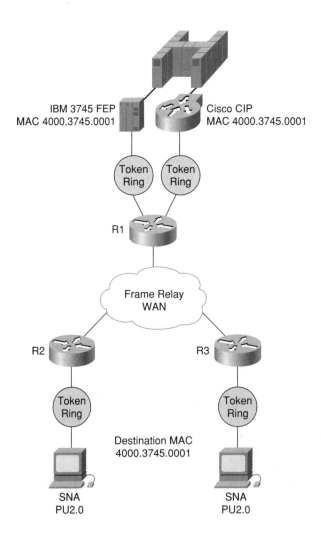

The workstation connecting through router R2 in Figure 12-6 establishes its SNA connection through the FEP. Next, the workstation connecting through router R3 sends a test frame looking for the MAC address attaching to the mainframe. R1 receives the test frame and will inspect the circuit cache for a duplicate MAC address. In this case, a duplicate is found and the R1 router will then determine the number of active circuits to each MAC address. In this scenario, the FEP has an active circuit and the CIP does not. Using load-balancing router R1 will establish the new circuit to the CIP. The workstation connecting through router R3 will then be assigned the path using the CIP by router R1. Using both an FEP and a CIP demonstrates the capability of these two technologies to work together and outlines a migration path from an FEP to the CIP. For a more detailed discussion on replacing FEPs with a Cisco CIP, read Chapter 16, "CIP Design and Configuration."

12.1.6 Use of Dynamic Peers

Standard DLSw requires that any router participating in DLSw must have a persistent TCP connection with any peer that it must communicate. DLSw+ dynamic peers, found in Cisco IOS Release 11.1 and higher, establish the TCP connection with a predefined DLSw peer only when circuits are being used between them. The TCP connections are dynamically established and exist as long as there is an active circuit between the DLSw peers. After the last circuit between the DLSw peers ends and a specified amount of time expires, the TCP connection is dynamically torn down.

Dynamic peers are suitable for the following network configurations:

- Large networks with minimal branch-to-branch communications

- Occasional communications between branch offices

- Dial-out error recovery for small networks or branch offices

12.1.7 Local Switching

The local-switching feature of DLSw+ enables the same functionality found with Cisco SDLLC. *Local switching* provides the conversion of SDLC frames to Token-Ring frames. This is useful for SDLC serial-attached devices connecting to an IBM host using a Token-Ring LAN connection. Likewise, the reverse configuration, serially attached IBM FEP or AS/400 to a router and remote Token-Ring–attached SNA devices, is possible. Using the reverse situation will avoid costly upgrades to the IBM FEP or AS/400 to support LAN interfaces.

12.2 DESIGN CONFIGURATIONS

The DLSw+ configurations discussed here represent the majority of configuration you will require for employing DLSw+ in your SNA network. The Cisco IOS commands specific to enabling these configurations are discussed in detail. The configuration examples depict the various transport methods for using DLSw+ connectivity to IBM SNA hosts using LANs, serial lines, and Frame Relay. Additionally we discuss examples using DLSw+ peer groups, load balancing, and the use of backup peers.

12.2.1 DLSw+ Using TCP Encapsulation

TCP encapsulation is the DLSw standard for transporting the DLSw peer connections. It is the baseline for delivering sequenced, error-free, and acknowledged connections. Figure 12-7 illustrates a DLSw+ peer connection using the TCP encapsulation method.

Figure 12-7
Delivering DLSw+ connections over TCP connections between peers using local acknowledgement.

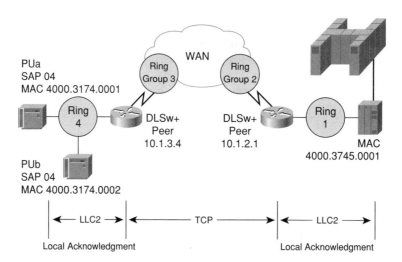

12.2.2 DLSw+ Using Direct Encapsulation

This form of encapsulation is used when the Cisco DLSw+ router is directly connected to another Cisco DLSw+ router via a serial connection. The serial connection is typically using Cisco proprietary implementation of HDLC. Figure 12-8 diagrams a direct encapsulation configuration for DLSw+ on Cisco routers.

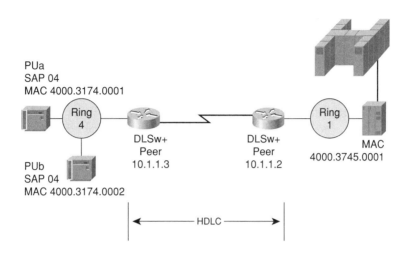

Figure 12-8
Establishing direct encapsulation for DLSw+ connectivity between two adjacent peers.

12.2.3 DLSw+ Using FST Encapsulation

Recall from previous discussions on encapsulation techniques that Fast Sequence Transport (FST) has lower overhead cost than does TCP encapsulation. The DLSw+ packet is encapsulated in IP datagrams and then routed across the network. FST encapsulation is a viable alternative to TCP if it can be determined that the datagrams will not cause out-of-sequence problems for the DLSw+ connection. Figure 12-9 illustrates the use of FST as the encapsulation technique for delivering DLSw+ packets.

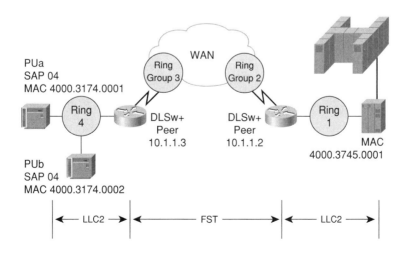

Figure 12-9
DLSw+ connections using FST encapsulation between peers.

12.2.4 DLSw+ with SDLC to Token Ring

The conversion of SDLC frames to Token-Ring frames is performed automatically by DLSw+ and is an advantage for preserving a corporation's investment in legacy SNA 3274/3174 SDLC-attached controllers. Typically, locations that use SDLC-attached controllers can now directly attach them to the serial ports on a router for delivery to a Token-Ring–attached IBM 3745 FEP. Conversely, to avoid the costly upgrade to supporting Token Ring on IBM 3745 FEPs, the FEP can attach to the serial port of a router while the remote IBM 3714 controller is Token Ring–attached to the Cisco router. Figure 12-10 diagrams a typical use of DLSw+ as the transport for delivering SNA data between an SDLC and Token-Ring–attached SNA devices. A Cisco CIP is also an option for connecting the SNA resources in this configuration to the mainframe.

Figure 12-10
SDLC-to-Token Ring with DLSw+ connections.

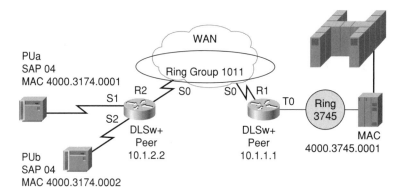

12.2.5 DLSw+ with Frame Relay

Frame relay supports the transport of SDLC- and LAN-attached IBM SNA controllers for communicating to the IBM mainframe. Figure 12-11 shows the use of DLSw+ as the connection for transporting the SNA data to the mainframe. The configuration supports IBM 3174 Token-Ring–attached controllers communicating to an IBM 3745 FEP over a Frame-Relay connection. A Cisco CIP can replace the FEP as the Frame-Relay connection to the mainframe.

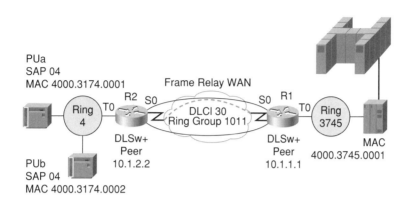

Figure 12-11
*SNA over
Frame Relay
using DLSw+
connectivity.*

12.2.6 DLSw+ Ethernet to Token Ring

DLSw+ inherently supports the translation of Ethernet MAC addressing to Token-Ring MAC addressing. Figure 12-12 provides a configuration where Token-Ring–attached IBM 5494 controllers communicate to an IBM AS/400 using an Ethernet LAN connection to a Cisco router. The Token-Ring–attached controllers define the destination station of the AS/400 in the noncanonical form. This is because the translation feature of DLSw+ will convert the MAC addresses to the canonical Ethernet form for MAC addressing. Therefore, the AS/400 MAC address 0800.5CED.1E4C is defined in the controllers as 1000.3AB7.7832 for the destination partner.

> **NOTES**
>
> Ethernet loops can ensue within a DLSw network if parallel spanning paths exist. Ethernet loop prevention is available with Cisco IOS Release 12.0(3)T.

12.2.7 DLSw+ Using Peer Groups

The configuration depicting the use of DLSw+ peer groups shown in Figure 12-13 illustrates the use of peer groups with border peers. Routers R1 and R2 are border peers in this sample network. The configuration shown depicts the physical network connections and not the logical DLSw+ peer connections.

Figure 12-12
*Ethernet-to-To
ken-Ring
translation
using DLSw+.*

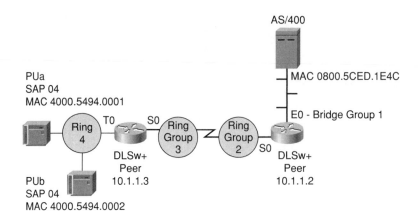

Figure 12-13
*Peer groups
and border
peer
configuration
for connecting
to a
mainframe.*

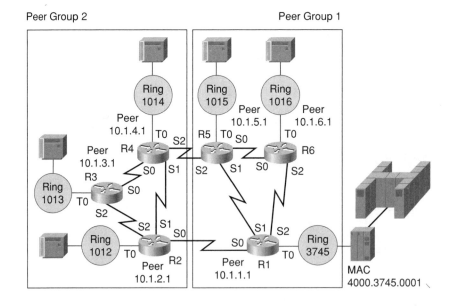

12.2.8 DLSw+ Using Load Balancing and Alternative Paths to an IBM Mainframe

The support in DLSw+ for duplicate MAC addressing of destination resources enhances a network designer's ability to build availability and load balancing into the network. Figure 12-14 illustrates the use of duplicate MAC addresses on IBM 3745 FEPs Token Ring attached to separate Token-Ring segments. Each Token-Ring segment is attached to a Cisco router residing in the data center. In this figure, router R1 demonstrates the support for alternative paths to the mainframe FEPs and the capability of DLSw+ to load balance the SNA sessions between the FEPs. A Cisco router with a CIP can replace the IBM 3745 FEP as the access to the mainframe SNA application. For more information on using the CIP, consult Chapter 16, "CIP Design and Configuration."

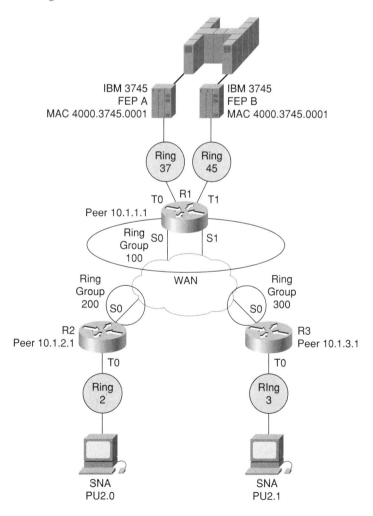

Figure 12-14
Duplicate MAC address configuration to mainframe supported using DLSw+ load balancing.

12.2.9 DLSw+ Using Backup Peer to AS/400

The use of backup DLSw+ peers is a fundamental design requirement for 24x7 data-center operations. Using DLSw+ backup peers enables the network designer to plan for unforeseen outages to the production routers. In Figure 12-15, we see the use of three Cisco routers at the data-center location supporting DLSw+ connections to two remote routers over a frame relay network. Router R2 will be acting as the backup peer for both routers R1 and R3.

Figure 12-15
DLSw+ backup peer configuration to an Ethernet-attac hed AS/400.

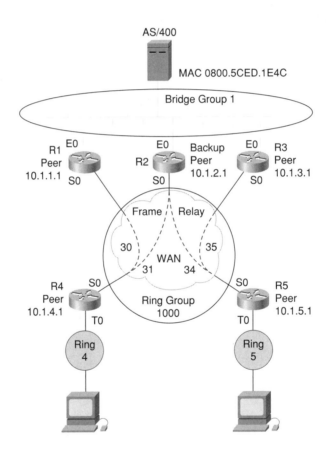

12.3 DEFINE THE SOURCE-BRIDGE RING GROUP

The source-bridge ring-group IOS command identifies the virtual ring number assigned to the ring-group being defined by the command. The format of the command is this:

```
source-bridge ring-group ring-group [virtual-mac-address]
```

The variable *ring-group* is the ring number being assigned to a virtual ring that is used by multiple routers for implementing SRB over a WAN. The value is a decimal range from 1 to 4095. The optional variable *virtual-mac-address* allows the assignment of a virtual MAC address to the ring group as seen by this router.

12.4 DEFINE THE DLSW+ LOCAL PEER

The DLSw+ local-peer is a global command that identifies the parameter values used by the DLSw+ peer instance on this router. The format of the command is this:

```
dlsw local-peer [peer-id ip-address] [group group] [border] [cost cost]
[lf size] [keepalive seconds] [passive] [promiscuous]
[ init-pacing-window size] [max-pacing-window size][biu-segment]
```

The peer-id keyword identifies the *ip-address* value used when DLSw+ is implementing FST or TCP. It is best to use the loop interface IP address for the DLSw+ *ip-address* value because the loopback interface does not rely on a physical port and is therefore always active.

If this router is being defined in a peer-group, the keyword group must be defined with a *group* value of the peer-group used for this router. The value of *group* is a decimal range of 1–255.

When participating in a peer-group it is possible for this router to act as the border peer. Border peer functionality is enabled using the border keyword of the dlsw local-peer command.

The capabilities exchange mechanism of DLSw+ includes the assignment of a weighted-cost for this router to successfully establish DLSw+ connections. The weighted-cost value is specified by the optional *cost* keyword. The *cost* value specified must be in the decimal range of 1–5. If defined, it is this value that is advertised to remote peers via the capabilities exchange. The *cost* value is useful when there are multiple peers to a destination. The value will determine which router is a preferred peer and which is a capable peer. The cost keyword is applicable only in fault-tolerance mode.

During capabilities exchange, the DLSw+ peers will also determine the largest frame size accepted over a connection. This is determined by the exchange of the *size* value specified for the optional lf keyword. The allowable maximum frame sizes that are coded for the size value are as follows:

```
516

1470

1500
```

```
2052

4472

8144

11407

11454

17800
```

The DLSw+ peers will negotiate the largest frame size based on the lowest value defined for each peer.

The optional keyword keepalive specifies the default remote peer keepalive interval in seconds. The default value for keepalive should the keepalive keyword not be coded is 30 seconds. The valid range is 0 to 100 seconds. A value of 0 indicates that there are no keepalive messages exchanged between the peers.

The passive optional keyword indicates that this router will not be the initiator of peer connections to configured remote peers. It will only establish peer connections when requested by another peer.

Specifying the optional keyword promiscuous enables this router to act as a dynamic peer for connecting to nonconfigured remote peers.

Using the biu-segment optional keyword causes each end station of the circuit to send the largest frame size it is capable of sending. This keyword is a performance and utilization enhancement that allows efficient use of the WAN links. If a frame received at a peer from a remote peer is larger than that capable of the end station to handle, DLSw+ will segment the frame prior to sending it to the end station. Implementing this function requires the definition of biu-segment on both DLSw+ peers.

The RFC 1795 defines an initial pacing window size variable with a valid range of 1—2000. The optional keyword init-pacing-window size value enables you to specify this variable.

The keyword max-pacing-window specifies the maximum size of the pacing window set forth by RFC 1795. The value is set by specifying the size variable following the keyword. The valid value is the range 1–2000.

An example of using the dlsw local-peer is as follows:

```
dlsw local-peer peer-id 10.1.2.1 group 1 border
```

In the example, the router being defined identifies a specific IP address as the DLSw+ peer. The router is assigned to peer group 1 and is acting as a border peer within that group.

12.5 SPECIFY THE DLSW+ RING OR PORT LIST

The dlsw ring-list command is an optional command that enables you to define multiple ring numbers to a ring list for segregating traffic of local interfaces to remote peers. The format of the command is this:

```
dlsw ring-list list-number rings ring-number(s)
```

The *list-number* variable specifies the ring list number being defined. The value is in the range of 1–255.

The rings keyword denotes the beginning of the list of physical and virtual rings assigned to the ring list. The positional variable *ring-number(s)* denotes the ring numbers being assigned to the list. The ring numbers must be in the decimal range of 1–4095.

Traffic received from local interfaces is forwarded to peers only if the input ring number is in the ring list for the remote peer definition.

The following is an example of using the dlsw ring-list command:

```
dlsw ring-list 10 rings 4 5 100
```

In the example, for dlsw ring-list the list is assigned the number 10 and is comprised of rings 4, 5, and 100. In this case, 100 is a virtual ring.

The dlsw port-list optional command enables the engineer to map traffic of local interfaces to remote peers. The format of the dlsw port-list command is this:

```
dlsw port-list list-number type number
```

The *list-number* parameter identifies the number assigned to the port list. Again, the valid range for the *list-number* is 1–255.

The *type* parameter identifies the interface type being used. The valid values are as follows:

- Tokenring
- Ethernet
- Serial
- Frame Relay
- ATM

The *number* value identifies the port or slot/port position of the interface being assigned to the port list.

Remote peer traffic received by this router is forwarded to only the ports in the port list. Local interface traffic is forwarded to peers only if the input port number of the local interface is in the port list for the remote peer definition.

The following example of the `dlsw port-list` command specifies Token-Ring port number 1 as a member of the port-list number 10.

```
dlsw port-list 10 token-ring 1
```

12.6 IDENTIFY A DLSW+ BRIDGE GROUP LIST

Bridge groups map local Ethernet bridge groups to remote peers. The command used for this mapping is the `dlsw bgroup-list` command. The format is as follows:

```
dlsw bgroup-list list-number bgroups number(s)
```

The `list-number` parameter identifies the number used for the bridge-group list. The value coded here is used in the `dlsw remote-peer` command to define the bridge group segment applying to this command. The valid range is 1–255.

An example of the `dlsw bgroup-list` command is this:

```
dlsw bgroup-list 1 bgroups 1 2 3
```

The example specifies the bridge-group list is using number 1 and attaches Ethernet bridge groups 1, 2, 3.

The `bgroups` keyword and its subsequent variable `number(s)` identifies the transparent bridge groups attaching to DLSw+. The bridge groups are defined using the following command:

```
dlsw bridge-group number
```

The `number` parameter of the `dlsw bridge-group` command identifies the Ethernet bridge group attaching to DLSw+. The valid range for the number variable is 1–63. This value should match an Ethernet bridge group defined on an Ethernet interface. Multiple bridge groups are defined by issuing multiple `dlsw bridge-group` commands specifying each Ethernet bridge group.

An example of the `dlsw bridge-group` command is this:

```
dlsw bridge-group 1

dlsw bridge-group 2

dlsw bridge-group 3
```

The example demonstrates the use of the `dlsw bridge-group` command for defining three Ethernet bridge groups to DLSw+.

12.7 DEFINE THE DLSW+ REMOTE PEERS

Three types of encapsulation techniques provide connectivity between DLSw+ peers:

- Direct
- FST
- TCP

These three techniques share many optional parameters and are discussed in the subsection 12.4. The remaining subsections discuss the parameters specific to each type of encapsulation technique.

12.7.1 Direct Encapsulation with HDLC and Frame Relay

Recall that direct encapsulation is possible when routers are connected without intermediate routers between the source and destination resources. Direct encapsulation is the fastest and most efficient means for transporting SNA data. However, it limits the design possibilities to a strict point-to-point configuration. DLSw+ participates in direct encapsulation using HDLC and Frame Relay. The format for enabling direct encapsulation over HDLC is as follows:

```
dlsw remote-peer list-number interface serial number
[backup-peer [ip-address ¦ frame-relay interface serial number dlci-number
¦ interface name]] [bytes-netbios-out bytes-list-name] [cost cost]
[dest-mac mac-address] [dmac-output-list access-list-number]
[host-netbios-out host-list-name] [keepalive seconds] [lf size]
[linger minutes] [lsap-output-list list] [passive] [pass-thru]
```

The `dlsw remote-peer list-number` parameter identifies the specific `dlsw-ring-list` used for connecting to the dlsw remote peer. The valid range for the `list-number` is 1–255. If a `dlsw ring-list` has not been specified, the default value 0 is used. A `list-number` value of 0 denotes that all ports or bridge groups with DLSw+ enabled forward explorer packets to establish connectivity to the remote peer. If a value other than

0 is specified, the value must match the number you specified on a dlsw ring-list, dlsw port-list, or dlsw bgroup-list command.

The *number* value following the dlsw remote-peer keywords interface serial identifies the physical serial port used for direct encapsulation of DLSw+ packets. The value is any valid port of slot/port combination used on the router that connects to the remote peer router.

An example of using direct HDLC encapsulation to a remote DLSw+ router is this:

```
dlsw remote-peer 0 interface 0/1
```

The example specifies that all rings are available for connecting to the remote peer found at the remote side of the connection on slot 0 and port 1 serial interface processor of the router.

The major distinction with defining remote DLSw+ peers between HDLC and Frame Relay is the inclusion of the frame-relay keyword and the *dlci-number* parameter on the dlsw remote-peer command. The format for enabling direct frame relay encapsulation of DLSw+ is as follows:

```
dlsw remote-peer list-number frame-relay interface serial number dlci-number
[backup-peer [ip-address ¦ frame-relay interface serial number dlci-number
¦ interface name]] [bytes-netbios-out bytes-list-name] [cost cost]
[dest-mac mac-address] [dmac-output-list access-list-number]
[host-netbios-out host-list-name] [keepalive seconds] [lf size]
[linger minutes] [lsap-output-list list] [passive] [pass-thru]
```

The *list-number* parameter is again the ring-list used for mapping traffic to and from the remote peer being defined. Its value can range from 1–255 with a value of 0 denoting all ports and bridge groups using DLSw+ will forward explorer packets to establish connectivity to the remote peer. If a value other than 0 is specified, the value must match the number you specified on a dlsw ring-list, dlsw port-list or dlsw bgroup-list command. The frame relay interface serial positional parameter *number* identifies the Frame-Relay port, slot/port or subinterface of a port used for direct connection to the remote peer. The *number* parameter must be followed by the positional *dlci-number* parameter which identifies the Frame-Relay DLCI of the remote router used for connecting to the remote peer.

An example of using the dlsw remote-peer command for direct Frame-Relay encapsulation is this:

```
dlsw remote-peer 0 frame relay interface serial 0/1.30 30
```

This dlsw remote-peer frame relay command specifies the use of the Frame-Relay subinterface 30 on port 1 of slot 0 using DLCI 30 as the connection identifier to the remote peer.

There is a common optional parameter specific only to the use of direct encapsulation. This parameter is the pass-thru parameter. Specifying the pass-thru parameter disables the local-acknowledgement feature of DLSw+ and therefore passes SNA RR and RNR polling from end-to-end.

12.7.2 FST Encapsulation

DLSw+ uses FST encapsulation when the dlsw remote-peer command is issued using the fst keyword. The format for using FST encapsulation with DLSw+ is as follows:

```
dlsw remote-peer list-number fst ip-address
[backup-peer [ip-address ¦ frame-relay interface serial number dlci-number
¦ interface name]] [bytes-netbios-out bytes-list-name] [cost cost]
[dest-mac mac-address] [dmac-output-list access-list-number]
[host-netbios-out host-list-name] [keepalive seconds] [lf size] [linger minutes]
[lsap-output-list list] [passive]
```

The list-number parameter is the ring-list used for mapping traffic to and from the remote peer being defined. Its value can range from 1–255 with a value of 0 denoting all ports and bridge groups using DLSw+ will forward explorer packets to establish connectivity to the remote peer. If a value other than 0 is specified, the value must match the number you specified on a dlsw ring-list, dlsw port-list, or dlsw bgroup-list command.

The ip-address parameter following the fst keyword specifies the IP address of the remote peer being defined for which this router may establish a peer connection. An example of enabling FST encapsulation with DLSw+ is as follows:

```
dlsw remote-peer 1 fst 10.2.1.1
```

The example identifies the ports and bridge groups assigned to ring-list 1 are used for forwarding explorer packets when discovering a destination SNA device. The remote peer to receive these explorer packets is identified by IP address 10.2.1.1.

12.7.3 TCP Encapsulation

DLSw+ uses TCP encapsulation to a remote peer through the defining of the dlsw remote-peer command with the tcp keyword specified. The format for enabling DLSw+ to use TCP encapsulation is as follows:

```
dlsw remote-peer list-number tcp ip-address

[backup-peer [ip-address ¦ frame-relay interface serial number dlci-number ¦ interface name]]

[bytes-netbios-out bytes-list-name] [cost cost] [dest-mac mac-address]

[dmac-output-list access-list-number] [dynamic] [host-netbios-out host-list-name]

[keepalive seconds] [lf size] [linger minutes] [lsap-output-list list]

[no-llc minutes] [passive] [priority] [tcp-queue-max size] [timeout seconds]
```

The list-number parameter is the ring-list used for mapping traffic to and from the remote peer being defined. Its value can range from 1–255 with a value of 0 denoting all ports and bridge groups using DLSw+ will forward explorer packets to establish connectivity to the remote peer. If a value other than 0 is specified, the value must match the number you specified on a dlsw ring-list, dlsw port-list, or dlsw bgroup-list command.

The ip-address parameter following the tcp keyword specifies the IP address of the remote peer being defined for which this router may establish a peer connection. An example of enabling TCP encapsulation with DLSw+ is as follows:

```
        dlsw remote-peer 0 tcp 10.2.2.1
```

The example identifies indicates that all ports and bridge groups will forward explorer packets due to the 0 coded for the list-number positional parameter. The remote peer to receive these explorer packets is identified by IP address 10.2.2.1.

TCP encapsulation has five optional parameters that are specific to the dlsw remote-peer command. These are as follows:

```
[dynamic] [no-llc minutes] [priority] [tcp-queue-max size] [timeout seconds]
```

Using the optional `dynamic` keyword allows DLSw+ to establish peer connections only when they are needed with the remote peer. After there is no more DLSw+ data to be sent to the remote peer, the TCP connection is torn down.

The `no-llc` keyword is used when you want the peer connection to the defined remote peer to disconnect after all LLC2 connections have been terminated. The *minutes* value for the `no-llc` keyword is must be a valid number in the range of 1–300 in minutes. The default time if the `no-llc` keyword is not coded is five minutes. The function of the `no-llc` keyword is implemented only when the `dynamic` keyword is specified.

Using the `priority` keyword enables TCP prioritization by port number. The TCP ports and their analogous priority are listed in Table 12.1. Traffic is assigned to the ports based on the priority group assignments. APPN over DLSw+ carries the APPN Class of Service (COS) characteristics through the routed network by mapping the APPN COS to the TCP TOS for SNA TOS.

Table 12-1 *Valid port numbers for TCP connections.*

Priority	Port
High	2065
Medium	1981
Normal	1982
Low	1983

The `tcp-queue-max` keyword is used to tune the performance of the TCP encapsulation for the defined peer. The *size* parameter indicates the maximum number of output TCP segments allowed to be queued for the remote peer. The valid range is 10–200. The default is 100.

If acknowledgement of a TCP segment is not received from the remote peer within 90 seconds, the router will retransmit the segment. This default is modified by specifying a new retransmit time limit using the `timeout` keyword. The retransmit time limit for TCP can range anywhere from 5–1200 seconds. The default is 90 seconds.

12.7.4 Common DLSw+ Encapsulation Parameters

Eleven common parameters for the three encapsulation techniques used by DLSw+ may affect the delivery of SNA data. The following shows the format of these common parameters:

```
[backup-peer [ip-address | frame-relay interface serial number dlci-number | interface name]]

[cost cost] [dest-mac mac-address] [dmac-output-list access-list-number] [keepalive seconds] [lf size]
```

```
[linger minutes] [lsap-output-list list] [passive]
```

Recovery of SNA connections when a remote peer becomes disconnected is possible through the use of backup peers. *Backup peers* are defined using the backup-peer keyword on the dlsw remote-peer command. The *ip-address* parameter identifies the IP address of the remote peer being backed up by the dlsw remote-peer statement being defined, as follows:

```
dlsw remote-peer 0 tcp 10.2.1.1

dlsw remote-peer 0 tcp 10.2.2.1 backup-peer 10.2.1.1
```

The remote peer 10.2.2.1 will serve as the backup peer for the primary remote peer 10.2.1.1 should the TCP connection to 10.2.1.1 fail.

The frame-relay interface serial or interface subkeywords of the backup-peer keyword enable you to identify which Frame-Relay or HDLC interface is being backed up by this remote peer command. For the Frame-Relay interface serial subkeyword, the *number* variable is the port, slot/port pair, of subinterface number identifying the Frame-Relay connection and the *dlci-number* parameter is the DLCI used by the remote peer being backed up. The *name* parameter of the interface subkeyword is the port, slot/port pair, of the serial line being backed up by this peer. In the following example, interface serial port 2 on slot 3 is the primary remote peer connection. The backup peer uses TCP encapsulation through the WAN should the primary direct encapsulation peer connection fail. The commands are entered as follows:

```
dlsw remote-peer 0 interface 3/2

dlsw remote-peer 0 tcp 10.3.2.1 backup-peer interface 3/2
```

The capabilities exchange mechanism of DLSw+ includes the assignment of a weighted cost for this router to successfully establish DLSw+ connections. The weighted cost value is specified by the optional cost keyword. The *cost* value specified must be in the decimal range of 1–5. If defined, it is this value that is advertised to remote peers via the capabilities exchange. The *cost* value is useful when there are multiple peers to a destination. The value will determine which router is a preferred peer and which is a capable peer. The cost keyword is applicable only in fault-tolerance mode.

Specifying the dest-mac keyword activates the establishment of a connection to the remote peer being defined only when an explorer frame with the destination MAC address matching the *mac-address* parameter is passed to the router. The *mac-address* parameter is written in dotted-triple decimal format.

The dmac-output-list keyword enables peer connections to the remote peer being defined only when the destination MAC address of an explorer frame passes through the access list specified by the variable *access-list-number*. The *access-list-number* value must match a number defined on an access-list command. Using this keyword will enable the connection to the peer for multiple destination MAC addresses but not all destination MAC addresses.

The optional keyword keepalive specifies the default remote peer keepalive interval in seconds. The default value for keepalive should the keepalive keyword not be coded is 30 seconds. The valid range is 0 to 100 seconds. A value of 0 indicates that there are no keepalive messages exchanged between the peers.

During capabilities exchange, the DLSw+ peers will also determine the largest frame size accepted over a connection to avoid frame segmentation on the circuit. This is determined by the exchange of the *size* value specified for the optional lf keyword. The allowable maximum frame size coded for the *size* value are as follows:

516

1470

1500

2052

4472

8144

11407

11454

17800

The DLSw+ peers will negotiate the largest frame size based on the lowest value defined for each peer.

The linger keyword and its subsequent variable *minutes* indicates the length of time before the backup peer connection remains active after the primary peer connection has been recovered. The default time is 5 minutes. The range for linger is 1 to 300 minutes.

IEEE 802.5-encapsulated packets may be filtered using the lsap-output-list optional keyword. The valid range for the *list* parameter is 200–299, which specifies a defined access-list number.

The passive optional keyword indicates that this router will not be the initiator of peer connections to configured remote peers. It will only establish peer connections when requested by another peer.

12.8 ENABLING DLSW+

Each type of DLSw+ transport mechanism has a specific command for enabling DLSw+ functionality. This section describes the dlsw commands required for Frame Relay, Token Ring, Ethernet, and SDLC.

12.8.1 DLSw+ over Frame Relay

Frame Relay is configured for DLSw+ in either direct encapsulation into the Frame-Relay frame itself or via the RFC 1490 Frame Relay Forum Version 3 (FRF.3) LLC2 encapsulation technique. For direct encapsulation the following commands are required:

```
frame-relay map dlsw dlci-number

dlsw remote-peer list-number frame-relay interface serial number dlci-number
```

The frame-relay map dlsw command uses the dlci-number parameter to specify a valid Frame-Relay DLCI number used by this router. The dlsw remote-peer command with the frame-relay interface serial keyword maps to the ring-list being used for the Frame-Relay connection and identifies the actual Frame-Relay interface on the router and the DLCI number of the remote peer. The pass-thru keyword can be used to allow keepalives and SNA polls to pass through the Frame-Relay network. Using pass-thru causes less overhead on the link and on router CPU utilization than does local acknowledgement.

Using RFC 1490 FRF.3 LLC2 encapsulation requires the following command to be specified on the Frame-Relay interface definition:

```
frame-relay map llc2 dlci-number
```

The frame-relay map llc2 command indicates that DLSw+ RFC 1490 FRF.3 is to be used for delivering SNA frames. The DLSw+ packets are to use the DLCI specified by the dlci-number parameter value.

12.8.2 DLSw+ and Token Ring

DLSw+ employs the use of ring numbers and therefore requires the SRB mapping information from a Token Ring. The source-bridge command must be defined on the Token-Ring interface that will use DLSw+. The format of the command is this:

```
source-bridge local-ring bridge-number ring-group
```

The *local-ring* parameter is the ring number of the attached physical Token-Ring LAN. The *ring-group* number is the virtual ring defined by the global source-bridge ring-group command. The *bridge-number* is the virtual bridge connecting the physical Token-Ring LAN to the virtual ring-group.

12.8.3 DLSw+ and Ethernet

DLSw+ enables the use of Ethernet bridge groups through the use of the dlsw bridge-group global command. The format of the command is as follows:

```
dlsw bridge-group group-number
```

The *group-number* parameter must match at least one bridge-group number defined on an Ethernet LAN interface definition. The range for *group-number* is 1 through 63. For Ethernet to use bridge groups, the global bridge protocol command must also be defined specifying neither *ieee* or *ibm* as the BPDU format. An example of establishing DLSw+ for an Ethernet LAN is as follows:

```
dlsw local-peer peer-id 1.1.1.1

dlsw remote-peer 0 tcp 2.2.2.2

dlsw bridge-group 1

interface Ethernet0

 bridge-group 1

bridge 1 protocol ieee
```

12.8.4 DLSw+ and SDLC

SDLC-attached devices are mapped to DLSw+ using the sdlc dlsw command on the serial interface defining the SDLC connection to the device. The format of the command is this:

```
sdlc dlsw {sdlc-address ¦ default ¦ partner mac address [inbound ¦ outbound]}
```

The *sdlc-address* parameter is the hexadecimal SDLC station address of the device(s) connected to the SDLC-attached serial interface on the router. The default keyword indicates that an unlimited number of SDLC addresses map to DLSw+. The partner keyword value *mac-address* identifies the default MAC address of the destination partner used by the SDLC-attached device(s). Typically this is the MAC address of the IBM 3745 Token-Ring interface or the internal Token-Ring adapter of a channel attached Cisco CIP router. The inbound keyword indicates to DLSw+ that the partner will initiate the SNA session while the outbound keyword indicates that the SDLC-attached device(s) will initiate the connection to the partner.

An example of defining three SDLC devices on a single SDLC connection is as follows:

```
sdlc dlsw C1 C2 C3
```

12.9 DUPLICATE PATH SPECIFICATION

Enhanced availability of SNA connectivity is accomplished by designing a network with duplicate paths to the IBM SNA mainframe. The dual paths are designed using two FEPs or CIPs, two Token Rings, two routers, and two WAN connections to the data center. Specifying duplicate path configuration use for DLSw+ is accomplished by entering the global command:

```
dlsw duplicate-path-bias [load-balance]
```

The dlsw duplicate-path-bias global command without the optional load-balance keyword will favor session establishment for the SNA resources over the preferred path to the duplicate MAC address. The *preferred path* is the path over which the first explorer response is received or the peer connection with the least-cost value. Using the load-balance keyword enables DLSw+ to establish SNA sessions with the mainframe in a round-robin manner between the two paths.

12.10 DLSw+ CONFIGURATION EXAMPLES

The DLSw+ examples illustrated in this section depict the most common configurations used for transporting SNA in corporate networks. The examples review the usage of the DLSw+ commands previously discussed and explore some of the advanced features of DLSw+. The configurations shown display only those parameters and commands pertinent to DLSw+ transport for SNA. An interior gateway routing protocol must also be defined for routing of DLSw+ segments to take place.

12.10.1 DLSw+ Using TCP Encapsulation

The configurations shown in Figure 12-16 define the use of TCP encapsulation between two DLSw+ peers using local acknowledgement. Each configuration employs the use of the loopback interface as the TCP peer IP address to use for connectivity. This is a good practice to use because the loopback interface is always considered to be active. Routers with multiple WAN and LAN connections therefore have a high availability for establishing DLSw+ peer connections. This is especially true if the `dlsw remote-peer` `list-number` parameter as shown in Figure 12-16 is equal to 0.

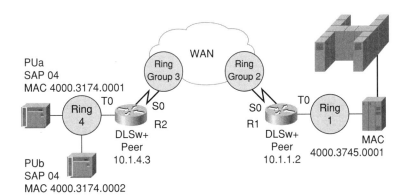

Figure 12-16
DLSw+ configuration example for TCP encapsulation with local-acknowledgement between DLSw+ peers.

R2 Configuration

```
source-bridge ring-group 3
!
dlsw local-peer peer-id 10.1.4.3
dlsw remote-peer 0 tcp 10.1.1.2
!
interface loopback 0
 ip address 10.1.4.3 255.255.255.0
!
interface tokenring 0
 no ip address
 ring-speed 16
 source-bridge 4 1 3
 source-bridge spanning
```

R1 Configuration

```
source-bridge ring-group 2
!
dlsw local-peer peer-id 10.1.1.2
dlsw remote-peer 0 tcp 10.1.3.4
!
interface loopback 0
 ip address 10.1.1.2 255.255.255.0
!
interface tokenring 0
 no ip address
 ring-speed 16
 source-bridge 1 1 2
 source-bridge spanning
```

12.10.2 DLSw+ Using Direct Encapsulation

Figure 12-17 illustrates the use of HDLC direct encapsulation with DLSw+. In this configuration, we use the IP address assigned to the serial interfaces of each router as the DLSw+ remote peer. The DLSw+ remote peer is tied to the serial interface of each router in this example because no other WAN interfaces can possibly connect the two routers.

Figure 12-17
DLSw+ configuration example for direct HDLC encapsulation between DLSw+ peers.

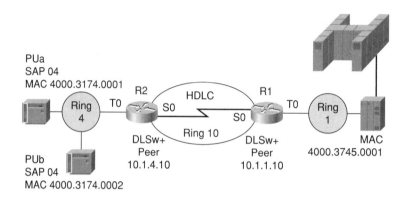

R2 Configuration

    source-bridge ring-group 10
    dlsw local-peer peer-id 10.1.4.10
    dlsw remote-peer 0 interface serial 0
    !
    interface serial 0
      ip address 10.1.4.10 255.255.255.0
    !
    interface tokenring 0
      ring-speed 16
      source-bridge 4 1 10

R1 Configuration

    source-bridge ring-group 10
    dlsw local-peer peer-id 10.1.1.10
    dlsw remote-peer 0 interface serial 0
    !
    interface serial 0
      ip address 10.1.1.10 255.255.255.0
    !
    interface tokenring 0
      ring-speed 16
      source-bridge 1 1 10

12.10.3 DLSw+ Using FST Encapsulation

There is little difference between defining TCP encapsulation and FST encapsulation for DLSw+ peers. The only true difference is the use of the fst keyword on the dlsw remote-peer command. Use FST only if the design will limit the delivery of out-of-sequence datagrams to a minimum.

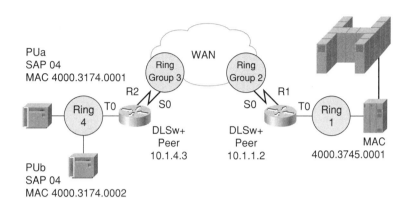

Figure 12-18
*DLSw+
configuration
example for
using FST
encapsulation
between
DLSw+ peers.*

R2 Configuration

```
source-bridge ring-group 3
!
dlsw local-peer peer-id 10.1.4.3
dlsw remote-peer 0 fst 10.1.1.2
!
interface loopback 0
  ip address 10.1.4.3 255.255.255.0
!
interface tokening 0
  no ip address
  ring-speed 16
  source-bridge 4 1 3
  source-bridge spanning
```

R1 Configuration

```
source-bridge ring-group 2
!
dlsw local-peer peer-id 10.1.1.2
dlsw remote-peer 0 fst 10.1.3.4
!
interface loopback 0
  ip address 10.1.1.2 255.255.255.0
!
interface tokenring 0
  no ip address
  ring-speed 16
  source-bridge 1 1 2
  source-bridge spanning
```

12.10.4 DLSw+ with SDLC to Token-Ring

For many installations, legacy controllers (such as the IBM 3174 that were connected to the IBM 3745 using 56Kbps lines) avoid upgrades for Ethernet or Token-Ring attachment by connecting them directly to the interfaces on a Cisco router. Typically, the IBM 3745 is Token Ring–attached as shown in Figure 12-19. The local dlsw peer for router R1 is the IP address of the Token-Ring interface to the IBM 3745 Token-Ring LAN. The local peer for the remote router R2 is the WAN serial interface IP address.

Figure 12-19
*DLSw+
configuration
example for
enabling
DLSw+ with
SDLC to
Token-Ring
translation.*

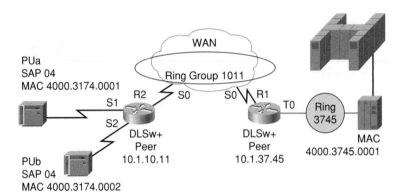

R2 Configuration

source-bridge ring-group 1011
dlsw local-peer peer-id 10.1.10.11
dlsw remote-peer 0 tcp 10.1.37.45
!
interface serial 0
  ip address 10.1.10.11 255.255.255.0
!
  interface serial 1
  no ip address
  encapsulation sdlc
  no keepalive
  clock rate 5600
  sdlc role primary
  sdlc vmac 400.3174.1000
  sdlc address c1
  sdlc xid C1 01731741
  sdlc partner 4000.3745.001 C1
  sdlc dlsw C1
!
interface serial 2
  no ip address
  encapsulation sdlc
  clockrate 56000
  sdlc role primary
  sdlc vmac 4000.3174.2000
  sdlc address C2
  sdlc xid C2 01731742
  sdlc partner 4000.3745.0001
  sdlc dlsw C2

R1 Configuration

source-bridge ring-group 1011
dlsw local-peer-id 10.1.37.45
dlsw remote-peer 0 tcp 10.1.10.11
!
interface serial 0
  ip address 10.1.10.10 255.255.255.0
!
interface tokenring 0
ip address 10.1.37.45 255.255.255.0
  ring-speed 16
  source-bridge 3745 1 1011
  source-bridge spanning

12.10.5 DLSw+ with Frame Relay

The example configuration shown in Figure 12-20 illustrates the use of DLSw+ over Frame Relay with local-acknowledgement. Local-acknowledgement would not be used if the passthru keyword were specified on the dlsw remote-peer frame-relay command used on both routers.

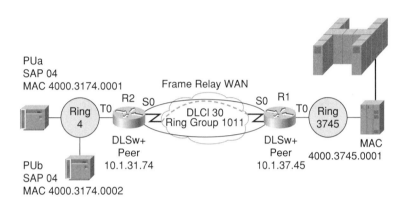

Figure 12-20
DLSw+ configuration example for enabling DLSw+ with Frame Relay.

R2 Configuration

```
source-bridge ring-group 1011
dlsw local-peer peer-id 10.1.31.74
dlsw remote-peer 0 frame-relay interface serial 0 30
!
interface serial 0
no ip address
  encapsulation frame-relay
  frame-relay lmi-type ansi
  frame-relay map llc2 30
!
interface tokenring 0
  ip address 10.1.31.74 255.255.255.0
  ring-speed 16
  source-bridge 4 1 1011
```

R1 Configuration

```
source-bridge ring-group 1011
dlsw local-peer peer-id 10.37.45
dlsw remote-peer 0 frame-relay interface serial 0 30
!
interface serial 0
no ip address
  encapsulation frame-relay
  frame-relay lmi-type ansi
  frame-relay map llc2 30
!
interface tokenring 0
  ring-speed 16
  source-bridge 3745 1 1011
```

12.10.6 DLSw+ Ethernet to Token Ring

In many installations, you will find that there is a mix of Token-Ring and Ethernet LANs with attached SNA devices. In this example, Figure 12-21, an Ethernet attached AS/400 IBM host computer is communicating with IBM 5494 PU T2.1 devices attached to a Token-Ring LAN. The example illustrates the use of the `dlsw bridge-group` command and its associated required interface command `bridge-group` and the global command bridge protocol.

Figure 12-21
*DLSw+
configuration
example for
translating
Token-Ring to
Ethernet.*

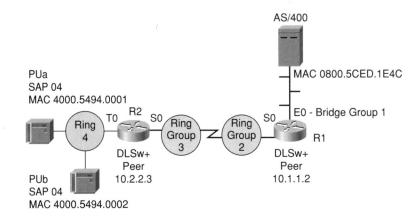

R2 Configuration

    source-bridge ring-group 3
dlsw local-peer peer-id 10.2.2.3
dlsw remote-peer 0 tcp 10.1.1.2 if 1500
!
interface serial 0
ip address 10.2.2.3 255.255.255.0
!
    interface tokenring 2/0
no ip address
ring-speed 16
source-bridge 4 1 3
source-bridge spanning

R1 Configuration

    source-bridge ring-group 2
dlsw local-peer peer-id 10.1.1.2
dlsw remote-peer 0 tcp 10.2.2.3 if 1500
dlsw bridge-group 1
!
interface serial 0
ip address 10.2.2.2 255.255.255.0
!
interface ethernet 0
 ip address 10.1.1.2 255.255.255.0
 bridge-group 1
!
bridge 1 protocol ieee

12.10.7 DLSw+ Using Peer Groups

This example illustrates the use of dynamic peers along with peer groups and border peers. Each router in Figure 12-22 will dynamically accept a peer connection to DLSw+ peers not configured due to the inclusion of the `promiscuous` keyword on the `dlsw local-peer` command. This not only allows dynamic peer connection establishment, but also reduces configuration overhead and maintenance while at the same time reducing WAN overhead because the peer connections are only established when required.

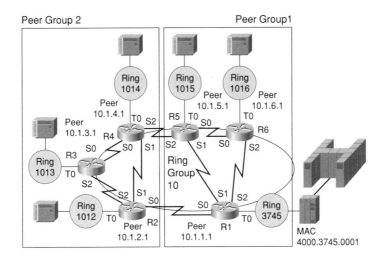

Figure 12-22
*DLSw+
configuration
example
depicting the
use of peer
groups and
border peers.*

R2 Configuration
source-bridge ring-group 10
dlsw local-peer peer-id 10.1.2.1 group 2 border promiscuous
   dlsw remote-peer 0 tcp 10.1.1.1
   dlsw remote-peer 0 tcp 10.1.3.1
   dlsw remote-peer 0 tcp 10.1.4.1
!
  interface loopback 0
  ip address 10.1.2.1 255.255.255.0
interface tokenring 0
  source-bridge 1012 1 10

R3 Configuration
source-bridge ring-group 10
dlsw local-peer peer-id 10.1.3.1 group 2 border promiscuous
   dlsw remote-peer 0 tcp 10.1.2.1
   dlsw remote-peer 0 tcp 10.1.4.1
!
  interface loopback 0
  ip address 10.1.3.1 255.255.255.0
interface tokenring 0
  source-bridge 1013 1 10

R4 Configuration
source-bridge ring-group 10
dlsw local-peer peer-id 10.1.4.1 group 2 border promiscuous
   dlsw remote-peer 0 tcp 10.1.3.1
   dlsw remote-peer 0 tcp 10.1.2.1
   dlsw remote-peer 0 tcp 10.1.5.1
!
  interface loopback 0
  ip address 10.1.4.1 255.255.255.0
interface tokenring 0
  source-bridge 1014 1 10

R1 Configuration
source-bridge ring-group 10
dlsw local-peer peer-id 10.1.1.1 group 1 border promiscuous
   dlsw remote-peer 0 tcp 10.1.5.1
   dlsw remote-peer 0 tcp 10.1.6.1
   dlsw remote-peer 0 tcp 10.1.2.1
!
  interface loopback 0
  ip address 10.1.1.1 255.255.255.0
interface tokenring 0
  source-bridge 3745 1 10

R6 Configuration
source-bridge ring-group 10
dlsw local-peer peer-id 10.1.6.1 group 1 border promiscuous
   dlsw remote-peer 0 tcp 10.1.1.1
   dlsw remote-peer 0 tcp 10.1.5.1
!
  interface loopback 0
  ip address 10.1.6.1 255.255.255.0
interface tokenring 0
  source-bridge 1016 1 10

R5 Configuration
source-bridge ring-group 10
dlsw local-peer peer-id 10.1.5.1 group 1 border promiscuous
   dlsw remote-peer 0 tcp 10.1.4.1
   dlsw remote-peer 0 tcp 10.1.6.1
   dlsw remote-peer 0 tcp 10.1.1.1
!
  interface loopback 0
  ip address 10.1.5.1 255.255.255.0
interface tokenring 0
  source-bridge 1015 1 10

Within a group, however, each DLSw+ peer must be defined two the border peers. This is shown in the configuration for router R6 in peer group 1 and R3 in peer group 2. Each border peer must have predefined definitions for DLSw peers to all members of the group, any other border peer with in the group, and at least one border peer of the adjoining peer group. Border peers of routers R1, R2, R4, and R5 all demonstrate this configuration requirement. Definitions of the serial interfaces for each router have been removed from the sample configurations for purposes of highlighting only the DLSw+ commands for establishing peer groups and border peers.

12.10.8 DLSw+ Using Load Balancing to IBM Mainframe

Figure 12-23 shows the use of the dlsw duplicate-path-bias global command with the load-balance keyword specified. Using this feature of DLSw+ enables us to provide high availability and load balancing to the IBM mainframe through two IBM 3745 FEPs using the same Token-Ring MAC address. Each FEP is attached to a different Token-Ring segment with each segment having a unique network wide ring number. Router R1 in the configuration will round-robin the SNA session setup requests to the mainframe between Token-Ring ports 0 and 1. The FEPs in this configuration can be replaced by using CIP on a channel-attached Cisco router. For more on using the CIP, consult Chapter 16, "CIP Design and Configuration."

12.10.9 DLSw+ Using Backup Peer to AS/400

The backup peer feature of DLSw+ allows a remote router to rediscover the destination MAC address for SNA session establishment through a predefined backup DLSw+ peer. Figure 12-24 diagrams such a configuration. The figure lists only the router configurations specific to supporting the backup peer feature of DLSw+. We can see from the configuration that the Frame-Relay interfaces on remote routers R4 and R5 have predefined connectivity to the backup peer router R2. The R2 router defines its local peer as promiscuous, and therefore only establishes peer connections when they are requested from the remote peers. The backup peer connection will terminate after all the LLC2 sessions using the connection terminate.

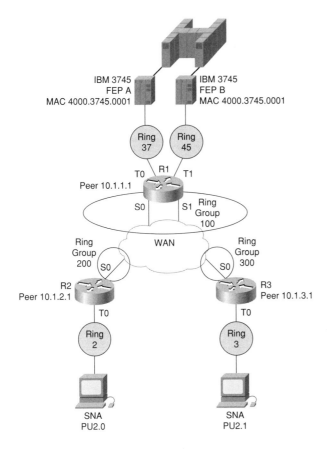

R1 Configuration
source-bridge ring-group 100
!
dlsw local-peer peer-id 10.1.1.1
dlsw remote-peer 0 tcp 10.1.2.1
dlsw remote-peer 0 tcp 10.1.3.1
    dlsw duplicate-path-bias load-balance
!
interface loopback 0
  ip address 10.1.1.1 255.255.255.0
!
interface serial 0
  ip address 10.2.2.1 255.255.255.0
!
interface serial 1
  ip address 10.3.2.1 255.255.255.0
!
interface tokenring 0
  no ip address
  ring-speed 16
  source-bridge 3 1 300
  source-bridge spanning

R3 Configuration
source-bridge ring-group 300
!
dlsw local-peer peer-id 10.1.3.1
dlsw remote-peer 0 tcp 10.1.1.1
!
interface loopback 0
  ip address 10.1.3.1 255.255.255.0
interface serial 0
  ip address 10.3.2.2. 255.255.255.0
!
interface tokenring 0
  no ip address
  ring-speed 16
  source-bridge 3 1 300
  source-bridge spanning

Figure 12-23
*DLSw+
configuration
example
utilizing
duplicate paths
for load
balancing to an
IBM
mainframe.*

R2 Configuration
source-bridge ring-group 200
!
dlsw local-peer peer-id 10.1.2.1
dlsw remote-peer 0 tcp 10.1.1.1
!
interface loopback 0
  ip address 10.1.2.1 255.255.255.0
!
interface serial 0
  ip address 10.2.2.2 255.255.255.0
!
interface tokenring 0
  no ip address
  ring-speed 16
  source-bridge 2 1 200
  source-bridge spanning

Figure 12-24
*DLSw+
configuration
example using
backup peer
connectivity to
an
Ethernet-attac
hed AS/400
host computer.*

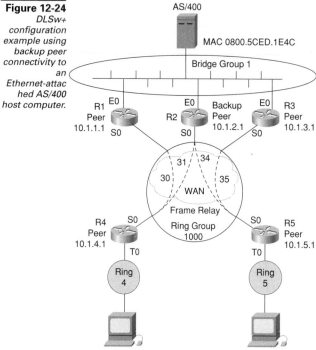

AS/400

MAC 0800.5CED.1E4C

Bridge Group 1

R1 E0
Peer
10.1.1.1 S0

E0   Backup   E0   R3
R2   Peer   Peer
       10.1.2.1 S0 10.1.3.1
S0

31 / 34
30   35
WAN
Frame Relay
Ring Group
1000

R4 S0
Peer
10.1.4.1
T0

Ring
4

S0 R5
Peer
10.1.5.1
T0

Ring
5

R2 Configuration
source-bridge ring-group 1000
dlsw local-peer peer-id 10.1.2.1 promiscuous
dlsw remote-peer 0 frame-relay interface serial 0 31
  dlsw remote-peer 0 frame-relay interface serial 0 34
  dlsw bridge-group 1
!
interface serial 0
no ip address
  encapsulation frame-relay
  frame-relay lmi-type ansi
  frame-relay map llc2 30
  frame-relay map llc2 31
!
interface ethernet 0
  no ip address
  bridge-group 1
    !
  bridge 1 protocol iee

R4 Configuration
source-bridge ring-group 1000
dlsw local-peer peer-id 10.1.4.1
dlsw remote-peer 0 frame-relay interface serial 0 30
  dlsw remote-peer 0 frame-relay interface serial 0 31
    backup-peer frame-relay interface serial 0 30
!
interface serial 0
no ip address
  encapsulation frame-relay
  frame-relay lmi-type ansi
  frame-relay map llc2 30
  frame-relay map llc2 31
!
interface tokenring 0
  no ip address
  ring-speed 16
  source-bridge 4 1 1000

R5 Configuration 1000
source-bridge ring-group 1000
dlsw local-peer peer-id 10.1.5.1
dlsw remote-peer 0 frame-relay interface serial 0 35
  dlsw remote-peer 0 frame-relay interface serial 0 34
    backup-peer frame-relay interface serial 0 35
!
interface serial 0
no ip address
  encapsulation frame-relay
  frame-relay lmi-type ansi
  frame-relay map llc2 34
  frame-relay map llc2 35
!
interface tokenring 0
  no ip address
  ring-speed 16
  source-bridge 5 1 1000

13

APPN Design and Configuration

APPN is IBM's peer-to-peer architecture. Akin to TCP/IP and the use of routers for determining paths through a network, APPN routes pure SNA traffic using network nodes (NN). As we will find in our discussion, it is the number of network nodes and their connectivity that requires careful design and planning. APPN can be considered as being a "network of hosts," where each routing entity has the same structure as an application node. As it is not possible uncouple these processes (topology and resource), scalability becomes an issue. Too many NNs in an APPN network can lead to an over-complex design that reduces the network's capability to provide a viable delivery system and can also create performance issues.

13.1 DESIGN CRITERIA

We know from earlier chapters that Cisco IOS software is capable of delivering SNA frames over an IP router network through various encapsulation techniques. In determining the design criteria for an APPN network on Cisco routers, it is important to explore and understand the alternative methods for delivering SNA data over Cisco routers as compared to APPN. The reason is that APPN comes at a performance and memory cost on a Cisco router enabled for APPN network node support. To determine the design criteria, we must first determine the applicability of using APPN in the network.

13.1.1 APPN in the Overall Design Solution

APPN network nodes make all the routing decisions in APPN. Each NN updates the network topology upon determining network changes. In turn, each NN will send *topology database updates (TDUs)* to all other known network nodes. The more NNs in your network, the more you will see TDUs traversing the network using valuable bandwidth for routing updates versus delivering data. Cisco routers enabled for APPN act only as NNs and assist attached end nodes (ENs) in locating and selecting the path to the destination EN resource. NNs therefore must be strategically placed within the network design to minimize routing update overhead but allow for any-to-any connectivity.

Any-to-any connectivity is only required in a true peer-to-peer environment. APPN's most common use is in SNA hierarchical networks to replace the SNA switching layer provided by FEP/NCPs with the result that meshed, or any-to-any, networks are very uncommon.

APPN is advantageous over the SNA encapsulation techniques in the areas of supporting native SNA routing and guaranteed service using the SNA Class of Service (COS) delivery mechanism. APPN network nodes are generally more suitable for positioning in the data center and backbone routers. The data center and backbone are, in general, the preferred areas formatting APPN routing decisions. APPN is commonly used with DLSw+ for delivering SNA data from the branch office location to the Cisco router acting as the APPN NN where the routing decision is made. Placing APPN NNs for route decisions at the data center increases router utilization. In such a case, Cisco APPN can use DLSw+ for delivering SNA data to the data center. More often we see Cisco router APPN NNs residing in the backbone where the route decision is made using the alternative paths designed between the backbone routers.

Assigning NN functionality in a Cisco router located at a branch office is dependent on the needs of the branch office. If the branch office requires communication only with the data center, DLSw+ to either the backbone router acting as a NN or the data-center router using APPN NN functionality is the appropriate solution. If there is an on-going requirement that the branch office communicate with resources in other branch offices, however, it may be cost-justifiable to enable NN functionality on the branch office routers involved as long as they have a direct WAN link. With a direct link between branch offices, the branch office router will route the APPN traffic over the direct link rather than the backbone network node. Placing an APPN NN router at the branch office enables SNA COS functionality from the branch office to the data center through the entire Cisco WAN. This will ensure service levels for applications requiring guaranteed performance criteria.

> **NOTES**
>
> At first glance, it seems logical that all routers within the Cisco router network handling SNA traffic should implement APPN NN functionality. However, this could lead to TDU congestion and therefore network scalability issues. It is more prudent to keep the number of APPN network nodes to a minimum.

13.1.2 APPN Support on Cisco IOS

The Cisco IOS software supports all the functions of APPN. In addition, the Cisco IOS software features for transporting SNA are applicable to transporting APPN. Cisco support of APPN with these features is as follows:

- APPN support over pure IP router backbone networks is possible using DLSw+ or RSRB encapsulation and network transport.

- Use of the connection network concept is possible over DLSw+ and RSRB-based networks, Frame-Relay– and ATM-based networks, as well as Token-Ring and Ethernet LANs.

- APPN in concert with Downstream Physical Unit (DSPU) support of Cisco IOS software reduces the number of DSPUs required for VTAM definitions.

- Cisco IOS software provides priority queuing, custom queuing, and weighted fair queuing that can be used along with SNA COS, assisting in traffic prioritization and bandwidth reservation for SNA traffic over the WAN.

- Cisco APPN NN support on a channel-attached Cisco router allows VTAM to directly interface with the network as either an EN or NN.

- Cisco routers can act as an APPN Dependent Logical Unit Requestor (DLUR) to VTAM's Dependent Logical Unit Server (DLUS) functions, and thereby enable legacy non–APPN-capable SNA physical units to communicate to the mainframe over APPN.

- Cisco router APPN network nodes support both Intermediate Session Routing (ISR) and High Performance Routing (HPR).

The previously mentioned features support APPN along with SNA encapsulation techniques of:

- DLSw+ over Frame Relay

- BNN/BAN for Frame Relay

- Frame Relay Host

- Fast Sequenced Transport (FST)

- Direct encapsulation

They provide for a robust solution for using APPN in a Cisco router-based network.

13.1.3 Addressing APPN Scalability

APPN is based on nodes containing a complete map of the network topology. Each APPN NN contains information about all links attached to it, applications that reside within the NN, or applications registered to it by attached ENs. For the most part, APPN is a dynamic network building its topology database and COS tables as each NN learns of the addition, deletion, or modification of network resources.

The network topology information found in each NN is built on the receipt of TDUs from each active link of a NN. Large APPN networks containing many NNs can therefore use considerable amounts of bandwidth and processing just to maintain the topology databases. It is precisely for this reason that the size of the network will dictate its capability to scale without performance issues. Contributors to determining the appropriate size of an APPN network and the number of NNs required are the amount of traffic flowing through the network and the physical stability of the links that connect the network. To provide a stable and scalable APPN network, controls must be placed on reducing the number of TDUs flowing through the network.

Increasing the number of NNs proportionally increases the number of TDUs flowing through the network. TDU flows in APPN can be reduced through applying some or all of the following recommendations:

- Limit the number of links by using APPN Connection Networks.

- Minimize the number of CP-CP sessions for NN connectivity to two adjacent nodes.

- Place APPN NN functions at the edge employing DLSw+, FRAS BNN, or RSRB to deliver the SNA data to the mainframe via the APPN NN channel-attached router.

- Employ a Border Node (BN) into the design. This will create APPN subnetworks, enabling a scalable and more manageable network.

Recall that APPN ENs request assistance from their network node server (NNS) for locating a network resource during application-to-application establishment. The NNS first interrogates its own local directory. If the requested resource is not found in the local directory, the NNS then searches the distributed resources directory. If the location of the resource is still unknown, the NNS server issues a LOCATE search request over all the CP-CP sessions it maintains with other NNs. This dynamic search in large networks can again contribute to unforeseen bandwidth and processing utilization. Reducing the number of LOCATE search requests flowing through the network will also contribute to the successful scaling of large APPN networks. LOCATE search flow reduction is possible by using one or more of the following techniques:

- Employing the use of a tftp server for recovering the last-known directory cache of a Cisco APPN network node using the Safe-Store of Directory Cache function. A restarted Cisco NN obtains the resource directory from the tftp server instead of from broadcasting LOCATE requests throughout the network.

- Using partial directory entries coded within the Cisco router APPN configuration identifying the full resource name or a wildcard partial name, along with the name of the owning EN or NN.

- Defining VTAM as the Central Directory Server (CDS) and employing the CDS/Client function on Cisco APPN network nodes to query the CDS on VTAM for the location of a resource.

- EN resource registration requests NN to register the resource with the CDS. This will quickly populate the CDS and add to the reduction of LOCATE search flows.

The LOCATE search flows of an APPN network can cause greater performance issues than TDU flows. A detailed discussion of LOCATE search flows is found in Chapter 3, "Advanced Peer-to-Peer Networking (APPN)." Applying the enhanced features found on Cisco routers for reducing LOCATE search requests in addition to the techniques for reducing TDU flows through the network will greatly enhance stability, performance, and scaling of the APPN network.

13.2 DESIGN CONFIGURATIONS

APPN NN support in Cisco IOS software enables the transport of SNA over a Cisco router-based WAN natively. There is no requirement for encapsulating the SNA frames into DLSw+ or RSRB. As pointed out in the design criteria, however, sometimes it is desirable to use DLSw+ or RSRB for connecting the remote locations with an NN-enabled router. The design configurations described here provide a basis for the majority of configurations you will encounter when deploying APPN in your network.

At a minimum, the following four commands are required in a Cisco router to enable APPN NN functionality:

```
appn routing

appn control-point

appn link-station

appn port
```

The router must enable the use of APPN routing. The default routing used when the appn routing command is entered is ISR. HPR routing is enabled if the hpr command is applied to the appn control-point definition and subsequent link-station and port definitions of the control-point. Cisco routers have the capability to define a dynamic link-station upon receipt of a connection from another NN.

13.2.1 APPN over Token Ring

In this sample configuration, the router NN1 is the initiator for connecting to router NN2 over the Token-Ring LAN. Figure 13-1 diagrams the configuration. The link-station definition in NN2 for the NN1 is defined dynamically upon CP-CP session initiation.

Figure 13-1
APPN
Token-Ring
configuration
between two
Cisco routers
with dynamic
link-station
definitions on
NN2.

NN1

CPname NN1
Port TR0
Link Station NN2TR0

NN2

CPname NN2
Port TR0

13.2.2 APPN over Frame Relay

Figure 13-2 illustrates the use of a Frame-Relay connection between two Cisco routers enabled for APPN NN functionality. The definitions for both routers specify that each will establish a connection to the other at link activation.

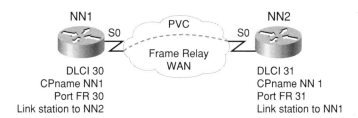

Figure 13-2
APPN Frame-Relay configuration between two Cisco routers with both routers attempting to establish CP-CP sessions at link activation.

13.2.3 APPN over SDLC

SDLC can be used for connecting two Cisco routers running APPN NN functionality. In Figure 13-3, we see that router NN1 establishes a CP-CP connection to router NN2. Each NN has an SDLC station address defined to the serial interface. NN1 specifies the link-station of NN2 in its configuration and will therefore attempt to connect to NN2. The definition in NN2 does not define the link-station for NN1 and will dynamically define the link-station upon an established connection from NN1.

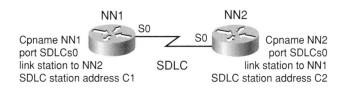

Figure 13-3
APPN SDLC configuration between two Cisco routers with dynamic link-station definitions on NN2.

13.2.4 APPN Using RSRB

APPN's implementation with RSRB uses a virtual station for RSRB communications. The use of RSRB encapsulation enables APPN to traverse an IP WAN router-based network. Figure 13-4 shows the use of a virtual station defining a ring number to the ring group used for connecting the routers over the IP WAN. Included in the configuration is the use of TCP encapsulation with local-acknowledgement for reducing WAN overhead of SNA RR, RNR, and REJ supervisory frames.

Figure 13-4
APPN with RSRB for traversing an IP-only WAN router topology.

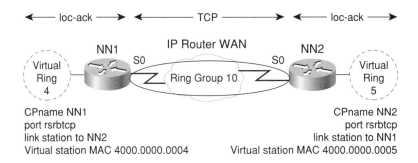

13.2.5 APPN Using DLSw+

DLSw+ in combination with Cisco Virtual Data Link Control (VDLC) allows for a connection between APPN nodes separated by non-APPN nodes over an IP-only WAN router backbone. This configuration is diagrammed in Figure 13-5. As seen in the figure, EN1 has defined a link and port to NN3. The physical connection to NN3 is via the local Token-Ring–attached router (R1) employing DLSw+. The NN3 router has both APPN and DLSw+ enabled. DLSw+ will perform the Token Ring-to-Ethernet translation for the connection.

Figure 13-5
APPN using DLSw+ to connect an EN and its NN over an Ethernet backbone.

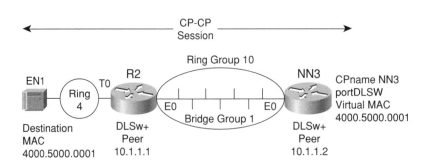

13.2.6 APPN Using a Connection Network over Ethernet

In this example, we demonstrate the use of an APPN connection network. The three routers attached to an Ethernet in Figure 13-6 all connect to a virtual routing node (VRN) named NETA.CONNET. The connection network of each router APPN definition defines NETA.CONNET as the connection network routing node. In this example, routers NN1, NN2, and NN3 must all connect over the Ethernet to establish connectivity. Using the connection network concept, only CP-CP sessions from NN1 to NN2 and NN3 are required. Each has a virtual connection to the connection network VRN. NN2 and NN3 communicate via a direct connection without the need for CP-CP sessions due to the use of the connection network.

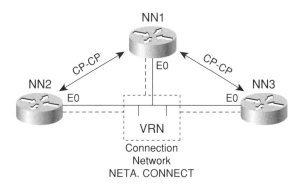

Figure 13-6
Cisco APPN network nodes using a connection network configuration over Ethernet.

13.2.7 APPN Using HPR

HPR uses LLC2 frames over Frame Relay and is mapped to the Frame-Relay DLCI number of the partner router. HPR uses LLC2 (connection-oriented) frames for control sessions. For SNA data transmission, it encapsulates the FID2 RU inside a FID5 header (NHDR). The RTP components handle the sequencing and flow control of the UI frames through the network. Figure 13-7 illustrates the mapping of HPR to the DLCI 30 between NN1 and NN2 over a Frame-Relay network. NN1 maps to NN3 over DLCI 31 and NN3 maps to NN2 using DLCI 32. In this example, the DLCI numbers assigned to the partners matches; however, the DLCI numbers do not need to match for a Frame-Relay connection. The `appn control-point` command must include the `hpr` keyword to enable HPR over the Frame-Relay connection. Failing to include the `hpr` keyword on the `appn control-point` definitions defaults APPN routing to ISR. If ISR were used in the configuration, a disruption of the connection from NN1 to NN2 requires the ENs to reestablish their session over the NN1-to-NN3-to-NN2 connection. HPR reroutes the active session over NN1 to NN3 to NN2 without session disruption.

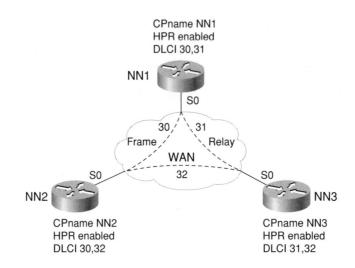

13.2.8 APPN over ATM

Although we have not addressed Asynchronous Transfer Mode (ATM) in great detail, it is important to note that APPN on Cisco routers can use ATM as the transport mechanism between Cisco router APPN NNs. ATM uses virtual circuits for establishing connectivity between ATM devices. Cisco IOS software supports ATM, and the APPN functions can use ATM interfaces for transporting native APPN/SNA frames. The appn link-station definition ATM destination address maps to the virtual circuit descriptor defined on an ATM interface used by the router. Figure 13-8 illustrates an APPN/ATM configuration.

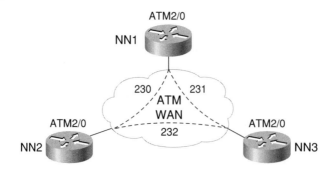

13.2.9 APPN over ATM Ethernet LAN Emulation

ATM LAN Emulation (LANE) enables you to logically extend a LAN in one building or location to another building or location over an ATM WAN. Using LANE removes the need for routing decisions because the LAN is "bridged" through the ATM WAN. Cisco IOS software support for APPN supports the use of an ATM LANE configuration for connecting APPN connections. Figure 13-9 depicts an Ethernet LANE configuration between two locations separated by an ATM WAN. NN1 connects to the ENs in the figure using direct CP-CP sessions. LANE is applicable to ISR in pre-Cisco IOS Release 11.3. HPR over ATM LAN is supported as of Cisco IOS Release 11.3.

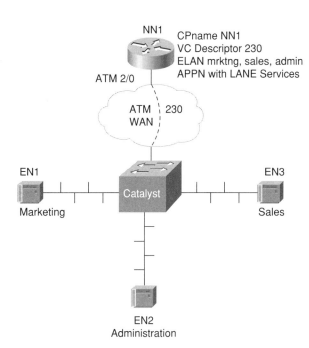

Figure 13-9
Ethernet ATM LANE configuration for connecting APPN nodes over a WAN.

13.2.10 APPN with DLUR/DLUS

Cisco IOS software that uses APPN functions supports the transport of legacy non-APPN PU2.0 devices to VTAM over an APPN network through the use of DLUR/DLUS. In Figure 13-10, the Token-Ring–attached SNA PU 2.0 device requires connectivity to the mainframe over an APPN network. The attached Cisco router NN1 envelopes the SNA PU2.0 frames into an LU6.2 connection using the DLUR function. The frames are then transported to the associated DLUS function of VTAM residing on the mainframe. The APPN code in the Cisco router identifies the name of the primary and secondary DLUS for which this DLUR router will establish the LU6.2 session with for transporting legacy SNA PU2.0.

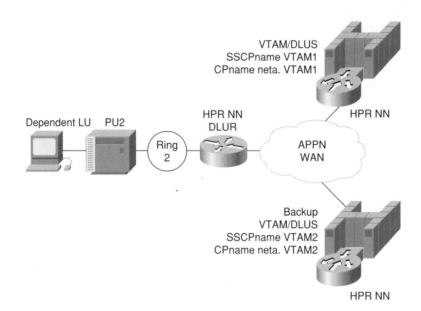

Figure 13-10
DLUR/DLUS configuration for supporting legacy SNA PU2.0 device communication over APPN networks.

13.3 COMPLETING AND MODIFYING APPN DEFINITIONS

The implementation of APPN with Cisco IOS software requires an acknowledgement of the definitions prior to committing them to the APPN subsystem. Specifying this commitment is accomplished by issuing the `complete` command under every APPN definition.

The update of an APPN definition or the deletion of an APPN definition is not performed until the `complete` command is entered. When modifying a definition you must perform the following tasks in order:

1. Stop the link or port being changed.

2. Enter the definition as it currently exists.

3. Enter the `no complete` command.

4. Change any of the parameters of the definition desired.

5. When finished with the changes, enter the `complete` command to commit the new definitions to the APPN subsystem.

6. Start the link or port that was changed.

At this point, the definition will take effect by the APPN subsystem applying the changes to the configuration.

13.4 ENABLING APPN

The Cisco IOS software becomes aware of APPN functionality by entering the `appn routing` global command. The router at startup will execute the APPN subsystem upon reading the `appn routing` command. The APPN subsystem can also be started and stopped manually by entering the `privileged execute` commands `appn start` and `appn stop`. For access to the `privilege execute` commands, consult with your Cisco router administrators. Specifying APPN routing automatically enables ISR functionality. HPR functions must be defined on the APPN control-point definitions for the router to use HPR as the preferred APPN routing protocol.

13.5 DEFINE THE ENCAPSULATION MODE

APPN must have the capability to communicate over the serial-line connections to this router. As such, the serial interfaces supporting APPN are as follows:

- ATM
- Frame Relay
- PPP
- SDLC
- SMDS
- X25
- ISDN (via PPP)

Of these serial interface encapsulation types, the most popular are ATM, Frame Relay, and SDLC. Therefore, our discussion focus on these three interfaces. The APPN port definitions point to the interfaces used for connecting APPN nodes over the network.

Cisco routers can also transport APPN frames over DLSw+ or RSRB connections. For this to take place, the router configuration must properly define the DLSw+ or RSRB definitions. When using RSRB, the `source-bridge ring-group` global command must be defined with either the `tcp`, `fst`, or `interface` keywords specified to determine the encapsulation method. The APPN port using RSRB defines the LAN interface being associated with RSRB. The RSRB LAN interface definition defines the source-bridge connection to the virtual ring group defined on the `source-bridge ring-group` global command.

DLSw+ support is also provided for transporting APPN traffic through the use of Cisco's VDLC. The VDLC definition under the `appn port` specification points to the ring group used by DLSw+ for transporting SNA over the WAN. Details on the RSRB and DLSw+ specific commands and parameters used on the `appn port` specification are found in Section 13.6.7 of this chapter.

13.6 DEFINING APPN CONTROL POINT

APPN cannot be used in the Cisco router unless an APPN control point is defined. Only one control point can be defined per router. The `appn control-point` command defines the fully qualified control-point name for the node. Recall that the *fully qualified name* is comprised of a network identifier and a control-point name. There is only one control-point definition per router. The format of the `appn control-point` command is as follows:

```
appn control-point netid.cpname
```

The `netid.cpname` identifies to which network this node is a member of and the networkwide unique control-point name assigned to this router. The `netid` variable must match the `netid` variable of any other NN connecting to this router. If the `netid` does not match, CP-CP sessions will not be established. Both the `netid` and `cpname` variables are one to eight alphanumeric characters in length separated by a period. The variable name cannot begin with a numeric value. Following characters are valid for use in the `netid` and `cpname` variables:

- Alphabetic characters: A–Z, a–z, $, #, @
- Numeric characters: 0–9

In the following example, we have defined a control-point name NYCNN1 as part of the network NETUSA.

```
appn control-point NETUSA.NYCNN1

complete
```

The fully qualified control-point name is not case sensitive. It is in uppercase here for display purposes only. The `complete` command is shown in the example to illustrate that the `appn control-point` definition is not committed unless the `complete` command is entered.

13.6.1 Central Resources Registration (CRR)

The earlier discussion on design criteria for APPN focused on reducing the number of `LOCATE` search broadcasts issued by NNs through the APPN network on behalf of requesting ENs. One way discussed is by having Cisco router NNs automatically register the applications owned by the ENs attaching to the router after the ENs have registered their applications with the router NN services. The Cisco APPN subsystem defaults *central resource registration (CRR)* as being active upon control-point definition. CRR can be disabled using the following command under control-point mode:

```
no central-resource-registration
```

This command disables automatic updates to the CDS NN on VTAM. This command is only used when VTAM is not performing CDS functions. Issuing the following command under control-point mode enables CRR after it was disabled:

```
central-resource-registration
```

The Cisco APPN subsystem is aware of the CDS functions of a NN through the capabilities exchange that occurs during CP-CP session establishment. Currently, VTAM is the only NN that supports CDS functionality.

13.6.2 Defining DLUR/DLUS Services for the CP

Enabling the transport of legacy SNA PU2.0 devices to communicate with an SSCP on a VTAM NN is accomplished by issuing the `dlur` command under control-point mode. Along with specifying the `dlur` command to enable DLUR functional support, you must specify the fully qualified control-point name of the VTAM SSCP providing the services. Entering the following command under control-point mode provides this specification:

```
dlus netid.cpname
```

The `netid.cpname` parameter must match the fully qualified control-point name of the SSCP providing the primary DLUS services. A backup DLUS may also be defined, allowing recovery of SSCP sessions should the primary DLUS fail. Entering the following command specifies the backup:

```
backup-dlus netid.cpname
```

Should the primary DLUS connection fail, the router APPN subsystem will attempt to establish a DLUR/DLUS LU6.2 session pipe with the SSCP defined by the *netid.cpname* entered on the backup-dlus command. The dlur and dlus commands must be specified prior to defining the backup-dlus command. The backup-dlus command may also be entered on the appn link-station definition. The value defined on the link-station definition overrides the value specified for the control point. This allows for assigning different link-stations to different DLUS backup SSCPs.

NOTES

VTAM's netid and cpname are defined in the VTAM start options list. The netid is the NETID parameter value, and the cpname for VTAM is the SSCPNAME parameter value specified in the ATCCON00 member of the SYS1.VTAMLST partitioned data set. The values can also be found by issuing the VTAM operator command DISPLAY NET, VTAMOPTS.

13.6.3 Safe-Store of Directory Database

As part of our discussion on scalability, we introduced the use of the safe-store feature used on Cisco routers for saving the directory database to a TFTP server. Enabling this feature is accomplished by specifying the safe-store-host command under control-point mode. The format of the command is as follows:

```
safe-store-host ip-address tftp-ip-address directory path
```

The safe-store-host command specifies the IP address of the TFTP server used for storing the directory database. The directory keyword parameter *path* identifies the file directory used on the TFTP server for writing the directory database.

The safe-store-cycle command enables you to define the number of stored instances saved on the TFTP server before overwriting the first stored instance. The safe-store feature uses a file-naming standard for storing the directory database instances. The format of the safe-store-cycle command is as follows:

```
safe-store-cycle number
```

The *number* parameter defines the number of stored instances on the TFTP server before overwriting the first stored instance. The range for the *number* parameter is 1 to 99. The default `safe-store-cycle` value is two instances. The stored files are written to the TFTP server using the following naming convention:

```
cpname.dnn
```

The *cpname* value of the control point is used as the low-level name of the filename. The high-level value of the naming convention begins with the letter *d* followed by two decimal digits. The *nn* value is the number of the stored cycle. If the *cpname* is NYCNN1 and the `safe-store-cycle` number parameter is specified as 3, for example, the following files will be written to the TFTP server:

```
NYCNN1.d01

NYCNN1.d02

NYCNN1.d03
```

NOTES

Some TFTP servers (UNIX flavors) require the file being written to previously exist. If this is the case for the TFTP server being used on your network, predefine the files using the naming convention described here. Although the name of the control point is not case sensitive for the establishment of CP-CP sessions, its entered format for the *cpname* variable of the `appn control-point` command is used in creating the stored filename on the TFTP server. If the preceding *cpname* were entered on the `appn control-point` command as NYCnn1, for example, the filename written to the TFTP server would be NYCnn1.d01.

Controlling the frequency of storing the intervals is accomplished by specifying the `safe-store-interval` command. The default interval for stored instances on a TFTP server is 20 minutes. You can use the `safe-store-interval` command to increase or decrease the default interval. The format of the `safe-store-interval` command is as follows:

```
safe-store-interval interval
```

The *interval* is expressed in minutes and is in the range of 0 to 32767. Specifying a value of 0 indicates that the safe-store feature will in effect be disabled. The use of this command enables you to effectively manage router processor usage. Although long intervals considerably reduce processor utilization, they may reduce the accuracy of the stored directory database.

The following is an example of defining the safe-store feature:

```
safe-store-host ip-address 10.10.1.254 directory APPNDB

safe-store cycle 3

safe-store-interval 30
```

The example defines the TFTP server at IP address 10.10.1.254 with the location for storing the directory database at APPNDB. Three instances of the directory database are stored images on the TFTP server. The router will copy the directory database to the TFTP server every 30 minutes. Therefore, on the fourth iteration, the first stored instance will be rewritten. If the router recycles, it will TFTP the most recent iteration of the directory database from the defined TFTP server.

13.6.4 Specifying High-Performance Routing (HPR)

HPR defined on the control point enables HPR functions for the router. HPR is enabled on the router by entering the control-point command hpr under control-point configuration mode. Channel-attached Cisco routers using CIP require the channel to be defined using MPC. The following four optional HPR commands can be entered under control-point configuration mode for controlling HPR characteristics:

```
hpr max-sessions

hpr retries

hpr timers liveness

hpr timers path-switch
```

The hpr max-sessions command enables you to reduce the number of RTP connections from the default value of 65535. The format of the hpr max-sessions command is as follows:

```
hpr max-sessions num-sessions
```

The num-sessions variable is a decimal number in the range of 1 to 65535.

The hpr retries optional command, if specified, defines the number of times the NN will retry sending packets before initiating a path switch for the RTP connection. The format of the hpr retries command is as follows:

```
hpr retries low-retries medium-retries high-retries network-retries
```

All four variables default to a value of 6 if the hpr retries command is not specified. Each variable has a valid range of 0 to 10. The *low-retries* variable defines the retry count for sending low-priority packets before a path switch is initiated. The *medium-retries* variable is the count for retrying to send medium-priority packets. Likewise, the *high-retries* value is the number of retries for sending a high-priority packet before deciding to switch the path used by RTP. The *network-retries* value specifies the send retry count for network-priority packets before initiating a path switch for the RTP connections.

Much akin to using the hpr retries command is the hpr timers liveness command. The hpr timers liveness command sets the wait time in seconds for the node to send an HPR status request after not receiving a packet for the four different data traffic priorities. The format of the hpr timers liveness command is as follows:

```
hpr timers liveness low-time medium-time high-time network-time
```

For each of the variables, the time is specified in seconds. The value for each variable ranges from 1 to 180 seconds. If the hpr timers liveness command is not specified, the timers default to 45 seconds for all. After the timer has expired, the node will send an HPR status request up to the number of retries specified in the hpr retries command. The node will initiate path switching for the RTP connection after the retries count has been reached for the priority in question.

After HPR timers and retries have been exhausted, HPR sets a time limit on the amount of seconds it takes to reestablish the RTP connection over a different path. The format for specifying the path-switch time limit is as follows:

```
hpr timers path-switch low-time medium-time high-time network-time
```

The default value for *low-time* is 480 seconds. Medium-priority default value for *medium-time* is 240 seconds. The *high-time* default value is 120 seconds. Network priority RTP connections default to a *network-time* value of 60 seconds. Each value for the variables of the hpr timers path-switch command can range from 0 to 7200 seconds. A value of 0 indicates that the RTP connections will not be switched. In this case, the connections will just be torn down.

13.6.5 Locate Throttling

The locate throttling feature of the Cisco APPN NN function is enabled by using the locate-queuing command under control-point configuration mode. The locate throttling feature issues one LOCATE broadcast search for a destination LU requested by multiple source LUs. This minimizes the number of searches performed for the same LU from the same network node server. Locate throttling is disabled by default.

13.6.6 Negative Caching

Cisco APPN NN functionality further protects the network from LOCATE broadcast search requests by caching a list of LUs that were determined to be unreachable. If a request for a destination LU comes into the NN and the LU is found on the negative cache list, the NN immediately replies to the requesting EN that the destination LU is unreachable. The format of the `negative caching` command is as follows:

```
negative-caching [time] time [threshold] threshold-value
```

The *time* variable is the time in seconds that an LU is considered unreachable. The default is 60 seconds, with a range of 0 to 3600. A value of 0 indicates that the LU is never reachable. The *threshold-value* variable defines the number of times a LOCATE search is rejected before removing the entry from the negative cache. The default is 20 searches and can range from 0 to 1000. A value of 0 indicates that the entry will never be removed from the negative cache. The `negative-caching` command applies to LOCATE requests from ENs of the NNS domain. Expiration of either variable will remove the negative cache entry for the destination resource. Upon removal, the next LOCATE request for the LU will be issued by the NN.

13.6.7 Defining the APPN Port

The APPN port definitions associate the APPN subsystem to an interface on the router. Any interface used for establishing connectivity to an APPN network requires a port definition. The `appn port` command associates a router interface to APPN for use by the control point. The format of the `appn port` command is as follows:

```
appn port portname interface
```

The *portname* variable is an assigned label for the port being defined. The *portname* parameter is usually eight alphanumeric characters long and identifies the type of connection, destination of connection or the interface used for APPN connectivity. The *interface* variable specifies the actual interface on the router being used for the port. For example, entering:

```
appn port T03745 tokenring 1/0
```

identifies slot 1 as a Token-Ring interface processor with a Token-Ring LAN attachment on port 0 of the card. The *portname* variable T03745 indicates that the Token Ring on slot 1 port 0 attaches to an IBM 3745 FEP.

13.6.8 Using RSRB

Employing RSRB as the APPN transport mechanism requires the rsrb keyword on the appn port command. The format of the appn port rsrb command is as follows:

```
appn port portname rsrb
```

For RSRB to function properly, a virtual MAC address and an associated virtual ring and bridge must be defined for connectivity to the ring group used by the RSRB connections. The format of the command defining the virtual RSRB station and ring is as follows:

```
rsrb-virtual-station mac-address local-ring bridge-number target-ring
```

The *mac-address* parameter value of the rsrb-virtual-station command is triple-dotted hexadecimal 12-digit representation of the MAC address of the virtual station used by the APPN port. The *local-ring* parameter is the virtual ring number of the APPN station associated with the port. The value for *local-ring* is a decimal value with the range of 1 to 4095. The *bridge-number* is a decimal number ranging from 1 to 15 and identifies the virtual bridge connecting the virtual station Token Ring to the ring group identified by the *target-ring* parameters. The *target-ring* parameter value must match a ring group virtual ring number defined on a source-bridge ring-group command used by this router. For example, if the following command were entered under the port configuration mode:

```
source-bridge ring-group 100
source-bridge remote-peer 100 tcp 10.1.1.1
appn control-point NYCnn1
complete
appn port VRNG rsrb
rsrb-virtual-station 4000.cdef.0001 200 1 100
complete
```

the virtual RSRB ring 200 bridges to the ring group 100 over bridge 1. The APPN traffic will be encapsulated in TCP segments and sent to the peer at 10.1.1.1.

13.6.9 Using DLSw+

APPN transport over DLSw+ requires the vdlc keyword at the end of the appn port command. The vdlc keyword indicates the use of the Cisco VDLC internal protocol for connecting DLSw+ to an APPN port. The format of the appn port for implementing DLSw+ is as follows:

```
appn port portname vdlc
```

Assigning the port to VDLC for DLSw+ again requires the mapping of the port to the source-bridge ring group used by DLSw+. The format of the command that associates the port of the ring group for DLSw+ to use is as follows:

```
vdlc ring-group [vmac vdlc-mac-address]
```

The *ring-group* variable must match a ring group used by DLSw+ on this router. The optional *vmac* keyword and its associated variable *vdlc-mac-address* assign a virtual MAC address to identify the APPN port being defined. If the following configuration included:

```
source-bridge ring-group 100
dlsw local-peer peer-id 10.8.1.1
dlsw remote-peer 0 tcp 10.8.2.1
appn control-point NYCnn1
complete
appn port DLSW vdlc
vdlc 100 vmac 4000.abcd.0001
complete
```

a virtual MAC address of 4000.abcd.0001 is used by the port named DLSW for connecting to the ring group 100.

If the APPN connection is over an SDLC interface, the appn port command requires the assignment of a secondary SDLC station address to the port. The format of the command is as follows:

```
sdlc-sec-addr address
```

The *address* variable of the sdlc-sec-addr command is a hexadecimal value ranging from 00 to FE. The default value used is 00. As an example, the following statements define a connection through an SDLC interface on port 2 of the Cisco router:

```
interface serial 2
  encapsulation sdlc
  sdlc address C1
appn control-point NYCnn1
  complete
appn port SDLC serial 2
  sdlc-sec-addr C1
  complete
```

The default Service Access Point (SAP) used by Automatic Network Routing (ANR) frames on an APPN port is the hexadecimal value C8. This value can be changed using the following:

```
hpr sap sap
```

The *sap* value can be any hexadecimal even number ranging from 02 to FE. The SAP value is used by all link-stations defined to the port.

13.6.10 Enabling Dynamic Link-Station Builds

Each port definition has a minimum of one link-station defined for use on the port. Cisco APPN NN allows for dynamic link-station definition based on the XID3 exchange between the NN and the EN connecting to other NNs. The appn port command supports dynamic link-station definitions for PU2.1 devices using the service-any command entered under the port configuration mode. The service-any command is the default for the port and will allow the NN to attempt to build a dynamic link-station definition for the incoming connection request. Specifying the no service-any command under port configuration mode disables dynamic link-station definitions and therefore requires a predefined link-station for using the port.

For dynamic link-station definitions concerning PU 2.0 devices, the null-xid-poll command must be entered under the port configuration definition. The router will issue a null XID over the port in an attempt to solicit an XID0 or XID3 response. Specifying the null-xid-poll command works for both PU 2.0 and PU 2.1 devices. The null-xid-poll command indicates to the router that it expects the partner PU 2.0 to issue an XID0 response upon which the NN function builds a link-station. PU 2.1 XID3 negotiation and exchange continues to function as normal. The default is XID3 polling.

NOTES

Configuring the null-xid-poll command to Cisco APPN NN routers connecting over a port results in a failed connection. Each router will expect the other to send an XID0 or XID3 response. Similar issues arise if null-xid-poll is defined on a port connecting to an IBM 3745 FEP configured for XID polling. Use the null-xid-poll command on ports connecting PU 2.0 devices that do not support XID3 polls.

13.6.11 Define the APPN Link-Station

APPN link-stations represent a connection or the capability to have a connection to another APPN node. Cisco IOS 11.3 enables complete dynamic link-station definitions if the partner node initiates the connection. Cisco APPN NNs will initiate connections if a link-station definition exists identifying a partner node for the link. The most frequently used link-station commands are discussed here. The appn link-station global command may also define link characteristics for the APPN connection regardless of which node initiates.

The format of the appn link-station global command is as follows:

```
appn link-station linkname
```

The *linkname* variable is a one-to-eight alphanumeric character string identifying the link established between two PU 2.1 or PU 2.0 devices over the associated port. The name cannot begin with a number. An APPN port is associated with a link-station using the port command under appn link-station configuration mode. The format of the port command is as follows:

```
port port-name
```

The port command under link-station configuration mode maps the access to the predefined link-station over a specific previously defined APPN port. The *port-name* variable must match the name assigned to an appn port definition. For example, connection to another NN over a serial line is defined as this:

```
appn port BOSTON serial 1
complete
appn link-station NYtoBOS
port BOSTON
complete
```

In the example interface, serial 1 on the router has an HDLC line from the NY office to the Boston office. The port name identified as BOSTON maps to the serial interface on the router that connects the two locations. The router being defined, residing in NY, defines the link-station name as NYtoBOS and maps the link-station to the port named BOSTON.

13.6.12 Configuring the Destination Address for the Link-Station

The initiation of a link requires the destination address of the link-station being connected on the associated port. The address assigned is also used for mapping the incoming connection to the link station matching the address. The media types discussed for our purposes are as follows:

- ATM

- Frame Relay

- Token Ring

- Ethernet

- SDLC

The format of the ATM link-station destination address is as follows:

```
atm-dest-address pvcid
```

The `atm-dest-address` command under link-station configuration mode identifies which interface provides the ATM PVC information being mapped for this link-station partner. The *pvcid* variable must match an ATM interface PVC previously defined. The *pvcid* value is the virtual circuit descriptor value of the previously defined interface command `atm pvc` found under the ATM interface. For example:

```
interface ATM 1/0
 atm pvc 244 1 12 aal5nlpid
 map-group atm-appn
!
appn control-point NETA.APPN
 complete
!
appn port ATM ATM 1/0
 complete
!
appn link-station ATMtoSNA
 port ATM
 atm-dest-address 244
 complete
```

The virtual circuit descriptor of the PVC used for the ATM connection is 244 in the preceding example.

For Frame-Relay interface support when defining the link-station, the following command defines the associated destination address:

```
fr-dest-address dlci [sap]
```

The *dlci* variable is the DLCI number used by the partner router attached to the Frame-Relay network. The value used for the *dlci* variable should match a previously defined Frame-Relay definition. The *sap* variable is optional and defines the SAP address used for identifying the link-station being defined when multiple link-stations are connected over the same Frame-Relay DLCI. The default *sap* value is hexadecimal 04, but can be coded in the range of 04 to EC as long as the number is divisible by four. The following example illustrates the use of the `fr-dest-address` command under the link-station:

```
interface serial 0
 encapsulation frame-relay IETF
 frame-relay map llc2 22
!
appn control-point neta.NYC
  complete
!
appn port framerly serial 0
  complete
!
appn link-station BOSTON
 port framerly
 fr-dest-address 22
  complete
```

In this example, the APPN link-station BOSTON is reached using the destination address 22, which maps the DLCI of the frame-relay map command found under router interface serial 0.

For Token-Ring and Ethernet link-station definitions, the lan-dest-address command under link-station configuration mode defines the MAC address and optionally the SAP address of the LAN-attached destination partner. The format of the command is as follows:

```
lan-dest-address mac-addr [sap]
```

The mac-addr variable defines the 12-digit, triple-dotted hexadecimal value of the MAC address assigned to the destination partner LAN interface. The optional sap variable, which defaults to 04, allows for multiplexing connections over the link-station using SAP addresses. The sap value must be within the hexadecimal range of 04 to EC and must be divisible by four. The following example defines the destination partner attached to Token-Ring interface 0, has a MAC address of 4000.1234.1234, and uses the default SAP address of 04:

```
interface tokenring 0
!
appn control-point neta.NYNN1
  complete
!
appn port tr0 tokenring 0
  complete
!
appn link-station NYNN2
 port tr0
 lan-dest-address 4000.1234.1234
  complete
```

SDLC-attached nodes over serial interfaces use the SDLC station address for establishing connectivity. The value of the destination partner is defined using the `sdlc-dest-address` command under link-station configuration mode. The format for defining the destination SDLC station address is as follows:

```
sdlc-dest-address address
```

The value of the *address* variable is a two-digit hexadecimal number in the range of 00 to FE. The value used here must match the SDLC address value defined on the serial interface of the partner node. The following illustrates the use of the `sdlc-dest-address` command:

```
Configuration for NY

interface serial 0
 encapsulation sdlc
 sdlc address c2
!
appn control-point neta.NY
  complete
!
appn port sdlc serial 0
 sdlc-sec-addr c2
  complete
!
appn link-station Boston
 port sdlc
 sdlc-dest-address c1
  complete

Configuration for Boston

interface serial 1
 encapsulation sdlc
 sdlc address c1
!
appn control-point neta.BOSTON
  complete
!
appn port sdlc serial 1
 sdlc-sec-addr c2
  complete
```

In the preceding example, the SDLC station address defined on interface serial 1 of the Boston router matched the SDLC destination station address defined on the NY router `sdlc-dest-address link-station` command.

13.7 USING THE APPN CONNECTION NETWORK FEATURE

The connection network concept is available on Cisco APPN for providing any-to-any connectivity on shared media without defining any-to-any link-station connectivity. The NN function of a Cisco router supports connection network for Token-Ring, Ethernet, FDDI, DLSw+, and RSRB networks. For a router to join the connection network, the `appn connection-network` global command must be entered. The format of the command is as follows:

```
appn connection-network netid.cnname
```

The *netid.cnname* is the name of the VRN used for the connection network. All nodes on the shared media using the same connection network must specify the same VRN name. Both the *netid* and *cnname* variables may be one to eight alphanumeric characters in length and concatenated by the use of a period.

The connection network for each router supports up to five port mappings for access to the connection network. Typically, a single port is suitable for connecting. However, in some instances—for example, alternative routing and redundancy to the same shared media—multiple ports are assigned. Defining which ports are used for connecting to the connection network is accomplished by entering the following command under connection network configuration mode:

```
port portname
```

The value for *portname* is a previously defined APPN port that maps to any of the supported shared media interface types or DLSw+ VDLC or RSRB virtual station used in transporting the APPN traffic. An example of defining the connection network to a Token-Ring LAN is as follows:

```
appn connection-network NETA.TOKRNG
 port INTtok1
  complete
```

13.8 DEFINING THE APPN CLASS OF SERVICE

For most implementations of APPN on Cisco routers, the default COS characteristics predefined by the APPN specifications meet the requirements for LU-LU sessions. The COS names that defined the standard definitions are as follows:

#BATCH	#INTERSC
#BATCHSC	SNASVCMG
#CONNECT	CPSVCMG
#INTER	

The #BATCH and #BATCHSC COS names are more commonly used for file transfer or print connections. These types of connections tend to be bursty and use excessive bandwidth for a brief period. Having the EN application assign a COS of #BATCH or #BATCHSC to the connection will ensure that more time-sensitive connections will not be impacted, because the #BATCH and #BATCHSC COS have a low priority.

The #INTER and #INTERSC COS characteristics are applicable to real-time interactive connection, such as credit verification or online ad hoc reports. The #INTER and #INTERSC COS are considered by APPN to have a high priority for delivery. APPN traffic marked as high will be delivered before traffic marked as medium or low.

The COS entries SNASVCMG and CPSVCMG provide the top priority over an APPN network. These COS characteristics are typically reserved for management traffic and control-point traffic.

If for some reason the default COS characteristics are not applicable to connections within your network, you can define new COS characteristics or modify the defaults. It is highly recommended that you use the default COS names and characteristics connections over the APPN network. This will reduce the complexity of defining the APPN COS in all NN routers throughout the network. If a special COS is required, however, it is recommended that a new COS name and characteristic be defined. To define a COS for use by APPN, the following global command must be entered:

```
appn class-of-service cosname
```

The *cosname* variable is a one-to-eight alphanumeric character string not beginning with a number.

13.8.1 Node and Transmission Group (TG) Row Definitions

Following the definition of the appn class-of-service command, there must be at least one node row, a TG row, and a transmission priority definition. There can be up to eight rows for both the node-row and TG-row definitions. If defining more than one row, the following row definitions, in succession, should specify a higher weight but be less restrictive. The format for defining the node row is as follows:

```
node-row index weight weight congestion {yes ¦ no} {yes ¦ no} route-additional-resistance min max
```

The *index* value is the row number of the node row being defined. The range for index is 1 to 8. The *weight* value is the criteria given to this row for calculating the best path to a destination. The *weight* value ranges from decimal 0 to 255. The weight assigned to the row being defined must be less than the following row definition.

The congestion keyword and subsequent yes¦no value pairs define three types of consideration for the transmission group servicing this node:

- Specifying yes yes indicates that only congested transmission groups will match this row.

- Specifying no yes pair indicates the congestion will not affect the COS row in deciding on the best path.

- Having a no no pair indicates that only noncongested transmission groups will match this row. The value pair no no is the default.

The route-additional-resistance keyword enables you to add resistance for the minimum and maximum calculation for deciding on the best route for this node. The range for min and max is 0 through 255 with both values defaulting to 0.

The tg-row command specifies the characteristics used for selecting the appropriate TG for connecting the LU session over the network. The format of the tg-row command is as follows:

```
tg-row index weight weight byte min max time min max capacity min max delay min max
security min max user1 min max user2 min max user3 min max
```

The *index* variable is the number of the row being defined. The clause is in the range of 1 to 8. The *weight* value is the criteria given to this row for calculating the best path to a destination. The *weight* value ranges from decimal 0 to 255. The weight assigned to the row being defined must be less than the following row definition.

All the *min* and *max* variables have a range of 0 to 255. The byte keyword variables *min* and *max* define the cost per byte for measuring the efficiency of the TG. The time keyword *min* and *max* variables specify the cost per connect time. The capacity keyword *min* and *max* values specify the effective capacity of the TG. The delay keyword *min* and *max* values enable you to specify a propagation delay. The security keyword *min* and *max* values denote the security of the TG link and must match one of the user keywords user1, user2, and user3 min and max values. The user *min* and *max* values range from 1 to 255.

13.8.2 Defining Transmission priority

The COS being defined must have a transmission priority assigned to it. This is done with the `transmission-priority` command under the COS configuration mode. The format of the command is as follows:

```
transmission-priority priority
```

The *priority* variable may have a value of `network`, `high`, `medium`, or `low`. The `network` value is reserved for CP and SNA control traffic and should not be specified for LU-LU sessions. The remaining three values are applicable to LU-LU session traffic.

13.9 SPECIFYING THE APPN MODE

The `appn mode` command is used when mapping Low Entry Networking (LEN) node BIND requests to an existing COS name. This is accomplished using the following two commands:

```
appn mode modename
  class-of-service cosname
```

The APPN specification has eight possible mode names for use by APPN:

```
#BATCH              #CPSVCMG

#BATCHSC            #SNASVCMG

#INTER              #CPSVRMG

#INTERSC            [blank]
```

These mode names can not be modified in any way. The `appn mode` command is used when LEN nodes request connections through the NNS residing on the router. The LEN BIND request contains the name of a mode for use by the requested session. Specifying the LEN mode name for the *modename* variable on the `appn mode` command enables you to map the requested mode to a defined COS as specified by the associated `class-of-service` command under `appn mode` configuration services. The default COS used for a defined *modename* is the APPN provided COS #CONNECT. In the following example, an LEN has requested a BIND with the mode name TSO specified. The `appn mode` mapping associates the LEN TSO mode request with the COS #INTER:

```
appn mode TSO
 class-of-service #INTER
 complete
```

13.10 USING APPN PARTNER LU LOCATION

LOCATE broadcast searches are reduced over the APPN WAN through defining part-ner LU requests for all attached ENs and LENs of this Cisco APPN NN. The format of APPN partner LU location command is as follows:

```
appn partner-lu-location netid.luname
```

The *netid.luname* is the fully qualified name for the destination LU partner being defined. Using this command defines an entry in the directory database. All LEN node resources must be defined using this command set for them to be reachable by other nodes within the APPN network.

NOTES

Although APPN is known for dynamically learning the locations of LUs, it may be prudent—as in the case with LEN nodes—to predefine the location of destination LUs.

To complete the definition of a partner LU location, each defined LU must have an asso-ciated owning-cp command identifying the name of the CP that controls the LU. The format for the owning-cp command is as follows:

```
owning-cp netid.cpname
```

The *netid.cpname* variable is the name of the control point that manages the partner LU. The CP name may be that of a LEN, EN, or NN. If the control point defined is not the NNS for the resource, you can further define the location of the partner LU by spec-ifying the NNS being used for the resource. The command for defining the NNS of the partner LU is as follows:

```
serving-nn netid.cpname
```

The *netid.cpname* variable of the serving-nn command is the CP name of the NNS that has the details of where the partner LU actually resides.

When defining the *luname* of the appn partner-lu-location command, it is possible to use an abbreviated name that will capture multiple requests. The APPN subsystem is aware of the abbreviation by use of the wildcard command under partner-lu-location configuration mode. If the *luname* variable were specified as APC0, for example, any LU partner beginning with APC0 would have a directed search sent to the associated owning CP of the partner-lu-location definition. An LU request for APC1 would result in a LOCATE broadcast search rather than a directed search. The following is an example of defining a partner LU location for the applications named TSOA, TSOB, and TSOC on a APPN mainframe:

```
appn partner-lu-location neta.TSO
 owning-cp neta.VTAMCMC
 wildcard
 complete
```

13.11 APPN Configuration Examples

The following are examples of using APPN with Cisco routers in various topologies. The examples demonstrate many of the connectivity options discussed as well as the different types of encapsulation techniques.

13.11.1 Connecting Two Cisco APPN NNs over Token Ring

In this sample configuration, the routers NN1 and NN2 are not using a connection network. In this case, there is no need for a connection network because the two routers are the only devices on the Token-Ring LAN segment. Figure 13-11 diagrams the configuration. The link-station definition for NN2 in router NN1 indicates that NN1 will try to contact NN2 at link activation time. NN2 will dynamically define the NN1 link-station found on the APPN port TR0. The routers in this example are using ISR routing because the hpr command is not defined for the control-point definition.

13.11.2 APPN over Frame Relay

The Frame-Relay example shown in Figure 13-12 illustrates the use of the link-station definition in both attaching routers. Each router will attempt to initiate the connection at link activation time. Note that in this configuration the DLCI numbers associated with the Frame-Relay connections are different for each router.

Figure 13-11
*A direct
isolated
Token-Ring
segment
attaching two
Cisco APPN
NN routers.*

NN1   NN2

CPname NN1   CPname NN2
Port TR0   Port TR0
Link Station NN2TR0

NN1 Configuration   NN2 Configuration

interface tokenring 0   interface tokenring 0
mac-address 400.000.1000   mac-address 4000.0000.2000
!   !
appn control-point neta. NN1 appn control-point neta. NN2
  complete   complete
!   !
appn port TR0 tokenring 0   appn port TR0 tokenring 0
  complete   complete
!   !
appn link-station NN2TR0   appn routing
  port TR0
  lan-dest-address 4000.0000.200
  complete
!
appn routing

Figure 13-12
*APPN over
Frame Relay
with defined
link-stations.*

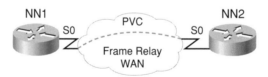

NN1   NN2

NN1 Configuration   NN2 Configuration

interface serial 0   interface serial 0
encapsulation frame-relay ietf encapsulation frame-relay ietf
frame-relay map llc2 30   frame-relay map llc2 31
!   !
appn control-point neta. NN1 appn control-point neta. NN2
  complete   complete
!   !
appn port FR30 serial 0   appn port FR31 serial 0
  complete   complete
!   !
appn link-station NN2   appn link-station NN1
  port FR30   port FR31
  fr-dest-address 30   fr-dest-address 31
  complete   complete
  !   !
  appn routing   appn routing

13.11.3 APPN over SDLC

SDLC can be used for connecting two Cisco routers running APPN NN functionality. Figure 13-13 shows that router NN1 establishes a CP-CP connection to router NN2. Each NN has an SDLC station address defined to the serial interface. Both NNs define the SDLC station using address C2 as the secondary SDLC station on the link. NN1 specifies the link-station of NN2 in its configuration and will therefore attempt to connect to NN2. The definition in NN2 does not define the link-station for NN1 and will dynamically define the link-station upon an established connection from NN1.

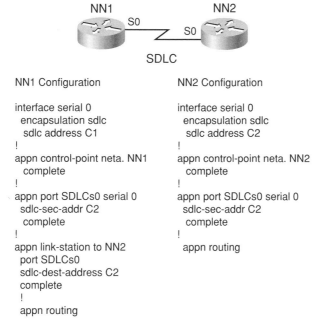

NN1 Configuration

```
interface serial 0
  encapsulation sdlc
  sdlc address C1
!
appn control-point neta. NN1
  complete
!
appn port SDLCs0 serial 0
  sdlc-sec-addr C2
  complete
!
appn link-station to NN2
  port SDLCs0
  sdlc-dest-address C2
  complete
!
appn routing
```

NN2 Configuration

```
interface serial 0
  encapsulation sdlc
  sdlc address C2
!
appn control-point neta. NN2
  complete
!
appn port SDLCs0 serial 0
  sdlc-sec-addr C2
  complete
!
appn routing
```

13.11.4 APPN Using RSRB

APPN's implementation with RSRB utilizes a virtual port for the RSRB communications. The use of RSRB encapsulation enables APPN to traverse an IP-only WAN router-based network. Figure 13-14 shows the use of a virtual ring defining a ring number to the ring group used for connecting the routers over the IP WAN. Included in the configuration is the use of TCP encapsulation with local-acknowledgement for reducing WAN overhead of SNA RR, RNR, and REJ supervisory frames.

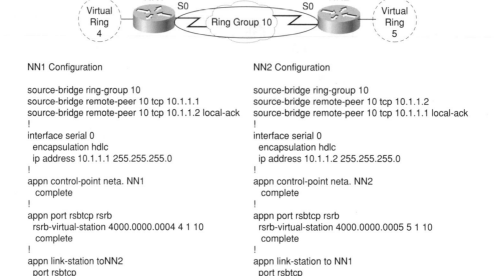

Figure 13-14
RSRB transport of APPN using TCP with local-acknowledgement.

NN1 Configuration

```
source-bridge ring-group 10
source-bridge remote-peer 10 tcp 10.1.1.1
source-bridge remote-peer 10 tcp 10.1.1.2 local-ack
!
interface serial 0
  encapsulation hdlc
  ip address 10.1.1.1 255.255.255.0
!
appn control-point neta. NN1
  complete
!
appn port rsbtcp rsrb
  rsrb-virtual-station 4000.0000.0004 4 1 10
  complete
!
appn link-station toNN2
  port rsbtcp
  lan-dest-address 4000.0000.0005
   complete
   !
   appn routing
```

NN2 Configuration

```
source-bridge ring-group 10
source-bridge remote-peer 10 tcp 10.1.1.2
source-bridge remote-peer 10 tcp 10.1.1.1 local-ack
!
interface serial 0
  encapsulation hdlc
  ip address 10.1.1.2 255.255.255.0
!
appn control-point neta. NN2
  complete
!
appn port rsbtcp rsrb
  rsrb-virtual-station 4000.0000.0005 5 1 10
  complete
!
appn link-station to NN1
  port rsbtcp
  lan-dest-address 4000.0000.0004
   complete
   !
   appn routing
```

13.11.5 DLSw+ Connecting an EN and Its NNs

DLSw+ in combination with Cisco VDLC allows for a connection between APPN nodes separated by non-APPN nodes over an IP-only WAN router backbone. This configuration is diagrammed in Figure 13-15. As seen in the figure, EN1 has defined a link and port to NN3. The physical connection to NN3 is via the local Token-Ring–attached router (R1). Router R1 employs DLSw+ through the IP only WAN to NN3. The router NN3 functions with APPN and DLSw+ enabled. DLSw+ will perform the Token Ring–to–Ethernet translation for the connection.

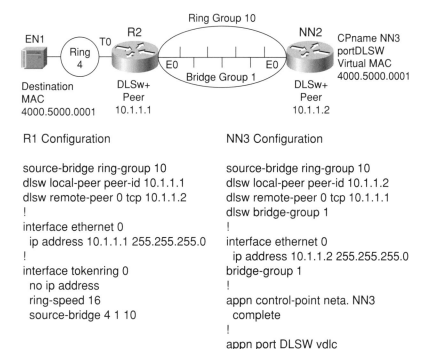

Figure 13-15
*APPN using
DLSw+ to
connect an EN
and its NN over
an Ethernet
backbone.*

R1 Configuration

source-bridge ring-group 10
dlsw local-peer peer-id 10.1.1.1
dlsw remote-peer 0 tcp 10.1.1.2
!
interface ethernet 0
  ip address 10.1.1.1 255.255.255.0
!
interface tokenring 0
  no ip address
  ring-speed 16
  source-bridge 4 1 10

NN3 Configuration

source-bridge ring-group 10
dlsw local-peer peer-id 10.1.1.2
dlsw remote-peer 0 tcp 10.1.1.1
dlsw bridge-group 1
!
interface ethernet 0
  ip address 10.1.1.2 255.255.255.0
bridge-group 1
!
appn control-point neta. NN3
  complete
!
appn port DLSW vdlc
  vdlc 10 vmac 4000.5000.0001
  complete
!
  appn routing
  !
bridge 1 protocol ieee

13.11.6 APPN Using a Connection Network over Ethernet

In this example, we demonstrate the use of an APPN connection network. The three routers attached to an Ethernet in Figure 13-16 all connect to a VRN named NETA.CONNET. The connection network of each router APPN definition defines NETA.CONNET as the connection network routing node. In this example, routers NN1, NN2, and NN3 must all connect over the Ethernet to establish connectivity. Using the connection network concept, only CP-CP sessions from NN1 to NN2 and NN3 are required. Each has a virtual connection to the connection network VRN. NN2 and NN3 communicate via a direct connection without the need for CP-CP sessions due to the use of the connection network.

Figure 13-16
APPN connection network over Ethernet.

NN1 Configuration

interface Ethernet 0
  no ip address
  mac-address 4000.E000.0001
!
appn control-point NETA. NN1
  complete
!
appn port ETHER0 Ethernet 0
   complete
!
appn connection-network NETA. CONNET
  port ETHER0
  complete
!
appn link-station to NN2
  port ETHER0
  lan-dest-address 4000.E000.0002
  complete
!
appn link-station to NN3
  port ETHER0
  lan-dest-address 4000.E000.0003
   complete
!
  appn routing

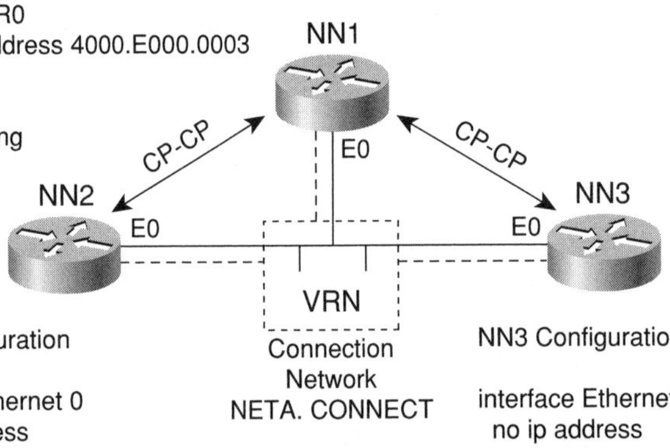

NN2 Configuration

interface Ethernet 0
  no ip address
  mac-address 4000.E000.0002
!
appn control-point NETA NN2
   complete
!
appn port ETHER0 Ethernet 0
   complete
!
  appn connection-network NETA. CONNET
  port ETHER0
  complete
!
appn link-station TONN3
  port ETHER0
  lan-dest-address 4000.E000.0003
   complete
   !
   appn routing

NN3 Configuration

interface Ethernet 0
  no ip address
  mac-address 4000.E000.0003
!
appn control-point NETA NN3
   complete
!
appn port ETHER0 Ethernet 0
   complete
!
appn connection-network NETA. CONNET
  port ETHER0
  complete
!
appn link-station TONN2
  port ETHER0
  lan-dest-address 4000.E000.0002
   complete
  !
  appn routing

13.11.7 APPN Using HPR over Frame Relay

As with transmitting SNA LLC2 frames over Frame Relay, HPR must be mapped to the Frame-Relay DLCI number of the partner router. Figure 13-17 illustrates the mapping of HPR to the DLCI 30 between NN1 and NN2 over a Frame-Relay network. NN1 maps to NN3 over DLCI 31, and NN3 maps to NN2 using DLCI 32. The `appn control-point` command must include the `hpr` keyword to enable HPR over the Frame-Relay connection. Failing to include the `hpr` keyword on the `appn control-point` definitions defaults APPN routing to ISR. If ISR were used in the configuration, a disruption of the connection from NN1 to NN2 requires the ENs to reestablish their session over the NN1-to-NN3-to-NN2 connection. HPR reroutes the active session over NN1 to NN3 to NN2 without session disruption.

13.11.8 APPN over ATM

Although we have not addressed ATM in great detail, it is important to note that APPN on Cisco routers can use ATM as the transport mechanism between Cisco router APPN network nodes. ATM uses virtual circuits for establishing connectivity between ATM devices. Cisco IOS software supports ATM and the APPN functions can use ATM interfaces for transporting native APPN/SNA frames. The appn link-station definition ATM destination address maps to the virtual circuit descriptor defined on an ATM interface used by the router.

13.11.9 APPN over ATM Ethernet LAN Emulation

ATM LANE enables you to logically extend a LAN in one building or location to another building or location over an ATM WAN. Using LANE removes the need for routing decisions because the LAN is "bridged" through the ATM WAN. Cisco IOS software support for APPN supports the use of an ATM LANE configuration for connecting APPN connections. Figure 13-19 depicts an Ethernet LANE configuration between two locations separated by an ATM WAN. The ENs are connected to the network using a Cisco Catalyst 5000 Ethernet Switch. NN1 connects to the ENs in the figure using direct CP-CP sessions. LANE is applicable to only ISR.

NN1 Configuration

```
interface serial 0
  encapsulation frame-relay ietf
  no keepalive
  frame-relay map llc2 30
  frame-relay map hpr 30
  frame-relay map llc2 31
  frame-relay map hpr 31
!
appn control-point neta. NN1
  hpr
  hpr timers liveness 1200 600 300 60
  complete
!
appn port FRAMEs0 serial 0
  complete
!
appn link-station to NN2
  port FRAMEs0
  fr-dest-address 30
    complete
!
appn link-station to NN3
  port FRAMEs0
  fr-dest-address 31
  complete
  !
  appn routing
```

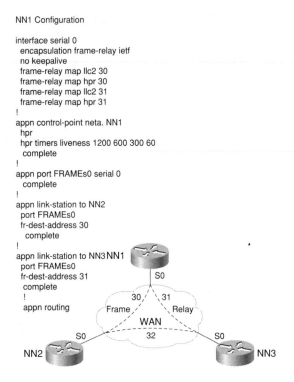

```
NN2 Configuration

interface serial 0
  encapsulation frame-relay ietf
  frame-relay map llc2 30
  frame-relay map hpr 30
  frame-relay map llc2 32
  frame-relay map hpr 32
!
appn control-point neta.NN2
  hpr
  hpr timers liveness 1200 600 300 60
  complete
!
appn port FRAMEs0 serial 0
  complete
!
appn link-station to NN1
  port FRAMEs0
  fr-dest-address 30
complete
!
appn link-station to NN3
  port FRAMEs0
  fr-dest-address 32
    complete
    !
    appn routing
```

```
NN3 Configuration

interface serial 0
  encapsulation frame-relay ietf
  frame-relay map llc2 31
  frame-relay map hpr 31
  frame-relay map llc2 32
  frame-relay map hpr 32
!
appn control-point neta. NN3
  hpr
  hpr timers liveness 1200 600 300 60
  complete
!
appn port FRAMEs0 serial 0
  complete
!
appn link-station to NN1
  port FRAMEs0
  fr-dest-address 31
complete
!
appn link-station to NN2
  port FRAMEs0
  fr-dest-address 32
  complete
  !
  appn routing
```

NN1 Configuration

```
interface ATM2/0
  atm pvc 230 0 3 aal5nlpid
  atm pvc 231 1 3 aal5nlpid
  map-group appn
!
appn control-point neta. NN1
  hpr
  complete
!
appn port ATM20 ATM 2/0
  complete
!
appn link-station to NN2
  port ATM20
  atm-dest-address 230
  complete
!
appn link-station to NN3
  port ATM20
  atm-dest-address 231
  complete
    !
    appn routing
```

Figure 13-18
ATM transport of APPN between two Cisco APPN network nodes.

NN2 Configuration

```
interface ATM2/0
  atm pvc 230 0 3 aal5nlpid
  atm pvc 232 2 3 aal5nlpid
  map-group appn
!
appn control-point neta.NN2
  hpr
  complete
!
appn port ATM 20 ATM 2/0
  complete
!
appn link-station to NN1
  port ATM20
  atm-dest-address 230
  complete
!
appn link-station to NN3
  port ATM20
  atm-dest-address 232
  complete
    !
    appn routing
```

NN3 Configuration

```
interface ATM2/0
  atm pvc 231 0 3 aal5nlpid
  atm pvc 232 2 3 aal5nlpid
  map-group appn
!
appn control-point neta. NN1
  hpr
  complete
!
appn port ATM 20 ATM 2/0
  complete
!
appn link-station to NN1
  port ATM20
  atm-dest-address 231
  complete
!
appn link-station to NN2
  port ATM20
  atm-dest-address 232
  complete
    !
    appn routing
```

Figure 13-19
*Ethernet LANE
configuration
supporting
APPN to a
Cisco NN over
an ATM WAN.*

NN1 Configuration

interface ATM2/0
  atm pvc 230 0 3 aal5nlpid
  map-group appn
!
interface ATM2/0.1
  lane client ethernet mrktng
!
interface ATM2/0.2
  lane client ethernet admin
!
interface ATM2/0.3
  lane client ethernet sales
!
appn control-point neta. NN1
  complete
!
appn port ATM20 ATM2/0
  complete
!
appn port ATM201 ATM 2/0.1
  complete
!
  appn link-station to MRKTNG
port ATM201
atm-dest-addresss 230
!
appn port ATM202 ATM 2/0.2
  complete
!
  appn link-station to ADMIN
port ATM202
atm-dest-address 230
!
appn port ATM203 ATM 2/0.3
  complete
  !
appn link-station to SALES
  port ATM203
  atm-dest-address 230
  complete
    !
  appn routing

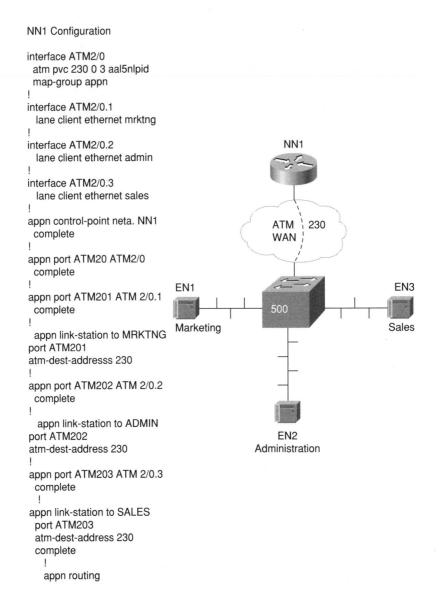

13.11.10 APPN with DLUR/DLUS

In Figure 13-20, the Token-Ring–attached SNA PU 2.0 device requires connectivity to the mainframe over an APPN network. The attached Cisco router NN1 envelopes the SNA PU2.0 frames into an LU6.2 connection using the DLUR function. The primary DLUS in the example is VTAM1. The backup DLUS is VTAM2. Both VTAMs are at V4.2. The frames are then transported to the associated DLUS function of VTAM residing on the mainframe. The APPN code in the Cisco router identifies the name of the primary and secondary DLUS with which this DLUR router will establish the LU6.2 session for transporting legacy SNA PU2.0.

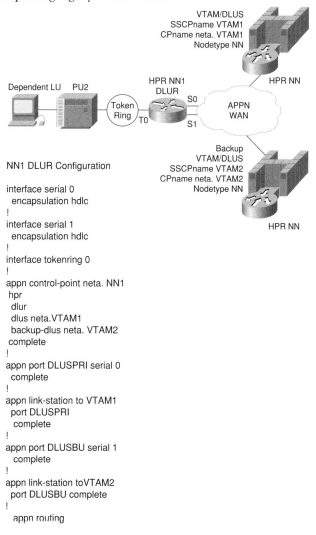

Figure 13-20
DLUR/DLUS configuration for supporting legacy SNA PU2.0 device communication over APPN networks.

VTAM/DLUS
SSCPname VTAM1
CPname neta. VTAM1
Nodetype NN

HPR NN

Dependent LU   PU2

HPR NN1
DLUR

Token
Ring   T0   S0

S1

APPN
WAN

Backup
VTAM/DLUS
SSCPname VTAM2
CPname neta. VTAM2
Nodetype NN

HPR NN

NN1 DLUR Configuration

```
interface serial 0
  encapsulation hdlc
!
interface serial 1
  encapsulation hdlc
!
interface tokenring 0
!
appn control-point neta. NN1
hpr
 dlur
 dlus neta.VTAM1
 backup-dlus neta. VTAM2
 complete
!
appn port DLUSPRI serial 0
  complete
!
appn link-station to VTAM1
  port DLUSPRI
  complete
!
appn port DLUSBU serial 1
  complete
!
appn link-station toVTAM2
  port DLUSBU complete
!
  appn routing
```

CHAPTER 14

NCIA Design and Configuration

By now, you must be aware that internetworking traditional SNA networks with IP router backbone networks uses encapsulation techniques. The most widely used techniques in a Cisco router-based network are SRB/RSRB and DLSw+. The encapsulation techniques take the SNA frame and place it in the data field of a TCP or IP packet. The techniques discussed to this point apply to the SNA path information unit (PIU) level of the SNA architecture. Typically, this is the SSCP-PU communication between VTAM on the mainframe and the cluster controller (IBM 3174) type device. Encapsulating the SNA frame allows it to be routable across the WAN.

Native Client Interface Architecture (NCIA) takes the encapsulation technique out to the actual end station requesting an SNA session. As shown in Figure 14-1, there are several techniques for the SNA logical unit (LU) representation on a workstation to access an SNA application residing on the mainframe. The most popular has been the use of Novell IPX protocol as the transport to a Novell server. The Novell server in turn then acts as an SNA PU Type 2 device to VTAM.

Another method has been the use of NetBEUI protocol to a Microsoft SNA server acting as an SNA PU Type 2 device for servicing the downstream LUs with access to the mainframe applications. Usually the servers in these two examples are located locally to the end-user site because neither protocol is a suitable WAN protocol. Novell IPX, although a routable protocol, has scaling issues over WANs. NetBEUI is Microsoft's implementation of NetBIOS and is typically used with source-route bridging requiring either RSRB or DLSw+ for transport over the WAN.

Figure 14-1
*IPX, NetBEUI,
and NCIA
techniques for
delivering SNA
LU frames to
the mainframe.*

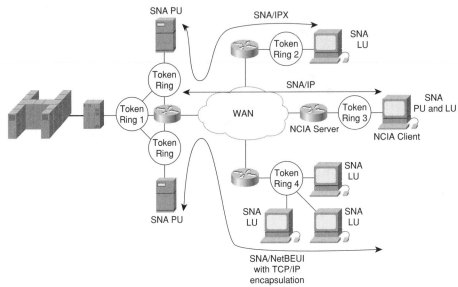

NCIA transports the SNA PU PIU frame in TCP/IP packets and thereby enables a scalable routable protocol for transporting SNA frames over the WAN for connectivity to SNA applications. Cisco routers, beginning with Cisco IOS 11.2, act as a server for the SNA NCIA client workstation. The NCIA server (router) communicates with the NCIA client (workstation). The NCIA client supports both SNA PU and LU functionality. NCIA enables network engineers to truly keep only one protocol stack on the workstations, reducing troubleshooting methodologies and limiting maintenance to only IP protocol issues.

14.1 DESIGN CRITERIA

NCIA, on its own, can serve connections over the backbone from a remote workstation, running NCIA client services, to the SNA computer. Recall that each NCIA client representing an SNA LU has a circuit established with the NCIA server. In large networks, this may encompass 10,000 or more SNA LU sessions. Each session will have an established circuit over the backbone to the NCIA server residing on a channel-attached or LAN-attached router for access to the SNA host computer. The server must service and poll the LU NCIA client as part of its function. This type of traffic can cause excessive overhead on the WAN due to the large number of circuits required.

NCIA is scalable using central-site RSRB or DLSw+ peer connections between the NCIA server and the SNA mainframe. In our example, shown in Figure 14-2, the distribution layer of the internetworking layer model becomes an ideal selection for NCIA servers being implemented with either RSRB or DLSw+ transport to the data-center router. Using RSRB or DLSw+ peering, 10,000 LU circuits may be reduced to 100 peer connections to multiple data-center routers. Because each NCIA client is an SNA PU, however, it must be defined in VTAM and polled. The sheer number of polling on the WAN will drive up WAN utilization.

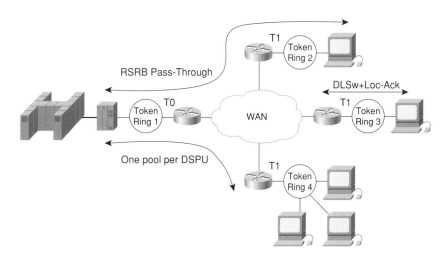

Figure 14-2
Scaling NCIA circuits using RSRB, DLSw+ peer connections, and DSPU services.

Using DLSw+ enables the use of local-acknowledgement to the NCIA clients to reduce polling overhead over the WAN. RSRB implementation with NCIA only support pass-through mode for polling. Further reduction of connections is possible using *downstream PU (DSPU)* configurations at the access router level in conjunction with NCIA as the transport for the DSPU. The importance of using DSPU is to further reduce of NCIA circuits through DSPU concentration at the access routers. Further detail on the NCIA/DSPU configuration is found in Chapter 15, "DSPU Design and Configuration."

14.2 DESIGN CONFIGURATIONS

NCIA can provide direct connection to the SNA host computer for the downstream SNA LUs through LAN- or channel-attached routers acting as the NCIA server. In support of scaling in large networks or in assisting in migration from an RSRB to a DLSw+ transport network, NCIA is capable of providing an end-to-end SNA solution.

14.2.1 LAN Attached NCIA Server

In the design example depicted with Figure 14-3, we see a remote workstation employing NCIA client services connecting to an IBM 3745 FEP using a Cisco LAN-attached NCIA server. The workstation communicates over the WAN IP backbone using TCP/IP to the NCIA server. Connectivity to the IBM 3745 is through LLC2 using SRB with DLSw+. NCIA requires the use of DLSw+ on the local level for communication over the LAN. Note that the remote router R2 in this configuration does not employ SRB because the ring supports only IP protocol for the transport of SNA data. For NCIA server channel attachment using a Cisco CIP, consult Chapter 16, "CIP Design and Configuration."

Figure 14-3
NCIA client/server configuration using a LAN-attached Cisco router as the NCIA server.

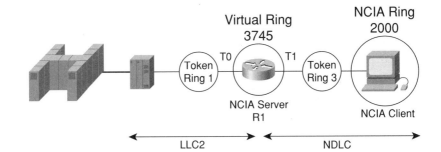

14.2.2 DLSw+ Transport for NCIA

The use of DLSw+ over the WAN for connecting to the LAN-attached IBM 3745 FEP requires a virtual ring definition over the WAN. Figure 14-4 illustrates the use of DLSw+ for transporting the NCIA server connection to the SNA host computer.

Figure 14-4
NCIA and DLSw+ transport configuration over the WAN.

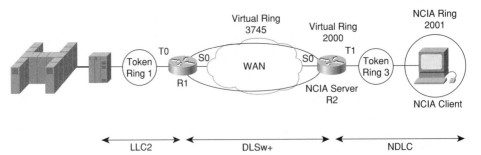

14.2.3 RSRB Transport for NCIA

RSRB employs the use of DLSw+ local switching and a virtual ring for the WAN. The NCIA server definition in router R1 connects the NCIA instance to the FEP Token Ring through a virtual ring. The NCIA virtual ring bridges to the DLSw+ virtual ring to connect to the FEP.

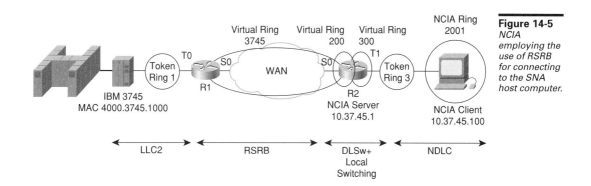

Figure 14-5
NCIA employing the use of RSRB for connecting to the SNA host computer.

14.3 IMPLEMENTING NCIA WITH RSRB AND DLSW+ ON CISCO ROUTERS

Implementing NCIA on Cisco routers requires the definition of virtual rings for RSRB and DLSw+ support. RSRB and/or DLSw+ peers must also be defined for providing the conduit through which NCIA is able to deliver the SNA data. The non–NCIA-specific commands required for supporting NCIA with RSRB and DLSw+ are as follows:

```
source-bridge ring-group

source-bridge remote-peer

dlsw local-peer

dlsw remote-peer

source-bridge
```

The initial four entries of the list are global commands that affect characteristics for use by all interfaces on the router. The last entry is specific to interface definitions. For more information on the `source-bridge ring-group`, `source-bridge remote-peer` and `source-bridge` commands, consult Chapter 9, "RSRB Design and Configuration." The `dlsw local-peer` and `dlsw remote-peer` commands are discussed in Chapter 11,

"DLSw+ Design and Configuration." For detailed information on using NCIA with DSPU, consult the examples provided in Chapter 15, "DSPU Design and Configuration."

14.4 DEFINE THE NCIA SERVER CHARACTERISTICS

There are three specific configuration commands for defining NCIA server capabilities on a Cisco router. These global commands are as follows:

```
ncia server

ncia client

ncia rsrb
```

Let's discuss each command along with their parameters.

14.4.1 The ncia server Global Command

Specifying the ncia server global command enables the NCIA server function. This command must be entered prior to entering any other NCIA command. Upon entering the ncia server command, the NCIA task within the router is operational. The format of the ncia server global command is as follows:

```
ncia server server-number server-ip-address
        server-virtual-mac-address virtual-mac-address
```

```
virtual-mac-range [inbound-only] [keepalive seconds] [tcp_keepalive minutes]
```

The NCIA server instance is identified by a number assigned using the *server-number* variable. Although this variable indicates multiple instances for NCIA servers, the current implementation supports only one instance. Hence the server-number variable must be equal to a 1.

The *server-ip-address* variable is any valid IP address used on this router for initiating (outgoing) or accepting (incoming) NCIA client connections. Again, we see a good use for the loopback interface IP address to provide this function.

NCIA server uses a virtual MAC address for providing the connection to the NCIA client. This value is specified for the positional parameter *server-virtual-mac-address*.

Each circuit established uses a virtual MAC address to designate the connection between the NCIA server and the NCIA client. NCIA server uses a virtual MAC address pool for assignment to the NCIA client connection. The variable *virtual-mac-address* value is the beginning MAC address for the pool. The variable *virtual-mac-range* is the number of virtual MAC addresses in the pool that can be allocated by this NCIA server.

The *virtual-mac-range* value may range from 1–4095. The virtual MAC address is incremented sequentially from the last dotted-decimal value of the MAC address. If the *virtual-mac-address* value is 4000.1212.0001 and the *virtual-mac-range* is 4, for example, the virtual MAC addresses assigned to the first four NCIA client connections are as follows:

```
4000.1212.0001
4000.1212.0002
4000.1212.0003
4000.1212.0004
```

In a DSPU configuration, the *server-virtual-mac-address* value must be defined as the destination MAC address within the NCIA client configuration at the workstation.

During NCIA client session establishment, the NCIA server and NCIA client perform a *capabilities exchange*. During this exchange, the NCIA server determines whether the NCIA client is using a MAC address or requires a MAC address from the pool. If the NCIA client has its own preconfigured MAC address, the server will use the NCIA client-provided MAC address. Otherwise, it will assign one from the pool.

Specifying the inbound-only optional keyword indicates to the NCIA server function that it will not initiate connections to clients. If this keyword is specified, the NCIA server cannot make outgoing connections. The default is to allow both connection options.

The keepalive *seconds* variable is the number of seconds to wait between sending keepalive messages to the NCIA client that may not have a lot of SNA activity. This keeps the connection established between the NCIA server and NCIA client as long as the NCIA client has not disconnected. The value for *seconds* is from 0 to 1200. A value of 0 disables the keepalive function. Not coding keepalive also disables the function.

The tcp_keepalive *minutes* variable ensures the TCP connection between the NCIA server and the NCIA client remains connected even when the NCIA client is idle. The default value is 20 minutes. The *minutes* variable may range from 0 to 99. TCP keepalive messages can be stopped by setting the *minutes* variable of the tcp_keepalive keyword to 0.

NOTES

Prior to issuing the ncia server command, a dlsw local-peer must be defined.

14.4.2 The `ncia client` Global Command

An NCIA client must be predefined for the NCIA server to connect out to the work-station. This is accomplished by using the `ncia client` command. The format of the command is as follows:

```
ncia client server-number client-ip-address virtual-mac-address [sna | all]
```

The *server-number* identifies the instance of the NCIA server this client will connect. Currently, the only available value is 1 due to the constraint of only one NCIA server instance per router.

The *client-ip-address* is the IP address of the NCIA client you wish the NCIA server to initiate a connection with. The *virtual-mac-address* is an assigned MAC address for the NCIA client should it be determined that the NCIA client does not have an assigned virtual MAC address for use with NCIA. If the NCIA client possesses a valid MAC address, the *virtual-mac-address* value defined on the `ncia client` command must match the actual MAC address presented by the NCIA client during capabilities exchange.

The keywords sna and all denote the type of traffic supported on the connection. Spec-ifying all enables the NCIA server to transport SNA, NetBIOS, NetBEUI, and any other type of nonroutable protocol. Specifying the sna keyword denotes that only SNA protocol will be used on the NCIA connection. The default is SNA-only support.

14.4.3 The `ncia rsrb` Global Command

Enabling NCIA support with RSRB is accomplished by associating virtual rings for use by NCIA for connecting to the DLSw+ virtual ring. This virtual path is defined using the `ncia rsrb` global command. The format of the command is as follows:

```
ncia rsrb virtual-ring local-bridge local-ring ncia-bridge ncia-ring virtual-mac-address
```

A minimum of two `source-bridge ring-group` commands is required to define RSRB for NCIA use. The *virtual-ring* variable of the `ncia rsrb` command maps to the `source-bridge ring-group` virtual ring that spans the WAN backbone. The *local-bridge* variable is a virtual bridge number connecting the WAN `ring-group` vir-tual ring with the logical *local-ring* defined for the DLSw+ peer connection. The *ncia-bridge* variable is a bridge number that connects the DLSw+ *local-ring* to the *ncia-ring* virtual ring number. The *ncia-ring* value must match a `source-bridge ring-group` virtual ring number that represents the NCIA ring to RSRB. The *virtual-mac-address* is the MAC address assigned to the NCIA server on the local ring.

NOTES

Although Cisco supports RSRB for NCIA, it does not encourage the use of RSRB for NCIA. It is supported in an effort to assist corporations employing NCIA in an RSRB environment to ease migration to DLSw+, the preferred transport mechanism for SNA traffic over IP backbones.

14.5 NCIA CONFIGURATION EXAMPLES

The following sections describe three configuration examples for using NCIA. These examples concentrate on having the NCIA server directly attached to the mainframe via a local Token-Ring connection, on remote NCIA server functionality through the use of DLSw+, and on RSRB for delivering SNA to the mainframe. Configurations concerned with DSPU are discussed in Chapter 15, "DSPU Design and Configuration." For NCIA server channel attachment to the mainframe using a Cisco CIP connection consult Chapter 16, "CIP Design and Configuration."

14.5.1 DLSw+ Support for NCIA over the WAN

Figure 14-6 illustrates the configurations for possible use when connecting the remote NCIA server to the IBM 3745 FEP. In the diagram, the DLSw+ virtual ring is the same on both routers. Because the RIF field under DLSw+ ends with the DLSw+ virtual ring, however, it is not a requirement for the virtual ring definitions to match.

14.5.2 Local Token Ring Using DLSw+

In this configuration, we see the use of local DLSw+ switching for connecting the attached Token-Ring segment to the IBM 3745 FEP Token-Ring segment. The DLSw+ local switching uses the virtual ring 3745 for the connection.

Figure 14-6
*NCIA and
DLSw+
transport
configuration
over the WAN.*

R1 Configuration

source-bridge-ring-group 3745
dlsw local-peer 10.254.1.1
  dlsw remote-peer 0tcp 10.254.1.2
  !
interface serial 0
  encapsulation hdlc
  ip address 10.254.1.1 255.255.255.0
  !
interface tokenring 0
  ring-speed 16
  source-bridge 1 3 3745

NCIA Client Configuration

NCIA Server 10.37.45.1
NCIA Ring 2000
NCIA Bridge 2
Local Ring 3
Destination MAC 4000.3745.1000
SAP Address 04

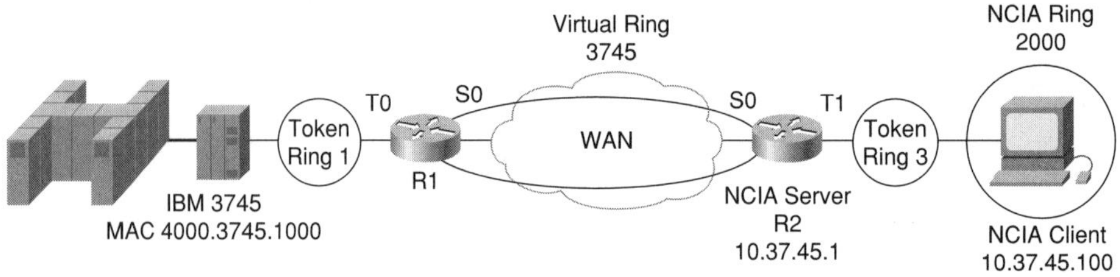

R2 Configuration

source-bridge ring-group 3745
dlsw local-peer 10.254.1.2
  dlsw remote-peer 0 tcp 10.254.1.1
  ncia server 1 10.37.45.1 4000.3745.0001 4000.00CC.0001 128
!
interface serial 0
  encapsulation hdlc
  ip address 10.254.1.2 255.255.255.0
!
interface tokenring 1
  ip address 10.37.45.1 255.255.255.0
  source-bridge 3 1 3745

14.5.3 RSRB use with NCIA over WAN

Figure 14-8 shows the use of RSRB and the router configuration to support it. Notice that two additional virtual rings are used for connecting the NCIA client to the IBM 3745 FEP. Virtual ring 300 represents the ring to which the NCIA server is attached. The NCIA server communicates with the RSRB virtual ring 3745 through the internal DLSw+ local ring 200.

NCIA Client Configuration

Figure 14-7
*NCIA server
LAN attached
to IBM 3745
FEP.*

NCIAS Server 10.37.45.1
NCIA Ring 2000
NCIA Bridge 2
Local Ring 3
Destination MAC 4000.3745.1000
SAP Address 04

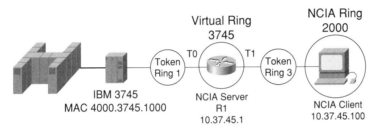

IBM 3745
MAC 4000.3745.1000

Virtual Ring
3745

NCIA Server
R1
10.37.45.1

NCIA Ring
2000

NCIA Client
10.37.45.100

R1 Configuration

```
source-bridge ring-group 3745
dlsw local-peer
ncia server 1 10.37.45.1 4000.3745.0001 4000.00CC.0001  128
!
interface tokenring 0
  ring-speed 16
  source-bridge 1 3 3745
!
interface tokenring 1
  ip address 10.37.45.1 255.255.255.0
  source-bridge 3 1 3745
```

Figure 14-8
*RSRB
configuration
for
transporting
NCIA
connections.*

R1 Configuration

source-bridge ring-group 3745
source-bridge remote-peer 3745 tcp 10.254.1.2
source-bridge remote-peer 3745 tcp 10.254.1.1
!
interface serial 0
  encapsulation hdlc
  ip address 10.254.1.1 255.255.255.0
!
interface tokenring 0
  ring-speed 16
  source-bridge 1 3 3745

NCIA Client Configuration

NCIA Server 10.37.45.1
NCIA Ring 2000
NCIA Bridge 2
Local Ring 3
Destination MAC 4000.3745.1000
SAP Address 04

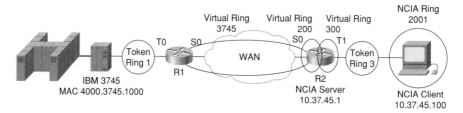

R2 Configuration

source-bridge ring-group 3745
  source-bridge ring-group 300
source-bridge remote-peer 3745 tcp 10.254.1.2
source-bridge remote-peer 3745 tcp 10.254.1.1
  dlsw local-peer
  ncia server 1 10.37.45.1 4000.3745.0001 4000.00CC.0001 128
ncia rsb 3745 2 200 1 300 4000.EEEE.0000
!
interface serial 0
  encapsulation hdlc
  ip address 10.254.1.2 255.255.255.0
!
interface tokenring 1
  ip address 10.37.45.1 255.255.255.0
  source-bridge 3 3 300

CHAPTER 15

DSPU Design and Configuration

Downstream physical unit (DSPU) is an SNA mechanism that enables LAN-attached devices to receive SNA services from the router for entrance into the network. The router provides the PU2 connection between upstream hosts and downstream PUs. The gateway to the mainframe can be an FEP or Cisco CIP. Figure 15-1 illustrates this technique.

Figure 15-1
*DSPU
configuration
with Cisco
routers.*

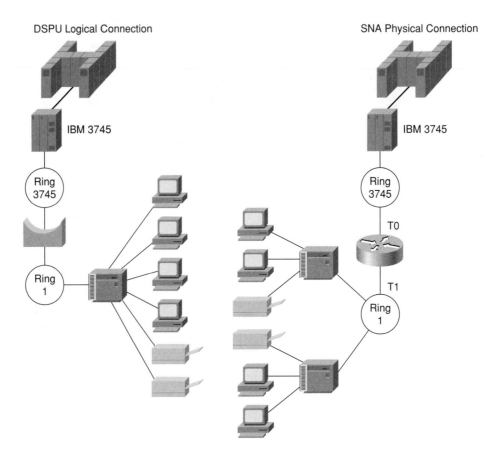

15.1 DESIGN CRITERIA

The tactical placement of DPSU SNA services on Cisco routers is at the access layer—in other words, the router providing services to a remote location. Use of DSPU is quite beneficial when implementing a migration from two data networks, one routing and one using SDLC lines, into one routing network. Figure 15-2 illustrates this.

Planning such a migration requires investigation into the topology of the remote location and the WAN. Some of the criteria to investigate include the following:

- What is the number of SNA PU Type 2 controllers based at the location?
- How many LUs are serviced at the location?
- How many LUs are serviced by each PU?

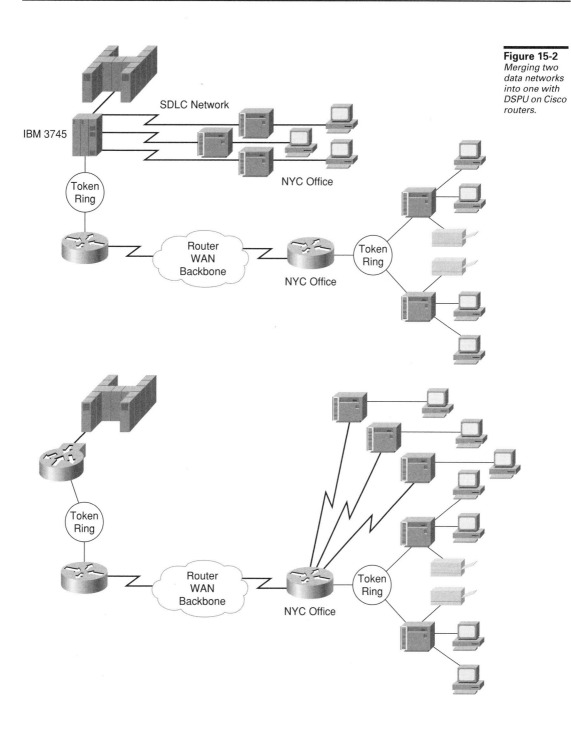

Figure 15-2
*Merging two
data networks
into one with
DSPU on Cisco
routers.*

- How many LUs are printers rather than terminals?
- What is the ratio of printers to terminals on each PU?
- How many PUs are connected over SDLC serial lines?
- Is the SDLC line a multidrop configuration?
- How many PUs are connected using a LAN?

This information is required to determine the number of serial and LAN ports needed to make the downstream PU connections without incurring added costs on the downstream devices. Secondly, the number of LUs being serviced will provide you with an indication of the amount of processing need on the router to service the LUs so as to not reduce their current performance. Instead, the design should meet their current performance or exceed this performance.

One way to assist in meeting the expected performance is to remember to implement local-acknowledgement for the SNA connections. This will enable the routers to respond to the SNA polls locally, reducing WAN bandwidth overhead and at the same time providing faster service to PUs having data to send. Using local-acknowledgement requires the interfaces connecting the downstream PUs to act in primary link mode. The data-center routers connecting to the host computer must have their SNA interfaces defined using secondary link mode.

15.2 DESIGN CONFIGURATIONS

As with all networking solutions, one must ponder which options are pertinent to his design and which are not. Operating the router as the "SNA gateway" offers many choices in operation. Among these is the management of hundreds LUs through the use of a single PU. Let's look at the possibilities.

15.2.1 Dedicated LU

When defining the relationship between LUs and PUs, there are two choices to be made. The first is to have a static, or dedicated, relationship between one or a group of LUs to a specific PU. Every time the LU device becomes active on the network, it will receive the same LUNAME in this dedicated relationship. This is sometimes quite important when the host mainframe application is dependent on LUNAME for access to the application. Figure 15-3 illustrates this point. A good example of this would be an older application running under CICS that has a security relationship between the CICS TER-Mid and the VTAM LUNAME.

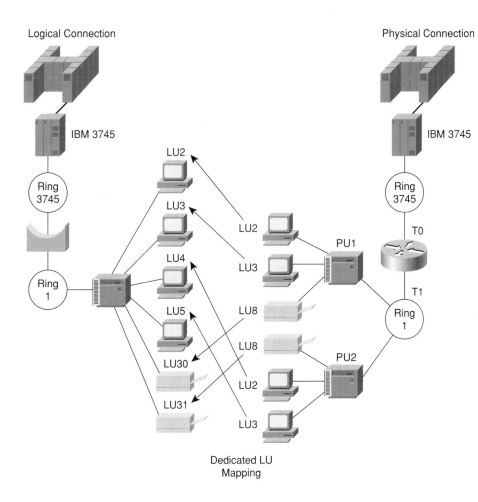

Figure 15-3
Use of dedicated LU addresses between the downstream PU and the upstream host.

Logical Connection

IBM 3745

Physical Connection

IBM 3745

Ring 3745

Ring 1

LU2
LU3
LU4
LU5
LU30
LU31

LU2
LU3
LU8
LU8
LU2
LU3

PU1

PU2

Ring 3745

T0

T1

Ring 1

Dedicated LU Mapping

15.2.2 Pooled LU

The alternative method for access from a DSPU would be for the router to pool the LUs and have them randomly assigned as the LU becomes active on the network. Every time the LU becomes active on the network, it may receive a different LUNAME. This involves less administration and lightens the definitions for the network personnel. Figure 15-4 depicts the use of pooled LUs.

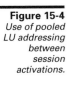

NOTES

Check with the SNA application team before selecting a method, you may be able to use pooled LUs or you may not. This will be based on the method by which LUNAMEs are used by the SNA application. In addition, LUs representing printers usually need to have a dedicated LU for the mainframe printer output.

Figure 15-4 shows dedicated mapping for the printer LUs of both PU1 and PU2. The printer LUs will always receive the same upstream host LU definition. This figure demonstrates the use of both dedicated and pooled LU methods.

Figure 15-4
Use of pooled LU addressing between session activations.

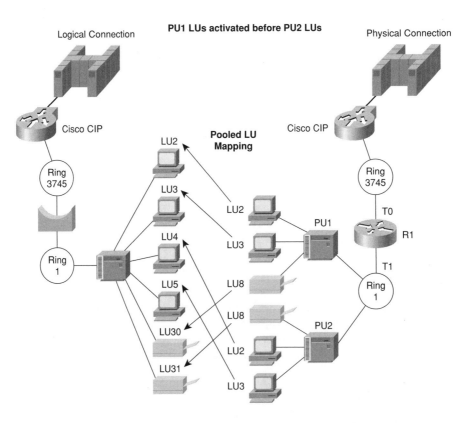

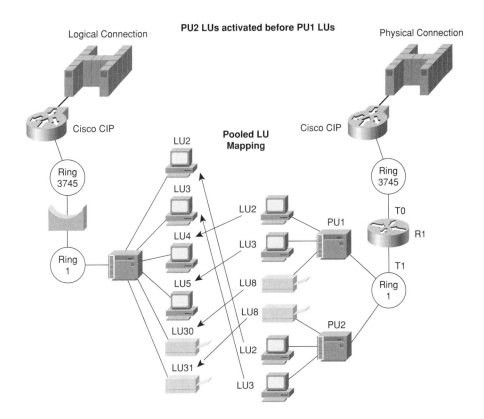

PU2 LUs activated before PU1 LUs

Logical Connection

Physical Connection

Figure 15-4
Continued.

15.2.3 Upstream Host Using RSRB

Parts of the definitions within the router define the upstream hosts. The *upstream host* is the destination for the LUs you are supporting. There are choices as to which transport mechanism you want to employ to create this session. Our first discussion, shown in Figure 15-5, uses remote source-route bridging (RSRB). Here we use the notion of a virtual token ring address that the Cisco IOS uses to maintain a physical representation on the Token Ring. This virtual MAC address allows for a means of communication between the downstream PU and the upstream LU. We are working with Token Ring and therefore our partners expect a Token-Ring address; hence, we create one. This must follow all traditional naming conventions and must be unique throughout the network. In addition, we must create a DSPU virtual ring number that is again unique throughout the network. Working together, the virtual MAC address and the DSPU virtual ring number identifies the data-link control interface to the network.

Figure 15-5
*RSRB
connecting
downstream
PUs and
upstream
hosts between
two Cisco
routers.*

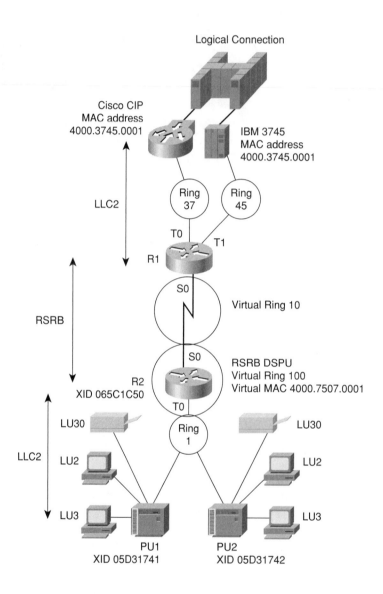

Also, one can further insulate the SNA endpoint from the emulation of the SNA net-work transported over a WAN by implementing local-acknowledgement. As described in the prior section on RSRB, we can prevent the SNA timers from expiring by spoofing the response at the local router. In this manner, we can answer the time sensitivity with SNA while still allowing the TCP/IP-routed network to manage its timers.

15.2.4 DSPU over DLSw+ Using VDLC

To configure a downstream PU while using DLSw+ with Virtual Data Link Control (VDLC), we need to create a VDLC interface. Figure 15-6 illustrates the use of VDLC with DLSw+ for DSPU support. Similar to RSRB, the VDLC interface uses a virtual Token-Ring address on the LAN to create a presence for the Cisco IOS software to interact with the downstream and upstream partners.

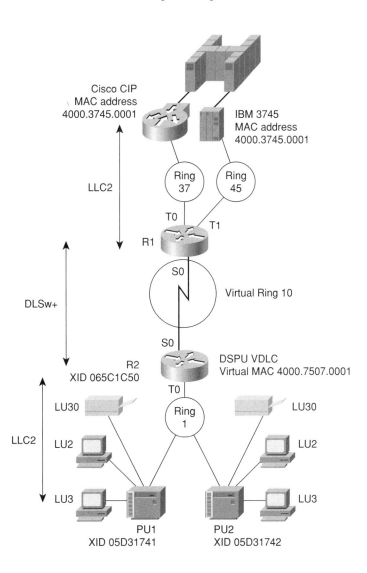

Figure 15-6
VDLC for connecting DSPU over DLSw+.

This is a Token-Ring topology, and the devices expect a Token-Ring MAC address for communication. Therefore, you must define a Token-Ring MAC address for the DSPU VDLC. This must be unique throughout the entire network.

We must also specify the source-route bridging virtual ring number with which the DSPU is participating.

Together, the virtual Token-Ring MAC address and the virtual ring number comprise the VDLC information that DLSw+ network needs.

15.2.5 DSPU over SDLC

We can extend our connections from not only LAN-attached venues, but also into the area of SDLC. We can attach devices over a serial interface after we define that interface to use SDLC. In this adaptation, we see three PUs connected over a serial line to a router. Figure 15-7 diagrams this topology. The router will be performing the SNA connectivity up to the host. The router will issue an SNA XID, exchange ID, to identify the PU on the network. In addition, we can define the DSPU to be able to initiate the session or not. To implement, we define an SDLC address and then enable it for either downstream or upstream capabilities.

Figure 15-7
SDLC connectivity for downstream PU to a LAN-attached IBM 3745 FEP.

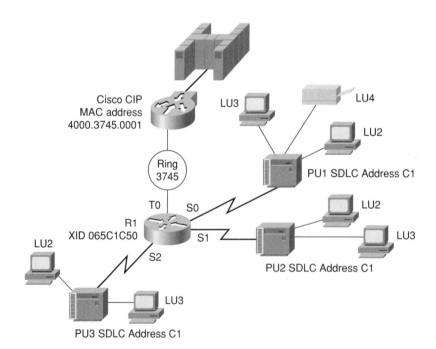

After all the definitions are in place, and each device knows its role as secondary, or primary link-station, normal SDLC Set Normal Response Mode (SNRM) processing will take place.

15.2.6 Upstream Host Using SDLC

Upstream connections provide entry points for the Cisco IOS software to be used by its downstream PUs. One upstream host PU can support 255 LUs. Cisco IOS DPSU feature supports multiple upstream hosts for each DSPU and therefore allows more than 255 LUs for DSPU connectivity. Connecting to the IBM 3745 from the data-center Cisco router is over a serial interface running SDLC.

In this case, the downstream PUs are Token Ring attached, and the upstream host PU is connected via a SDLC serial line between the Cisco router and the IBM 3745 FEP. Figure 15-8 illustrates this configuration. Such a configuration enables LAN connectivity to the IBM 3745 FEP without incurring the added expense of installing LAN adapters.

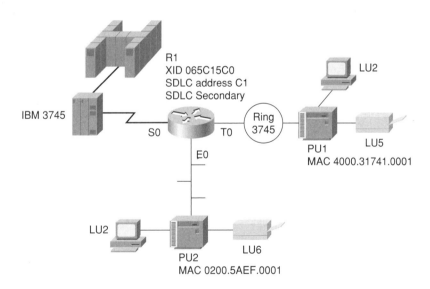

Figure 15-8
SDLC connectivity for upstream host to LAN attached downstream PUs.

15.2.7 Upstream Host Using Frame Relay

Again, when defining the environment that the router will communicate up to on behalf of the downstream devices, you need to define the host connection. Another choice for upstream connection is Frame Relay. Figure 15-9 shows a Frame-Relay network connecting the upstream host (IBM 3745 FEP) LAN attached to a data-center Cisco router. The data-center Cisco router uses Frame Relay to communicate with the DSPU Cisco router.

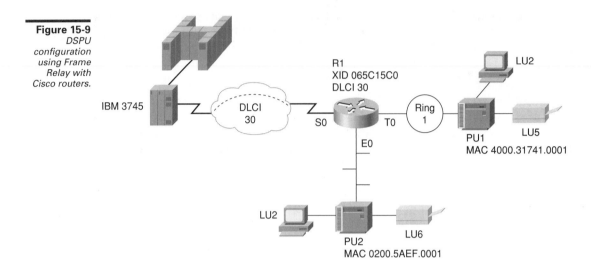

Figure 15-9
*DSPU
configuration
using Frame
Relay with
Cisco routers.*

15.2.8 DSPU Using NCIA

Downstream PUs can be configured to connect with *Native Client Interface Architecture (NCIA)*. In brief, NCIA is a Cisco mechanism to ease the use of SNA networking on the router backbone. Figure 15-10 diagrams the NCIA configuration using DSPU for connectivity to the IBM mainframe. It allows for the flexibility and scalability of SNA by implementing a client/server function between the end station and the router. The client/server approach transports SNA data from the downstream PU in TCP/IP packets. Therefore, the routers need to support only IP protocol over the LAN rather than multiple protocols on the LAN. To enable NCIA with DSPU, you need to define the DSPU connection as using NCIA for the transport mechanism and enable the local SAP on the NCIA server for use by the downstream PU.

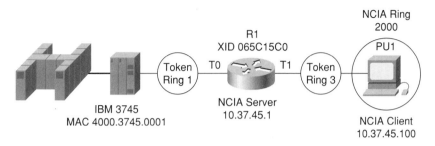

Figure 15-10
NCIA server using DSPU connectivity to the IBM 3745 FEP.

NCIA Client Configuration

NCIA Server 10.37.45.1
NCIA Ring 2000
NCIA Bridge 2
Local Ring 3
Destination MAC 4000.3745.0001
XID 05D31741
SAP Address 04

15.2.9 SNA Service Point

SNA service point is the mechanism to allow for SNA network management through the router from traditional mainframe based product—that is, IBM's NetView. You can issue commands from the router or the mainframe product to show status or view alerts. The following three commands are supported:

Alert	Sends unsolicited alerts up to the NetView console.
RUNCMD	Enables you to send/receive from the router up to NetView running on the host and back down to the router interface.
Vital Product Data	Can be sent to the NetView console via the router.

DSPUs can be managed with these mechanisms. Figure 15-11 illustrates the use of SNA service point in support of the three commands described.

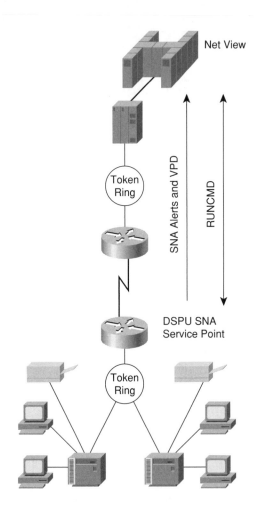

15.3 DEFINE DSPU UPSTREAM HOST

These connections are the LUs that the Cisco IOS will use to communicate with the upstream host on behalf of the downstream LUs. For our purposes, we will discuss the upstream host configurations for connections over Token Ring, Ethernet, RSRB, DLSw+ VDLC, SDLC and Frame Relay.

NOTES

Upstream connections can be supported over Token Ring, Ethernet, FDDI, RSRB, VDLC, SDLC, X.25/QLLC, and Frame Relay.

15.3.1 Upstream Host Using SDLC Connectivity

The upstream host connected over an SDLC line is defined using the following DSPU global command:

```
dspu host host-name xid-snd xid sdlc sdlc-addr [interface slot/port]

[window window-size] [maxiframe max-iframe] [retries retry-count]

[retry-timeout retry-timeout] [focalpoint]
```

The dspu host host-name variable is the name associated with the DSPU being defined in the router. For operational and administrative purposes, you should match the host-name variable with the name of the VTAM DSPU major node name.

The xid-snd xid variable should match the VTAM PU parameters named IDBLOCK and IDNUM found on the switch major node PU definition statement in VTAM. If the value here does not match a value in VTAM, the connection will fail.

The sdlc sdlc-addr variable is the hexadecimal SDLC station address assigned to the DSPU function within the router. This value should match the PU ADDR parameter of the VTAM switched major node definition representing the Cisco DSPU. In addition to this parameter, the SDLC address must be enabled using the dspu enable-host command for SDLC connectivity. This command is explained in Section 15.6.

The interface slot/port optional variable identifies which interface on the router is to be used for connecting to the DSPU host over SDLC.

The window window-size optional variable defines the number of SDLC frames to send and receive before requiring an acknowledgement. This value defaults to 7, and can range from 1 to 127. The value used here should match the PACING parameter found on the switched PU definition statement in VTAM.

The maxiframe max-iframe optional variable defines the largest SNA information frame (I-frame) that can be sent or received on this connection. The value ranges from 64 to 18432. A default of 1472 is used if the maxiframe keyword is not specified. Should an XID exchange occur where the maximum I-frame size differs, the smaller of the sizes is used.

The retries *retry-count* optional variable specifies the number of attempts the DSPU can use to reconnect to the upstream host after a lost connection. The range is 0 to 255. A value of 0 indicates that the DSPU will not attempt to retry on its own. In this case, it must wait for an activation request from VTAM. The default value of 255 indicates that the DSPU will keep retrying to establish the connection until the connection is made.

Specifying the retry-timeout *retry-timeout* optional variable indicates the number of seconds the DPSU will wait between retry attempts. The default is 30 seconds. The range is 1 to 600 in seconds.

The final optional keyword is focalpoint. This keyword indicates to the DSPU feature of Cisco IOS that the link being defined is to be used for SNA network management. At least one dspu host definition must have a focalpoint keyword defined.

15.3.2 Upstream Host Using Frame-Relay Connectivity

Using Frame Relay to connect the downstream PUs is made possible by associating the Frame-Relay DLCI used for the connection to the dspu host definition. The format of the command used for DSPU Frame-Relay connection is as follows:

dspu host *host-name* xid-snd *xid* dlci *dlci-number* [rsap *remote-sap*]

[lsap *local-sap*] [interface *slot/port*] [window *window-size*]

[maxiframe *max-iframe*] [retries *retry-count*] [retry-timeout *retry-timeout*] [focalpoint]

The dlci *dlci-number* variable is the required value used to associate the Frame-Relay connection with a DSPU upstream host definition. The value used here must match a DLCI used for connecting to this router.

The optional keyword rsap *remote-sap* variable is used by the Frame-Relay connection to establish the multiplexing of PU connections over the same DLCI. The value used here is the expected SAP address used by the destination Frame-Relay device at the other end of the Frame-Relay link. It is a two-digit hexadecimal value divisible by four. The default value of 04 is used for the rsap keyword value.

The final keyword specific to the Frame-Relay upstream host definition is the lsap *local-sap* variable. This value defines the SAP address used by Frame Relay for multiplexing PU sessions over the DLCI at this router. Cisco IOS uses a default value of 12 for the lsap value.

The remaining keywords and variables not discussed here are used in the same manner as that defined in Section 15.3.1, "Upstream Host Using SDLC Connectivity."

15.3.3 Upstream Host Using Token Ring, Ethernet, RSRB, VDLC with DLSw+

In defining the use of DSPU with LAN configurations, the MAC address of the upstream host must be defined. The format of the global `dspu host` command for connecting DSPU upstream hosts over LAN environments is as follows:

```
dspu host host-name xid-snd xid rmac remote-mac [rsap remote-sap] [lsap local-sap]
        [interface slot/port] [window window-size] [maxiframe max-iframe]

[retries retry-count] [retry-timeout retry-timeout] [focalpoint]
```

The `rmac` `remote-mac` variable defines the MAC address used for connecting to the upstream PU. In most installations this is either the MAC address of a LAN-attached IBM 3745 FEP or the internal LAN MAC address of the Cisco CIP router.

The optional variable `rsap` `remote-sap` is the SAP address value used by the upstream host for connecting to the downstream PUs. The default is hexadecimal `04`. This value must match the SAP parameter of the switched PU major node definition in VTAM for the DSPU definition.

The optional `lsap` `local-sap` variable defines the SAP address used by a downstream PU connecting to the upstream host. The default for this value is hexadecimal `12`.

The remaining keywords and variables not discussed here are used in the same manner as defined under section 15.3.1, "Upstream Host Using SDLC Connectivity."

15.4 DEFINE DOWNSTREAM PUs

You need to define a downstream PU when you want the router to initiate downstream connections or verification checking on incoming downstream sessions. Cisco IOS 11.3 and higher supports up to 1,024 downstream PUs. Downstream connections can be supported over the following:

Token Ring	NCIA
Ethernet	SDLC
FDDI	X.25/QLLC
RSRB	Frame Relay
VDLC	

For our discussion, we will be concerned with Token Ring, Ethernet, RSRB, VDLC, NCIA, SDLC, and Frame Relay.

The connection to downstream PUs from the router is verified when defining the dspu pu global command. Using the dspu pu command indicates explicit PU definition. Specifying the parameters in singular or combination form will determine the verification check. The verification is based on the following:

- *Specify xid-rcv only*—If the XID received from the downstream PU to the router does not match any of the PUs defined, the connection will fail.

- *Specify xid-rcv and interface only*—XIDs received on the defined interface must match; otherwise, the connection will fail.

- *Specifying addressing values only*—The addressing values for LAN connections (rmac, rsap, lsap), SDLC address for SDLC connections, or addressing values for Frame-Relay connections (dlci, rsap, lsap) must match the addressing used by the downstream PU.

- *Specify the xid-rcv and addressing values only*—With these values defined, the values for the downstream PU must match the xid-rcv value defined on the dspu pu command and the address values in accordance with the connection type. These would be either LAN connections (rmac, rsap, lsap), Frame-Relay connections (dlci, rsap, lsap), or SDLC address for SDLC connections. Failure to have any of the values match will abort connection establishment.

- *Specifying addressing and interface only*—In this scenario, the corresponding addressing values for the specified interface must match for successful connection. Downstream PUs presenting an address value on this interface that does not match will fail at the connection attempt.

- *Specifying xid-rcv, addressing and interface*—Both the xid-rcv and addressing values for the specified interface must match for a successful connection.

Downstream PUs can access the router DSPU functions without explicit definitions by using the exchange functions of the SNA devices. In this case the router will accept all downstream PU activation only when the dspu default-pu command is specified. Coding this command allows any downstream PU to connect even if it fails the previously noted verification checks. The format for defining the dspu default-pu global command is as follows:

```
dspu default-pu [window window-size] [maxiframe max-iframe]
```

The window window-size optional variable defines the number of SDLC frames to send and receive from the router to the downstream PU before requiring an acknowledgement. This value defaults to 7 and can range from 1 to 127. The value used here should match the PACING parameter found on the switched PU definition statement in VTAM that represents the default PU.

The maxiframe *max-iframe* optional variable defines the largest SNA I-frame that can be sent or received between the router and the downstream PU. The value ranges from 64 to 18432. A default of 1472 is used if the maxiframe keyword is not specified. Should an XID exchange occur where the maximum I-frame size differs, the smaller of the sizes is used.

At least one dspu lu command must be defined following the dspu default-pu command to identify from where the LUs are assigned.

```
dspu host host-name xid-snd xid rmac remote-mac [rsap remote-sap]
        [lsap local-sap] [interface slot/port] [window window-size]
        [maxiframe max-iframe]
```

NOTES

Not coding the dspu default-pu command will allow the DSPU function to reject any downstream PU connection if the verification check fails.

15.4.1 Downstream PU Using SDLC Connectivity

The mapping of the SDLC station address expected from the downstream PU connected to this router over an SDLC link is the key variable in making the downstream PU connection over SDLC. The format of the global command is as follows:

```
dspu pu pu-name sdlc sdlc-addr [xid-rcv xid] [interface slot/port]
        [window window-size] [maxiframe max-iframe] [retries retry-count]
        [retry-timeout retry-timeout]
```

The dspu pu *pu-name* variable is the name associated with the downstream PU connecting to this router. For operational and administrative purposes, you should match the pu-name variable with the name of the VTAM PU definition statement in VTAM representing the downstream PU device.

The sdlc *sdlc-addr* variable is the hexadecimal SDLC station address expected from a downstream PU within an XID. This value should match the PU ADDR parameter of the VTAM switched major node definition representing the downstream PU in the DSPU major node definition on VTAM. In addition to this parameter, the SDLC address must be enabled using the dspu enable-host command for SDLC connectivity. This command is explained in Section 15.6.

The xid-rcv *xid* optional variable indicates to the Cisco IOS to match the XID IDBLK and IDNUM values. These values should match the VTAM PU parameters named IDBLOCK and IDNUM found on the switch major node PU definition statement in VTAM. If the value here does not match a value in VTAM, the connection will fail.

The interface *slot/port* optional variable identifies which interface on the router is to be used for connecting the downstream PU to the router.

The window *window-size* optional variable defines the number of SDLC frames to send and receive from the router to the downstream PU before requiring an acknowledgement. This value defaults to 7 and can range from 1 to 127. The value used here should match the PACING parameter found on the switched PU definition statement in VTAM.

The maxiframe *max-iframe* optional variable defines the largest SNA I-frame that can be sent or received between the router and the downstream PU. The value ranges from 64 to 18432. A default of 1472 is used if the maxiframe keyword is not specified. Should an XID exchange occur where the maximum I-frame size differs, the smaller of the sizes is used.

The retries *retry-count* optional variable specifies the number of attempts the router DSPU can use to reconnect to the downstream PU after a lost connection. The range is 0 to 255. A value of 0 indicates that the router DSPU will not attempt to retry on its own. In this case it must wait for an activation request from VTAM. The default value is 4, indicating that the router DSPU will try to establish the connection four times before declaring the connection inoperable.

Specifying the retry-timeout *retry-timeout* optional variable indicates the number of seconds the router DSPU will wait between retry attempts for connecting to the downstream PU. The default is 30 seconds between retry attempts. The range is 1 to 600 in seconds.

15.4.2 Downstream PU Using Frame-Relay Connectivity

PUs downstream of the router connected over Frame Relay are defined through the mapping of the Frame-Relay DLCI number. The format of the command is as follows:

```
dspu pu pu-name dlci dlci-number [rsap remote-sap] [lsap local-sap] [xid-rcv xid]

[interface slot/port] [window window-size] [maxiframe max-iframe] [retries retry-count]

[retry-timeout retry-timeout]
```

The dlci *dlci-number* variable is the required value used to associate the Frame-Relay connection between the router DSPU and the downstream PU. The value used here must match a DLCI used for connecting the router to the downstream PU.

The optional keyword `rsap` *remote-sap* variable is used by the Frame-Relay connection to establish the multiplexing of downstream PU connections over the same DLCI. The value used here is the expected SAP address used by the downstream PU at the other end of the Frame-Relay link. It is a two-digit hexadecimal value divisible by four. The default value of `04` is used for the `rsap` keyword value.

The final keyword specific to the Frame-Relay `dspu` `pu` definition is the `lsap` *local-sap* variable. This value defines the SAP address used by Frame Relay for multiplexing PU sessions over the DLCI at this router. Cisco IOS uses a default value of `08` for the `lsap` value.

The remaining keywords and variables not discussed here are used in the same manner as that defined in Section 15.4.1, "Downstream PU Using SDLC Connectivity."

15.4.3 Downstream PU Using Token Ring, Ethernet, RSRB, VDLC, or NCIA

The `dspu` `pu` definition for downstream PUs over Token Ring, RSRB, VDLC, and NCIA indicates that we are explicitly defining the PU parameter connection requirements. The format of the command is as follows:

```
dspu pu pu-name [rmac remote-mac] [rsap remote-sap] [lsap local-sap] [xid-rcv xid]

[interface slot/port] [window window-size] [maxiframe max-iframe] [retries retry-count]

[retry-timeout retry-timeout]
```

The `rmac` *remote-mac* variable defines the MAC address used by the connecting downstream PU. If this value is defined in the DSPU definitions of the router, the value specified must match to establish the connection.

The optional variable `rsap` *remote-sap* is the SAP address value used by the downstream PU for connecting to the router DSPU. If the receiving SAP address from the downstream PU does not match, the connection establishment will fail. The default is hexadecimal `04`. This value must match the SAP parameter of the switched PU major node definition in VTAM for the DSPU definition.

The optional `lsap` *local-sap* variable defines the SAP address used by the router DSPU for connecting to the downstream PU. The default for this value is hexadecimal `08`.

The remaining keywords and variables not discussed here are used in the same manner as defined in Section 15.3.1, "Upstream Host Using SDLC Connectivity."

15.5 DEFINE DSPU LUs

There are two methods for defining LUs to the router: They can be either *dedicated* or *pooled*. In the dedicated mode, a single LU or a range of dedicated LUs can be defined. The format of the dedicated dspu lu command is as follows:

```
dspu lu lu-start [lu-end] {host host-name host-lu-start | pool pool-name} [pu pu-name]
```

The *lu-start* variable is the LU address for a specific LU or the beginning of an LU address pool dedicated to a host. The optional *lu-end* variable is the ending address of the LU pool or LUs dedicated to the host. The host *host-name* optional variable indicates that each LU in the range of LUs is dedicated to a host LU identified by the *host-name* variable. The *host-lu-start* variable value is the beginning range of the host LU addresses. A pool of LUs can be specified rather than the host itself. In this case, a *pool-name* variable is used to give a unique name to the LU pool. The pool and host keywords are mutually exclusive. The optional pu *pu-name* variable value is the dspu pu *pu-name* value of a previously defined downstream PU to which the LU pool is applied.

NOTES

If the dspu lu command follows a dspu pu command, the dspu lu definition applies to the *previous* dspu pu definition. In this case, if you are defining a dspu lu for the previously defined dspu pu, do not use the explicit pu *pu-name* variable on the dspu lu command.

Defining the LUs in a pooled methodology requires the use of the following command:

```
dspu pool pool-name host host-name lu lu-start [lu-end]

[inactivity-timeout inactivity-minutes]
```

The dspu pool *pool-name* variable identifies the name of the pool. The host *host-name* variable specifies the name of a previous host that owns this pool. The lu *lu-start* and optional *lu-end* variables define the LU pool range address range. The inactivity-timeout *inactivity-minutes* optional variable is the number of minutes of no activity prior to the session being disconnected.

If using the pooled LU methodology, following a dspu pool command you should enter the following dspu lu command:

```
dspu lu lu-start [lu-end] pool pool-name pu pu-name
```

The lu *lu-start* and optional *lu-end* variables define the LU pool range address range. The pool *pool-name* variable assigns the name of the LU pool used for selecting an LU. The pu *pu-name* variable identifies to which downstream explicitly defined PU this dspu lu command applies.

15.6 SPECIFY THE DATA LINK CONTROL

For the various methods of connecting DSPUs to the router the data link control must be enabled.

15.6.1 LAN Interface Required DSPU Commands

Configure the LAN data link controls that are used to communicate with both the downstream and upstream connections. Use the following interface commands:

```
dspu enable-host [lsap local-sap]
spu enable-pu [lsap local-sap]
dspu start
```

The dspu enable-host interface command enables the local SAP address for use on establishing upstream PU connections. Using the lsap *local-sap* optional parameter ensures that the SAP address defined is used for receiving activation requests from VTAM and activation requests to VTAM from downstream PUs. The default used by Cisco IOS is SAP address 12.

The dspu enable-pu interface command enables the use of a SAP address for connecting to the downstream PU. The default *local-sap* value on the dspu enable-pu interface command is SAP address 08.

Issuing the dspu start interface command signals the router to attempt to start a session with the upstream host or downstream PU available on the interface. If the resource address is incorrect or missing, the attempt will fail.

15.7 RSRB CONNECTIVITY DSPU DATA LINK COMMANDS

Configure the RSRB data link controls that are used to communicate with both the downstream and upstream connections. Use the following interface commands:

```
source-bridge ring-group ring-group [virtual-mac-address]
source-bridge remote-peer ring-group tcp ip-address [local-ack]
dspu rsrb local-virtual-ring bridge-number target-virtual-ring virtual-macaddr
dspu rsrb enable-host [lsap local-sap]
dspu-rsrb enable-pu [lsap local-sap]
dspu rsrb start {host-name | pu-name}
```

The source-bridge global commands are required for establishing RSRB on the router. Use of the local-ack keyword of the source-bridge remote-peer global command enables the use of local-acknowledgement for use by the DSPU on the interface connected using RSRB.

The dspu rsrb interface command defines the virtual ring used by the DSPU (the local-virtual-ring variable) over a virtual bridge (bridge-number) to the ring-group (target-virtual-ring). The DSPU uses a virtual MAC address (virtual-macaddr) as its interface to the local-virtual-ring.

The dspu rsrb enable-host global command identifies the use of a SAP address for receiving requests from the upstream host or for starting connections to the upstream host. The default for the local-sap optional variable is 12.

The dspu rsrb enable-pu global command defines a SAP address to establish connections to the downstream PUs on the interface or for accepting requests from the downstream PU. The default for the local-sap optional variable is 08.

To have the DSPU function initiate the sessions with either upstream hosts or downstream PUs use the global command dspu rsrb start. Use either host-name or pu-name for this command. Each command entered specifies activation to the upstream host identified by the host-name value or the downstream PU identified by the pu-name value.

15.7.1 VDLC Connectivity DSPU Data Link Commands

Prior to configuring VDLC for DSPU, a virtual ring group must be defined using the source-bridge ring-group global command. In addition, DLSw+ local and remote peer statements must be entered to establish DLSw+ connections for transporting the DSPU data.

To configure DSPUs with use of VDLC, issue the follow set of commands:

```
dspu vdlc ring-group virtual-mac-address
dspu vdlc enable-host [lsap local-sap]
dspu vdlc enable-pu [lsap local-sap]
dspu vdlc start {host-name | pu-name}
```

The dspu vdlc interface command defines the virtual ring used by the DSPU (*ring-group*) and a virtual MAC address (*virtual-mac-address*) as its interface to the *ring-group*. The *ring-group* variable must match a source-bridge ring group defined on this router.

The dspu vdlc enable-host global command identifies the use of a SAP address for receiving requests form the upstream host or starting connections to the upstream host. The default for the *local-sap* optional variable is 12.

The dspu vdlc enable-pu global command defines for use a SAP address to establish connections to the downstream PUs on the interface or for accepting requests from the downstream PU. The default for the *local-sap* optional variable is 08.

To have the DSPU function initiate the sessions with either upstream hosts or downstream PUs use the global command dspu vdlc start. Use either *host-name* or *pu-name* for this command. Each command entered specifies activation to the upstream host identified by the *host-name* value or the downstream PU identified by the *pu-name* value.

15.7.2 SDLC Connectivity DSPU Data Link Commands

To configure DSPUs with use over SDLC, issue the follow set of commands:

```
encapsulation sdlc
sdlc role {none | primary | secondary | prim-xid-poll}
sdlc address sdlc-address
dspu enable-host sdlc sdlc-address
dspu enable-pu sdlc sdlc-address
dspu start {host-name | pu-name}
```

First the serial interface being used for the SDLC connection of the DSPU must enable SDLC by using the encapsulation sdlc interface command. Second, depending on the type of activation establishment required, the sdlc role interface command must be defined. The caveats for defining this interface command with DSPU are as follows:

- The router establishing connection without XID exchange uses sdlc role primary.

- The router is secondary or none when downstream PU is initiating the connection.

- When XID is required, the router must be defined as `prim-xid-poll` or `none` to initiate the connection.

- If XID is required and the DSPU initiates the connection, the router interface must be defined as `sdlc role none`.

An SDLC station address used by the DSPU is defined to identify itself to the router. The `sdlc address` *sdlc-address* interface command identifies downstream PUs that will use the SDLC router interface by specifying the SNA station address for the *sdlc-address* variable value. The value specified must match an SNA PU station address connected to the router SDLC serial interface. This same *sdlc-address* value is used in the interface commands `dspu enable-host sdlc` and `dspu enable-pu sdlc` for the *sdlc-address* variables.

If the router is to initiate connections to the DSPUs on the SDLC serial interface, it can do so by entering the `dspu start` command. On the `dspu start` global command, enter either the *host-name* or a *pu-name* of a predefined upstream host or downstream PU.

15.7.3 Frame-Relay Connectivity DSPU Data Link Commands

To configure DSPUs with use of Frame Relay, the following set of commands are required:

```
encapsulation frame-relay [ietf]
frame-relay map llc2 dlci-number
dspu enable-host [lsap local-sap]
dspu enable-pu [lsap local-sap]
dspu start [host-name | pu-name]
```

The router serial interface connecting to the Frame-Relay network must be enabled for Frame Relay by entering the `encapsulation frame-relay ietf` command. The DLCI used by the router for connecting to the remote device must map to LLC2. This is done by entering the global command `frame-relay map llc2` *dlci-number*. The *dlci-number* variable must be a valid DLCI used for connecting with the remote device.

The `dspu enable-host` interface command is used for connecting a predefined `dspu host` definition to the Frame-Relay interface being defined. The variable `lsap` *local-sap* is the SAP used for communicating with the remote host. The default for the `local-sap` value is 12.

The `dspu enable-pu` interface command specifies the name of a predefined `dspu pu` global command. The `lsap` *local-sap* value is used for identifying the SAP address used for connecting with the downstream PU over the Frame-Relay DLCI. The default is 08.

Specifying the global command `dspu start` for a *host-name* or *pu-name* of a Frame-Relay connection allows the router to initiate the connection.

15.7.4 Frame-Relay Connectivity DSPU Data Link Commands

To configure DSPUs for use with NCIA, issue the follow set of commands:

```
dspu ncia server-number
dspu ncia enable-pu [lsap local-sap]
```

After defining an NCIA server, use the global command `dspu ncia server-number` to identify the NCIA server using DPSU functionality. Currently, only a value of 1 can be used for the *server-number* value.

NCIA enables the SAP address for use by DSPU through the `dspu ncia enable-pu` global command. The default for this value is `08` for incoming connection requests from downstream PUs. The default is overridden by specifying a value for the `lsap local-sap` variable.

15.8 DEFINE OUTSTANDING ACKNOWLEDGMENTS

Under DSPU, we can define the number of outstanding activation RUs that can be sent to the upstream or downstream PU before receiving a response. To do so, the following command is defined:

```
dspu activation-window window-size
```

The *window-size* value is the number of outstanding activation RUs sent without receiving a response back from the upstream or downstream PU. The default value is `5` with a range of 1 to 255.

The *window-size* is a means of pacing the activation of resources to avoid buffer depletion at activation time. Increasing the window activates more resources in a smaller period of time assuming enough buffers are available. Decreasing the window limits the number of resources that can be activated in a certain amount of time; however, it ensures that buffers will not be depleted. Typically, this option is not used.

15.9 SPECIFY SNA SERVICE POINT SUPPORT

The simplest way for defining an SNA service point is to specify one of the `dspu host` definitions as a focal point. Some of the benefits of using this is the ability to embed the location of the router and an associated name for the interface in SNA network-management messages. To define the location of the router, use the following global command:

```
location location-description
```

The *location-description* is up to 50 alphanumeric characters, including blanks and punctuation marks.

To assign a name to a LAN interface for use in SNA network management messages use the following command:

```
lan-name lan-name
```

The *lan-name* variable is up to eight alphanumeric characters in length. The default *lan-name* used by the router when sending SNA network-management messages concerning the LAN interface is the router terminology for the interface. As an example, a Token-Ring interface on slot2 port 0 will have a *lan-name* value of tr2/0.

15.10 DSPU CONFIGURATION EXAMPLES

The following configuration examples use the commands and variables previously discussed. Each example has been put into context for its use.

15.10.1 Dedicated LU

In this example, Figure 15-12, the downstream PU, PU1, sends an XID of 05D31741 to the Cisco router on Token-Ring interface 0. The LU1 on PU1 maps to the Cisco router dedicated LU number 2. The LU2 using a downstream LU address of 2 will be mapped to upstream LU3. Downstream PU1 LU3 maps to LU address 20 on the upstream PU definition. A second downstream PU connects to the router using an XID of 05D31742. PU2 has its first three LUs mapped to the upstream PU LU addresses 4, 5, and 21, respectively.

15.10.2 Pooled LU

Taking the dedicated LU example and changing it to a pooled LU algorithm, we find that the LUs on both PU1 and PU2 use the next available LU in the pool for the upstream PU definition. Figure 15-13 lists the Cisco IOS configuration for using pooled LUs. Each downstream LU is assigned an upstream LU address based on the activation sequence. Therefore, if LU1 of PU1 activates after LU1 of PU2, it will receive the upstream LU address of 3 based on the LU pool definitions and algorithms.

15.10.3 Upstream Host Using RSRB with Local-Acknowledgement

In this example, Figure 15-14, we employ the use of RSRB for delivering the SNA traffic used for DSPU. The local-acknowledgement feature is enabled for responding to SNA supervisory RR, RNR, and REJ SNA frames to the attached Token-Ring downstream PUs.

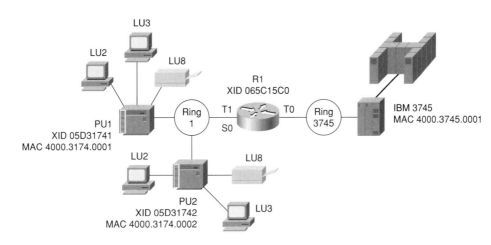

Figure 15-12
Dedicated LU configuration example.

R1 Configuration

```
dspu host R1 xid-snd 065C15C0 rmac 4000.3745.0001
dspu pu PU1 xid-rcv 05D31741 rmac 4000.3745.0001
dspu lu 2 host R1 2
dspu lu 3 host R1 3
dspu lu 8 host R1 30
dspu pu PU2 xid-rcv 05D31742 rmac 4000.3174.0002
dspu lu 2 host R1 4
dspu lu 3 host R1 5
dspu lu 8 host R1 31
!
interface TokenRing 0
no ip address
ring-speed 16
source-bridge 3745 1  1
!
interface TokenRing 1
no ip address
ring-speed 16
  dspu enable-pu
source-bridge 1  1 3745
```

In this example, we use both pooled and dedicated LUs. The SNA printer attached to PU1 uses LU address 30. Likewise, the SNA printer attached to PU2 uses LU address 30. As addressed earlier, because these are print devices and their CICS and JES2 usage requires a specific SNA LUNAME, we dedicate these to upstream LU addresses 30 and 31, respectively. Within the configuration, we define an RSRB connection for the DSPU virtual ring to the source-bridge ring group to connect to the IBM 3745 FEP.

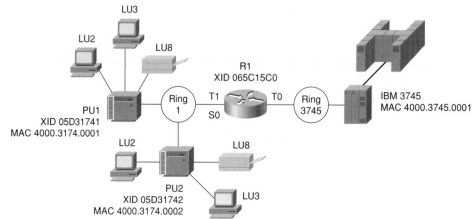

Figure 15-13
*LU pool
configuration
for the DSPU
function.*

R1 Configuration

```
dspu host R1 xid-snd 065C15C0 rmac 4000.3745.0001
dspu poll lupool host R1 lu 2 31
dspu pu PU1 xid-rcv 05D31741 rmac 4000.3745.0001
dspu lu 1 3 pool lupool
dspu pu PU2 xid-rcv 05D31742 rmac 4000.3174.0002
dspu lu 1 3 pool lupool
!
interface TokenRing 0
no ip address
ring-speed 16
source-bridge 3745 1  1
!
interface TokenRing 1
no ip address
ring-speed 16
 dspu enable-pu
source-bridge 1  1 3745
```

15.10.4 DSPU over DLSw+ Using VDLC

In this example, Figure 15-15, DSPU is using DLSw+ and VDLC for connecting to the IBM 3745 FEP. We have defined the default PU definition for any PUs not explicitly defined or in case the addresses or the XID defined in the router does not match. In the case of these PUs, only the LUs with addresses 2–10 will receive upstream LU addresses from the pool named LUPOOL. For communicating to the downstream PU, the router will use SAP address 08. The downstream PU is defined as using SAP address 04. The dspu host named NYCNM1 will receive SNA network management messages from the router and the downstream PUs because it has the focalpoint keyword specified.

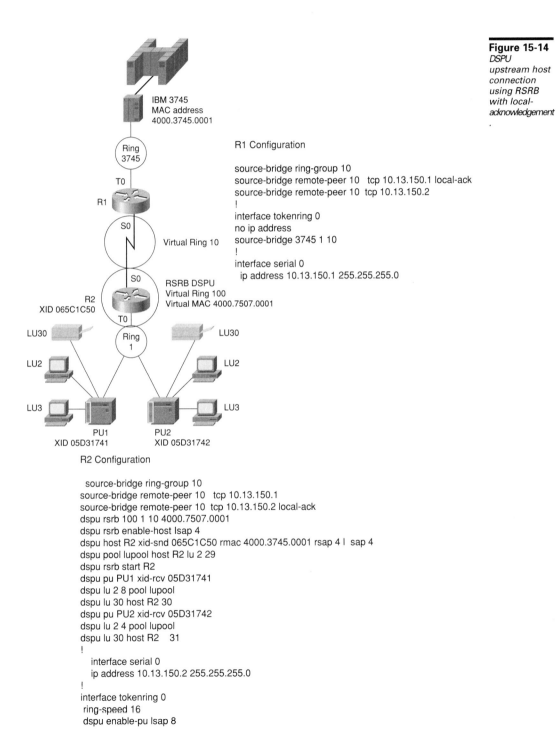

Figure 15-14
DSPU upstream host connection using RSRB with local-acknowledgement

IBM 3745
MAC address
4000.3745.0001

Ring 3745

T0

R1

S0

Virtual Ring 10

S0

R2
XID 065C1C50

RSRB DSPU
Virtual Ring 100
Virtual MAC 4000.7507.0001

T0

Ring 1

LU30
LU2
LU3

LU30
LU2
LU3

PU1
XID 05D31741

PU2
XID 05D31742

R1 Configuration

source-bridge ring-group 10
source-bridge remote-peer 10   tcp 10.13.150.1 local-ack
source-bridge remote-peer 10   tcp 10.13.150.2
!
interface tokenring 0
no ip address
source-bridge 3745 1 10
!
interface serial 0
   ip address 10.13.150.1 255.255.255.0

R2 Configuration

   source-bridge ring-group 10
   source-bridge remote-peer 10   tcp 10.13.150.1
   source-bridge remote-peer 10   tcp 10.13.150.2 local-ack
   dspu rsrb 100 1 10 4000.7507.0001
   dspu rsrb enable-host lsap 4
   dspu host R2 xid-snd 065C1C50 rmac 4000.3745.0001 rsap 4 l sap 4
   dspu pool lupool host R2 lu 2 29
   dspu rsrb start R2
   dspu pu PU1 xid-rcv 05D31741
   dspu lu 2 8 pool lupool
   dspu lu 30 host R2 30
   dspu pu PU2 xid-rcv 05D31742
   dspu lu 2 4 pool lupool
   dspu lu 30 host R2   31
   !
      interface serial 0
      ip address 10.13.150.2 255.255.255.0
   !
   interface tokenring 0
   ring-speed 16
   dspu enable-pu lsap 8

Figure 15-15
*DSPU using
DLSw+ and
VDLC for
connecting to a
LAN-attached
IBM 3745 FEP.*

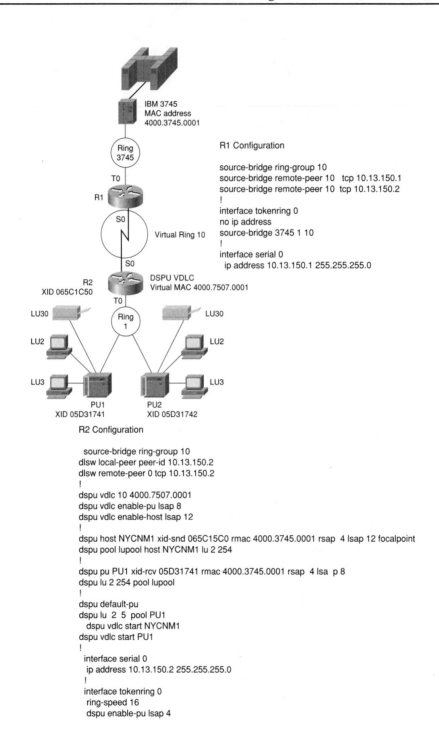

IBM 3745
MAC address
4000.3745.0001

Ring
3745

R1 Configuration

T0

source-bridge ring-group 10
source-bridge remote-peer 10 tcp 10.13.150.1
source-bridge remote-peer 10 tcp 10.13.150.2
!
interface tokenring 0
no ip address
source-bridge 3745 1 10
!
interface serial 0
   ip address 10.13.150.1 255.255.255.0

R1

S0

Virtual Ring 10

S0

R2
XID 065C1C50

DSPU VDLC
Virtual MAC 4000.7507.0001

T0

LU30

Ring
1

LU30

LU2

LU2

LU3

LU3

PU1
XID 05D31741

PU2
XID 05D31742

R2 Configuration

```
 source-bridge ring-group 10
dlsw local-peer peer-id 10.13.150.2
dlsw remote-peer 0 tcp 10.13.150.2
!
dspu vdlc 10 4000.7507.0001
dspu vdlc enable-pu lsap 8
dspu vdlc enable-host lsap 12
!
dspu host NYCNM1 xid-snd 065C15C0 rmac 4000.3745.0001 rsap  4 lsap 12 focalpoint
dspu pool lupool host NYCNM1 lu 2 254
!
dspu pu PU1 xid-rcv 05D31741 rmac 4000.3745.0001 rsap  4 lsa  p 8
dspu lu 2 254 pool lupool
!
dspu default-pu
dspu lu  2  5  pool PU1
  dspu vdlc start NYCNM1
dspu vdlc start PU1
!
 interface serial 0
 ip address 10.13.150.2 255.255.255.0
 !
 interface tokenring 0
 ring-speed 16
 dspu enable-pu lsap 4
```

15.10.5 DSPU over SDLC and Upstream Host Using Token Ring

In this example, Figure 15-16, a Token-Ring–attached upstream host communicates to downstream PUs over an SDLC line. In this example, the location previously used three 9.6Kbps SDLC lines—one for each of the IBM 3174 controllers. Using DSPU, these controllers are merged on to a single 56Kbps line.

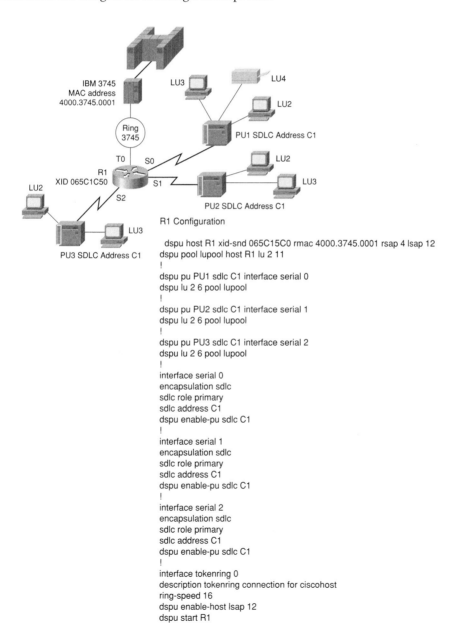

Figure 15-16
Three downstream PUs connecting to a Token-Ring–attached IBM 3745 FEP using Cisco router DSPU functionality.

R1 Configuration

```
 dspu host R1 xid-snd 065C15C0 rmac 4000.3745.0001 rsap 4 lsap 12
dspu pool lupool host R1 lu 2 11
!
dspu pu PU1 sdlc C1 interface serial 0
dspu lu 2 6 pool lupool
!
dspu pu PU2 sdlc C1 interface serial 1
dspu lu 2 6 pool lupool
!
dspu pu PU3 sdlc C1 interface serial 2
dspu lu 2 6 pool lupool
!
interface serial 0
encapsulation sdlc
sdlc role primary
sdlc address C1
dspu enable-pu sdlc C1
!
interface serial 1
encapsulation sdlc
sdlc role primary
sdlc address C1
dspu enable-pu sdlc C1
!
interface serial 2
encapsulation sdlc
sdlc role primary
sdlc address C1
dspu enable-pu sdlc C1
!
interface tokenring 0
description tokenring connection for ciscohost
ring-speed 16
dspu enable-host lsap 12
dspu start R1
```

15.10.6 Upstream Host Using SDLC

In this example, Figure 15-17, we see an upstream host IBM 3745 FEP attached to the router using an SDLC connection. The downstream PUs are Token Ring and Ethernet attached.

Figure 15-17
SDLC attached
FEP servicing
LAN-attached
DSPUs
through a
Cisco router.

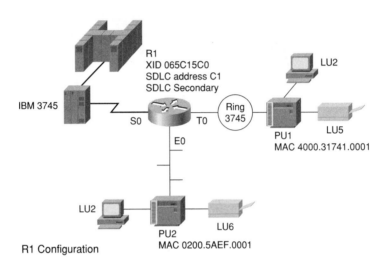

R1 Configuration

```
 dspu host R1 xid-snd 065C15C0 sdlc C1 interface serial 0
 dspu pool lupool host R1 lu 2 12
 !
 dspu pu PU1 rmac 4000.3174.0001 rsap 4 lsap 8
 dspu pool lu 2 6 pool lupool
 !
 dspu pu pu-ether rmac 4000.3174.0001 rsap 4 lsap 8
 dspu lu 2 6 pool lupool
 !
 interface serial 0
 encapsulation sdlc
 sdlc role secondary
 sdlc address C1
 dspu enable-host sdlc C1
 !
 interface tokenring 0
  ring-speed 16
  dspu enable-pu lsap 8
 !
 interface ethernet 0
 dspu enable-pu lsap 8
```

15.10.7 Upstream Host Using Frame Relay

In Figure 15-18, an upstream host connects to the downstream PUs over a Frame-Relay network connection. The downstream PUs are Token Ring and Ethernet attached. The Frame-Relay connection is between a Cisco router and a Frame-Relay–attached IBM 3745 FEP.

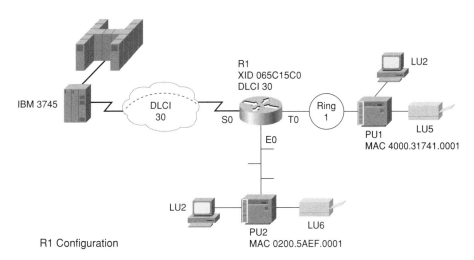

Figure 15-18
Frame Relay between a Cisco router connecting to an upstream host attached via a Frame-Relay IBM 3745 FEP.

R1 Configuration

```
    dspu host R1 xid-snd 065C15C0 dlci 30 rsap 4 lsap 12
dspu pool lupool host R1 lu 2 12
!
dspu pu PU1 rmac 4000.3174.0001 rsap 4 lsap 8
dspu lu 2 6 pool lupool
!
dspu pu PU2 rmac 0200.5AEF.0001 rsap 4 lsap 8
dspu lu 2 6 pool lupool
!
interface serial 0
 encapsulation frame-relay ietf
 frame-relay map llc2 30
 dspu enable-host lsap 12
 dspu start R1
!
interface tokenring 0
ring-speed 16
 dspu enable-pu lsap 8
!
interface ethernet 0
 dspu enable-pu lsap 8
```

15.10.8 DSPU Using NCIA

In this example, shown in Figure 15-19, we see NCIA connections from a LAN-attached workstation access the SNA host through DSPU connectivity. In this example, the NCIA server resides on the Cisco router Token Ring attached to the IBM 3745 FEP.

Figure 15-19
NCIA server using DSPU for connecting to the upstream host.

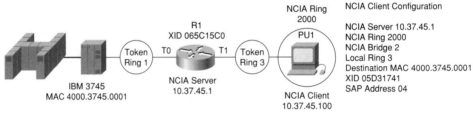

R1 Configuration

```
    ncia server 1 10.37.45.1 4000.3745.0001 4000.7513.0001 128
    !
    dspu ncia 1
    dspu ncia enable-pu lsap 8
    !
    dspu host R1 xid-snd 065C15C0 rmac 4000.3745.0001 rsap 4 ls  ap 4
    !
    dspu host PU1 xid-rcv 05D31741
    dspu lu 2 6 host R1
    !
    interface TokenRing 0
    ring-speed 16
    dspu enable-host R1 lsap 4
    dspu start R1
     !
    interface TokenRing 1
    ring-speed 16
    dspu enable-host PU1 lsap 4
```

CHAPTER 16

CIP Design and Configuration

The Cisco *Channel Interface Processor (CIP)* and the *Channel Port Adapter (CPA)* enable direct channel connection to the IBM mainframe. The CIP is available on Cisco 7000 and 7500 router platforms. The CPA is available only on the Cisco 7200 router platform. For purposes of this text, we will refer only to the CIP for connecting to the mainframe. However, all features, functions, and commands used for connecting resources to the mainframe through a Cisco router using the CPA are supported and specified as discussed for the CIP.

Direct connection of a channel-attached Cisco router to the mainframe enables a Cisco router to perform functions previously only available to IBM 3745 FEPs and IBM 3172 Interconnect Controllers. These features are as follows:

- Connection of LAN-attached devices to TCP/IP or SNA applications residing on the mainframe

- Support for the TCP/IP Offload facility of IBM TCP/IP for MVS or Cisco IOS for S/390

- Support for the Multipath Channel (MPC) feature

- Common Link Access for Workstations (CLAW) for TCP/IP access to mainframes

- Cisco SNA (CSNA) which allows the transport of SNA, APPN ISR to VTAM

- Cisco Multipath Channel (CMPC) for the support of APPN ISR and APPN HPR data to VTAM

- Attachment via a parallel channel adapter (PCA)

- Attachment via an Enterprise System Connection (ESCON) channel adapter (ECA)

In addition to these features, the Cisco IOS software support advances connectivity options through the following supported features not found on the IBM 3745 FEP or IBM 3172 Interconnect Controller. These enhancements are as follows:

- TCP Assist for offloading mainframe TCP/IP checksum processing cycles

- Support for a TN3270 server residing on the router

- IP precedence and IP TOS mapping for TN3270 connections

- Support for APPN/HPR on the Cisco router

- Support for NCIA server on the Cisco router

- Support for DLSw+ on the Cisco router

- Support for APPN DLUR/DLUS

Full support of all these features along with all the features previously discussed for transporting SNA data over multimedia WANs enables the Cisco channel-attached router as a full-function replacement of an IBM 3745 or IBM 3172 and most other gateway channel devices.

NOTES

Although the CIP supports SNA, APPN, and TCP/IP connectivity concurrently to the mainframe, this chapter discusses SNA and APPN connectivity options only.

16.1 DESIGN CRITERIA

The Cisco CIP supports many features for connecting to the IBM mainframe for SNA. The capability to use ESCON allows for multiple IBM mainframe connectivity from one Cisco CIP, and thereby increases availability for downstream SNA sessions. The mainframe must be using EMIF to allow the CIP to connect multiple logical partitions (LPARs) using a single channel connection. The following concerns are some of the criteria that must be addressed when implementing Cisco CIP:

- Which of the many SNA transport features supported by Cisco IOS software are currently implemented and which features are planned?

- Which layer of the Cisco router internetworking architecture is most appropriate for supporting the SNA transport to the Cisco CIP router: core, access, or distribution?

- How many CIP routers and CIP interfaces are required to support the SNA traffic to the mainframe?

- What is the impact on the router processing memory and CIP memory requirements to support the SNA traffic over the CIP connection? This is important when LLC2 frames are to be transported to the CIP connection via a bridging methodology.

- Is the SNA network a mix of SNA sub-area routing and APPN ISR/HPR or a variant of this configuration?

- What is the need of uninterrupted or automated recovery to the mainframe through high-availability configurations?

There are three typical functional configurations for implementing Cisco CIP routers, as discussed in the following sections.

16.1.1 All in One

The Cisco CIP router provides all the functions necessary for connecting to the mainframe. This may include all the varied SNA transport features: DLSw+, RSRB, SDLLC, STUN, Frame Relay, and APPN, along with TCP/IP support. Figure 16-1 depicts this type of configuration. If this solution is entertained, it is best for use in small networks with a maximum of 50 remote locations. In addition, to ensure availability, more than one CIP router must be employed to provide primary support for some of the remote locations.

Figure 16-1
*All-in-one CIP
connectivity to
the IBM
mainframe.*

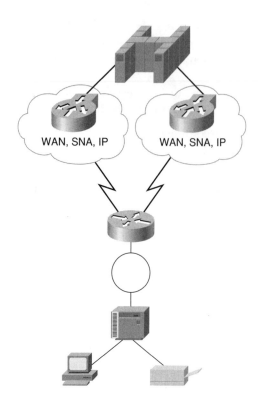

16.1.2 CIP and SNA Combined

In networks where minimal non-SNA connections are used through the CIP (that is, FTP, TCP) to the mainframe, offloading the WAN processing to LAN-attached routers ensures performance and throughput of the CIP router. Using the configuration illustrated in Figure 16-2, the CIP router can support hundreds of remote locations. This functional design segregates multiprotocol broadcast replication from the SNA processing. In addition, it increases the options for availability design by having a data-center backbone LAN with multiple CIP routers attached to multiple WAN routers for connecting to the WAN locations. In this configuration, the CIP routers are processing LLC2 frames along with IP packets.

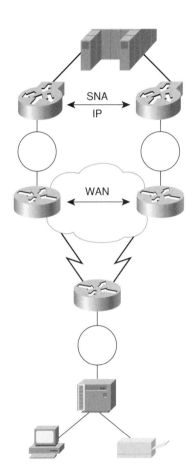

Figure 16-2
*CIP and SNA
connectivity to
the IBM
mainframe.*

16.1.3 CIP Solo

Using the CIP for processing SRB LLC2 traffic and IP only is possible through further segregation of services. SRB traffic in a router is switched instead of DLSw+ or APPN/DLUR, which are processed by the router's main processor. In such a configuration, as shown in Figure 16-3, SNA-only routers on the data-center backbone LAN are the DLSw+ peers for the remote locations. These routers then transport the SNA frames to the CIP routers using SRB. Meanwhile, WAN routers deliver IP-based traffic directly to the CIP router. The CIP can handle upwards of 6,000 SNA PU sessions when using this type of connection.

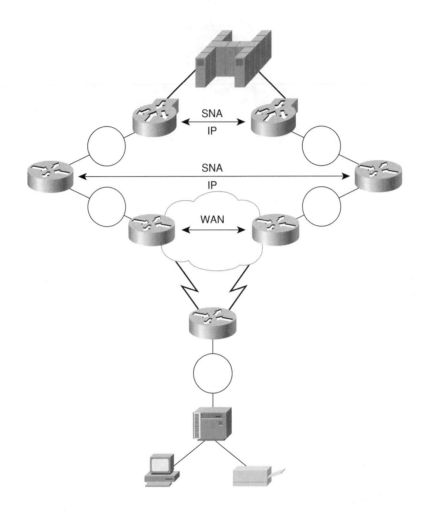

Figure 16-3
SRB and IP-only connectivity to the IBM mainframe.

16.2 DESIGN CONFIGURATIONS

The design configuration shown here represents the use of a Cisco CIP router for mainframe connectivity in place of the IBM 3745 FEP. The configurations cover many of the previous SNA transport mechanisms discussed by using the CIP rather than the IBM 3745 as the destination MAC address for the SNA connection establishment.

16.2.1 ESCON, PCA and MPC Configurations

Figure 16-4 illustrates using the mainframe via the various connectivity options from a Cisco CIP router to the IBM mainframe. Router R1 connects directly to the IBM mainframe using a bus-and-tag Parallel Channel Adapter (PCA) connection. Throughput on a PCA connection is approximately 4.5MBps.

Router 2 in Figure 16-4 diagrams the CIP connection using ESCON Channel Adapters (ECAs). The one CIP connection from R2 connects directly to the mainframe using ECA. The second CIP connection on the R2 router connects to a mainframe using the ESCON Director. *ESCON Directors* allow access to multiple logical partitions (LPARs) or multiple mainframes using a single ESCON connection from the router. In essence, the ESCON Director is a switch. Both PCA and ECA adapters use a single channel for reading and writing to the mainframe.

NOTES

The CIP also works with EMIF to allow access to multiple LPARs without using an ESCON Director.

The router R3 in the diagram depicts the use of Cisco MPC (CMPC) support for connecting to the mainframe over ESCON. CMPC enables the use of a pair of channels. One channel of the pair is used for reading; the second channel in the pair is used for writing. The pair of channels is referred to as a *transmission group (TG)*. If you have a CIP with two channel adapters installed, one adapter can be dedicated to reading and the other can be dedicated to writing. CMPC can also use a subchannel pair within a single physical channel.

16.2.1.1 High Availability Using RSRB to Mainframe Using Dual CIP Routers

RSRB caches the RIF field for all destination MAC address connections successfully made through the router. Figure 16-5 shows the use of RSRB between a remote location serviced by router R3 and two data-center routers R1 and R2 channel attached to the mainframe using a Cisco CIP. The internal LAN definitions on the CIP routers address connectivity to the mainframe using the same internal MAC address of 4000.7513.0001 on different internal CIP ring numbers.

Figure 16-4
PCA, ESCON and MPC connectivity configurations for CIP to mainframe.

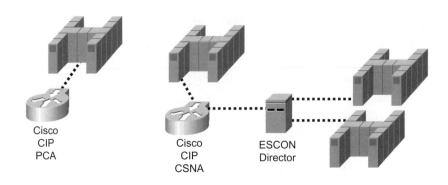

Cisco
CIP
PCA

Cisco
CIP
CSNA

ESCON
Director

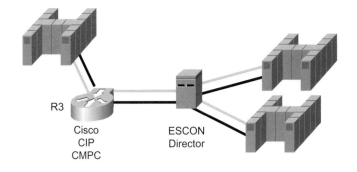

R3

Cisco
CIP
CMPC

ESCON
Director

—— Read Channel
—— Write Channel
•••••• Read/Write Channel

The cache in R3 will maintain two RIF entries to the destination MAC address: one through R1 and one through R2. The first entry in the cache is the entry used by the remote location. If the router R1 or its channel connection were to fail the cache entry, the R1 router will expire and all new sessions will establish their SNA connectivity through the R2 router.

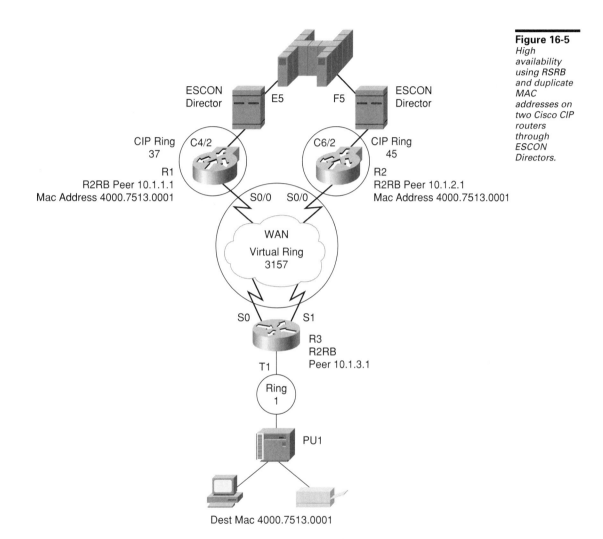

Figure 16-5
*High
availability
using RSRB
and duplicate
MAC
addresses on
two Cisco CIP
routers
through
ESCON
Directors.*

16.2.1.2 High Availability and Load Balancing
Using DLSw+ to Dual CIP Routers

In Figure 16-6, we can answer the RIF cache problem by implementing DLSw+-to-WAN routers and using SRB to connect to the CIP routers. In this scenario, the remote location PU1 connects to MAC address 4000.7513.0001 using DLSw+. The DLSw+ learns of two unique paths through the network. The data-center routers R4 and R5 will provide round-robin connectivity over the dual Token Rings that attach the WAN routers R4 and R5 to the channel-attached routers R1 and R2. Recall that the round-robin is pertinent to SNA session establishment only.

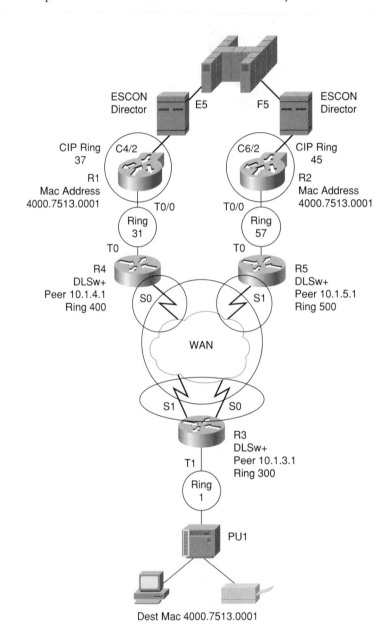

ESCON Director E5

F5 ESCON Director

CIP Ring 37 C4/2

C6/2 CIP Ring 45

R1
Mac Address
4000.7513.0001

R2
Mac Address
4000.7513.0001

T0/0

T0/0

Ring 31

Ring 57

T0

T0

R4
DLSw+
Peer 10.1.4.1
Ring 400

R5
DLSw+
Peer 10.1.5.1
Ring 500

S0

S1

WAN

S1

S0

R3
DLSw+
Peer 10.1.3.1
Ring 300

T1

Ring 1

PU1

Dest Mac 4000.7513.0001

16.2.1.3 VTAM-to-VTAM Communications
Through a Single CIP Router with Two CIPs

VTAM-VTAM communications is often used in networks with more than one VTAM running. Figure 16-7 illustrates the use of VTAM-VTAM connectivity over two CIPs in the same router. The performance is enhanced through the use of the CMPC protocol. This configuration can also be accomplished by using two different CIP routers with a single connection to one of the VTAMs. These routers would then communicate over a high-speed backbone such as Fast Ethernet, ATM, or FDDI using the same mechanism as shown with the single CIP router configuration.

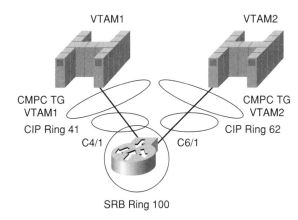

Figure 16-7
VTAM-VTAM communications over a single CIP router with two CIPs.

16.2.1.4 TN3270 Session Switching Using
DLUR/DLUS with VTAM Host Redundancy

The Cisco CIP support for TN3270 enables IBM 3270 data stream traffic to pass through an IP backbone. The TN3270 server support on the Cisco CIP offloads TCP/IP processing from TN3270 termination on the mainframe and presents the TN3270 connections to VTAM as LUs of a LAN-attached PU.

Figure 16-8 illustrates the use of TN3270 server functionality with the added functionality of switching TN3270 connections from one VTAM to another should the primary VTAM become inoperative. The switched major nodes on VTAM must represent the direct PU connections for the TN3270 server along with a definition used for session switching. The configuration uses the APPN Virtual Routing Node for connecting the three mainframe APPN nodes. The transport between the two CIP routers is DLSw+.

Figure 16-8
*TN3270
session
switching
using
DLUR/DLUS
and host
redundancy.*

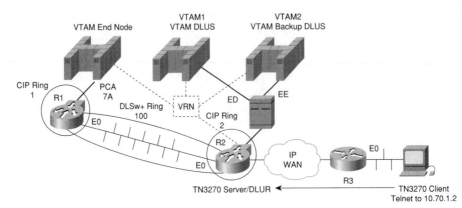

16.2.1.5 CMPC ESCON Connection for APPN HPR to VTAM

In this configuration, Figure 16-9, the CIP router communicates with VTAM and the APPN WAN using HPR. The CIP router defines the channel and Token-Ring ports as APPN links to establish the end-to-end connection. This same connection can also support APPN ISR. The CIP router does not have to be an APPN NN in this configuration; it is labeled as such to show function.

Figure 16-9
*ESCON CMPC
channel
configuration
using APPN
HPR.*

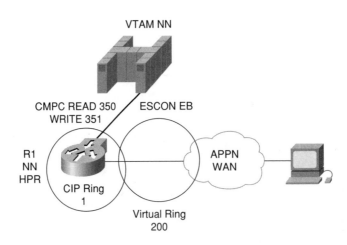

16.2.2 Loading the CIP Microcode

As of Cisco IOS Software Release 11.1, microcode for the CIP (or *CIP image*) is unbundled from the Cisco IOS software release. The route processor (RP) of the Cisco 7000 or the router switch processor (RSP) of the Cisco 7200/7500 router must have flash memory installed. A minimum of 8MB of RAM is required on the CIP itself to use the IBM channel attach features of Cisco IOS Software Release 11.1 and later.

NOTES

The CIP image is preloaded on flash cards for all Cisco 7000 with RSP7000, Cisco 7500, and Cisco 7200 series routers ordered with the CIP/CPA option for Cisco IOS Software Release 11.1 and later.

The Cisco CIP microcode is found on the Cisco Web site under "Support." After finding the appropriate microcode for your CIP or CPA, it is TFTP'd to a viable TFTP server within your network. Execute the following commands in Listing 16.1 to transfer the CIP microcode from a TFTP server to a flash card on the router.

Listing 16.1.—Example of transferring the CIP microcode to the CIP router.

```
Router-r1#copy tftp slot0:
Enter source file name: cip25-8.bin
6843800 bytes available on device slot0, proceed? [confirm]
Address or name of remote host [tftpserver.domain.com]? 10.1.254.2
Accessing file "cip25-8.bin" on 10.1.254.2 ...FOUND
Loading cip25-8.bin from 10.1.254.2 (via Ethernet2/3): !
--- expanding multi-segment file ---
slot0:cip25-8.bin_kernel_hw4 size = 257888
!!!!!!!!!!!!!!!!!!!!!!!!!!!!!!!!!!!!!!!!!!!!!!!!!!!!!!!!CCCCCCC
--- expanding multi-segment file ---
slot0:cip25-8.bin_kernel_hw5 size = 256914
!!!!!!!!!!!!!!!!!!!!!!!!!!!!!!!!!!!!!!!!!!!!!!!!!!!!!!!!CCCCCCC
--- expanding multi-segment file ---
slot0:cip25-8.bin_seg_802 size = 233792
!!!!!!!!!!!!!!!!!!!!!!!!!!!!!!!!!!!!!!!!!!!!!!!!!!!!!!CCCCCCC
--- expanding multi-segment file ---
```

```
slot0:cip25-8.bin_seg_csna size = 85896
!!!!!!!!!!!!!!!!!!CC
--- expanding multi-segment file ---
slot0:cip25-8.bin_seg_eca size = 461408
!!!!!!!!!!!!!!!!!!!!!!!!!!!!!!!!!!!!!!!!!!!!!!!!!!!!!!!!!!!!
!!!!!!!!!!!!!!!!!!!!!!!!!!!!!!!!!!!!CCCCCCCCCCCCCC
--- expanding multi-segment file ---
slot0:cip25-8.bin_seg_offload size = 64656
!!!!!!!!!!!!!!C
--- expanding multi-segment file ---
slot0:cip25-8.bin_seg_pca size = 69360
!!!!!!!!!!!!!!!CC
--- expanding multi-segment file ---
slot0:cip25-8.bin_seg_push size = 13752
!!!
--- expanding multi-segment file ---
slot0:cip25-8.bin_seg_tcpip size = 182032
!!!!!!!!!!!!!!!!!!!!!!!!!!!!!!!!!!!!!!!!!CCCCC
--- expanding multi-segment file --
slot0:cip25-8.bin_seg_tn3270 size = 542392
!!!!!!!!!!!!!!!!!!!!!!!!!!!!!!!!!!!!!!!!!!!!!!!!!!!!!!!!!!!
!!!!!!!!!!!!!!!!!!!!!!!!!!!!!!!!!!!!!!!!!!!!!!!!CCCCCCCCCCCCCCCCCC
```

The router configuration file must have a pointer to the CIP microcode name and location. This is accomplished by entering configuration mode on the router and entering the microcode configuration command as shown in Listing 16.2.

Listing 16.2.—Configuration command to point to CIP microcode.

```
microcode CIP flash slot0:cip25-8.bin
microcode reload
```

The microcode global command defines the interface processor being loaded, where the microcode resides, and the name of the microcode to load. The microcode reload global command will load the CIP immediately.

16.3 DEFINING CSNA SUPPORT

The Cisco SNA (CSNA) feature communicates with VTAM on the mainframe using the External Channel Adapter (XCA) driver of VTAM. In support of SNA, the CSNA uses a single channel address for reading and writing to the mainframe. The CSNA function utilizes the CIP virtual interface x/2 for defining internal virtual LANs used for connectivity through LLC2.

16.3.1 Assigning CSNA to an I/O Device Address

The cnsa command uses the channel path and the device address. The format of the csna interface command is as follows:

```
csna path device [maxpiu value] [time-delay value] [length-delay value]
```

The csna *path* parameter is subdivided into three arguments: logical path, channel logical address, and control unit address.

- The logical path (2 hexadecimal digits) constitutes the address of the physical connection from the mainframe point of view, one hexadecimal digit for the control unit address, and one hexadecimal digit for the device address. The PCA channel connections require the first two digits of the path value to be 01. The second two digits are configured in the IOCP generation file and should correspond to the appropriate device.

- The ESCON *logical-channel* argument of the csna *path* parameter must match the ESCON PATH input port value as defined in the IOCP generation. When using ESCON Directors, this is the port connecting to the mainframe. Without ESCON Directors (direct ESCON attachment to the mainframe), the *logical-channel* argument is 01. The IOCP/HCD macro definition CHPID points to the logical partition by a named value on the PART parameter. The IOCP/HCD RESOURCE macro defining the named partition specifies the LPAR number of the partition. Coding a value of shared for the channel path identifier (CHPID) macro requires the specification of the LPAR number attaching to the csna definition through a ESCON Director. If an ESCON Director is not used, the path value is 01.

- The *control-unit-address* argument of the csna *path* parameter is a single hexadecimal digit that must match the IOCP/HCD CUADD parameter of the CNTLUNIT macro. If the CUADD parameter was not coded in the IOCP/HCD CNTLUNIT macro for this channel, the default value of 0 is used for the *control-unit-address* argument of the csna *path* parameter.

- The csna *device* parameter represents the position of the CIP interface as a device attached to the channel. The value here is from the UNITADD parameter of the CTLUNIT macro in the IOCP/HCD definitions.

If given, the IOCP IODEVICE address of EB2 and the UNITADD parameter of the corresponding CTLUNIT macro specified EB0 and the UNITADD IOCP parameter begins at 00. The csna interface command would be defined as follows:

```
csna E220 02
```

where the ESCON port address connecting to the mainframe is E2. The LPAR using this connection is LPAR number 2 and the CUADD value defaults to 0. The CIP is connected as the third device on the channel (counting from 0) because the device parameter is 02.

Suppose the IODEVICE address is 97A. The IODEVICE ADDRESS parameter specifies a beginning IO address of 920 for 64 addresses (IODEVICE ADDRESS=(0920,64)). The corresponding UNITADD parameter begins at 20 for 64 devices (UNITADD=((20,64))). The csna device parameter is the difference between 7A and 20, which equals 5A. The corresponding csna command would be coded as follows:

```
csna E220 5A
```

The optional maxpiu keyword value denotes the largest packet size in bytes that can be placed on the channel being defined. This can be thought of as equivalent to SNA MAX-DATA and IP MTU size. The value defaults to 20470 if not coded and ranges from 4096 to 65535 bytes. The format is as follows:

```
maxpiu value
```

The optional time-delay keyword value is in milliseconds and specifies the delay used prior to transmitting a received packet on the interface. The default is 10 milliseconds, with a range of 0 to 100 milliseconds. The format is as follows:

```
time-delay value
```

The optional length-delay keyword value is the number of bytes to buffer before placing the data on the interface for transmission. The default is 20470 and the valid range is 0 to 65535. The format is as follows:

```
length-delay value
```

16.3.2 Defining the Internal Virtual LAN

SNA communications over the CIP with CSNA requires an internal virtual LAN definition. Define the internal virtual LAN under the ENABLE mode using the CONFIG TERM terminal operator command. Listing 16.3 illustrates a sample configuration using internal virtual LAN.

Listing 16.3.—Internal virtual LAN definition for CSNA services.

```
source-bridge ring-group 4
!
interface Channel 4/0
no ip address
csna E220 02
!
interface Channel4/2
 no ip address
 no keepalive
    LAN Tokenring 0
    source-bridge 6 1 4
    adapter 0 4000.C15C.0001
```

Using the listing, the CIP virtual interface Channel 4/2 is used for defining the internal virtual LAN. CSNA does not require an IP address for connectivity to the mainframe and therefore it is not defined. This is denoted by the command no ip address. Because this is a virtual interface and is considered up and active only when the physical interface Channel 4/0 is up, there is no need for keepalive messages. We denote this by using the no keepalive command.

NOTES

The CPA of a Cisco 7200 router does not use a virtual interface. Therefore, the commands discussed under the CIP virtual interface will hold true for a physical interface on the CPA.

The internal virtual LAN interface is defined using the LAN command. The LAN command can specify FDDI, Ethernet, and Tokenring. Tokenring is currently the only supported internal LAN at this time. The value 0 following the LAN Tokenring parameter indicates to the CIP that this is virtual LAN interface 0. The number of LAN interfaces can range from 0–31. The virtual Channel 4/2 interface can have multiple virtual LAN interfaces assigned to it.

The source-bridge statement following the LAN Tokenring statement defines the connection between this LAN virtual ring and the WAN virtual ring. The WAN virtual ring is the value defined on the source-bridge ring-group global command. The statement in Listing 16.3 identifies ring number 6 as the ring number for the LAN virtual ring segment. The source-bridge statement therefore in Listing 16.3 defines connectivity between the internal LAN virtual ring segment (ring number 6) and the WAN virtual ring segment (4) through bridge 1.

The last statement required for CSNA connectivity is the adapter statement. The adapter statement identifies the relative adapter number (RAN) and the MAC address assigned to the RAN for use on the internal virtual LAN segment. The RAN value ranges from 0–17 and must match the VTAM XCA major node parameter ADAPNO. The CIP allows multiple virtual adapters defined to the internal LAN virtual Token-Ring segment.

The internal LAN virtual MAC address as defined in Listing 16.3 is 4000.C15C.0001 on adapter 0. This MAC address will be the destination MAC address for devices connecting to the mainframe using SNA.

16.3.3 Defining the VTAM XCA Major Node

The CIP2 communicates with VTAM using an *External Communications Adapter (XCA)*. Four parameters in the XCA definition are pertinent to establishing communications with the CIP2. These are the ADAPNO, CUADDR, SAPADDR, and MEDIUM.

Listing 16.4 details an XCA definition for the CIP2 CSNA defined in Listing 16.3. The PORT statement identifies the RAN using the ADAPNO parameter. The value coded for the XCA ADAPNO parameter must match the value defined for the first variable on the CIP adapter command. For the examples shown, this value is 0.

The XCA CUADDR parameter on the PORT statement specifies the I/O device address VTAM will use to communicate with the CIP. The value specified in Listing 16.4 is EB2. This value must be the I/O device address referenced by the device-address variable of the CSNA statement defined for the CIP Channel 4/0 interface.

The SAPADDR parameter on the PORT statement specifies the Service Access Point (SAP) address this VTAM XCA major node will use for communicating with devices over the channel connection. The SAPADDR value of 4 specified on the XCA must be matched in the SNA PU controller definitions of the devices that will communicate with VTAM through the CIP2.

The final parameter of the XCA PORT statement, MEDIUM, specifies the type of LAN in use. This value must reflect the type of virtual LAN defined on the CIP for communicating to VTAM. In the examples given, the value RING on the XCA identifies the use of a Token-Ring LAN defined by the LAN statement on the CIP2 virtual interface Channel 4/2.

Listing 16.4.—Example of the VTAM XCA Major Node definition for CIP connection.

```
XCAR1    VBUILD TYPE=XCA
CIPEB21  PORT   ADAPNO=0,CUADDR=EB2,SAPADDR=4,MEDIUM=RING,TIMER=60
*  PU2/PU2.1 SWITCHED RESOURCES *
GEB2101  GROUP DIAL=YES,ISTATUS=ACTIVE,AUTOGEN=(50,L,P)
```

16.4 DEFINING TN3270 SERVER SUPPORT

The modifications to the CSNA configuration in supporting TN3270 server functions involve the following additions:

- An IP address for the Channel 4/2 interface

- A second virtual adapter for use on the virtual Token-Ring interface

- TN3270 PU definitions to represent the PU functions for the LUs assigned by VTAM using Dynamic Definition Dependent LUs (DDDLUs)

The assignment of an IP address to the virtual Channel 4/2 interface enables IP services as seen in Listing 16.5. The statement max-llc2-sessions specifies the maximum number of active SNA LLC2 sessions at any given time through this virtual Channel 4/2 interface. The TN3270 server uses a second virtual adapter on the virtual LAN. RAN 1 and MAC address 4000.3270.7006 define the addresses for the TN3270 server adapter.

Listing 16.5.—Additional statements required on the CIP Channel 4/2 interface for TN3270 server function.

```
source-bridge ring-group 4
interface channel 4/0
csna 0110 00
!
interface Channel 4/2
 ip address 192.168.6.1 255.255.255.0
 no keepalive
 max-llc2-sessions 2000
  LAN Tokenring 0
  source-bridge 6 1 4
  adapter 0 4000.0000.7006
  adapter 1 4000.3270.7006
 tn3270-server
  maximum-lus 4000
  pu PUEB2001 017FABC0 192.168.6.2 token-adapter 1 04 luseed LUTNS###
```

Entering the `tn3270-server` command enables the TN3270 server functions. The TN3270 server may handle a maximum of 30,000 LU sessions. The `maximum-lus` statement limits the number of LUs supported by the TN3270 server. In the example, the maximum number of LUs is 4000. The previous `max-llc2-sessions` value thereby limits the number of active LUs to only 2000 at any given time.

The core of the TN3270 server functions is the definition of the SNA PU. The `PU` statement defines the variables required to establish PU and LU sessions with the VTAM on the mainframe. The format of the statement is as follows:

```
PU puname idblkidnum ip-address adapter-type ran lsap luseed lunamestem
```

The *puname* on the TN3270 PU statement for the router matches the name of the VTAM switched PU name. The *idblkidnum* value must match the `IDBLK` and `IDNUM` values specified on the VTAM PU definition statement defined for the TN3270 PU representation. The *ip-address* is the IP address used by the TN3270 client for connecting to the TN3270 server PU. This IP address is known as the *IP Listening Address*. The `adapter-type` value must match the virtual LAN type defined for the Channel 4/2 interface. The *ran* value identifies the adapter used for connectivity to the mainframe.

The *lsap* variable of the TN3270 PU statement identifies the SAP used for communication over this virtual interface for this specific PU. If a second PU were defined under the TN3270 server using the same virtual adapter, a different SAP value would be assigned to the second PU definition. Usually, the SAP value for SNA begins with `04` and increments by four. Therefore, a second PU using the same `rmac` address would use a `lsap` value of `08`. Because it is customary to use SAP `04` for the CSNA connections, a value of SAP `08` is more appropriate for the TN3270 connection.

The `luseed` keyword indicates that the VTAM DDDLU feature will be used to define LU names and their associated characteristics dynamically. The names are based on the value given to the *lunamestem* variable. In Listing 16.6, the suggested variable for dynamic LU names is `LUTNS###`. The `###` positions are replaced by VTAM during definition time with the decimal value of the LU's local address (`LOCADDR`) value as assigned by VTAM in the switched major node. The `###` `LUSEED` will output the seed in decimal. Using only two hashes —`##`—can generate a hex output for the LU name. If LUSEED is used, it is recommended that the seeds specified in VTAM and on the server match.

Listing 16.6.—Switched PU definition to support DDDLU for TN3270 server.

```
* CIP switch DEFINTIION
SWEB200  VBUILD TYPE=SWNET,MAXGRP=4,MAXNO=80
PUEB2001 PU  ADDR=01,PUTYPE=2,MAXPATH=4,ANS=CONT,LOGAPPL=NMT,
             ISTATUS=ACTIVE,MAXDATA=521,IRETRY=YES,MAXOUT=7,
             PASSLIM=5,IDBLK=017,IDNUM=FABC0,MODETAB=SDLCTAB,
             LUSEED=LUTNS###,LUGROUP=EB2LUGRP,USSTAB=TESTUSS
  PATHEB2  PATH   DIALNO=01400032707006,GRPNM=GEB2001
 *LUTNS001  LU     LOCADDR=1
 *LUTNS002  LU     LOCADDR=2
 *LUTNS003  LU     LOCADDR=3
 *LUTNS004  LU     LOCADDR=4
```

Listing 16.6 illustrates the resulting LU name for the first four LUs on the switched major node representing the TN3270 server PU defined in the router. The * denotes a comment line to VTAM. Note that the router *luseed* value must match the LUSEED value specified in the VTAM switched major node. The LUGROUP value in the switched major node points to a list that identifies the LU model type.

Listing 16.7 lists a sample LUGROUP major node for VTAM.

Listing 16.7.—VTAM LUGROUP major node definition to support DDDLU model types for TN3270 server.

```
TN3270G  VBUILD TYPE=LUGROUP
*
*  PU2/PU2.1 SWITCHED RESOURCES *
*                                              *
*  THIS IS A TEST XCA LUGROUP MAJOR NODE FOR CISCO CIP  *
*  TN3270 SESSIONS                             *
*
EB2LUGRP LUGROUP
327802   LU    DLOGMOD=D4C32782,
               MODETAB=ISTINCLM,SSCPFM=USS3270,LOGAPPL=NMT
327803   LU    DLOGMOD=D4C32783,
               MODETAB=ISTINCLM,SSCPFM=USS3270,LOGAPPL=NMT
327804   LU    DLOGMOD=D4C32784,
               MODETAB=ISTINCLM,SSCPFM=USS3270,LOGAPPL=NMT
327805   LU    DLOGMOD=D4C32785,
               MODETAB=ISTINCLM,SSCPFM=USS3270,LOGAPPL=NMT
```

```
327902    LU    DLOGMOD=D4C32782,
                 MODETAB=ISTINCLM,SSCPFM=USS3270,LOGAPPL=NMT
327903    LU    DLOGMOD=D4C32783,
                 MODETAB=ISTINCLM,SSCPFM=USS3270,LOGAPPL=NMT
327904    LU    DLOGMOD=D4C32784,
                 MODETAB=ISTINCLM,SSCPFM=USS3270,LOGAPPL=NMT
327905    LU    DLOGMOD=D4C32785,
                 MODETAB=ISTINCLM,SSCPFM=USS3270,LOGAPPL=NMT
327802E   LU    DLOGMOD=SNX32702,
                 MODETAB=ISTINCLM,SSCPFM=USS3270,LOGAPPL=NMT
327803E   LU    DLOGMOD=SNX32703,
                 MODETAB=ISTINCLM,SSCPFM=USS3270,LOGAPPL=NMT
327804E   LU    DLOGMOD=SNX32704,
                 MODETAB=ISTINCLM,SSCPFM=USS3270,LOGAPPL=NMT
327805E   LU    DLOGMOD=SNX32705,
                 MODETAB=ISTINCLM,SSCPFM=USS3270,LOGAPPL=NMT
327902E   LU    DLOGMOD=SNX32702,
                 MODETAB=ISTINCLM,SSCPFM=USS3270,LOGAPPL=NMT
327903E   LU    DLOGMOD=SNX32703,
                 MODETAB=ISTINCLM,SSCPFM=USS3270,LOGAPPL=NMT
327904E   LU    DLOGMOD=SNX32704,
                 MODETAB=ISTINCLM,SSCPFM=USS3270,LOGAPPL=NMT
327905E   LU    DLOGMOD=SNX32705,
                 MODETAB=ISTINCLM,SSCPFM=USS3270,LOGAPPL=NMT
3278S2    LU    DLOGMOD=D4C32782,
                 MODETAB=ISTINCLM,SSCPFM=USSSCS,LOGAPPL=NMT
3278S3    LU    DLOGMOD=D4C32783,
                 MODETAB=ISTINCLM,SSCPFM=USSSCS,LOGAPPL=NMT
3278S4    LU    DLOGMOD=D4C32784,
                 MODETAB=ISTINCLM,SSCPFM=USSSCS,LOGAPPL=NMT
3278S5    LU    DLOGMOD=D4C32785,
                 MODETAB=ISTINCLM,SSCPFM=USSSCS,LOGAPPL=NMT
3279S2    LU    DLOGMOD=D4C32782,
```

```
                       MODETAB=ISTINCLM,SSCPFM=USSSCS,LOGAPPL=NMT
       3279S3   LU     DLOGMOD=D4C32783,
                       MODETAB=ISTINCLM,SSCPFM=USSSCS,LOGAPPL=NMT
       3279S4   LU     DLOGMOD=D4C32784,
                       MODETAB=ISTINCLM,SSCPFM=USSSCS,LOGAPPL=NMT
       3279S5   LU     DLOGMOD=D4C32785,
                       MODETAB=ISTINCLM,SSCPFM=USSSCS,LOGAPPL=NMT
       3278S2E  LU     DLOGMOD=SNX32702,
                       MODETAB=ISTINCLM,SSCPFM=USSSCS,LOGAPPL=NMT
       3278S3E  LU     DLOGMOD=SNX32703,
                       MODETAB=ISTINCLM,SSCPFM=USSSCS,LOGAPPL=NMT
       3278S4E  LU     DLOGMOD=SNX32704,
                       MODETAB=ISTINCLM,SSCPFM=USSSCS,LOGAPPL=NMT
       3278S5E  LU     DLOGMOD=SNX32705,
                       MODETAB=ISTINCLM,SSCPFM=USSSCS,LOGAPPL=NMT
       3279S2E  LU     DLOGMOD=SNX32702,
                       MODETAB=ISTINCLM,SSCPFM=USSSCS,LOGAPPL=NMT
       3279S3E  LU     DLOGMOD=SNX32703,
                       MODETAB=ISTINCLM,SSCPFM=USSSCS,LOGAPPL=NMT
       3279S4E  LU     DLOGMOD=SNX32704,
                       MODETAB=ISTINCLM,SSCPFM=USSSCS,LOGAPPL=NMT
       3279S5E  LU     DLOGMOD=SNX32705,
                       MODETAB=ISTINCLM,SSCPFM=USSSCS,LOGAPPL=NMT
       @        LU     DLOGMOD=D4C32782,
                       MODETAB=ISTINCLM,SSCPFM=USSSCS,LOGAPPL=NMT
```

16.4.1 TN3270 with DLUR/DLUS Support

The TN3270 server function can also be employed by using the DLUR/DLUS features of Cisco IOS and VTAM. The DLUR function of the TN3270 feature allows the TN3270 PU to appear as an APPN end node. The commands applicable to DLUR are as follows:

```
dlur fq-cpname fq-dlusname
dlus-backup dlusname2
```

```
preferred-nnserver name
lsap type adapter-number [lsap]
link name [rmac rmac] [rsap rsap]
vrn vrn-name
pu pu-name idblk-idnum ip-address
```

The dlur command follows the usage as discussed for APPN connections. The *fq-cpname* is a fully qualified control-point name (netid) and the LU name used for the session switching. The *fq-dlusname* is the name of the control point providing the DLUS services.

The dlus-backup command identifies the fully qualified CP name of the VTAM DLUS providing backup. There can be only one dlus-backup per CIP.

The preferred-nnserver *name* specifies the name of the APPN network node server to which this DLUR definition belongs. The name is the CP name of an adjoining NN. This is an optional parameter and is not required for SNA switching to take place.

The lsap *type adapter-number* [*lsap*] is the local SAP address definition for the DLUR end node. The *type* parameter identifies the type of internal LAN adapter in use for the DLUR. The only valid value at this time is token-adapter. The *adapter-number* parameter identifies which adapter on the internal LAN is being used for the DLUR connection. The optional *lsap* variable is the local SAP address used by the DLUR ranging from 04 to FC in multiples of four. The value selected must be unique for all LLC2 connections traversing the adapter. The default value is C0.

The link name [rmac *rmac*] [rsap *rsap*] command defines an APPN link to the host for the end node DLUR. The *name* parameter is the eight-character alphanumeric string identifying the link. This name must be unique for the DLUR being defined. The *rmac* value is optional and defines the remote MAC address used for connecting the end node. The *rsap* value is the SAP address used for communicating to the DLUS over the link. The default here is 04 and ranges from 04 to FC in multiples of four.

The vrn *vrn-name* identifies the name of the virtual routing node for connecting the DLUR to the DLUS and possible backup DLUS. The DLUS and backup-DLUS must have the same VRN name specified in the VTAM switched major node representing the DLUR; otherwise, the switch will fail.

The pu *pu-name idblk-idnum ip-address* command defines the TN3270 DLUR PU used for connecting TN3270 clients. The *pu-name* parameter is a unique PU name assigned to the PU command. For operational and documentation purposes, the name should match the VTAM PU switch major node name defined for supporting the TN3270 PU definition. The *idblk-idnum* parameter must match the unique IDBLK and IDNUM parameters of the PU definition statement in VTAM that represents this TN3270 connection. The *ip-address* is the IP address used by the TN3270 client for connecting to the TN3270 server.

16.5 CIP CMPC DEFINITION

In taking advantage of IBM's Multipath Channel architecture, the following tasks must be completed on both VTAM and on the CIP router:

1. Define the VTAM Transport Resource List (TRL) major node.

2. Define a local SNA major node.

3. Specify the CMPC subchannels.

4. Specify the CMPC TGs.

5. Define the internal CIP virtual LAN for CMPC. The LAN interface definition parameters are the same as those used by CSNA.

16.5.1 Transport Resource List Major Node

The *VTAM TRL major node* identifies to VTAM that the MPC line control is to be employed on IO device address 2F0 and 2F1. The TRLE statement defines which IO device address is for reading (READ) and which is for writing (WRITE). These IO device address values and properties must be matched on the CMPC definition within the CIP router. Listing 16.8 is a sample TRL major node.

Listing 16.8.—VTAM TRL major node for CMPC support.

```
CIPTRL  VBUILD TYPE=TRL
TRL2F0    TRLE  LNCTL=MPC,MAXBFRU=8,REPLYTO=3.0,        X
             READ=(97A),                                X
             WRITE=(97B)
```

NOTES

Although an even/odd address pair is not required, it is prudent for understanding the relationships and to maintain IO address continuity.

16.5.2 Define the Local SNA Major Node

Because CMPC support is only for APPN, a MPC channel link is defined on the VTAM host for connecting to the CMPC router through the definition of a local SNA major node. The PU statement shown in Listing 16.9 points to the previously defined TRL major node. The TRLE parameter of the PU statement specifies the corresponding TRLE definition statement found on a previously defined TRL major node. In this example, the TRLE parameter points to the TRLE statement named TRL2F0. Also note that this local SNA major node defines the PU for XID required with CP-CP sessions using HPR routing.

Listing 16.9.—Local SNA major node for MPC channel link configuration to CMPC router from VTAM.

```
LAGLNA    VBUILD TYPE=LOCAL
  LAGPUA     PU  TRLE=LAGTRLEA,                                    X
               ISTATUS=ACTIVE,                                     X
               XID=YES,CONNTYPE=APPN,CPCP=YES,HPR=YES
```

16.5.3 Defining the CMPC Subchannels

The cmpc command is specified on the physical interfaces of the CIP and not the logical interface x/2. This is because CMPC pairs subchannel addresses, so each subchannel may be defined on separate physical CIP interface ports of the same CIP. The format of the cmpc command is as follows:

```
cmpc path device tg-name {read | write}
```

The cmpc *path* and *device* parameters are defined exactly like that described for csna. The cmpc *tg-name* variable is a name associated with the subchannel being defined. A read and write subchannel must be defined to use CMPC. The *tg-name* value ties the two cmcp definitions together to form the CMPC TG. An example of coding the cmpc command is as follows:

```
interface channel 4/0
!
cmpc 97A 5A R1CIP read
cmpc 97B 5B R1CIP write
```

16.5.4 Defining the CMPC Transmission Group

The CMPC transmission group is defined by using the tg command under the virtual channel interface x/2 definition. The format of the tg command is as follows:

```
tg name llc type adapter-number lsap [rmac rmac] [rsap rsap]
```

The *name* parameter is the TG name used for a previously defined cmpc statement. This name ties the subchannel pair to the LLC2 driver for the internal LAN.

The llc keyword denotes connectivity to the LLC stack on the CIP.

The *type* parameter specifies the type of internal LAN defined for use by the TG. The only value allowed at this time is token-adapter.

The *adapter-number* parameter identifies which internal virtual LAN adapter definition is used by the TG.

The *lsap* parameter defines the local SAP address used for communicating to the host. The SAP address value used here must be unique within the router and host, along with any IEEE 802.2 clients using the specified adapter. The default is 04. However, it may be wise to specify the high end of the allowable range, FC, and move down for additional CMPC connections to avoid any unknown conflicts. The value is a multiple of four ranging from 04 to FC.

The optional keyword rmac and its associated variable *rmac* is a MAC address assigned for use by the CMPC driver for LLC2 connectivity.

The optional rsap keyword and variable *rsap* defaults to 04 and is the remote SAP address used by the driver for communications.

NOTES

To change any parameter on the tg command, the no tg command must first be entered. The new tg command with the altered parameters must then be entered for the definition to take effect.

16.6 CIP CONFIGURATION EXAMPLES

In this section, we address various network configurations using the Cisco CIP as the gateway to the mainframe. The configurations explore the use of the CIP with examples of the previously discussed SNA encapsulation techniques for connecting legacy SNA resources to the IBM mainframe.

16.6.1 High Availability Using RSRB to Mainframe Using Dual CIP Routers

In Figure 16-10 the CIP router acts as the gateway to the mainframe and also connects the WAN. RSRB is used for transporting the data from the remote locations to the mainframe through the CIP. Although RSRB and duplicate MAC addresses provide high availability, they do not enable load balancing. DLSw+ will support the load-balancing function.

Figure 16-10
Using RSRB to CIP WAN routers for high availability.

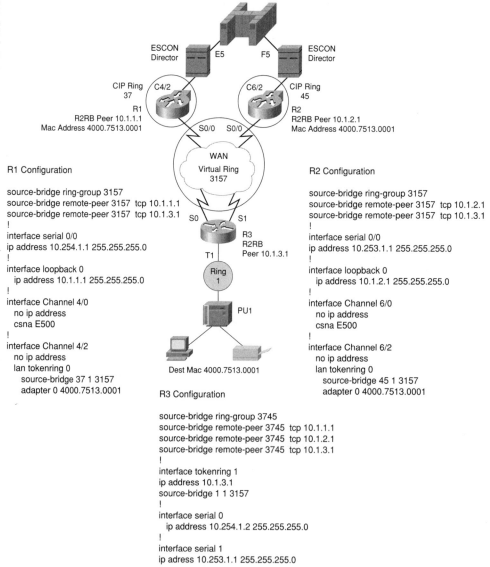

R1 Configuration

source-bridge ring-group 3157
source-bridge remote-peer 3157 tcp 10.1.1.1
source-bridge remote-peer 3157 tcp 10.1.3.1
!
interface serial 0/0
ip address 10.254.1.1 255.255.255.0
!
interface loopback 0
  ip address 10.1.1.1 255.255.255.0
!
interface Channel 4/0
  no ip address
  csna E500
!
interface Channel 4/2
  no ip address
  lan tokenring 0
    source-bridge 37 1 3157
    adapter 0 4000.7513.0001

R2 Configuration

source-bridge ring-group 3157
source-bridge remote-peer 3157 tcp 10.1.2.1
source-bridge remote-peer 3157 tcp 10.1.3.1
!
interface serial 0/0
ip address 10.253.1.1 255.255.255.0
!
interface loopback 0
  ip address 10.1.2.1 255.255.255.0
!
interface Channel 6/0
  no ip address
  csna E500
!
interface Channel 6/2
  no ip address
  lan tokenring 0
    source-bridge 45 1 3157
    adapter 0 4000.7513.0001

R3 Configuration

source-bridge ring-group 3745
source-bridge remote-peer 3745 tcp 10.1.1.1
source-bridge remote-peer 3745 tcp 10.1.2.1
source-bridge remote-peer 3745 tcp 10.1.3.1
!
interface tokenring 1
ip address 10.1.3.1
source-bridge 1 1 3157
!
interface serial 0
  ip address 10.254.1.2 255.255.255.0
!
interface serial 1
ip adress 10.253.1.1 255.255.255.0

16.6.2 High Availability and Load Balancing Using DLSw+ to Dual CIP Routers

Figure 16-11 shows the router configurations necessary for supporting high availability and load balancing using DLSw+ and dual CIP routers. The WAN routers at the data center offload all processing from the CIP routers except for SRB. This type of configuration enables duplicate MAC addressing for load balancing and redundancy should either CIP router fail.

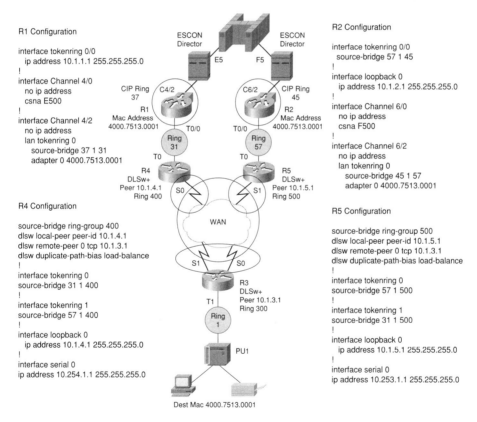

Figure 16-11
High availability using duplicate MAC addresses with load balancing via DLSw+ on two Cisco CIP routers through ESCON Directors.

R1 Configuration

```
interface tokenring 0/0
  ip address 10.1.1.1 255.255.255.0
!
interface Channel 4/0
  no ip address
  csna E500
!
interface Channel 4/2
  no ip address
  lan tokenring 0
    source-bridge 37 1 31
    adapter 0 4000.7513.0001
```

R4 Configuration

```
source-bridge ring-group 400
dlsw local-peer peer-id 10.1.4.1
dlsw remote-peer 0 tcp 10.1.3.1
dlsw duplicate-path-bias load-balance
!
interface tokenring 0
source-bridge 31 1 400
!
interface tokenring 1
source-bridge 57 1 400
!
interface loopback 0
  ip address 10.1.4.1 255.255.255.0
!
interface serial 0
ip address 10.254.1.1 255.255.255.0
```

R2 Configuration

```
interface tokenring 0/0
  source-bridge 57 1 45
!
interface loopback 0
  ip address 10.1.2.1 255.255.255.0
!
interface Channel 6/0
  no ip address
  csna F500
!
interface Channel 6/2
  no ip address
  lan tokenring 0
    source-bridge 45 1 57
    adapter 0 4000.7513.0001
```

R5 Configuration

```
source-bridge ring-group 500
dlsw local-peer peer-id 10.1.5.1
dlsw remote-peer 0 tcp 10.1.3.1
dlsw duplicate-path-bias load-balance
!
interface tokenring 0
source-bridge 57 1 500
!
interface tokenring 1
source-bridge 31 1 500
!
interface loopback 0
  ip address 10.1.5.1 255.255.255.0
!
interface serial 0
ip address 10.253.1.1 255.255.255.0
```

ESCON Director E5 F5

CIP Ring 37 C4/2 C6/2 CIP Ring 45

R1 Mac Address 4000.7513.0001 T0/0 T0/0 R2 Mac Address 4000.7513.0001

Ring 31 Ring 57

T0 T0

R4 DLSw+ Peer 10.1.4.1 Ring 400 S0 S1 R5 DLSw+ Peer 10.1.5.1 Ring 500

WAN

S1 S0

R3 DLSw+ Peer 10.1.3.1 Ring 300 T1 Ring 1

PU1

Dest Mac 4000.7513.0001

16.6.3 CMPC Connectivity Between Two VTAMs over a Single CIP Router

Figure 16-12 shows an example of using a single CIP router for communications between two VTAMs. Each VTAM is connected to a different CIP on the same router. CMPC is used here to support APPN node-to-node communications between the VTAMs. The configuration shown demonstrates the use of the *rmac* and *rsap* values on the tg command. The tg named VTAM1 has the rmac point to the MAC address of the adapter used for connecting VTAM2. Likewise, the tg named VTAM2 has its rmac point to the MAC address of the adapter used for connecting VTAM1. Likewise, the *rsap* values reflect the SAP addresses used for the other VTAM connection to the CIP.

16.6.4 TN3270 Session Switching Using DLUR/DLUS with VTAM Host Redundancy

The Cisco CIP support for TN3270 enables IBM 3270 data stream traffic to pass through an IP backbone. The TN3270 server support on the Cisco CIP offloads TCP/IP processing from TN3270 termination on the mainframe and presents the TN3270 connections to VTAM as LUs of a LAN-attached PU.

Figure 16-13 illustrates the use of TN3270 server functionality with the added functionality of switching TN3270 connections from one VTAM to another should the primary VTAM become inoperative. The switched major nodes on VTAM must represent the direct PU connections for the TN3270 server along with a definition used for session switching. The configuration uses the APPN virtual routing node for connecting the three mainframe APPN nodes. The transport between the two CIP routers is DLSw+.

16.6.5 VTAM-to-APPN NN Using HPR over CMPC

In this configuration, Figure 16-14, the CIP router uses an ESCON CMPC connection to VTAM. The CIP router uses HPR for communications to VTAM and the APPN network.

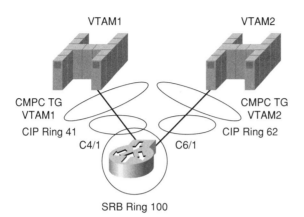

Figure 16-12
*CMPC
configuration for
VTAM-VTAM
communications
over a single
router with two
CIPs.*

SRB Ring 100

```
source-bridge ring-group 100

interface Channel4/1
 no ip address
 no keepalive
 cmpc C010 40  VTAM1  READ
 cmpc C010 41  VTAM1  WRITE
!
interface Channel4/2
 no ip address
 no keepalive
 lan TokenRing 0
 source-bridge 41  5  100
 adapter 4  4000.0000.CC42
tg VTAM1 llc token-adapter 4  34  rmac 4000.000.CC62 rsap  30
!
interface Channel6/1
 no ip address
 no keepalive
 cmpc C020 F4    VTAM2  READ
 cmpc C010 F5  VTAM2  WRITE
!
interface Channel6/2
 lan TokenRing 0
 source-bridge 62  3  100
    adapter 6  4000.0000.CC62
tg VTAM2 llc token-adapter 6   30  rmac 4000.000.CC42 rsap  34
```

Figure 16-13
Configuration for TN3270 session switching using DLUR/DLUS and host redundancy.

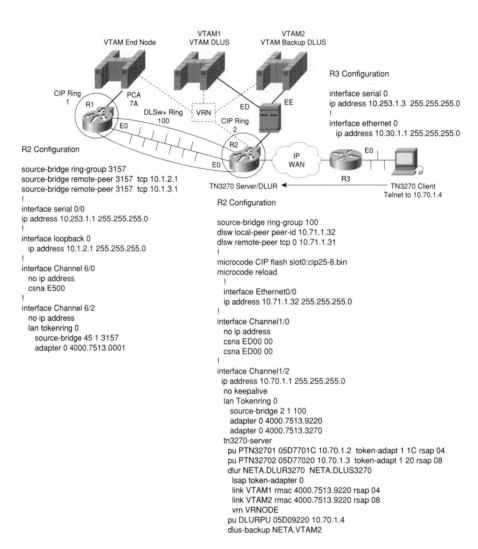

R2 Configuration

```
source-bridge ring-group 3157
source-bridge remote-peer 3157 tcp 10.1.2.1
source-bridge remote-peer 3157 tcp 10.1.3.1
!
interface serial 0/0
ip address 10.253.1.1 255.255.255.0
!
interface loopback 0
 ip address 10.1.2.1 255.255.255.0
!
interface Channel 6/0
 no ip address
 csna E500
!
interface Channel 6/2
 no ip address
 lan tokenring 0
   source-bridge 45 1 3157
   adapter 0 4000.7513.0001
```

R3 Configuration

```
interface serial 0
ip address 10.253.1.3 255.255.255.0
!
interface ethernet 0
 ip address 10.30.1.1 255.255.255.0
```

R2 Configuration

```
source-bridge ring-group 100
dlsw local-peer peer-id 10.71.1.32
dlsw remote-peer tcp 0 10.71.1.31
!
microcode CIP flash slot0:cip25-8.bin
microcode reload
 !
 interface Ethernet0/0
 ip address 10.71.1.32 255.255.255.0
!
interface Channel1/0
 no ip address
 csna ED00 00
 csna ED00 00
!
interface Channel1/2
 ip address 10.70.1.1 255.255.255.0
 no keepalive
 lan Tokenring 0
   source-bridge 2 1 100
   adapter 0 4000.7513.9220
   adapter 0 4000.7513.3270
   tn3270-server
     pu PTN32701 05D7701C 10.70.1.2  token-adapt 1 1C rsap 04
     pu PTN32702 05D77020 10.70.1.3  token-adapt 1 20 rsap 08
     dlur NETA.DLUR3270  NETA.DLUS3270
       lsap token-adapter 0
       link VTAM1 rmac 4000.7513.9220 rsap 04
       link VTAM2 rmac 4000.7513.9220 rsap 08
       vrn VRNODE
     pu DLURPU 05D09220 10.70.1.4
     dlus-backup NETA.VTAM2
```

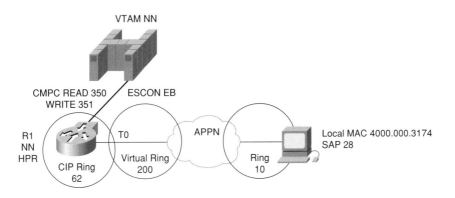

Figure 16-14
*ESCON CMPC
configuration
for connecting
the APPN WAN
to VTAM using
HPR.*

R1 Configuration

```
source-bridge ring-group 200
!
interface tokenring 0
 source-bridge 10  1  200
!
 interface Channel6/1
no ip address
no keepalive
cmpc EB10 50 VTAM1 READ
cmpc EB10 51 VTAM1 WRITE
!
interface Channel6/2
no ip address
no keepalive
lan Tokenring 0
  source-bridge 62    2   200
  adapter 0 4000.7513.0061
lan Tokenring 1
tg VTAM1 llc token-adapter 0  20 rmac 4000.7513.eb10 rsap  24
!
  appn control-point neta.R1
    hpr
    complete
!
appn port CMPC rsrb
    local-sap 24
    rsrb-virtual-station 4000.7513eb10  50  3  200
  complete
!
appn link-station PC
    port CMPC
    lan-dest-address 4000.0000.3174  28
complete
!
appn routing
```

PART III

Appendixes

Migration Scenarios

NOTES

This appendix is provided by Cisco Systems. It is included as an appendix to provide further information on migrating an IBM FEP based approach to Cisco CIP based configuration. The text is also available on the Cisco website at http://www.cisco.com/warp/public/731/data/data3_rg.htm.

This chapter describes basic configuration and shows several sample networks. For each network, it describes the network design, explains when and why to use that network design, and in some cases briefly describes how to migrate from or coexist with a FEP. Examples include:

- Single CIP to a single host
- Dual CIP to a single host
- Multi-LPAR single CIP
- APPN network
- APPN in a sysplex environment
- SNI-to-APPN border node migration

SNA COMMUNICATION OVER CSNA

SNA nodes communicate to the CIP using LLC2, a connection-oriented data link protocol for LANs. An LLC2 stack on the CIP card communicates with either the adjacent SNA device (over a physical Token Ring) or to DLSw+ or APPN running in the channel-attached router, as illustrated in Figure A-1.

Figure A-1
Communication between CSNA in the CIP and SNA Nodes

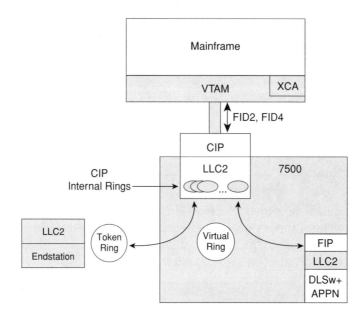

The CIP running CSNA will support multiple internal LAN interfaces, each of which looks like a LAN port to VTAM. (VTAM supports a maximum of 18 LAN ports.) However, only a single LAN port is required. CSNA also supports up to 256 open LLC2 SAPs per LAN port.

VTAM DEFINITIONS

The CIP running CSNA is not an SNA addressable node—it has no PU or LU appearance. CSNA is defined to the host control program (MVS or VM) as a channel-to-channel machine (a 3088). This provides VTAM a physical connection out to the LAN through a subchannel.

To enable VTAM communication over the CIP to SNA devices, you must configure an XCA major node and a switched major node to VTAM. The XCA major node allows VTAM to communicate with the CIP, and the switched major node definition allows SNA devices to communicate with VTAM over the CIP.

External Communication Adapter Major Node Definition

Define an XCA major node for each connection (port) between VTAM and a CSNA connection. A single XCA major node can support up to 4096 LLC2 connections, although experience has shown that better results are achieved with 3000 or fewer LLC2 connections per XCA major node. If more LLC2 connections are needed, define additional XCA major nodes. Multiple XCA major nodes can also be configured for availability, with each one pointing to a different CIP.

The CSNA feature is defined to the host control program (MVS or VM) as being a channel-to-channel adapter or machine (CTCA), for example, a 3088. VTAM identifies the CSNA gateway through a combination of the following:

- ADAPNO—Adapter number

- CUADD—Subchannel address

- SAPADDR—SAP address

```
XCANAME VBUILD TYPE=XCA            ** EXTERNAL COMMUNICATION ADAPT**

PORTNAME PORT ADAPNO=?,            ** RELATIVE ADAPTER NUMBER     ** X
                 CUADDR=???,       ** CHANNEL UNIT ADDRESS        ** X
                 MEDIUM=RING,      ** LAN TYPE                    ** X
                 SAPADDR=4         ** SERVICE ACCESS POINT ADDRESS**

GRPNAME GROUP ANSWER=ON,           ** PU DIAL INTO VTAM CAPABILITY** X
                 AUTOGEN=(5,L,P),  ** AUTO GENERATE LINES AND PUS ** X
                 CALL=INOUT,       ** IN/OUT CALLING CAPABILITY   ** X
                 DIAL=YES,         ** SWITCHED CONNECTION         ** X
                 ISTATUS=ACTIVE    ** INITIAL ACTIVATION STATUS   **
```

Switched Major Node Definition

Configure one or more switched major nodes. Within a switched major node definition, configure every SNA PU that will access VTAM through the CIP. For each PU configure its associated LUs. Many networks today already have the SNA devices defined in a switched major node. For example, if the devices attach to a FEP over Token Ring, they are already defined as part of a switched major node. In this case, the only change is to add the XCA major node.

Example:

```
SWMSNAME  VBUILD    TYPE=SWNET,       **                              X
                    MAXGRP=14,        **                              X
                    MAXNO=64          **

PUNAME    PU        ADDR=01,          **                              X
                    PUTYPE=2          **                              X
                    IDBLK=???         **                              X
                    IDNUM=???         **                              X
                    ISTATUS=ACTIVE    **                              X
LUNAME1   LU        LOCADDR=02
LUNAME2   LU        LOCADDR=03
LUNAME3   LU        LOCADDR=04
LUNAME4   LU        LOCADDR=05
LUNAME5   LU        LOCADDR=06
```

ROUTER CONFIGURATION

The router must be configured to:

- Bridge traffic from a physical LAN or a router component (DLSw+, SRB, SR/TLB, and so forth) onto the router virtual ring

- Bridge data from the router virtual ring to one of the CIP internal rings, or connect a data link user (APPN, DSPU) to one of the CIP internal rings

- Connect the CIP to VTAM

Figure A-2 shows the major configuration parameters of the CIP and of the Token Ring interfaces and how they are logically combined using the source-bridge definition. The CIP ring is referred to as an internal ring. The RSP ring is referred to as a virtual ring.

Configure an adapter on the CIP to be associated with the XCA major node definition. For each adapter configured CSNA creates an internal Token Ring. A virtual bridge connects the CSNA internal ring to a virtual ring group in the router. The Token Ring interface processor (TRIP) is also configured to connect to the same virtual ring group as the CIP.

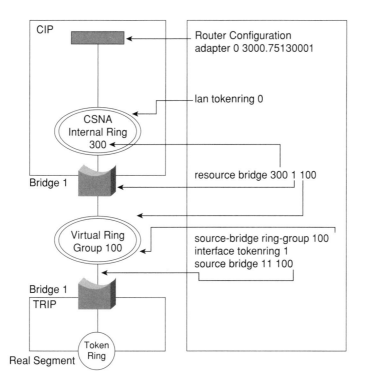

Figure A-2
Using Virtual Rings to Provide Connectivity

Configuration Relationships in the ESCON Environment

Figure A-3 shows the relationship among router configuration, VTAM parameters, and MVS IOCP generation commands when the CIP connects via an Escon director. Figure A-4 shows the relationship among router configuration, VTAM parameters, and MVS IOCP generation commands when the CIP connects via bus and tag.

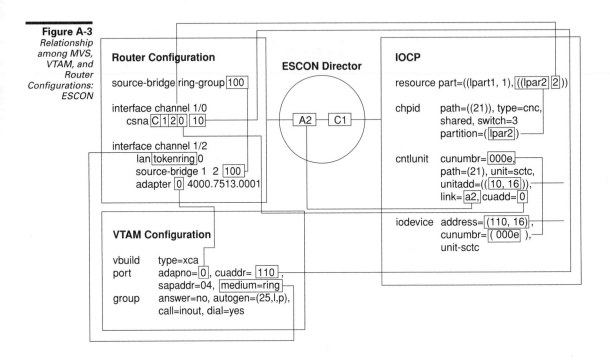

Figure A-3
Relationship among MVS, VTAM, and Router Configurations: ESCON

Configuration Relationships in the Bus and Tag Environment

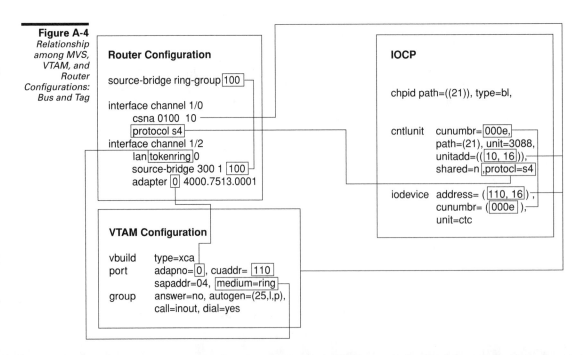

Figure A-4
Relationship among MVS, VTAM, and Router Configurations: Bus and Tag

SCENARIO 1: SINGLE CIP TO SINGLE HOST

The first scenario is a network that replaces a FEP with a CIP. As shown in Figure A-5, there is a single mainframe in this network. Historically, IBM SNA networks were built using the IBM FEP and remote terminals were connected via SDLC links. In the Before scenario a second FEP was in place for backup only.

In the After scenario one FEP has been replaced with a channel-attached router with a CIP. Both the CIP and the remaining FEP have the same MAC address. Eventually the second FEP will also be replaced but for now it provides SNI connectivity to a supplier and can also function as a backup to the CIP. DLSw+ is used to transport SNA traffic from remote sites to the central site.

Once data reaches the headquarters site DLSw+ sends most traffic to the CIP which will typically be the first to respond to explorers, but in the event that the CIP is not available, the FEP is automatically used.

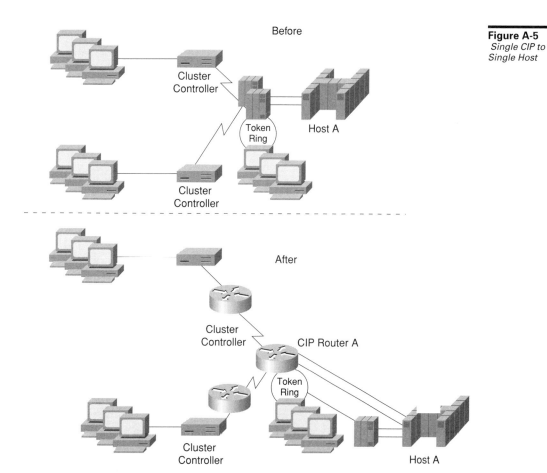

Figure A-5
Single CIP to Single Host

Reasons for Change

The FEP was at capacity and the customer preferred to use their information services dollars on technology that would carry them into the future as well as address today's requirements. In addition, the Cisco channel-attached router replacing the leased FEP would pay for itself in 18 months—with savings coming from lease costs and monthly NCP licensing costs. Migrating from an SDLC/FEP network to a LAN/channel-attached router network simplified SNA system configuration significantly and reduced the downtime for planned outages. Finally, the customer planned to use TCP mainframe applications in the near future and wanted to build an infrastructure that enabled them to do that.

Design Choices

This customer opted to combine SNA functionality (DLSw+) and WAN connections in the CIP router because the network was very small (25 sites). The design provides a very safe fallback to the FEP but at the same time enables SRB dynamics and configuration simplicity.

Configuration

XCA Major Node Configuration

```
XCANODE    VBUILD TYPE=XCA
PRTNODE    PORT   ADAPNO=0,CUADDR=770,SAPADDR=04,MEDIUM=RING,TIMER=30
*
GRPNODE    GROUP  ANSWER=ON,                                           X
                  AUTOGEN=(100,L,P),                                   X
                  CALL=INOUT,                                          X
                  DIAL=YES,                                            X
                  ISTATUS=ACTIVE
```

Router Configuration

```
!
source-bridge ring-group 100
!
interface tokenring 1/0
 no ip address
 no ip route-cache
```

```
    ring-speed 16
    source-bridge 200 1 100
!
interface Channel1/0
 no ip address
 csna 0100 70
!
interface Channel1/2
 no ip address
 no keepalive
 lan TokenRing 0
   source-bridge 300 1 100
   adapter 0 4000.7000.0001
 !
end
```

Implementation Overview

The first step is to implement DLSw+ from the remote site to the central site and to change the FEP access from SDLC to Token Ring. As part of this step, configure the VTAM switched major nodes. Once that is done, the following steps enable the CIP in this configuration:

1. Perform IOCP generations to configure the channel definitions, as shown in either Figure A-3 or Figure A-4.

2. Configure VTAM XCA major node.

3. Configure the attached router with the CIP definitions and bridge traffic from the internal ring group to the CIP virtual ring.

4. Vary the channel online (Vary E00,ONLINE).

5. Confirm the CIP is online (Display U,,,E00,1).

6. Activate the VTAM XCA (Vary NET,ACT,ID=name_of_member).

SCENARIO 2: REDUNDANT CIP TO SINGLE HOST

Initially this site had a 3745-410 running in twin-standby mode to provide better network resiliency. In this case there is one active NCP while the second one is in standby mode. The second NCP takes over only if the first NCP has problems. This allows quick recovery from storage-related failures and from a CCU hardware check. Note that the idle CCU is totally inactive unless a failure is detected. With the inclusion of duplicate Token Ring addressing this design can also provide another level of network redundancy.

Optionally, the 3745-410 could be configured in twin-backup mode where each CCU controls approximately half the network. It is the equivalent of having two 210s running at half capacity. If there is a failure in one CCU the other CCU can take over just as in the first example. However, only half the resources are impacted and hence recovery is faster.

Irrespective of the configuration in use, the use of CSNA on two Cisco 7500 series routers with one or more CIP cards can provide better load sharing and redundancy features.

The After scenario is designed so there is no single point of failure in the network. The redundant CIP to a single host scenario is often used when the end systems cannot afford the downtime of a failure. For many companies that require online access to provide 24/7 customer support, the loss of host access for even a short period of time can incur a significant loss in both income and credibility. It is important for these networks to implement a solution that will avoid or minimize the amount of downtime due to network problems.

Also for these companies the redundancy option provides the necessary network configuration to perform maintenance or configuration changes to the network with minimal impact to the end-system users.

Providing redundancy to the single CIP to single host solution is quite straightforward. In Figure A-6 two Cisco 7500 routers, each with a CIP, are deployed in place of the 3745-410. In this example both CIPs have the same virtual MAC address. When one router is not available, the SNA end system will automatically find the backup router using standard SRB protocols. Note that in both the Before and the After networks, loss of a channel-attached gateway is disruptive.

Reasons for Change

The 3745-410 did not have the capacity to support the entire network if one of the processors was down. During outages, the entire network slowed down. To address this problem with more FEPs was not cost-effective. In addition, this enterprise was considering migrating their campus to FDDI, which the 3745 does not support. With the Cisco channel-attached routers, they could migrate their campus to either FDDI or ATM in the future.

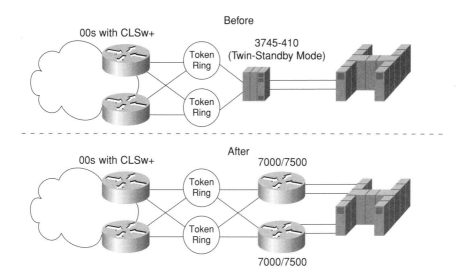

Figure A-6
Redundant CIPs to Single Host

Design Choices

In this network they opted to separate DLSw+ from the channel-attached router. This minimizes both scheduled and unscheduled outages in their network. Also, they already had DLSw+ installed in these routers before they installed the CIPs. Hence, this simplified migration. Finally, as their DLSw+ routers (Cisco 4700s) reach capacity, it is less costly to add a Cisco 4700 router than a Cisco 7500 with a CIP. Either of the channel-attached routers can handle their entire capacity today, and if the network grows, they have sufficient slots in their 7500s to add CIPs to their channel-attached routers.

The network uses load balancing across central site DLSw+ routers and duplicate Token Rings to ensure there is no single point of failure, as shown in Figure A-7.

Router Configuration

This configuration uses the same MAC address on internal Token Ring LANs of two different routers.

```
RTRA
!
source-bridge  ring-group  100
int  tok  0/0
source-bridge  200  1  100
int  tok  0/1
source-bridge  201  2  100
!
```

```
interface  Channel1/0
  no  ip  address
  csna  0100  70
!
lan  TokenRing  0
  source-bridge  300  1  100
  adapter  0  4000.0000.0001
!
  RTRB
!
source-bridge  ring-group  101
int  tok  0/0
source-bridge  200  1  101
int  tok  0/1
source-bridge  201  2  101
!
interface  Channel1/0
  no  ip  address
  csna  0100  80
!
lan  TokenRing  0
    source-bridge  400  1  101
    adapter  0  4000.0000.0001
!
```

SCENARIO 3: SINGLE CIP TO MULTIPLE HOST

This scenario shows a legacy SNA network with several remote sites connected via SDLC links to cluster controllers. Also, a high-speed line was connected to a remote 3745 at a site that demanded high-speed connection back to the mainframe and had more remote users than a cluster controller could support. This enterprise also had a separate multiprotocol network running in parallel.

At the data center there are two VTAMs. One is used primarily for production and the other used primarily for testing. There is little, if any, cross-domain routing. Figure A-8 shows the Before and After networks.

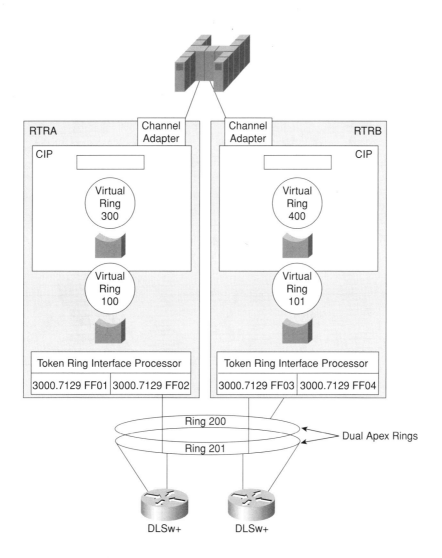

Figure A-7
Dual Routers with Duplicate MACs

Reasons for Change

The primary reasons for change were to minimize costs and increase throughput and flexibility. The remote 3745 was replaced with a lower-cost Cisco 4500 router to eliminate recurring NCP and maintenance charges, consolidate multiprotocol and SNA WAN traffic, and simplify network configuration. The central site FEP was replaced with a channel-attached router to increase channel throughput and to enable TCP/IP on the mainframe in the future.

Figure A-8
*Replacing a
Single FEP
with a
Channel-
Attached
Router*

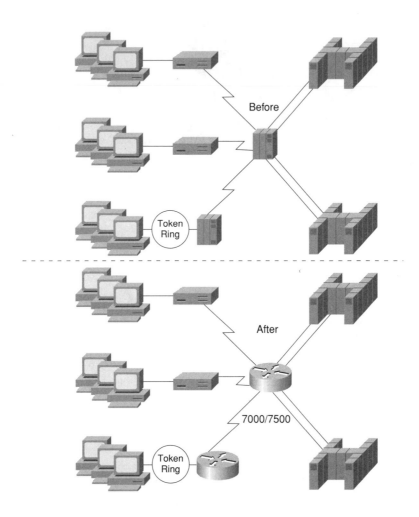

Design Choices

This enterprise chose not to implement APPN even though they had multiple main-frames. The reason is that all SNA sessions were in the same domain. The VTAM in the second mainframe was simply used for testing and backup. They chose not to imple-ment two channel-attached routers for redundancy, but they did select to use two CIPs in a single channel-attached router. This created higher availability than they had pre-viously, and provided an option in the future to separate CIP functionality across mul-tiple CIPs. In the future they plan to add TN3270 server capability to the CIP to allow access to VTAM applications from Web-based clients, and they also anticipate a need for TCP/IP on the mainframe. Figure A-9 shows the logical configuration.

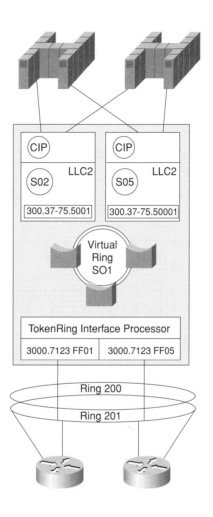

Figure A-9
Dual CIPs in a Single Router

Router Configuration

```
!
source-bridge  ring-group  501
int  tok  0/0
  source-bridge  200  1  501
int  tok  0/1
source-bridge  201  2  501
!
interface  Channel1/0
  no  ip  address
  csna  0100  70
```

```
!
interface  Channel1/1
  no  ip  address
  csna  0101  80
!
interface  Channel1/2
  no  ip  address
  no  keepalive
  lan  TokenRing  0
    source-bridge  502  1  501
    adapter  0  4000.3745.5001
lan  TokenRing  1
    source-bridge  505  1  501
    adapter  1  4000.3745.5001
!
```

SCENARIO 4: MIGRATING TO APPN

In the Before environment, the FEP provided SNA routing. The FEP can be replaced without loss of function by implementing APPN in a channel-attached router. APPN was being considered for this data center even if the FEP were not being replaced. Recent enhancements to VTAM's APPN implementation simplify network definition and enhance availability.

This scenario shows the replacement of the FEP with a Cisco router running APPN/DLUR. One host is configured as an NN and the other as an EN. The NN provides NN server function for the EN and provides DLUS functionality. Figure A-10 illustrates this scenario.

NOTES

For more detail on APPN, refer to the Cisco *APPN Design and Implementation* guide.

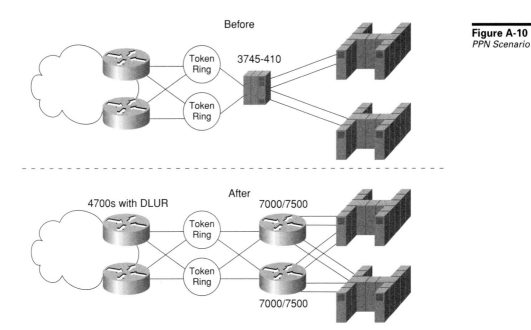

Before

3745-410

After

4700s with DLUR   7000/7500

7000/7500

Reasons for Change

This enterprise was interested in simplifying their SNA network and reducing their FEP dependency to reduce costs. They also wanted to improve throughput at the data center. Although they were starting with APPN/ISR routing, they intend to migrate to HPR in the future. With HPR, loss of a channel gateway, LAN adapter, or channel adapter can be dynamically recovered without disrupting end-user sessions.

Design Choices

This enterprise chose to put DLUR functionality in their existing data center routers to maximize the scalability of their channel-attached routers and minimize the cost of their total network. In addition, when they migrate to HPR, this design will allow them to nondisruptively reroute around the failure of a channel-attached router by configuring the channel-attached router as an ANR node.

Router Configuration

This partial router configuration shows that there are three required parameters and one optional parameter for defining an APPN connection. Refer to the VTAM configuration manuals for more details on the changes required to VTAM.

The APPN CONTROL-POINT command is used to identify the router.

The LINK-STATION defines the connection to the router. (This statement is required in at least one of two APPN nodes connected over a link.)

The PORT defines a point of connection into the APPN network.

The APPN ROUTING command is optional and will automatically start APPN routing when the router is started.

4700 Router Configuration

```
version  11.0
!
hostname  RTRA
!
enable  password  cisco
!
appn  control-point  NETA.RTRA
dlus  NETA.VTAMA
  dlur
  complete
!
!
appn  link-station  linkA
complete
!
appn  port  porta  dlsw
complete
!
appn  routing
!
end
```

APPN IN A PARALLEL SYSPLEX ENVIRONMENT

APPN is required in VTAM, at a minimum, in order to take advantage of a Parallel Sysplex environment. In the Before picture illustrated in Figure A-11, APPN is implemented in each VTAM host, while the FEPs and the rest of the network continue to use subarea protocols. This environment allows SNA sessions to take advantage of generic resources. The Generic Resource feature of VTAM enables end-user sessions to be dynamically spread across alternate, identical images of an application. The end user logs on to a generic resource (for example, CICS), and the CMC host (which is also an ICN) establishes the session with a specific application (perhaps CICS01) running in one of the migration data hosts. The CMC/ICN balances CICS sessions across all the sysplex processors, and recovery from the failure of any single processor is disruptive but dynamic. In VTAM V4R4 and the latest CICS, this recovery will be nondisruptive, using a facility know as Multi-Node Persistent Sessions (MNPS).

In the After picture shown in Figure A-11, data center routers provide DLUR function for legacy traffic. The Cisco channel-attached router can handle the capacity of multiple FEPs, so there are only two channel-attached routers in the After picture. The DLUR function was installed in existing data center routers to maximize scalability and availability. The DLUR router routes traffic directly to the correct migration data host using APPN routing. (In the After picture, if there were really no FEPs, you could convert the ICNs to NNs and the MDHs to ENs.)

SCENARIO 5: MIGRATING FROM SNI TO APPN

In the Before environment, Enterprise A connected to a value-added network over a back-to-back SNI connection. Enterprise A had a small network with a single FEP. They wanted to eliminate the FEP, but they were using it for SNI.

In the After environment, the FEP in Enterprise A has been replaced with a Cisco channel-attached router. In the first phase, the router was configured for local DLSw+ conversion from LAN to SDLC. In the second phase, for which the configuration in Figure A-12 applies, APPN/DLUR functionality was added to allow the channel-attached router to directly route all steady-state session traffic going to the value-added network, without requiring VTAM. In the value-added network, VTAM migrated to become an ICN. It continues to use subarea protocols for attaching to other networks, but uses APPN for attaching to this network. In the future, as more enterprises select this connectivity option, the value-added network provider hopes to replace some FEPs with Cisco channel-attached routers.

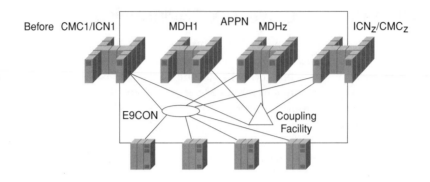

For more detail on APPN, refer to the Cisco *APPN Design and Implementation* guide.

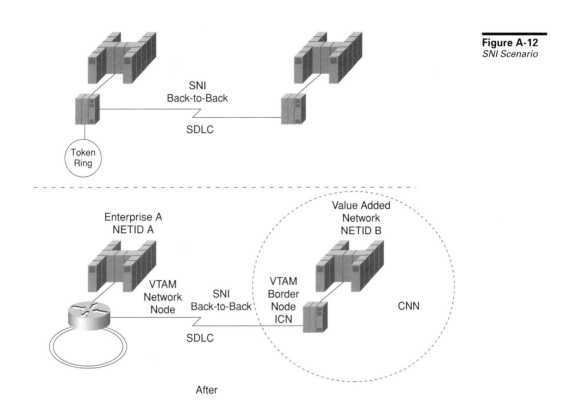

Figure A-12
SNI Scenario

Reasons for Change

Enterprise A was interested in reducing their FEP costs. The value-added service provider had a large number of FEPs supporting SNI, and by migrating one customer, they only put a small dent in their FEP SNI traffic. However, they also recognized that as soon as one migration was successful, they could offer this alternative to other clients. They were willing to do this for Enterprise A in the hopes that it would allow them to migrate other customers in the future.

Design Choices

Enterprise A and the value-added service provider chose to use the border node (BN) function of APPN. They selected this alternative because Enterprise A was already migrating to APPN/DLUR, and this option gave them the most application flexibility (either session end could initiate the connection) while at the same time providing topology independence.

Router Configuration

The following shows the router configuration in the final phase:

```
interface  Channel  1/0
  no  ip  address
  no  keepalive
  csna  0100  00
interface  Channel  1/2
  no  ip  address
  no  keepalive
  lan  TokenRing  0
  source-bridge  7  1  1000
  adapter  0  4000.7507.0000
interface  Serial4/0
  no  ip  address
  encapsulation  sdlc
  no  ip  route-cache  optimum
  bandwidth  64
  no  keepalive
  nrzi-encoding
  sdlc  vmac  4000.3745.0000
  sdlc  address  01
  sdlc  partner  4000.7507.0000  01
  sdlc  dlsw  1
appn  control-point  NETA.CP7507
  dlus  NETA.VTAMA
  dlur
  complete
!
appn  port  CIP  rsrb
  desired-max-send-btu-size  1500
  max-rcv-btu-size  1500
  retry-limit  infinite
  rsrb-virtual-station  4000.7507.0001  6  1  1000
  complete
!
appn  port  SDLC0  Serial4/0
  sdlc-sec-addr  02
  complete
!
appn  link-station  VANFEP
```

```
    port  SLDC0
    retry-limit  infinite
    sdlc-dest-address  0
    complete
!
appn  link-station  VTAMA
  port  CIP
lan-dest-address  4000.7507.0000
retry-limit  infinite
complete
!
appn  routing
!
end
```

APPN Memory Requirements

NOTES

This appendix is provided by Cisco Systems. It is included to assist in developing the memory requirements of Cisco routers when implementing IBM APPN services. The text is also available on the Cisco website at

http://www.cisco.com/warp/public/731/Protocol/appnm_wp.htm

The purpose of this paper is to provide guidelines for calculating APPN memory requirements. The information is presented in a format that assumes someone is upgrading from an existing Cisco IOS environment to APPN. Obviously, if this is a new router additional memory will be required to handle the interfaces, other protocols, and the base IOS.

It is important to point out that this reflects only one aspect of a router's performance. Memory alone cannot determine how many routers must be used for a particular size network. The throughput rate of the router will be a factor. Line speed, packet size, and pacing window size will also impact performance. Unique to SNA environments, recovery time—the length of time it takes to restore user sessions after an outage occurs—will also be a critical factor. Other aspects of performance will be addressed separately.

RECOMMENDATIONS

As part of the APPN launch, it was announced that a minimum of 16 megabytes of DRAM and 8 megabytes of flash would be required to support APPN. Subsequent testing has shown us that this will not always be the case. In general, the following guidelines should be your starting point:

- With the 2500 family, 8 megabytes of DRAM and 8 megabytes of flash should be the initial estimate. Generally, the limiting factors in this environment will be the number of sessions that can be supported by the CPU and the number of interfaces.

- With the 4000 and 4000 M, 16 megabytes of DRAM, 4 megabytes of flash, and 4 megabytes of shared DRAM are the minimum amounts of memory required.

- With the 4500, 32 megabytes DRAM, 4 megabytes of flash, and 16 megabytes of shared DRAM will support most configurations. For the 4500 M, 16 megabytes of DRAM, 4 megabytes of flash and 16 megabytes of shared DRAM provide the minimum memory configuration. Larger networks will require 32 megabytes of DRAM.

- For the 7000 family, 16 megabytes of DRAM may be adequate for very small networks, although 64 megabytes of DRAM will be more likely in most installations.

The following memory formula was created as part of the testing of APPN in Cisco's Engineering lab. These are considered rough estimates, but these are accurate enough to provide predictable results. Total APPN memory requirements can be calculated by using these estimates:

Memory Requirements	Kbytes
To start APPN (control blocks, stacks, etc.)	760.0
Each APPN port defined	1.5
Each local APPN link, defined but not active	1.5
Each active APPN/LEN (Low Entry Networking)/ subarea link which does not have CP-CP (Control Point-to-Control Point) sessions	6.5
Each APPN link which has CP-CP sessions	12.5
Each connection network defined	1.5
Each network node in the network topology which is not adjacent to this node	0.4
Each connection between network nodes in the network topology (do not include connections of which this node is an end point)	0.9
Each PU (physical unit) served by DLUR (Dependent LU Requester) on this node	1.5
Each LU (logical unit) served by DLUR on this node	0.9
Each DLUS (Dependent LU Server) with which this node has a DLUR/S connection active	15.0
Each active intermediate session	1.3
Each cached or registered resource in the APPN directory	0.3

The above calculations represent memory requirements in "idle" status–no data traffic is flowing. As sessions are started, data begins flowing, APPN searches are in progress, and APPN consumes additional memory to communicate between components and with other APPN nodes. This "operational" portion of memory usage is much harder to estimate since it depends on things such as the number of searches outstanding at any one time and other elements which depend on network traffic and usage. We have observed during testing that the total storage rarely exceeds double the "idle" time storage, so we will double our estimates in the examples shown to conservatively allow for this operational memory.

The above numbers also do not address buffers required. On the 4000 series, where buffers are carved from shared memory, APPN can run small to medium networks on routers with 4 megabytes of shared memory. Larger APPN networks (more than 100 or so attached APPN or LEN nodes or many sessions) will require additional shared memory. With IOS 11.0 each interface carves out interface-specific private buffer pools, leaving less memory for public buffer growth.

On the 2500 and 7000 series, buffers should be taken into account when planning for main memory usage. The number of CP-CP sessions and end user sessions will influence this.

EXAMPLES

The following examples are included to give you some idea of how the memory formula works. Each represents an actual customer that Cisco is working with to implement APPN in their network.

Example 1—Large Hierarchical Network

This customer is a large government agency. There are eight mainframes in the data center, one of which is a network node and the remainder are either end nodes or LEN nodes. These are channel-attached to controllers that interface to an FDDI LAN. One hundred twenty-five Cisco routers are also attached to the FDDI LAN and provide data center access to the remote sites.

Each Cisco router at the data center is attached to four remote sites. Each remote site has a single Cisco router attached to a token ring with 30 Communications Manager/2 (CM/2) end nodes. Each end node has 20 mainframe sessions: 4-3270 sessions requiring DLUR on the remote Cisco router and 16 LU 6.2 sessions. While connections to four remote routers may seem like a small number, the large number of end user sessions dictates memory usage in this case.

Figure B-1
Full APPN Network

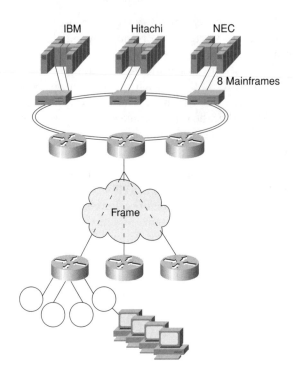

With 625 network nodes in the network, border node is required to create smaller sub-networks. Without border node, the topology database would become too large and topology exchange traffic would be the predominant network traffic. Five subnetworks have been created, each with 125 network nodes–25 central site routers and 100 remote routers.

This exercise assumes that each remote router has 31 pairs of CP-CP session: 30 pairs of NN-EN sessions with attached CM/2 nodes and 1 pair with the central site router. The central site routers each have 6 pairs of CP-CP sessions: 4 with remote routers and 2 with other central-site routers for redundancy.

The topology database for each network will show 125 network nodes and 101 TGs: 100 TGs between the 25 central-site routers and their remote nodes and the FDDI connection network.

Each remote router supports 600 sessions: 480 LU 6.2 sessions and 120-3270 sessions requiring DLUR. For the DLUR support, each CM/2 node is assumed to be a single PU with 4 LUs–one for each 3270 session. Each central site router supports 2400 intermediate sessions.

There is currently no peer-to-peer traffic between remote sites, but future plans call for this capability.

The following chart estimates APPN memory requirements for resources in the remote routers in this example. In addition to the network characteristics mentioned above, it reflects the following assumptions:

- The base memory includes port definitions and the base control blocks and processes required to initialize APPN.

- The number of NNs and TGs in the topology database was determined by taking the total number of NNs or TGs in a single network and subtracting the ones directly attached to the given node. For example, there is a total of 101 TGs in a network and one was subtracted for the TG connecting the router to the data center router. Likewise, for the NNs, one was subtracted for this router and one for the data center router it's attached to.

- Only one mainframe serves as the DLUS node and manages all 3270 sessions.

- Once the memory is determined using the formula, it's doubled to include the operational memory necessary to communicate between components and with adjacent nodes.

Example 1–Remote Router

Feature	Mbytes each	Total number	Total Mbytes
Base memory to run APPN	1	1	1
Active link, no CP-CP session	0.0065	0	0
Active link, CP-CP session	0.0125	31	0.3875
Connection network	0.0015	0	0
Each non-adjacent NN in topology database	0.0004	123	0.0492
Each non-adjacent TG in topology database	0.0009	100	0.09
DLUR PU served by this router	0.0015	30	0.045
DLUR LU served by this router	0.0009	120	0.108
DLUS VTAM	0.015	1	0.015
Each active session	0.0013	600	0.78
Each resource in directory	0.0003	700	0.21
APPN resources memory requirement			2.6847
APPN operational memory w/o buffers			5.3694

Additional memory will be required for buffers for session data. This will be dependent on the frequency of messages and size of packets. Given this, it's reasonable to assume that APPN will add 8 or 16 megabytes of memory to this router. This memory will be in addition to that needed to support the base IOS and any other protocols needed in the box. Because of this memory requirement this customer has chosen 4X00 routers with 16 or 32 megabytes of memory.

The following chart summarizes the memory formula for the data center routers:

Example 1–Data Center Router

Feature	Mbytes each	Total number	Total Mbytes
Base memory to run APPN	1	1	1
Active link, no CP-CP session	0.0065	0	0
Active link, CP-CP session	0.0125	6	0.075
Connection network	0.0015	1	0.0015
Each non-adjacent NN in topo database	0.0004	118	0.0472
Each non-adjacent TG in topo database	0.0009	96	0.0864
DLUR PU served by this router	0.0015	0	0
DLUR LU served by this router	0.0009	0	0
DLUS VTAM	0.015	0	0
Each active session	0.0013	2400	3.12
Each resource in directory	0.0003	1000	0.3
APPN resources memory requirement			4.6301
APPN			

C

CIP Configuration Examples for Mapping Cisco IOS-IBM VTAM-IBM IOCP Parameters

This appendix provides configuration-mapping examples. These examples are provided by Cisco Systems and are extremely useful in understanding the interplay among the various parameter values associated with Cisco IOS, IBM VTAM, and IBM OS/390 (MVS) IOCP.

EXAMPLE 1: APPN OVER TOKEN RING TO CIP ROUTER

This example configuration depicts the physical and logical views of connecting an APPN network over a Token-Ring interface of a channel-attached router. In the example, the router labeled NETA.ZAPHOD is an APPN NN connecting to the channel-attached router over a Token-Ring Interface Processor (TRIP). The channel-attached router is defined as an APPN NN with the name NETA.ARTHUR connecting to the VTAM APPN NN NET.CPAC using an ESCON Director.

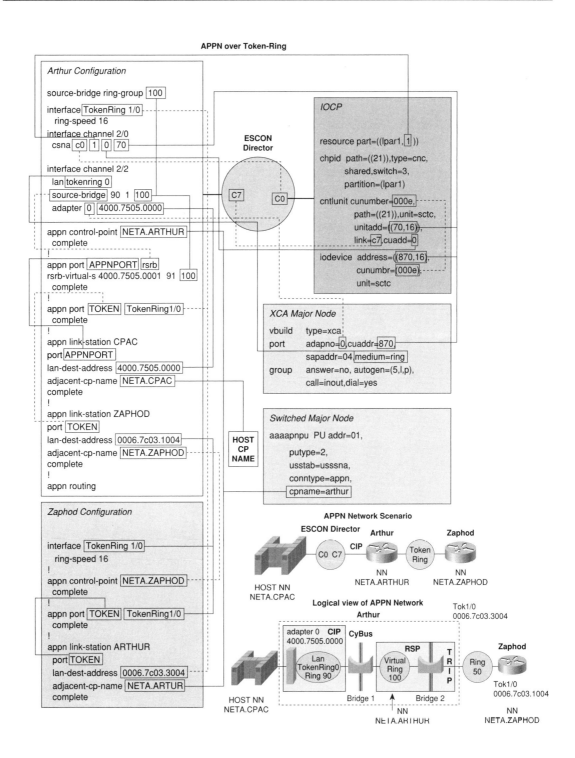

EXAMPLE 2: APPN OVER ATM

This example configuration depicts the physical and logical views of connecting an APPN network over an ATM interface of a channel attached router. In the example, the router labeled NETA.ZAPHOD is an APPN NN connecting to the channel attached router over an ATM Interface Processor (AIP). The channel-attached router is defined as an APPN NN with the name NETA.ARTHUR connecting to the VTAM APPN NN NET.CPAC using an ESCON Director.

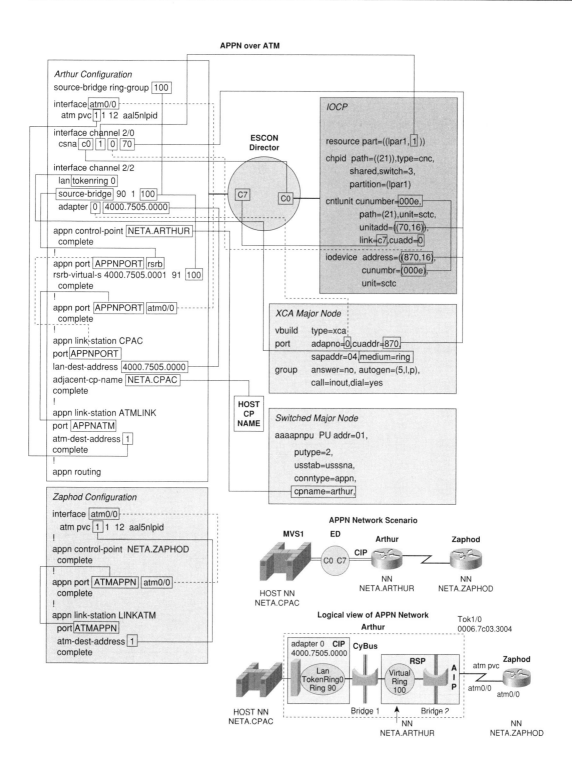

APPN over ATM

Arthur Configuration
source-bridge ring-group 100

interface atm0/0
  atm pvc 1 1 12 aal5nlpid

interface channel 2/0
  csna c0 1 0 70

interface channel 2/2
  lan tokenring 0
  source-bridge 90 1 100
  adapter 0 4000.7505.0000

appn control-point NETA.ARTHUR
complete
!
appn port APPNPORT rsrb
rsrb-virtual-s 4000.7505.0001 91 100
  complete
!
appn port APPNPORT atm0/0
  complete
!
appn link-station CPAC
port APPNPORT
lan-dest-address 4000.7505.0000
adjacent-cp-name NETA.CPAC
complete
!
appn link-station ATMLINK
port APPNATM
atm-dest-address 1
complete
!
appn routing

Zaphod Configuration
interface atm0/0
  atm pvc 1 1 12 aal5nlpid
!
appn control-point NETA.ZAPHOD
  complete
!
appn port ATMAPPN atm0/0
  complete
!
appn link-station LINKATM
port ATMAPPN
atm-dest-address 1
complete

ESCON Director
C7   C0

HOST CP NAME

IOCP
resource part=((lpar1, 1))
chpid path=((21)),type=cnc,
       shared,switch=3,
       partition=(lpar1)
cntlunit cunumber=000e,
       path=(21),unit=sctc,
       unitadd=((70,16)),
       link=c7,cuadd=0
iodevice address=((870,16),
       cunumbr=000e,
       unit=sctc

XCA Major Node
vbuild type=xca
port   adapno=0,cuaddr=870
        sapaddr=04,medium=ring
group   answer=no, autogen=(5,l,p),
        call=inout,dial=yes

Switched Major Node
aaaapnpu PU addr=01,
        putype=2,
        usstab=usssna,
        conntype=appn,
        cpname=arthur,

APPN Network Scenario

MVS1   ED   Arthur   Zaphod
       C0 C7   CIP
                      NN   NN
HOST NN   NETA.ARTHUR   NETA.ZAPHOD
NETA.CPAC

Logical view of APPN Network
Arthur   Tok1/0
                                0006.7c03.3004
adapter 0 CIP   CyBus
4000.7505.0000   Zaphod
       Lan   RSP   A   atm pvc
       TokenRing0 Virtual I
       Ring 90   Ring   P   atm0/0
                   100   atm0/0

HOST NN   Bridge 1   Bridge 2
NETA.CPAC   NN   NN
                  NETA.ARTHUR   NETA.ZAPHOD

EXAMPLE 3: APPN OVER FRAME RELAY

This example configuration depicts the physical and logical views of connecting an APPN network over a Frame-Relay connection of a channel-attached router. In the example, the router labeled NETA.ZAPHOD is an APPN NN connecting to the channel-attached router over a Fast Serial Interface Processor (FSIP) used for the Frame-Relay connection. The channel-attached router is defined as an APPN NN with the name NETA.ARTHUR connecting to the VTAM APPN NN NET.CPAC using an ESCON Director.

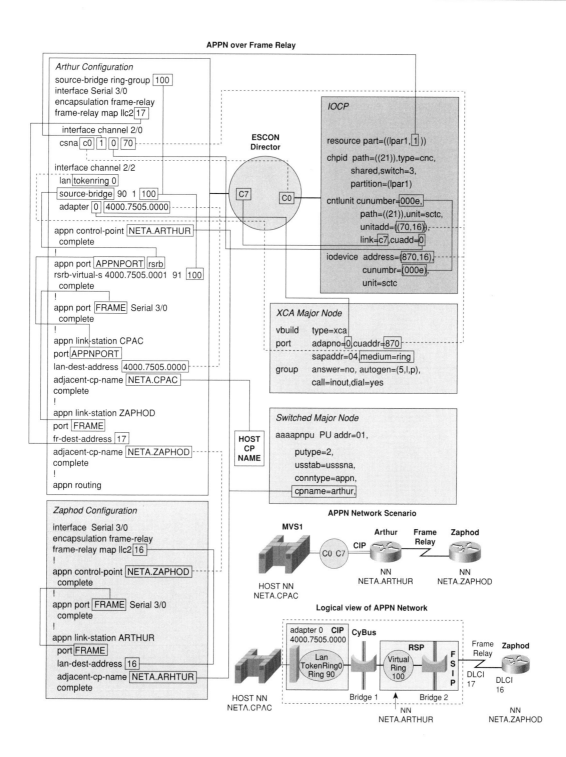

APPN over Frame Relay

Arthur Configuration

source-bridge ring-group 100
interface Serial 3/0
encapsulation frame-relay
frame-relay map llc2 17

interface channel 2/0
csna c0 1 0 70

interface channel 2/2
lan tokenring 0
source-bridge 90 1 100
adapter 0 4000.7505.0000

appn control-point NETA.ARTHUR
complete
!
appn port APPNPORT rsrb
rsrb-virtual-s 4000.7505.0001 91 100
complete
!
appn port FRAME Serial 3/0
complete
!
appn link-station CPAC
port APPNPORT
lan-dest-address 4000.7505.0000
adjacent-cp-name NETA.CPAC
complete
!
appn link-station ZAPHOD
port FRAME
fr-dest-address 17
adjacent-cp-name NETA.ZAPHOD
complete
!
appn routing

ESCON Director

C7   C0

IOCP

resource part=((lpar1, 1))

chpid path=((21)),type=cnc,
        shared,switch=3,
        partition=(lpar1)

cntlunit cunumber=000e,
        path=((21)),unit=sctc,
        unitadd=((70,16)),
        link=c7,cuadd=0

iodevice address=((870,16)),
        cunumbr=(000e),
        unit=sctc

XCA Major Node

vbuild   type=xca
port   adapno=0,cuaddr=870
          sapaddr=04,medium=ring
group   answer=no, autogen=(5,l,p),
          call=inout,dial=yes

Switched Major Node

aaaapnpu PU addr=01,
          putype=2,
          usstab=usssna,
          conntype=appn,
          cpname=arthur,

HOST
CP
NAME

Zaphod Configuration

interface Serial 3/0
encapsulation frame-relay
frame-relay map llc2 16
!
appn control-point NETA.ZAPHOD
complete
!
appn port FRAME Serial 3/0
complete
!
appn link-station ARTHUR
port FRAME
lan-dest-address 16
adjacent-cp-name NETA.ARHTUR
complete

APPN Network Scenario

MVS1   Arthur   Frame   Zaphod
                               Relay

C0 C7   CIP

HOST NN   NN   NN
NETA.CPAC   NETA.ARTHUR   NETA.ZAPHOD

Logical view of APPN Network

adapter 0 CIP   CyBus   RSP   Frame   Zaphod
4000.7505.0000   Relay

                    Lan   Virtual   F
                    TokenRing0   Ring   S
                    Ring 90   100   I   DLCI   DLCI
                                                P   17   16

                    Bridge 1   Bridge 2

HOST NN   NN   NN
NETA.CPAC   NETA.ARTHUR   NETA.ZAPHOD

EXAMPLE 4: APPN OVER DLSW

This example configuration depicts the physical and logical views of connecting an APPN network over a DLSw connection using a Token-Ring interface of a channel-attached router. In the example, the router labeled NETA.ZAPHOD is an APPN NN connecting to the channel-attached router over a Token-Ring Interface Processor (TRIP) used for the DLSw connection. The channel-attached router is defined as an APPN NN with the name NETA.ARTHUR connecting to the VTAM APPN NN NET.CPAC using an ESCON Director.

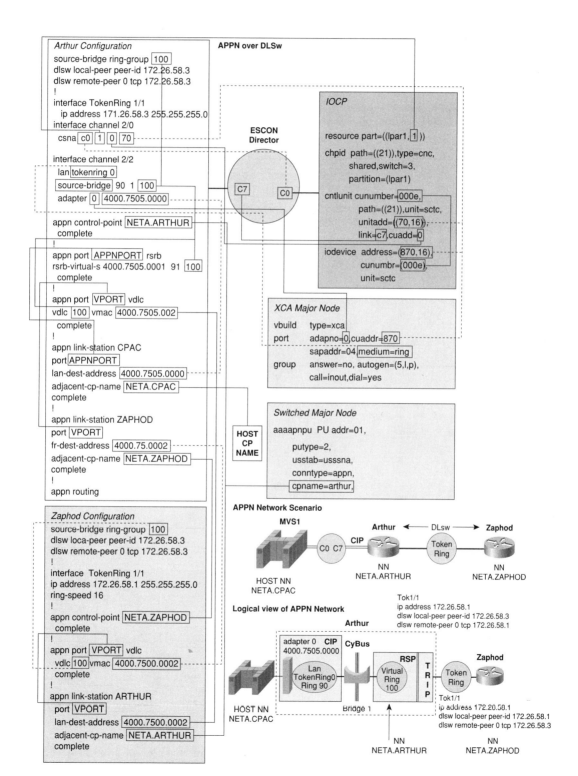

EXAMPLE 5: APPN/HPR OVER MULTIPATH CHANNEL (MPC)

This example configuration depicts the physical and logical views of connecting an APPN network over an MPC connection using the CIP interface of the channel-attached router. In the example, the channel-attached router is defined as an APPN NN with the name NETA.ARTHUR connecting to the VTAM APPN NN NET.CPAC using an ESCON Director.

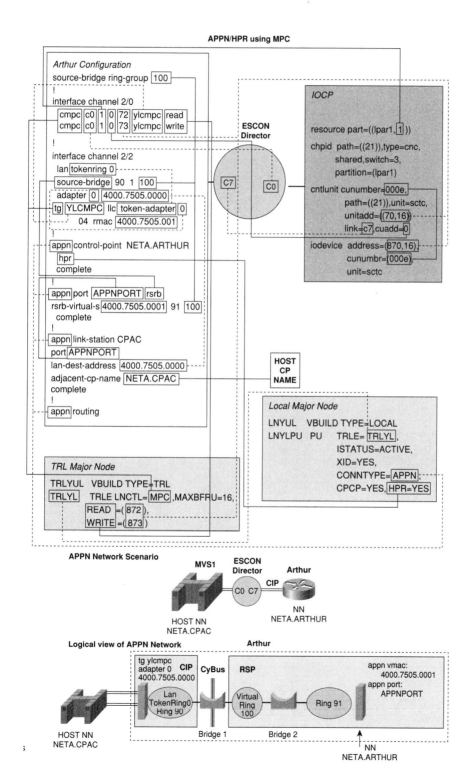

APPN/HPR using MPC

EXAMPLE 6: DIRECT-ATTACHED TOKEN-RING LLC2 SESSIONS USING CSNA

This example configuration depicts a PC attached to a Token-Ring LAN that is attached to the Cisco channel-attached router. In the example, the channel-attached router is using an ESCON Director.

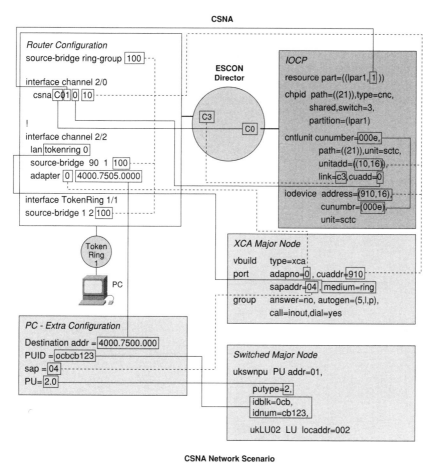

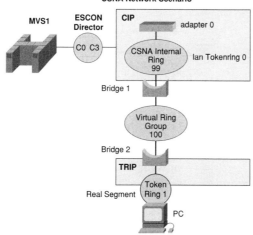

EXAMPLE 7: DOWNSTREAM PU USING VIRTUAL DATA LINK CONTROL TO CIP

This example configuration depicts a PC attached to a remote Token-Ring LAN. The router labeled Zaphod encapsulates the SNA traffic using DLSw+ to the channel-attached data-center router named Arthur. In the example, the channel-attached router is using an ESCON Director.

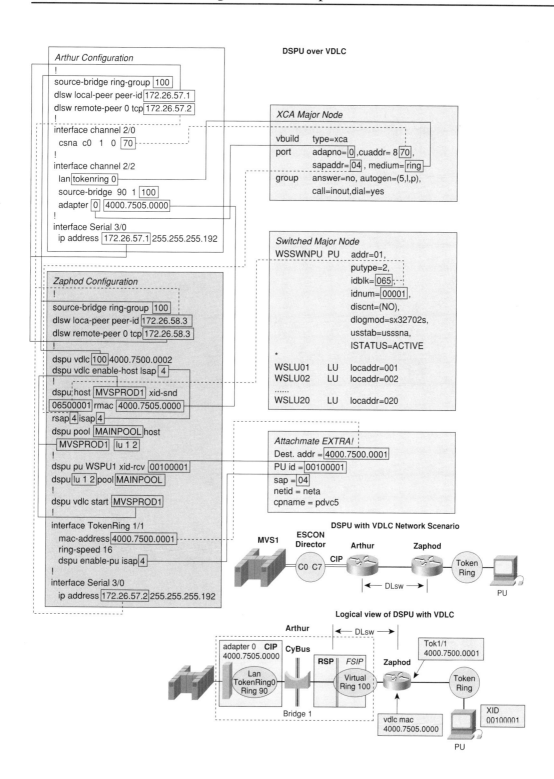

DSPU over VDLC

Arthur Configuration
```
!
source-bridge ring-group 100
dlsw local-peer peer-id 172.26.57.1
dlsw remote-peer 0 tcp 172.26.57.2
!
interface channel 2/0
  csna c0 1 0 70
!
interface channel 2/2
  lan tokenring 0
  source-bridge 90 1 100
  adapter 0 4000.7505.0000
!
interface Serial 3/0
  ip address 172.26.57.1 255.255.255.192
```

XCA Major Node
```
vbuild    type=xca
port      adapno= 0 ,cuaddr= 8 70 ,
          sapaddr= 04 , medium= ring
group     answer=no, autogen=(5,l,p),
          call=inout,dial=yes
```

Zaphod Configuration
```
!
source-bridge ring-group 100
dlsw loca-peer peer-id 172.26.58.3
dlsw remote-peer 0 tcp 172.26.58.3
!
dspu vdlc 100 4000.7500.0002
dspu vdlc enable-host lsap 4
!
dspu host MVSPROD1 xid-snd
06500001 rmac 4000.7505.0000
rsap 4 isap 4
dspu pool MAINPOOL host
 MVSPROD1 lu 1 2
!
dspu pu WSPU1 xid-rcv 00100001
dspu lu 1 2 pool MAINPOOL
!
dspu vdlc start MVSPROD1
!
interface TokenRing 1/1
  mac-address 4000.7500.0001
  ring-speed 16
  dspu enable-pu isap 4
!
interface Serial 3/0
  ip address 172.26.57.2 255.255.255.192
```

Switched Major Node
```
WSSWNPU  PU   addr=01,
              putype=2,
              idblk= 065 ,
              idnum= 00001 ,
              discnt=(NO),
              dlogmod=sx32702s,
              usstab=usssna,
              ISTATUS=ACTIVE
*
WSLU01   LU   locaddr=001
WSLU02   LU   locaddr=002
......
WSLU20   LU   locaddr=020
```

Attachmate EXTRA!
```
Dest. addr = 4000.7500.0001
PU id = 00100001
sap = 04
netid = neta
cpname = pdvc5
```

DSPU with VDLC Network Scenario

Logical view of DSPU with VDLC

Example 8: DLUR/DLUS over MPC

This example configuration depicts a PC attached to a local Token-Ring LAN. The router labeled Arthur is an APPN NN with the name NETA.ARTHUR and is providing DLUR services. VTAM on APPN NN NETA.CPAC is acting as the DLUS. The CIP is using MPC connectivity to the mainframe through an ESCON Director.

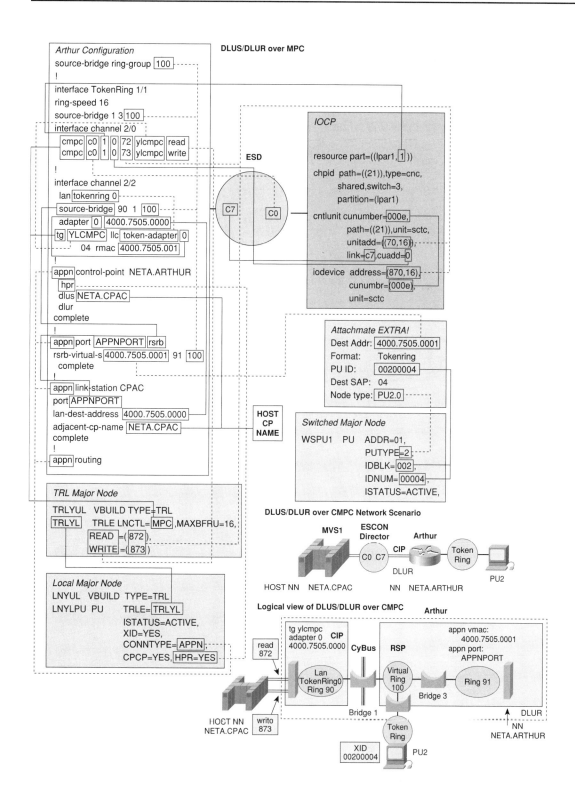

EXAMPLE 9: DLUR/DLUS BACKUP

This example configuration depicts a PC attached to a local Token-Ring LAN. The router labeled Zaphod is an APPN NN with the name NETA.ZAPHOD and is providing DLUR services. VTAM on APPN NN NETA.CPAC is acting as the primary DLUS executing on LAPR1. VTAM on APPN NN NETA.MVS is acting as the backup DLUS executing on LAPR2. The CIP is using MPC connectivity to the mainframe through an ESCON Director.

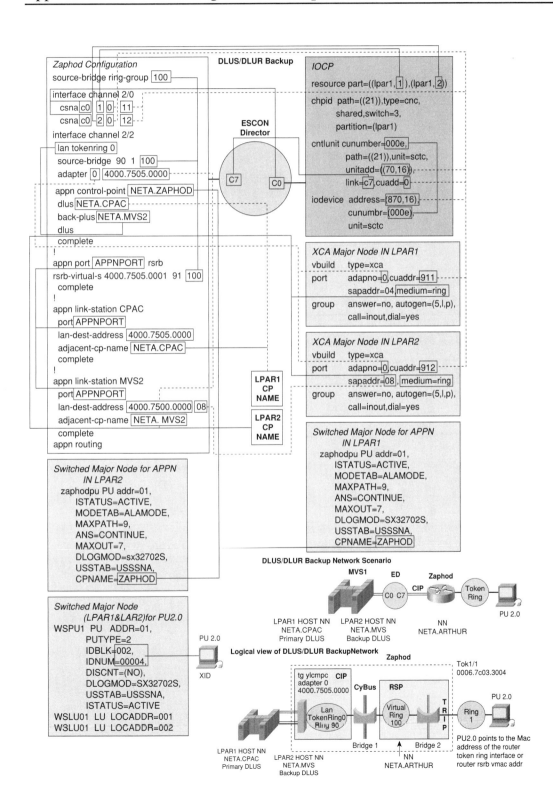

EXAMPLE 10: TN3270 SERVER

This example configuration depicts a PC attached to a local Token-Ring LAN. The PC is using TN3270 for connectivity to SNA applications residing on the mainframe. The router CIP card is running TN3270 server and is represented to VTAM as an SNA PU 2.0 device.

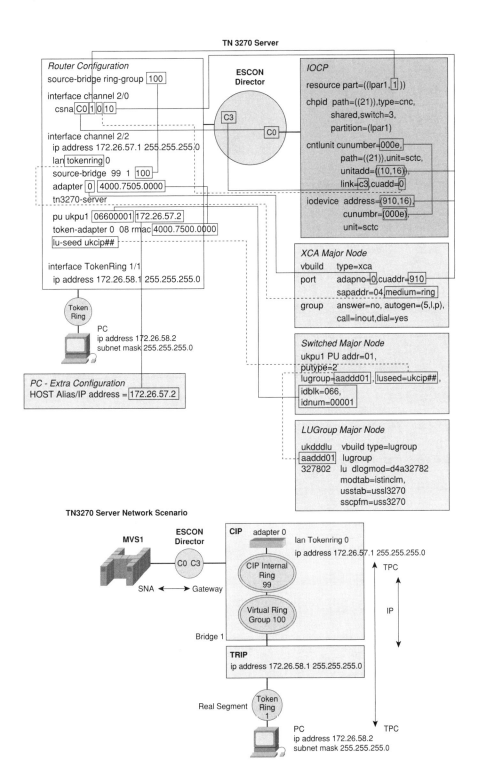

TN 3270 Server

Router Configuration
source-bridge ring-group 100

interface channel 2/0
 csna C0 1 0 10

interface channel 2/2
 ip address 172.26.57.1 255.255.255.0
 lan tokenring 0
 source-bridge 99 1 100
 adapter 0 4000.7505.0000
 tn3270-server

 pu ukpu1 06600001 172.26.57.2
 token-adapter 0 08 rmac 4000.7500.0000
 lu-seed ukcip##

interface TokenRing 1/1
 ip address 172.26.58.1 255.255.255.0

ESCON Director

C3

C0

IOCP
resource part=((lpar1, 1))
chpid path=((21)),type=cnc,
      shared,switch=3,
      partition=(lpar1)
cntlunit cunumber=000e,
      path=((21)),unit=sctc,
      unitadd=((10,16)),
      link=c3,cuadd=0
iodevice address=(910,16),
      cunumbr=000e,
      unit=sctc

XCA Major Node
vbuild   type=xca
port   adapno=0,cuaddr=910
          sapaddr=04,medium=ring
group   answer=no, autogen=(5,l,p),
          call=inout,dial=yes

Switched Major Node
ukpu1 PU addr=01,
putype=2
lugroup=aaddd01, luseed=ukcip##,
idblk=066,
idnum=00001

LUGroup Major Node
ukdddlu   vbuild type=lugroup
aaddd01   lugroup
327802   lu dlogmod=d4a32782
          modtab=istinclm,
          usstab=ussl3270
          sscpfm=uss3270

Token Ring

PC
ip address 172.26.58.2
subnet mask 255.255.255.0

PC - Extra Configuration
HOST Alias/IP address = 172.26.57.2

TN3270 Server Network Scenario

MVS1

ESCON Director

C0 C3

SNA ◄──► Gateway

CIP   adapter 0

lan Tokenring 0
ip address 172.26.57.1 255.255.255.0

CIP Internal Ring 99

Virtual Ring Group 100

Bridge 1

TRIP
ip address 172.26.58.1 255.255.255.0

Token Ring 1

Real Segment

PC
ip address 172.26.58.2
subnet mask 255.255.255.0

TPC

IP

TPC

D

IBM VTAM
APPN Code
Requirements

This appendix provides information on the minimum coding requirements for IBM VTAM to participate in an APPN network.

ALLOWING APPN RESOURCE TO CONNECT TO VTAM

VTAM requires a PU for each and every APPN device that connects to it. The PU may be created dynamically; if this method is chosen, however, the PU models must be set up such that APPN capabilities are enabled.

Critical are CONNTYPE, CPCP and DYNLU defined values.

MINIMUM VTAM START OPTIONS FOR APPN

Most of the APPN start options will default to the suitable requirements. Others will require modification. The following parameters require initial attention:

- CONNTYPE—Specifies whether APPN PUs are connected as either APPN or LEN. Suggested setting is APPN.

- CPCP—Specifies whether adjacent nodes use CP-CP with APPN Node support. Suggested setting is YES

- DYNADJCP—Specifies whether adjacent control points (ADJCP) can be dynamically created. Suggested setting is NO to allow flexibility of defining on specific link stations.

- DYNLU—Defines that LU resources do not require definition of link stations. Suggested setting is YES.

- HOSTSA—Defines subarea function is required. HOSTSA is required to be used in conjunction with NODETYPE to create an ICN (integrated connection node).

- NETID—Set the NETID value equal to the value specified for SSCPNAME.

- NODETYPE—Specifies the APPN type. Suggested setting is NN for ICN and EN for MDH.

- SSCPNAME—Ensure the NEITD value is the same as the SSCPNAME value.

Bibliography

http://www.cisco.com/universal/cc/td/doc/product/software/index.htm

Cisco IOS Configuration Fundamentals
Authors: Cisco Systems, Inc
ISBN: 1-57870-044-2
Publication date: December 1997
Cisco Press

Cisco IOS Wide Area Networking Solutions
Authors: Cisco Systems, Inc
ISBN: 1-57870-054-x
Publication date: March 1998
Cisco Press

Cisco IOS Bridging and IBM Network Solutions
Authors: Cisco Systems, Inc
ISBN: 1-57870-051-5
Publication date: June 1998
Cisco Press

ATM and Multiprotocol Networking
Authors: George C. Sackett, Christopher Y. Metz
ISBN: 0070577242
Publication date: 1997
McGraw Hill Text

Introduction to SNA Networking: A Professioal's Guide to VTAM/NCP, 2nd edition
Authors: Jay Ranade, George Sackett
ISBN: 0070515069
Publication date: 1995
McGraw Hill Text

Glossary

address translation gateway See *ATG*.

AIP ATM Interface Processor. ATM network interface for Cisco 7000 series routers designed to minimize performance bottlenecks at the UNI. The AIP supports AAL3/4 and AAL5. See also *AAL3/4* and *AAL5*.

APaRT automated packet recognition/translation. Technology that allows a server to be attached to CDDI or FDDI without requiring the reconfiguration of applications or network protocols. APaRT recognizes specific data link layer encapsulation packet types and, when these packet types are transferred from one medium to another, translates them into the native format of the destination device.

ATG address translation gateway. Cisco DECnet routing software function that allows a router to route multiple, independent DECnet networks and to establish a user-specified address translation for selected nodes between networks.

ATM Interface Processor See *AIP*.

ATM network Traditional Cisco ATM network built around BPX switches.

ATM network interface card ESP card that is used as the OC-3 interface to the BPX's BXM.

Automated Packet Recognition/Translation See *APaRT*.

autonomous switching Feature on Cisco routers that provides faster packet processing by allowing the ciscoBus to switch packets independently without interrupting the system processor.

BIGA Bus Interface Gate Array. Technology that allows the Catalyst 5000 to receive and transmit frames from its packet-switching memory to its MAC local buffer memory without the intervention of the host processor.

BOBI break-out/break-in. VNS feature that allows interworking between Euro-ISDN (ETSI) and other VNS-supported signaling variants, such as DPNSS and QSIG.

BPX Service Node Closely integrated BPX switch, AXIS interface shelf, and extended services processor designed to support ATM and Frame Relay switched virtual circuits, as well as traditional PVCs.

break-out/break-in See *BOBI*.

Bus Interface Gate Array See *BIGA*.

Call Detail Record See *CDR*.

CDP Cisco Discovery Protocol. Media- and protocol-independent device-discovery protocol that runs on all Cisco-manufactured equipment including routers, access servers, bridges, and switches. Using CDP, a device can advertise its existence to other devices and receive information about other devices on the same LAN or on the remote side of a WAN. Runs on all media that support SNAP, including LANs, Frame Relay, and ATM media.

CDR Call Detail Record. VNS record of voice or data SVCs, which includes calling and called numbers, local and remote node names, data and timestamp, elapsed time, and Call Failure Class fields.

CFRAD See *Cisco FRAD*.

Channel Interface Processor See *CIP*.

CIP Channel Interface Processor. Channel attachment interface for Cisco 7000 series routers. The CIP is used to connect a host mainframe to a control unit, eliminating the need for an FEP for channel attachment.

ciscoBus controller See *SP*.

Cisco Discovery Protocol See *CDP*.

Cisco FRAD Cisco Frame Relay access device. Cisco product that supports Cisco IOS Frame Relay SNA services and can be upgraded to be a full-function multiprotocol router. The Cisco FRAD connects SDLC devices to Frame Relay without requiring an existing LAN. However, the Cisco FRAD does support attached LANs and can perform conversion from SDLC to Ethernet and Token Ring. See also *FRAD*.

Cisco Frame Relay access device See *Cisco FRAD*.

CiscoFusion Cisco internetworking architecture that "fuses" together the scalability, stability, and security advantages of the latest routing technologies with the performance benefits of ATM and LAN switching, and the management benefits of VLANs. See also *Cisco IOS.*

Cisco IOS Cisco system software that provides common functionality, scalability, and security for all products under the CiscoFusion architecture. Cisco IOS allows centralized, integrated, and automated installation and management of internetworks, while ensuring support for a wide variety of protocols, media, services, and platforms. See also *CiscoFusion.*

Cisco Link Services See *CLS.*

Cisco Link Services Interface See *CLSI.*

CiscoView GUI-based device-management software application that provides dynamic status, statistics, and comprehensive configuration information for Cisco internetworking devices. In addition to displaying a physical view of Cisco device chassis, CiscoView also provides device monitoring functions and basic troubleshooting capabilities, and can be integrated with several leading SNMP-based network management platforms.

CLS Cisco Link Services. A front-end for a variety of data-link control services.

CLSI Cisco Link Services Interface. Messages that are exchanged between CLS and data-link users such as APPN, SNA service point, and DLSw+.

configuration register In Cisco routers, a 16-bit, user-configurable value that determines how the router functions during initialization. The configuration register can be stored in hardware or software. In hardware, the bit position is set using a jumper. In software, the bit position is set by specifying a hexadecimal value using configuration commands.

CPP Combinet Proprietary Protocol.

CxBus Cisco Extended Bus. Data bus for interface processors on Cisco 7000 series routers. See also *SP.*

Data Movement Processor See *DMP.*

Diffusing Update Algorithm See *DUAL.*

DistributedDirector Method of distributing Web traffic by taking into account Web server availability and relative client-to-server topological distances in order to determine the optimal Web server for a client. DistributedDirector uses the Director Response Protocol to query DRP server agents for BGP and IGP routing table metrics.

DLSw+ data-link switching plus. Cisco implementation of the DLSw standard for SNA and NetBIOS traffic forwarding. DLSw+ goes beyond the standard to include the advanced features of the current Cisco RSRB implementation, and provides additional functionality to increase the overall scalability of data-link switching. See also *DLSw* in the main glossary.

DMP Data Movement Processor. Processor on the Catalyst 5000 that, along with the multiport packet buffer memory interface, performs the frame-switching function for the switch. The DMP also handles translational bridging between the Ethernet and FDDI interfaces, IP segmentation, and intelligent bridging with protocol-based filtering.

DRP Director Response Protocol. Protocol used by the DistributedDirector feature in IP routing.

DSPU concentration Cisco IOS feature that enables a router to function as a PU concentrator for SNA PU 2 nodes. PU concentration at the router simplifies the task of PU definition at the upstream host while providing additional flexibility and mobility for downstream PU devices.

DUAL Diffusing Update Algorithm. Convergence algorithm used in Enhanced IGRP that provides loop-free operation at every instant throughout a route computation. Allows routers involved in a topology change to synchronize at the same time, while not involving routers that are unaffected by the change. See also *Enhanced IGRP*.

EIGRP See *Enhanced IGRP*.

EIP Ethernet Interface Processor. Interface processor card on the Cisco 7000 series routers. The EIP provides high-speed (10-Mbps) AUI ports that support Ethernet Version 1 and Ethernet Version 2 or IEEE 802.3 interfaces, and a high-speed data path to other interface processors.

Enhanced IGRP Enhanced Interior Gateway Routing Protocol. Advanced version of IGRP developed by Cisco. Provides superior convergence properties and operating efficiency, and combines the advantages of link state protocols with those of distance vector protocols. Compare with *IGRP*. See also *IGP*, *OSPF*, and *RIP*.

Enhanced Interior Gateway Routing Protocol See *Enhanced IGRP*.

Enhanced Monitoring Services Set of analysis tools on the Catalyst 5000 switch, consisting of an integrated RMON agent and the SPAN. These tools provide traffic monitoring and network segment analysis and management. See also *RMON* and *span*.

ESP Extended Services Processor. Rack-mounted adjunct processor that is co-located with a Cisco BPX/AXIS (all three units comprise a BPX service node) and has IP connectivity to a StrataView Plus Workstation.

Ethernet Interface Processor See *EIP*.

EXEC Interactive command processor of Cisco IOS.

Extended Services Processor See *ESP.*

Fast Ethernet Interface Processor See *FEIP.*

Fast Sequenced Transport See *FST.*

Fast Serial Interface Processor See *FSIP.*

fast switching Cisco feature whereby a route cache is used to expedite packet switching through a router. Contrast with *process switching.*

FDDI Interface Processor See *FIP.*

FEIP Fast Ethernet Interface Processor. Interface processor on the Cisco 7000 series routers. The FEIP supports up to two 100-Mbps 100BaseT ports.

FIP FDDI Interface Processor. Interface processor on the Cisco 7000 series routers. The FIP supports SASs, DASs, dual homing, and optical bypass, and contains a 16-mips processor for high-speed (100-Mbps) interface rates. The FIP complies with ANSI and ISO FDDI standards.

FRAS Frame Relay access support. Cisco IOS feature that allows SDLC, Token Ring, Ethernet, and Frame Relay-attached IBM devices to connect to other IBM devices across a Frame Relay network. See also *FRAD.*

FSIP Fast Serial Interface Processor. Default serial interface processor for Cisco 7000 series routers. The FSIP provides four or eight high-speed serial ports.

FST Fast Sequenced Transport. Connectionless, sequenced transport protocol that runs on top of the IP protocol. SRB traffic is encapsulated inside of IP datagrams and is passed over an FST connection between two network devices (such as routers). FST speeds up data delivery, reduces overhead, and improves the response time of SRB traffic.

Gateway Discovery Protocol See *GDP.*

GDP Gateway Discovery Protocol. Cisco protocol that allows hosts to dynamically detect the arrival of new routers as well as determine when a router goes down. GDP based on UDP. See also *UDP* in the main glossary.

generic routing encapsulation See *GRE.*

GRE generic routing encapsulation. Tunneling protocol developed by Cisco that can encapsulate a wide variety of protocol packet types inside IP tunnels, creating a virtual point-to-point link to Cisco routers at remote points over an IP internetwork. By connecting multiprotocol subnetworks in a single-protocol backbone environment, IP tunneling using GRE allows network expansion across a single-protocol backbone environment.

helper address Address configured on an interface to which broadcasts received on that interface will be sent.

High-Speed Communications Interface See *HSCI*.

HIP HSSI Interface Processor. Interface processor on the Cisco 7000 series routers. The HIP provides one HSSI port that supports connections to ATM, SMDS, Frame Relay, or private lines at speeds up to T3 or E3.

Hot Standby Router Protocol See *HSRP*.

HSCI High-Speed Communications Interface. Single-port interface, developed by Cisco, providing full-duplex synchronous serial communications capability at speeds up to 52 Mbps.

HSRP Hot Standby Router Protocol. Provides high network availability and transparent network topology changes. HSRP creates a Hot Standby router group with a lead router that services all packets sent to the Hot Standby address. The lead router is monitored by other routers in the group, and if it fails, one of these standby routers inherits the lead position and the Hot Standby group address.

HSSI Interface Processor See *HIP*.

IGRP Interior Gateway Routing Protocol. IGP developed by Cisco to address the issues associated with routing in large, heterogeneous networks. Compare with *Enhanced IGRP*. See also *IGP, OSPF,* and *RIP*.

interface processor Any of a number of processor modules used in the Cisco 7000 series routers. See *AIP, CIP, EIP, FEIP, FIP, FSIP, HIP, MIP, SIP (Serial Interface Processor),* and *TRIP*.

Interior Gateway Routing Protocol See *IGRP*.

Inter-Switch Link See *ISL*.

IOS See *Cisco IOS*.

ISL Inter-Switch Link. Cisco-proprietary protocol that maintains VLAN information as traffic flows between switches and routers.

Local adjacency Two VNSs that control different VSN areas, but communicate with one another through a Frame Relay PVC, are considered to be locally adjacent.

MICA Multiservice IOS Channel Aggregation. Technology that enables the simultaneous support of remote-access users through both analog modems and ISDN devices.

MIP MultiChannel Interface Processor. Interface processor on the Cisco 7000 series routers that provides up to two channelized T1 or E1 connections via serial cables to a

CSU. The two controllers on the MIP can each provide up to 24 T1 or 30 E1 channel-groups, with each channel-group presented to the system as a serial interface that can be configured individually.

MultiChannel Interface Processor See *MIP*.

native client interface architecture See *NCIA*.

NCIA native client interface architecture. SNA applications-access architecture, developed by Cisco, that combines the full functionality of native SNA interfaces at both the host and client with the flexibility of leveraging TCP/IP backbones. NCIA encapsulates SNA traffic on a client PC or workstation, thereby providing direct TCP/IP access while preserving the native SNA interface at the end-user level. In many networks, this capability obviates the need for a standalone gateway and can provide flexible TCP/IP access while preserving the native SNA interface to the host.

NetFlow Network flow is defined as a unidirectional sequence of packets between given source and destination endpoints. Network flows are highly granular: flow endpoints are identified both by IP address as well as by transport layer application port numbers. (NetFlow also uses IP Protocol, ToS and the input interface port to uniquely identify flows.) Conventional network layer switching handles incoming packets independently, with separate serial tasks for switching, security, services and traffic measurements applied to each packet. With NetFlow switching, this process is applied only to the first packet of a flow. Information from the first packet is used to build an entry in the NetFlow cache. Subsequent packets in the flow are handled via a single streamlined task that handles switching, services, and data collection concurrently.

NETscout Cisco network management application that provides an easy-to-use GUI for monitoring RMON statistics and protocol analysis information. NETscout also provides extensive tools that simplify data collection, analysis, and reporting. These tools allow system administrators to monitor traffic, set thresholds, and capture data on any set of network traffic for any segment.

NMP Network Management Processor. Processor module on the Catalyst 5000 switch used to control and monitor the switch.

NSP Network Service Point.

physical layer interface module See *PLIM*.

PLIM physical layer interface module. Interface that allows the AIP to a variety of physical layers, including TAXI and SONET multimode fiber-optic cable, SDH/SONET single-mode fiber cable, and E3 coaxial cable.

process switching Operation that provides full route evaluation and per-packet load balancing across parallel WAN links. Involves the transmission of entire frames to the router CPU, where they are repackaged for delivery to or from a WAN interface, with the router making a route selection for each packet. Process switching is the most resource-intensive switching operation that the CPU can perform. Contrast with *fast switching*.

proxy polling Technique that alleviates the load across an SDLC network by allowing routers to act as proxies for primary and secondary nodes, thus keeping polling traffic off of the shared links. Proxy polling has been replaced by SDLC Transport. See *SDLC Transport*.

Reliable SAP Update Protocol See *RSUP*.

Route Processor See *RP*.

Route/Switch Processor See *RSP*.

RP Route Processor. Processor module in the Cisco 7000 series routers that contains the CPU, system software, and most of the memory components that are used in the router. Sometimes called a supervisory processor.

RSP Route/Switch Processor. Processor module in the Cisco 7500 series routers that integrates the functions of the RP and the SP. See also *RP* and *SP*.

RSUP Reliable SAP Update Protocol. Bandwidth-saving protocol developed by Cisco for propagating services information. RSUP allows routers to reliably send standard Novell SAP packets only when the routers detect a change in advertised services. RSUP can transport network information either in conjunction with or independently of the Enhanced IGRP routing function for IPX.

SDLC broadcast Feature that allows a Cisco router that receives an all-stations broadcast on a virtual multidrop line to propagate the broadcast to each SDLC line that is a member of the virtual multidrop line.

SDLC Transport Cisco router feature with which disparate environments can be integrated into a single, high-speed, enterprise-wide network. Native SDLC traffic can be passed through point-to-point serial links with other protocol traffic multiplexed over the same links. Cisco routers can also encapsulate SDLC frames inside IP datagrams for transport over arbitrary (non-SDLC) networks. Replaces proxy polling. See also *proxy polling*.

SDLLC SDLC Logical Link Control. Cisco IOS feature that performs translation between SDLC and IEEE 802.2 type 2.

serial tunnel See *STUN*.

silicon switching Switching based on the SSE, which allows the processing of packets independent of the SSP (Silicon Switch Processor) system processor. Silicon switching provides high-speed, dedicated packet switching. See also *SSE* and *SSP (Silicon Switch Processor)*.

silicon switching engine See *SSE*.

Silicon Switch Processor See *SSP*.

SIP SMDS Interface Protocol. Used in communications between CPE and SMDS network equipment. Allows the CPE to use SMDS service for high-speed WAN internetworking. SIP is based on the IEEE 802.6 DQDB standard. See also *DQDB*.

SP Switch Processor. Cisco 7000-series processor module that acts as the administrator for all CxBus activities. SP is sometimes called ciscoBus controller. See also *CxBus*.

SPAN Switched Port Analyzer. Feature of the Catalyst 5000 switch that extends the monitoring abilities of existing network analyzers into a switched Ethernet environment. SPAN mirrors the traffic at one switched segment onto a predefined SPAN port. A network analyzer attached to the SPAN port can monitor traffic from any of the other Catalyst switched ports.

SPNNI connection Frame Relay connection between two VNSs in different areas or domains. The SPNNI connection gets its name from the proprietary Network-to-Network Interface protocol that operates over this connection.

SSE silicon switching engine. Routing and switching mechanism that compares the data link or network layer header of an incoming packet to a silicon-switching cache, determines the appropriate action (routing or bridging), and forwards the packet to the proper interface. The SSE is directly encoded in the hardware of the SSP (Silicon Switch Processor) of a Cisco 7000 series router. It can therefore perform switching independently of the system processor, making the execution of routing decisions much quicker than if they were encoded in software. See also *silicon switching* and *SSP*.

SSP Silicon Switch Processor. High-performance silicon switch for Cisco 7000 series routers that provides distributed processing and control for interface processors. The SSP leverages the high-speed switching and routing capabilities of the SSE to dramatically increase aggregate router performance, minimizing performance bottlenecks at the interface points between the router and a high-speed backbone. See also *silicon switching* and *SSE*.

STUN serial tunnel. Router feature allowing two SDLC- or HDLC-compliant devices to connect to one another through an arbitrary multiprotocol topology (using Cisco routers) rather than through a direct serial link.

supervisory processor See *RP*.

Switch Processor See *SP*.

TACACS+ Terminal Access Controller Access Control System Plus. Proprietary Cisco enhancement to Terminal Access Controller Access Control System (TACACS). TACACS rovides additional support for authentication, authorization, and accounting. See also *TACACS* in main glossary.

THC over X.25 Feature providing TCP/IP header compression over X.25 links, for purposes of link efficiency.

TRIP Token Ring Interface Processor. High-speed interface processor on the Cisco 7000 series routers. The TRIP provides two or four Token Ring ports for interconnection with IEEE 802.5 and IBM Token Ring media with ports independently set to speeds of either 4 or 16 Mbps.

two-way simultaneous See *TWS*.

TWS two-way simultaneous. Mode that allows a router configured as a primary SDLC station to achieve better utilization of a full-duplex serial line. When TWS is enabled in a multidrop environment, the router can poll a secondary station and receive data from that station while it sends data to or receives data from a different secondary station on the same serial line.

Versatile Interface Processor See *VIP*.

VIP 1. Versatile Interface Processor. Interface card used in Cisco 7000 and Cisco 7500 series routers. The VIP provides multilayer switching and runs Cisco IOS. The most recent version of the VIP is VIP2.

2. virtual IP. Function that enables the creation of logically separated switched IP workgroups across the switch ports of a Catalyst 5000 running Virtual Networking Services software. See also *Virtual Networking Services*.

virtual IP See *VIP*.

Virtual Networking Services Software on some Catalyst 5000 switches that enables multiple workgroups to be defined across switches and offers traffic segmentation and access control.

VNS See *Virtual Networking Services*.

WorkGroup Director Cisco SNMP-based network-management software tool. Workgroup Director runs on UNIX workstations either as a standalone application or integrated with another SNMP-based network management platform, providing a seamless, powerful management system for Cisco workgroup products. See also *SNMP*.

Index